Style and Necessity in Thucydides

Style and Necessity in Thucydides

TOBIAS JOHO

Great Clarendon Street, Oxford, OX2 6DP,
United Kingdom

Oxford University Press is a department of the University of Oxford.
It furthers the University's objective of excellence in research, scholarship,
and education by publishing worldwide. Oxford is a registered trade mark of
Oxford University Press in the UK and in certain other countries

© Tobias Joho 2022

The moral rights of the author have been asserted

First Edition published in 2022

Impression: 1

All rights reserved. No part of this publication may be reproduced, stored in
a retrieval system, or transmitted, in any form or by any means, without the
prior permission in writing of Oxford University Press, or as expressly permitted
by law, by licence or under terms agreed with the appropriate reprographics
rights organization. Enquiries concerning reproduction outside the scope of the
above should be sent to the Rights Department, Oxford University Press, at the
address above

You must not circulate this work in any other form
and you must impose this same condition on any acquirer

Published in the United States of America by Oxford University Press
198 Madison Avenue, New York, NY 10016, United States of America

British Library Cataloguing in Publication Data
Data available

Library of Congress Control Number: 2022935645

ISBN 978–0–19–881204–3

DOI: 10.1093/oso/9780198812043.001.0001

Printed and bound in the UK by
Clays Ltd, Elcograf S.p.A.

Links to third party websites are provided by Oxford in good faith and
for information only. Oxford disclaims any responsibility for the materials
contained in any third party website referenced in this work.

To Erika and Wolfgang Joho

Acknowledgements

It is a pleasure to acknowledge the help that this book has received from friends and colleagues over the years.

At each stage of the project, Chris Pelling read large sections of the work with his famed generosity and contributed the kind of expertise that is the hallmark of the great masters. His advice, whether on large conceptual issues or on philological minutia, has been the *sine qua non* of this book. I am also greatly indebted to Edith Foster and Arnd Kerkhecker for their crucial support. They contributed their thorough grasp of Thucydides and fine-grained understanding of the Greek language. Both commented on several chapters, discussed larger issues of organization, and offered encouragement when it was needed. In the early stages of this project, I was fortunate to count on the intellectual acumen, erudition, and untiring support of Elizabeth Asmis, Nathan Tarcov, and Mark Payne of the University of Chicago. The discussions with these scholars made a lasting impression on me, both by helping me to lay the foundations for my work on Thucydides and by leaving an enduring mark on my vision of the intellectual life. I have also benefited significantly from discussions with Helma Dik and Jonathan Hall. Later, once the structure of the present project became clear and I had begun to submit chapters to OUP, the anonymous readers engaged by the Press wrote thoughtful in-depth reports, which were pivotal in refining the conception and shape of the book. At a moment when the project had got stuck, Claudia Michel offered sound advice, which helped me get things back on track. I also derived great benefit from the insights of Michael Allen, Anthony Ellis, and Leon Wash, who made crucial comments on individual chapters.

I am profoundly grateful to several native speaker friends who were willing to read individual chapters with an eye to polishing my English. For their invaluable help I thank (in alphabetical order) Michael Allen, David DeMarco, Anthony Ellis, Edith Foster, Branden Kosch, Alex Lee, Diana Moser, Leon Wash, and Konrad Weeda. Moreover, Nina Cook, a professional translator and proofreader, read Chapters 4 and 7 and greatly improved their style. Special and heartfelt thanks are due to David DeMarco for his Herculean labours, especially his tireless willingness to go over the intricacies of particular phrases with me. All these people did this book a great service. Its remaining mistakes, whether concerning English idiom or substantive content, are my sole responsibility.

I also thank Charlotte Loveridge at OUP and her assistants (especially Jo Spillane) as well as the team of copy-editors (headed by Saraswathi Ethiraju) for their patience and reliability in guiding my book through the publication process.

At the University of Bern, my Swiss home institution, I have benefited from the congenial environment at the Department of Classics. Arnd Kerkhecker, the long-time department chair, has been invaluable in fostering a setting that allows intellectual pursuits to flourish. Moreover, this place would not be what it is without the other members of the academic staff: Gerlinde Huber-Rebenich, Katharina Brunner, Gerald Bechtle, René Bloch, and Gunther Martin. I especially thank Katharina for her extraordinary collegiality that enabled me to carve out time for working on the book during busy periods. I also thank my student research assistant Remo Zumstein for his excellent proofreading and formatting work. His post was thankfully funded by the Department of Classics at Bern. I am also very grateful to the Department's regular two student assistants, Janna Büchi and Vincent Hagenow, who checked the book's references to primary and secondary sources and worked on the index with immense diligence, a sharp eye for detail, and infatigable good cheer.

Over the years, my sister Livia and her family have been an inexhaustible source of what the Greeks called εὐφροσύνη. Markus Burger proved time and again that he is 'the man who solves problems'. Finally, I thank Christina Nurawar Sani (who knows the answer to Hölderlin's 'wozu Dichter?') for a host of things—not least for introducing me to the poem by Stefan George from which the epigraph of this book is taken.

I dedicate this work to my parents, Erika and Wolfgang Joho, in recognition of their boundless support, both moral and practical, since time immemorial. The dedication is in the spirit of our various trips to the lands of classical antiquity. Despite the success of these undertakings, I could never persuade them to join me on a staggeringly ambitious journey to the island of Sicily. I am tempted to presume a lesson from Thucydides.

Contents

Introduction ... 1
  0.1 Dionysius of Halicarnassus and the Problem of Thucydides' Style ... 1
  0.2 What Benefit Does Thucydides Derive from a Nominal Register? ... 8
  0.3 Two Contrary Strands in the *History*: Contingency vs. Necessity ... 17
  0.4 Determinism 'up to a point' ... 23

1. Thucydides' Abstract Nominal Style: The Main Features and Differences from the Plain Style ... 25
  1.1 Abstract Nominal Phrases in Ancient Greek ... 26
  1.2 Four Stylistic Devices Used by Thucydides to Foster Abstraction ... 29
  1.3 Corcyrean Stasis in Two Stylistic Registers ... 36
  1.4 Conclusion ... 45

2. The Implications of Thucydides' Abstract Style: The *Pathology* (3.82–3) ... 47
  2.1 Persons Treated as Things ... 47
  2.2 Impersonal Agents ... 52
  2.3 Reification of Action ... 55
  2.4 Passivity and Settled States ... 57
  2.5 Convulsions of 'Greekness' ... 60
  2.6 Predominance of General Forces ... 63
  2.7 Emphasis on Incidents Occurring as Opposed to People Acting ... 65
  2.8 Phrases Involving $\pi i\pi\tau\omega$ ... 67
  2.9 Conclusion ... 73

3. The Passivity of the Powerful ... 76
  3.1 The Thucydidean Standpoint: The *Archaeology* ... 79
  3.2 Thucydides and His Speakers ... 84
  3.3 Compulsion by 'The Three Greatest Things' ... 88

	3.4 The Process of Imperial Growth in the *Pentecontaetia*	93
	3.5 The Paradox of Empire: Power and Passivity	101
	3.6 Conclusion	105
4.	A World Governed by Neuters: 'The Human' as a Substitute for 'The Divine'	108
	4.1 The Mainsprings of Action: Natural Conditions and Impersonal Factors	109
	4.2 Human Nature Personified	120
	4.3 Collapsing the Duality Between Inner and Outer	124
	4.4 Divine Visitation and Natural Drives: Affinities Between Euripides and Thucydides	128
	4.5 The Juxtaposition of τὸ θεῖον and τὸ ἀνθρώπειον in the Melian Dialogue	137
	4.6 Neuter Phrases Referring to Divine Powers in Herodotus and Euripides	140
	4.7 Conclusion	155
5.	Decision-Making Overshadowed by Necessity	159
	5.1 The Outbreak of the War	160
	5.2 Spartan Fear: A Passive Imposition	166
	5.3 The Speech of the Spartan Ambassadors at Athens: Passivity of the Doers and the Margin of Choice	169
	5.4 Victors and Losers After Pylos: An Unlikely Similarity	176
	5.5 Athenian Desire for Sicily: A Force Beyond Human Control	184
	5.6 National Character and Human Nature	188
	5.7 Conclusion	193
6.	Dual Motivation: The Interaction of Necessity and Individual Choice	195
	6.1 The Decision in Favour of the Sicilian Expedition (I): the Paragon of Necessity	196
	6.2 The Decision in Favour of the Sicilian Expedition (II): the Strand of Individualism	201
	6.3 Croesus in Herodotus (I): Immanent Motivation Alongside Divine Interference	207
	6.4 Croesus in Herodotus (II): Who Is αἴτιος—Man or God?	218
	6.5 Conclusion: Two Motivational Strands in Thucydides	222

7. Necessity and Leeway for Choice: Homer, Herodotus, Thucydides ... 227
   7.1 Can Necessity Be Malleable? ... 228
   7.2 The Homecoming of Odysseus: Predestination with Blank Spots ... 233
   7.3 Herodotus on Divine and Human Action in Relation to Fate: Apollo's Intervention and Croesus' Contribution ... 242
   7.4 Causality Ancient and Modern: Interaction between Entities Versus Deterministic Laws of Nature ... 247
   7.5 Causation of the Greatest Events: Necessity Intertwined with Contingency ... 257
   7.6 Conclusion: Flexible Necessity ... 263

8. Pericles' Containment of Necessity and the Scope for Choice ... 270
   8.1 The Athenians Exposed to Invasion and Plague: Human Nature on the Rise ... 275
   8.2 Pericles Face to Face with Human Nature ... 278
   8.3 Realization of the Periclean Ideal in Language ... 282
   8.4 Restoring the Athenians' Power of Choice ... 290
   8.5 The Power of Choice: An Ever-Imperiled Faculty ... 295
   8.6 The Equivocalness of γνώμη ... 299
   8.7 Conclusion: Intimations of Periclean Pessimism ... 303

Conclusion: The Exception of Pericles and the Persistence of Necessity ... 309

Bibliography ... 317
Index of Passages ... 333
Subject Index ... 344
Greek Terms ... 353

Kein ding sei wo das wort gebricht.
Stefan George, 'Das Wort'

Introduction

0.1 Dionysius of Halicarnassus and the Problem of Thucydides' Style

Thucydides' style has been a cause célèbre since ancient times. Dionysius of Halicarnassus, for instance, expresses unceremoniously his dissatisfaction with the style of Thucydides. The unflattering labels used by Dionysius include: 'tortuous, convoluted, and hard to unravel'[1] (τά τε σκολιὰ καὶ πολύπλοκα καὶ δυσεξέλικτα, *Thuc.* 24.362.20–1), or 'labored and overdone' (τῷ περιέργῳ καὶ περιττῷ, *Thuc.* 28.372.3). Dionysius allows that Thucydides can achieve an impressive effect if he employs the chief features of his style with moderation and at the right moment (*Thuc.* 24.363.18–19 along with 24.363.23–364.2, *Thuc.* 51.411.3–5, *Dem.* 10.148.19-149.1). However, more often than not, Thucydides fails to do so, with the result that his various aberrations result in outlandish obscurity (*Thuc.* 24.363.20–3, *Thuc.* 51.411.5–7, *Dem.* 10.149.1–3).

Dionysius does not content himself with stating his disapproval. Rather, he illustrates his criticism by rewriting some extended portions of Thucydides' work in what he considers to be a less outré style. Among other passages, Dionysius turns his particular attention to the excursus on stasis, which abounds with Thucydidean idiosyncrasies (*Thuc.* 28.372.6–33.381.8). Dionysius' adaptations provide a helpful gauge for spotting and measuring the eccentricities of Thucydides' style.

Dionysius begins the consideration of the chapters on stasis with this quotation from Thucydides (3.82.3):

---

[1] For the translation of σκολιός, see Pritchett (1975: 109): 'The word σκολιός, applied to style, is translated by Roberts as "tortuous" (*DHTLL* 205), by Lockwood as "twisty" (*CQ* 31 [1937] 202). The meaning of the word is best illustrated in chap. 40 (392.25), where comparison is made with labyrinths: ποιεῖ τὸν Ἀθηναῖον ἀποκρινόμενον λαβυρίνθων σκολιώτερα.'

2 STYLE AND NECESSITY IN THUCYDIDES

ἐστασίαζέ τε οὖν τὰ τῶν πόλεων, καὶ τὰ ἐφυστερίζοντά που πύστει τῶν
προγενομένων πολὺ ἐπέφερε τὴν ὑπερβολὴν τοῦ καινοῦσθαι τὰς διανοίας
...

And thus, the affairs in the cities were being distracted by civil strife [more literally: 'engaged in civil strife'], and the events that came later, through realization, I suppose, of what had happened before, carried the extravagance in the invention of new schemes still much further...

The passage illustrates what Dionysius deplores as the 'labored and overdone' manner of the excursus on stasis. He would rephrase things this way (*Thuc.* 29.374.8 and 14–16):

ἐστασίαζον αἱ πόλεις..., οἱ δ' ὑστερίζοντες ἐπιπυνθανόμενοι τὰ
γεγενημένα παρ' ἑτέροις ἐλάμβανον ὑπερβολὴν ἐπὶ τὸ διανοεῖσθαί τι
καινότερον.

The cities were engaged in civil strife, and those who came later, when they realized what had happened among the inhabitants of other cities, resorted to extravagance in order to scheme something still more novel.

Dionysius' changes show that he disapproves of Thucydides' suppression of phrases that involve personal nouns and verbs. Thucydides prefers abstract noun phrases: τὰ τῶν πόλεων καὶ τὰ ἐφυστερίζοντα ('affairs in the cities and events that came later') and πύστει τῶν προγενομένων ('through realization... of what had happened before'). If we look more closely at how Dionysius rephrases Thucydides, the grounds for his objections become even clearer.

First, where Thucydides writes 'affairs in the cities' and 'events that came later' (τὰ τῶν πόλεων and τὰ ἐφυστερίζοντα), Dionysius makes 'cities' and 'those [sc. people] who came later' (αἱ πόλεις and οἱ ὑστερίζοντες) the subject of the sentence. The second of these changes is especially significant. Dionysius seems to note the incongruity between Thucydides' subject 'events that came later' (τὰ ἐφυστερίζοντα) and the actions expressed by the phrases 'through realization' (πύστει) and 'carried the extravagance further' (ἐπέφερε τὴν ὑπερβολήν). Thucydides' phrasing suggests that 'events that came later' play the role of the agents that carry out the acts of realization and exaggeration. Thucydides' way of putting the issue is jarring because these actions (i.e. 'to realize' and 'to exaggerate') usually presuppose a human subject. Contrary to this common assumption, Thucydides seems to imply that events themselves are in charge and set the agenda. What is more, Dionysius adds the personal phrase παρ' ἑτέροις ('among the inhabitants of other cities') to τὰ γεγενημένα: 'what had happened *among the inhabitants* of other cities'. Thus, the statements refers not just to events, but to the impact that events have on people. By contrast, Thucydides simply has τῶν προγενομένων, which is governed by πύστει: 'through realization of what had happened before'. As compared with Dionysius, Thucydides focuses attention on events alone. His phrasing suggests bald impersonality. Commenting on the various neuter phrases in this passage, Colin Macleod observes: 'Thucydides systematically avoids distinguishing persons from events. This aptly reinforces the notion behind the whole passage that circumstances tend to shape human behaviour.'[2]

Second, Dionysius uses the verbal expression 'realizing what had happened' (ἐπιπυνθανόμενοι τὰ γεγενημένα) in the place of the Thucydidean noun phrase 'through realization of what had happened before' (πύστει τῶν προγενομένων). Here Dionysius rejects how Thucydides chooses a nominal phrase to capture an action. Opting for the standard device—a verb—to express action, Dionysius replaces Thucydides' *nomen actionis* (a noun semantically equivalent to an articular active infinitive[3]) with a verbal construction based on a participial phrase. Dionysius' rephrasing emphasizes the activity of personal subjects, whereas Thucydides' abstract noun reifies action stripped of the centrality of human agents.

Finally, Dionysius also rephrases the verbal component of the sentence, consisting in the thought that the revolutionaries went over the top in their effort to devise new schemes. For Thucydides' πολὺ ἐπέφερε τὴν ὑπερβολὴν τοῦ καινοῦσθαι τὰς διανοίας, Dionysius substitutes the following: ἐλάμβανον ὑπερβολὴν ἐπὶ τὸ διανοεῖσθαί τι καινότερον. The

[2] Macleod 1983e [1979]: 132.   [3] See Long 1968: 13.

replacement of ἐπιφέρω by λαμβάνω is probably due to the latter's widespread use in nominal periphrasis, i.e. in phrases that combine a relatively unspecific verb with a noun that does the job of conveying the verbal content.[4] The use of ἐπιφέρω provides evidence for the considerable freedom that Thucydides takes in using this construction: he expands the number of verbs that allow him to have nouns express content that one would ordinarily associate with verbs.[5]

What is more, Dionysius has altered the construction of the articular infinitive (Thucydides: τοῦ καινοῦσθαι τὰς διανοίας vs. Dionysius: ἐπὶ τὸ διανοεῖσθαί τι καινότερον). For one thing, it is noticeable that Dionysius expresses the distinctively human activity of 'planning' by a verbal form (διανοεῖσθαι) whereas Thucydides captures it by a noun (τὰς διανοίας). Furthermore, Dionysius' use of ἐπί followed by an articular infinitive in the accusative is a relatively common construction in ancient Greek[6]: the preposition can be regarded as semantically equivalent to a conjunction introducing a subordinate clause. By contrast, Thucydides uses the articular infinitive τοῦ καινοῦσθαι as an objective genitive dependent on ὑπερβολήν. In this construction, the articular infinitive is not obviously equivalent to a phrase featuring a finite verb, so that it has a more pointedly nominal flavour. By having this infinitive govern τὰς διανοίας as direct object, Thucydides has made three abstract nominal phrases depend on each other (extravagance—invention—schemes). Dionysius' phrasing suggests action that proceeds from purposefully acting subjects ('they resorted to extravagance in order to scheme something still more novel'). By contrast, Thucydides' wording has different implications: the bulky edifice of abstract nouns highlights the prevalence of processes and states of affairs.

In sum, by recasting Thucydides' original phrasing, Dionysius tries to make the passage more personal, verbal, and action-centred. The comparison between Thucydides' nominal πύστει τῶν προγενομένων and Dionysius' verbal ἐπιπυνθανόμενοι τὰ γεγενημένα shows particularly well why Dionysius found the original phrasing 'tortuous and hard to

---

[4] For examples, see LSJ s.v. λαμβάνω A.II.3.
[5] On Thucydides' fondness of periphrasis, see Classen-Steup i. lxxiii.
[6] K-G ii. 39 list ἐπί among the standard prepositions that govern an articular infinitive in the accusative.

follow' (σκολιὰ καὶ δυσπαρακολούθητα, *Thuc.* 29.373.22-3). Dionysius' verbal phrase exhibits immediately transparent structures of grammatical dependence. In Thucydides' nominal phrase, on the other hand, it is not clear what entity the reader should regard as the subject of the activity denoted by πύστις. The context offers 'events that came later', an obviously incongruous subject for a verb expressing a mental act. The dependence of the objective genitive τῶν προγενομένων on πύστει is less obscure, but, qua dependent genitive, its role in the sentence is not as immediately apparent as Dionysius' accusative τὰ γεγενημένα after ἐπιπυνθανόμενοι. From Dionysius' point of view, Thucydides puts too many thoughts into too few words. The nominalizations put language under strain by compressing phrases and blurring structures of dependence. In his rewriting, one can observe Dionysius' attempt to relax what he considers to be the overstrained muscles of Thucydides' nominalized language.

Other adaptations by Dionysius of passages from the chapters on stasis feature similar tendencies to the ones observed. The following excerpt, which comes directly after the passage quoted above, is Thucydides' famous statement of the mutation of meaning under the pressure of civil war (3.82.4):

καὶ τὴν εἰωθυῖαν ἀξίωσιν τῶν ὀνομάτων ἐς τὰ ἔργα ἀντήλλαξαν τῇ δικαιώσει

Further, they exchanged the usual evaluations that words attach to deeds in accord with their belief about what was right.[7]

After Dionysius' reworking, the passage reads like this (*Thuc.* 29.375.3-4):

τά τε εἰωθότα ὀνόματα ἐπὶ τοῖς πράγμασι λέγεσθαι μετατιθέντες ἄλλως ἠξίουν αὐτὰ καλεῖν.

Altering the customary application of words to acts, they claimed the right to refer to these acts by different labels.

---

[7] This translation is based on: Wilson 1982a: 20.

In Dionysius' version, Thucydides' main verb (ἀντήλλαξαν) has become a circumstantial participle (μετατιθέντες). Both use verbal forms to express the idea that people have changed the relationship of words to deeds. However, Dionysius, by expressing this notion through a participle, has reserved the centre of the sentence, i.e. the main verb, for a different idea: he puts the statement's emphasis on the revolutionaries' conscious resolve to change their evaluative judgments (ἠξίουν... καλεῖν). By contrast, Thucydides' main verb emphasizes the act of transformation, not the resolution that precedes the change. Dionysius' rearrangement shows that Thucydides' phrasing runs counter to an ordinary assumption: Dionysius makes the revolutionaries' *decision* the hub of the assertion, thus implying that it is more fundamental than the acts prompted by it. By contrast, Thucydides uses an abstract noun in the instrumental dative to capture the decision responsible for the revolutionaries' realignment of evaluative terms: τῇ δικαιώσει ('in accord with their belief about what was right'). It turns out that Dionysius' revision of the sentence enables him to get rid of a Thucydidean abstract noun. What is more, Dionysius has replaced another abstract noun from Thucydides' original, the object ἀξίωσιν ('evaluation'), by a verbal phrase, the infinitive λέγεσθαι, which depends on the participle εἰωθότα. Whereas in Dionysius' version emphasis rests on verb forms, Thucydides has made the nominal form ἀξίωσιν the nodal point of his sentence: it governs a participial attribute (εἰωθυῖαν), a subjective genitive (τῶν ὀνομάτων), and a prepositional phrase (ἐς τὰ ἔργα). By normal Greek standards, it is quite unusual for an abstract noun to be governing so many dependent phrases.[8]

Whereas Thucydides' version features only one verbal form (ἀντήλλαξαν), Dionysius has four (λέγεσθαι, μετατιθέντες, ἠξίουν, καλεῖν). The main verbs of both passages have a personal subject (presumably 'the revolutionaries'), but the effect is different in each case. In Dionysius' version, the revolutionaries have made the resolution to change the relationship between words and deeds. For Thucydides, the

---

[8] Radford 1901: 7 (mentioning Thucydides, Antiphon, Isocrates, and Aeschines as exceptions from the general trend); Denniston 1952: 36.

main verb emphasizes the act of changing the use of language, but not a conscious resolve to do so. In Thucydides, the abstract noun phrase τῇ δικαιώσει provides the motive for the transformation. Because of its impersonal character, it has greater independence from the subject of the sentence than a corresponding verbal construction. This is the case because a verbal phrase would agree with an unambiguously personal subject. The same observation applies to the phrase τὴν...ἀξίωσιν, especially in light of its numerous dependent phrases. Thucydides' phrasing hints at the possibility that, in changing the use of words, the revolutionaries are subject to a process, captured by impersonal abstract nouns.

After this general statement, Thucydides goes on to refer to specific instances of shifts in the application of language. Dionysius also takes issue with the style of these passages. The following quotation juxtaposes Thucydides' original with Dionysius' adaptation:

Th. 3.82.4: τόλμα μὲν γὰρ ἀλόγιστος ἀνδρεία φιλέταιρος ἐνομίσθη, μέλλησις δὲ προμηθὴς δειλία εὐπρεπής

For irrational daring came to be considered as courage showing devotion to one's partisans, and provident hesitation as specious cowardice

Thuc. 29.375.13–15: τὴν μὲν γὰρ τόλμαν ἀνδρίαν ἐκάλουν, τὴν δὲ μέλλησιν δειλίαν

For they called daring courage, and hesitation cowardice

Dionysius has replaced Thucydides' passive main verb (ἐνομίσθη) by an active one (ἐκάλουν). Whereas Thucydides' version does not highlight agents responsible for the shifts in language, Dionysius' active main verb makes clear reference to personal agents. Thucydides, again, emphasizes process over agency. What is more, Dionysius has dropped the adjectival attributes that Thucydides attaches to each of the four abstract nouns. Except for εὐπρεπής ('specious'), the other three adjectives ('irrational,' 'showing devotion to one's partisans', 'provident') apply most naturally to the behaviour of human beings. In this way, Thucydides assimilates abstract nouns to persons, a feature that Dionysius apparently considers incongruous.

Dionysius makes clear that the idiosyncrasies of Thucydides' style represent a vast deviation from the normal practices of ancient Greek prose writers. Referring specifically to the chapters on stasis, Dionysius remarks that neither Thucydides' own generation nor the subsequent writers adopted a style resembling that of Thucydides (*Thuc.* 29.373.24–374.1). In another passage, Dionysius provides a list of Attic prose writers who were contemporaries of Thucydides and stresses once again that none of them wrote in a style that resembled the language favoured by Thucydides (*Thuc.* 51.410.17–411.3).[9]

0.2 What Benefit Does Thucydides Derive from a Nominal Register?

Scholarly literature describes as 'abstract noun phrases' what Thucydides favours over personal and verbal constructions. Long provides this definition of abstract nouns: 'Conventionally we label "abstract" those generalizing nouns which denote concepts, qualities, actions etc., in contrast with nouns which refer to physical objects.'[10] Personal nouns do not belong to the category of abstract substantives because they always refer to living beings that exist in the physical, sensory world. As Denniston writes, abstract nouns as a whole can 'be roughly divided into *adjectival*, those which express a quality, and *verbal*, those which express an action or event'.[11] For instance, the phrases τὰ ἐφυστερίζοντα and πύστις are examples of verbal abstracts, the former denoting events and the latter an action. On the other hand, ἀνδρεία is an adjectival abstract since it refers to a quality.

By objecting to Thucydides' frequent use of abstract nouns, Dionysius takes issue with what scholars have identified as one of the most

---

[9] Pritchett (1975: xxii) convincingly argues that one should trust Dionysius' assessment: 'As a Professor of Classics, with a complete mastery of Greek and wide acquaintance with the Greek classics, at the same time enjoying a privileged life with apparent ease of movement and communication, he [*sc.* Dionysius] had available a great amount of classical prose literature now lost... [I]n matters of style it seems perverse to challenge Dionysius' view that Thucydides was idiosyncratic and obscure.' See also Grube 1950: 109–10.
[10] Long 1968: 12.   [11] Denniston 1952: 24.

characteristic features of Thucydides' style.[12] Denniston stresses both the distinctiveness and the exceptionality of this tendency. After demonstrating that ancient Greek prose was far less comfortable with using abstract nouns than modern English,[13] Denniston remarks: 'Turning back to Thucydides, we find everywhere the exact opposite of this tendency, an evident preference for abstract expression wherever its employment is at all possible.'[14]

Dionysius of Halicarnassus himself already drew attention to Thucydides' liking of abstract nominal expressions and pointed out that Thucydides 'sometimes expresses a verbal idea in a nominal form' (καὶ νῦν μὲν τὸ ῥηματικὸν ὀνοματικῶς ἐκφέρων, *Thuc.* 24.361.20–1; see also *Amm.* II 5.426.15–16).[15] The rhetorician Hermogenes puts particular stress on this feature of Thucydides' style, making an explicit connection between nominal phrasing and Thucydides' elevated tone (Περὶ ἰδεῶν 249.12–19):

Ἔτι δὲ σεμνὴ λέξις ἥ τε ὀνοματικὴ καὶ αὐτὰ τὰ ὀνόματα. ὀνοματικὴν δὲ λέγω τήν τε ἀπὸ τῶν ῥημάτων εἰς ὀνόματα πεποιημένην καὶ τὴν διὰ μετοχῶν τε καὶ ἀντωνυμιῶν καὶ τῶν τοιούτων. ὡς ἐλάχιστα γὰρ ἐν σεμνότητι δεῖ χρῆσθαι τοῖς ῥήμασιν, ὥσπερ ὁ Θουκυδίδης σχεδὸν μὲν διόλου βούλεται ποιεῖν τοῦτο, καταφανῶς δὲ αὐτὸ ἐν τῇ τῆς στάσεως ἐκφράσει τῶν Κερκυραίων πεποίηκε.

---

[12] Blass 1887–98: i. 213–15; Finley 1942: 261–6; Denniston 1952: 28, 36–7, 40; Classen-Steup i. lxxiii; Schmid 1948: 182–3; Dover 1965a: xiv; Rusten 1989: 22–3.
[13] Denniston 1952: 23–8.   [14] Denniston 1952: 28.
[15] Dionysius goes on to point out that Thucydides also conversely substitutes verbs for nouns (*Thuc.* 24.361.21–2). This would seem to contradict the view that Thucydides tends to reduce the verbal element in his language. However, the challenge is merely apparent, as a closer look at Dionysius' example shows. The passage chosen by Dionysius to illustrate Thucydides' substitution of 'verbs for nouns' is the statement about the 'truest cause' of the Peloponnesian War (1.23.6). As Dionysius writes in the *Second Letter to Ammaeus*, Thucydides should have used the nouns ἀνάγκη and πόλεμος instead of the infinitives τὸ ἀναγκάσαι and τὸ πολεμεῖν (*Amm.* II 6.427.14–16). As I will show in Chapter 5 (pp. 165–6), the interplay of the two infinitives in this specific passage has a dual effect: the construction first raises the problem of agency and then suggests that events unfold according to the logic of a process that carries human beings along. Thus, based on Dionysius' example, Thucydides' purpose in substituting 'verbs for nouns' is not to emphasize personal agency, but to stress people's passivity vis-à-vis processes that run their course.

Moreover, the nominal style is grand, and so are nouns themselves. I call that style nominal which is fashioned by using verbs as nouns and that is made up of participles, pronouns, and other such forms. For, if one aims at stylistic grandeur, one must use verbs as little as possible, just as Thucydides almost always wishes to do this, and he has patently done it in his description of stasis among the Corcyraeans.

Several other ancient literary critics associate Thucydides' language with a striving for grandeur and austerity.[16] Despite all his criticism, Dionysius in fact goes along with this assessment.[17] He acknowledges that Thucydides represents the fullest development of the grand style, on which Dionysius' hero Demosthenes modelled his own style without going to Thucydidean extremes (*Dem.* 10.148.14–20, 149.3–13). On Dionysius' view, Thucydides' problem is that he lacks self-restraint as well as feel for the suitable occasion: he exaggerates stylistic tendencies that would have their justification if used with measure and at the right moment (*Dem.* 10.148.20–149.3).

Modern scholars have generally followed the explanation of ancient critics that Thucydides' tendency towards abstraction reflects his striving for *gravitas*.[18] While it is true that the nominal constructions enable Thucydides to raise the account of the Peloponnesian War to a lofty level, the identification of the nominal style with the quest for grandeur also has a shortcoming: its extreme degree of generality (nominal phrases generate the overall impression of an elevated tone) often fails when one asks what the specific point of a particular Thucydidean construction is.

---

[16] Demetr. *Eloc.* 40, 45, 65, 72; Longin. 14.11; Marcellin. *Vit. Thuc.* 35–9, 41, 50, 56.
[17] See *Dem.* 10.149.9–13, 39.213.19–21 with 39.214.17–19.
[18] Blass 1887–98: i. 213; Wolcott 1898: 143, 157; Norden 1898: i. 96; Classen-Steup i. lxxiii. In her monograph *Word and Concept in Thucydides*, June Allison frequently comments on Thucydides' use of abstract nouns. Her chief concern is to prove that Thucydides was a pioneer in recognizing the specific linguistic status of conceptual language, and that he developed 'a set of metalinguistic terms' which allowed him to articulate his insight (1997: 15). Important points of contact notwithstanding, Allison's work and the present study are concerned with different aspects of Thucydides' use of abstract nouns: Allison investigates what she takes to be Thucydides' self-conscious insight into the nature of abstract language, whereas I am concerned with the light shed by abstract nouns on Thucydides' presentation of events.

Contrary to the impression of apparent uniformity, Dionysius in fact draws on a wide range of attributes to characterize Thucydides' style. In combination, these terms allow an articulate and nuanced description of Thucydides' distinctive *gravitas*. They can be subdivided into specific categories.

The first group consists of terms designating emotional states, in particular 'fear' (τὸ φοβερόν),[19] 'terror' (τὸ δεινόν),[20] and 'passion' (τὸ παθητικόν).[21]

The second group of attributes comprises physical and sensory qualities that may also capture, in a metaphorical sense, a specific type of character: 'rough' and 'severe' (αὐστηρόν),[22] 'pungent' and 'harsh' (πικρόν),[23] 'weighty' and 'grave' (ἐμβριθές),[24] and 'tension' or 'intensity' (ὁ τόνος).[25]

Next, there are terms that can be classified as sensory, physical, or aesthetic without capturing dispositions of character. While some terms refer to compactness and solidity,[26] others suggest convulsion, excess, and entanglement.[27] Both the notion of compactness and the idea of convulsion presuppose the idea of compression under strain, as if an external force exerted pressure on Thucydides' language.

A final group, drawn from *On Demosthenes*, links Thucydides' style with the notions of the unfamiliar and the contrived.[28]

---

[19] *Thuc.* 24.363.15, *Pomp.* 3.240.19–20.
[20] τὸ δεινόν, *Thuc.* 24.363.14, *Pomp.* 3.240.9; τὰ δεινά, *Thuc.* 15.347.17 and 21; δεινότης, *Thuc.* 53.412.25–6, *Dem.* 10.149.11–12.
[21] τὸ παθητικόν, *Thuc.* 24.363.15; τὰ παθητικά, *Imit.* fr. VI, iii Usener, 207.14; τὰ πάθη, *Thuc.* 15.347.18, 53.412.25, *Pomp.* 3.239.19.
[22] αὐστηράν [sc. τὴν σύνθεσιν τῶν μορίων], *Thuc.* 24.361.9; τὸ αὐστηρόν, *Thuc.* 24.363.14.
[23] τὸ πικρόν, *Thuc.* 24.363.13 and 53.412.24, *Pomp.* 3.239.14.
[24] τὸ ἐμβριθές, *Thuc.* 24.363.14.   [25] τοὺς τόνους, *Thuc.* 53.412.24.
[26] στιβαρὰν καὶ βεβηκυῖαν, *Thuc.* 24.361.9–10; τό τε στριφνὸν καὶ τὸ πυκνόν, *Thuc.* 24.363.13; τὰς συστροφάς ('concentration' [see Pritchett 1975: 140 n. 3]), *Thuc.* 53.412.24; τὸ στριφνόν, *Thuc.* 53.412.25.
[27] τὰ...βεβιασμένα σχήματα, *Thuc.* 33.381.5–6; τά τε σκολιὰ καὶ πολύπλοκα καὶ δυσεξέλικτα, *Thuc.* 24.362.20–1; τῷ περιέργῳ καὶ περιττῷ, *Thuc.* 28.372.3. On the meaning of περιττός in this passage, Pritchett observes that it 'must be determined by the words with which it is coupled. Usually it is found with words denoting the grand style [in which case it means 'extraordinary, richly wrought, exceedingly good, unsurpassed' – cf. Pritchett 1975: 142 n. 5]. Here..., however, the meaning is pejorative: "excessive, superfluous"' (Pritchett 1975: 110 n. 1).
[28] ἡ μὲν οὖν ἐξηλλαγμένη καὶ περιττὴ καὶ ἐγκατάσκευος καὶ τοῖς ἐπιθέτοις κόσμοις ἅπασι συμπεπληρωμένη λέξις, *Dem.* 1.130.1–3; τὸν...ἐγκατάσκευον καὶ ἐξηλλαγμένον τοῦ συνήθους χαρακτῆρα, *Dem.* 10.149.9–11.

Roberts has pointed out that, 'whenever we speak of Dionysius as a literary critic, we are speaking of one who was, first and foremost, a teacher of rhetoric.'[29] Given his rhetorical preoccupations, Dionysius was primarily interested, not in the relation between style and content, but in the connection between style and specifically induced states of mind in the audience. Nonetheless, Dionysius implies on many occasions that the grand style must interlock with a corresponding awe-inspiring subject. On closer inspection, it turns out that all the major attributes by which Dionysius characterizes Thucydides' style can in fact be correlated with central features of Thucydides' representation of the Peloponnesian War.

To begin with, the various terms found in the first group (i.e. characterizations of Thucydides' style drawn from the semantic field of affects and emotions) can refer either to πάθη (i.e. passions or sufferings) portrayed by Thucydides or to emotions induced in the reader.[30] Contrasting the distinctive qualities of Thucydides and Herodotus in the *Letter to Pompey*, Dionysius points out that Thucydides surpasses Herodotus in the ability 'to portray passions' (τὰ πάθη δηλῶσαι, *Pomp.* 3.239.19). Similarly, in *On Thucydides*, Dionysius refers to Thucydides' frequent accounts of the capture and destruction of a city, pointing out Thucydides' unrivalled ability to present 'sufferings... as cruel and terrible and worthy of pity' (ὠμὰ καὶ δεινὰ καὶ οἴκτων ἄξια... τὰ πάθη, *Thuc.* 15.347.17–18). On the other hand, in another passage, Dionysius stresses Thucydides' 'δεινότης that arouses passions' (τὴν ἐξεγείρουσαν τὰ πάθη δεινότητα, *Thuc.* 53.412.25–6). Here πάθη clearly refer to the emotions felt by the reader. The dual employment of πάθος and related words seems to imply a direct link between emotions as well as sufferings portrayed and emotions evoked. The opposite ideas juxtaposed by this antithesis (i.e. representation vs. evocation of πάθη) are mediated by Thucydides' style.

Close attention to the term δεινότης, which Dionysius uses both in the last-mentioned passage and elsewhere, reinforces this impression. When

---

[29] Roberts 1901: 4–5.
[30] Compare the definition, offered by Lateiner (1977: 42), of the dual meaning of τὸ παθητικόν, as used by Dionysius in literary analysis: 'vividly portraying disaster and arousing the reader's feelings'.

ancient literary critics use δεινότης to characterize a specific kind of style, the word is usually best rendered as 'passionate force', 'intensity', and 'forcefulness'.[31] Dionysius uses the term in this sense when referring to Thucydides' 'δεινότης that arouses passions' (*Thuc.* 53.412.25–6) and in a passage from *On Demosthenes*, where Dionysius observes that 'the power [sc. of Thucydides' grand style] lay entirely in its δεινότης' (τὸ κράτος ἅπαν ἦν ἐν τῇ δεινότητι, *Dem.* 10.149.11–12). In the same way, Dionysius refers to τὸ δεινὸν καὶ φοβερόν as one pair in a general list of the *chrōmata* of Thucydides' style (*Thuc.* 24.363.12–15). Thus, in connection with Dionysius' discussion of Thucydides, δεινότης frequently refers to the author's 'forceful' rhetorical skill, which arouses the emotional value of intense passion in the reader.

At the same time, however, Dionysius also draws on the term δεινός as a label for the kind of events that play an especially important role in Thucydides: 'the capture and destruction of cities, the enslavement of their inhabitants and other disasters that are similar in kind' (πόλεών τε ἁλώσεις καὶ κατασκαφὰς καὶ ἀνδραποδισμοὺς καὶ ἄλλας τοιαύτας συμφοράς, *Thuc.* 15.347.15–16). Dionysius goes on to observe that Thucydides, if he is successful, 'makes these sufferings appear so cruel, terrifying, and worthy of pity that he leaves no scope for being surpassed' (οὕτως ὠμὰ καὶ δεινὰ καὶ οἴκτων ἄξια φαίνεσθαι ποιεῖ τὰ πάθη, ὥστε μηδεμίαν ὑπερβολὴν... καταλιπεῖν, *Thuc.* 15.347.17–20). The term translated as 'terrifying' is δεινός. In this passage, the word reflects the character of the events portrayed, which Thucydides manages to transmit adequately by his skill as a writer. Dionysius goes on to observe that in several other cases Thucydides falls shorts of similar events by trivializing them, thus failing to convey these 'horrors' (δεινῶν) to the reader's perception.[32] The passage shows clearly that the word δεινός refers to a particular quality of events.

---

[31] Grube 1961: 136–7; Pritchett 1975: 108 n. 4. Both scholars note that δεινότης also means 'rhetorical skill generally' in the writings of ancient literary critics. In Dionysius' discussions of Thucydides, however, the term usually does not seem to denote rhetorical skill as such, but Thucydides' 'forcefulnes's, understood as a particular manifestation of rhetorical skill.

[32] As Pritchett (1975: 65 n. 3) observes, the manuscripts have ἡμῶν instead of αὐτῶν, but the emendation seems justified.

Dionysius also summarizes his quotation of Thucydides' account of the battle in the Great Harbor of Syracuse by pointing out that it is a prime example of his authorial δεινότης (*Thuc.* 27.371.3–4). The term refers to Thucydides' brilliant rhetorical abilities, but this capacity again manifests itself in a passage concerned with intense passion and large-scale suffering. Finally, at the beginning of his *Life of Nicias*, Plutarch praises the qualities displayed by Thucydides' account of the Athenian disaster at Sicily in superlative terms: 'In dealing with this topic, he outdid himself in pathos, vividness, and variety' (αὐτὸς αὑτοῦ περὶ ταῦτα παθητικώτατος ἐναργέστατος ποικιλώτατος γενόμενος, *Nic.* 1.1). Plutarch, too, links the theme of pathos, again referring to both the depiction and the evocation of grand emotions, with Thucydides' 'terrible' skill as a writer (δεινότητι, *Nic.* 1.2). It thus turns out that Thucydides' awe-inspiring rhetorical power and his concern with the depiction of passion go hand in hand. The terms drawn from the register of emotion function on three levels. They refer to: (1) the events portrayed; (2) Thucydides' authorial character and rhetorical skill (i.e. the medium of presentation); and (3) the states induced in the reader. The diffusion of the same terminology across these three levels of analysis suggests that Dionysius posits continuity between style and content.

Correspondence between Thucydides' topic and mode of expression is also suggested by the other sets of terms used by Dionysius to characterize Thucydides' style. For the qualities of 'harshness' and 'severity', one only need think of the description of the Peloponnesian War as 'a violent teacher' (βίαιος διδάσκαλος, 3.82.2). Likewise, the terms suggesting compression, strain, and convulsion reflect, as already noted, the pressure of external forces. This phenomenon is a recurring theme in Thucydides' representation of the War. In the proem, Thucydides describes the War as the 'very greatest commotion' (κίνησις...μεγίστη δή, 1.1.2) that ever happened to the Greeks and a great part of mankind in general.[33] The thought returns in the chapters on stasis when Thucydides remarks that 'in effect the whole Greek world was convulsed'

---

[33] Jeffrey Rusten (2015: 36) has argued that κίνησις does not mean 'commotion' in this passage, but 'mobilization'. Despite Rusten's carefully argued case, the traditional rendition of κίνησις as 'commotion' still carries conviction, chiefly because it seems plausible to expect that

(καὶ πᾶν ὡς εἰπεῖν τὸ Ἑλληνικὸν ἐκινήθη, 3.82.1). Moreover, as we will see in more detail in Chapter 2 (pp. 67–70), Thucydides systematically represents the Peloponnesian War, as well as various events in which the War finds vivid expression, through phrases that suggest the attack of an overwhelming force.

Finally, the categories of unfamiliarity and contrived newness also respond to aspects of the War regularly highlighted by Thucydides. The War, the greatest and universal κίνησις that ever occurred (1.1.2), marks a new stage in human experience. It follows that the sufferings that come in its wake also have a scale that has not been paralleled up to now (1.23.1). Moreover, the plague marks the beginning, as Thucydides observes, of 'a greater lawlessness' (ἐπὶ πλέον ἀνομίας, 2.53.1) in the human community, and stasis at Corcyra is the harbinger (ἐν τοῖς πρώτη ἐγένετο, 3.82.1) of terrors that will soon be rampant throughout Greece. The Peloponnesian War marks the incursion of forces of a heretofore unknown magnitude into the Greek world, thus overthrowing what is time-honoured and familiar. The uncommon character of Thucydides' style is an attempt to articulate the experience of this radical overthrow of deep-seated assumptions.

Close correspondence thus obtains between Thucydides' representation of the War and Dionysius' description of his style. In light of this circumstance, it is reasonable to infer that the prominent abstract noun phrases, with their implications of impersonality and passivity, also mark a specific experiential feature of the Peloponnesian War. It is right to ask, with Colin Macleod and Adam Parry, whether the stylistic elements criticized by Dionysius are not, in fact, indispensable to the author's purpose and not the gratuitous idiosyncrasies that Dionysius would edit away.[34] The assertion that Thucydides' nominalizations induce an elevated tone may mark the beginning, rather than the end, of an answer to the problem posed by Thucydides' abstract style.

Thucydides himself states that he disdains those who sacrifice truthfulness to literary effect (1.21.1), and he insists on his painstaking effort

---

Thucydides' characterization of the War in the proem should resonate with his statement of the War's distinctive nature at 1.23. This link is based on κίνησις meaning 'commotion'. Cf. Munson 2015: 41–2.

[34] Parry 1970: 5; Macleod 1983e [1979]: 135.

to offer an account of the utmost precision (1.20.1, 21.1, 22.1, 22.2). W. R. Connor surely refers to Thucydides' self-imposed focus on precision when he offers the following explanation for his wilful style:

> The difficulties derive...from a desire to affirm his [*sc.* Thucydides'] respect for the complexity of historical events and human motives. In Thucydides we discover...a style that replicates the intractability of historical experience. It assures the reader that the author will not oversimplify or reduce events to cliché, antithesis, or dogma.[35]

Taking much the same view, John H. Finley pointed out that Thucydides' abstract phrases 'vividly reflect the impersonal yet compelling forces in human affairs which it was Thucydides' chief purpose to describe'.[36] He continues:

> Thucydides conceived of the social and psychological forces which he analyzed in his work as living, compulsive elements of the human mind, and [...] his style reflected his feeling. In reading the *History*, one has the impression of dealing not only with people and things but, even more, with the forces behind them which make them what they are.[37]

Finley does not, however, offer a detailed stylistic analysis that shows how Thucydides' abstractions enact the working of such forces.[38]

Picking up from where Connor and Finley left off, this book seeks to respond to Dionysius' dissatisfaction with Thucydides' abstract nominal

---

[35] Connor 1985: 7–8. Similar views with regard to the conundrum of Thucydides' style are expressed by Parry (1970: 6) and Macleod (1983e [1979]: 135).
[36] Finley 1942: 266.   [37] Finley 1942: 265.
[38] Adam Parry and Daniel Tompkins, adopting an approach similar to mine, have each provided a detailed analysis of the implications that specific Thucydidean stylistic choices have for his interpretation of events. Parry has shown that in the excursus on the plague the syntactical organization of various sentences has the effect of capturing the 'overwhelming force' of the plague and the helplessness of the victims (Parry 1969: 114–17). Tompkins analyses the sentence structure of the speeches given by Nicias and Alcibiades, and he shows that each speaker's character is correlated with his preferred mode of expression (1972: 188 and 204 [on Nicias], 210 [on Alcibiades]). In three further articles, Tompkins has explored how Thucydides' stylistic choices contribute to his characterization of Archidamus (1993b: 102–11), Diodotus (1993a: *passim*), and Pericles (2013: 448–57).

style. The provisional and rough interpretation, offered above, of the extracts from the stasis section paves the way for the book's central concern. Thucydides' choice to *enact* events through abstract nominal phrases reflects his purpose both in the chapters on stasis and in the work as a whole. He means to show, in this great commotion, the subjection of human agency to forces beyond any individual or personal control.

0.3 Two Contrary Strands in the *History*: Contingency vs. Necessity

The provisional thesis that the nominal style highlights the priority of forces that defy human control implies that events in the *History* are subject to some kind of necessity. At first blush, this position runs counter to a theme that scholars have shown to be a central concern of Thucydides: his emphasis on unpredictability and contingency. In recent years, James Morrison, Francis Dunn, and Jonas Grethlein have drawn particular attention to the role of chance.[39] On their account, Thucydides enables readers to experience the Peloponnesian War from the immediate perspective of the participants, bringing them face to face with the complexity and the fundamental openness of the course of events.

In making this argument, the scholars mentioned highlight a range of narrative techniques by which Thucydides evokes the effect variously described as 'presentness',[40] 'experiential quality',[41] or 'participatory experience for the "engaged" reader'.[42] One feature that stands out among the techniques employed for this purpose is so-called embedded or internal focalization by which the author, while recounting past events in a third person manner, still represents them from the perspective of

---

[39] In emphasizing the unpredictability of events, these scholars follow in the footsteps of two classic works of Thucydidean scholarship: Hans-Peter Stahl's *Thucydides: Man's Place in History* and Lowell Edmunds's *Chance and Intelligence in Thucydides*. It is worth emphasising, however, that Stahl (2003 [1966]: 152–3) and Edmunds (1975: 202–4) hold that Thucydides subscribed to a repetitive or cyclical view of history, so that, in their view, Thucydides' emphasis on chance and unpredictability cannot be identified with his commitment to a fundamentally open horizon of possibilities. As Stahl observes, the events portrayed by Thucydides exhibit a '*recurring* structure' (2003 [1966]: 123), which is compatible with the unpredictability of events and the irrationality of human behaviour.

[40] Dunn 2007: 141.   [41] Grethlein 2013: 31.   [42] Morrison 1999: 97.

the protagonists, thus enabling the reader to experience events from their angle.[43]

Closely connected with the issue of focalization is Thucydides' attempt, stressed by all three scholars, to place the reader in the 'virtual present'.[44] Describing events without immediately naming their ultimate significance, Thucydides keeps the reader uncertain about the reach of a given event at the time of its occurrence. The result is yet again that the reader's perspective resembles that of the actual contemporaries of the events described.

Dunn goes furthest in the conclusions that he draws from the analysis of these various narrative strategies. Based on the argument that 'a revised understanding of human responsibilities and human agency' arose in the late fifth century,[45] Dunn argues that, '[i]n Thucydides,... there is no suggestion of a general pattern or rule of change'.[46] In spelling out this claim, Dunn emphasizes that the notions of necessity and inevitability are quite foreign to Thucydides.[47] Thus, the emphasis of Thucydides' narrative on unpredictability, presentness, and open-endedness implies the contingency of events, whether small or large, in the Peloponnesian War.

These conclusions are hard to reconcile with Thucydides' statement, in the chapter on method and in the excursus on stasis, that the events experienced in the Peloponnesian War will recur, with some variation but in basically the same way, due to the influence of 'the human' or 'human nature' (1.22.4, 3.82.2). While these remarks leave some room for variation, they nonetheless commit Thucydides to the view that human affairs do not proceed against the backdrop of an entirely open horizon of possibilities. The notion of unqualified contingency does not sit well with this circular structure: if events can move in any direction, how can there be a predetermined recurrence of the same?

The emphasis on Thucydides' concern with the unpredictability and openness of events can be usefully contrasted with a rival interpretation.

---

[43] Morrison 1999: 121–4; Grethlein 2013: 34–6.
[44] Morrison 1999: 123; Dunn 2007: 124; Grethlein 2013: 39–40.
[45] Dunn 2007: 7.   [46] Dunn 2007: 142.   [47] Dunn 2007: 142–3.

This alternative approach foregrounds Thucydides' conviction that the outbreak and outcome of the Peloponnesian War is subject to necessity.

Scholars who have studied the meaning of ἀνάγκη and similar terms in Thucydides draw a fundamental distinction between two senses of these words. Following the terminology used by Fisher and Hoekstra, one can distinguish between 'practical' and 'hard necessity'.[48] Practical necessity obtains when people find that, after a consideration of all the factors involved, there is really only one acceptable course of action open to them. Other options entail costs that would be unacceptable. Paradigm cases of practical necessity are situations during military operations in which one of two alternative options would involve dire consequences.[49] The necessities arising in these situations exert some immediate pressure insofar as they involve questions of life and death, but they are not fully compulsory. This is confirmed by several Thucydidean references to individuals who rise above their survival instinct. Nicias is a case in point. When the Athenians have come to a deadlock at the river Assinarus during their retreat at Sicily and run the risk of being massacred to the last man, Nicias surrenders himself to Gylippus, the Spartan commander of the Syracusan troops, telling him that he should do with Nicias as he pleases, but that he should put an end to the slaughter of his men (7.85.1). Another example can be found in Thucydides' account of the plague at Athens. While the plague rages, some Athenians, moved by 'virtue' (ἀρετῆς, 2.51.5) and a 'sense of shame' (αἰσχύνῃ, 2.51.5), do not shrink from visiting their sick friends, fully aware of the likelihood that they will now catch the deadly disease in turn. A similar preparedness to endure death is shown by the fallen soldiers whom Pericles celebrates in the Funeral Oration: Pericles admires, more than anything else, the fallen men's clear-sighted willingness to sacrifice their lives for the city (2.42.4, 43.2, 43.5–6). Finally, Greeks generally assume that Spartans will never surrender, 'neither out of hunger nor any other necessity' (οὔτε λιμῷ οὔτ' ἀνάγκῃ οὐδεμιᾷ, 4.40.1). Although the Spartans at Pylos ultimately do surrender, the boundless surprise felt by the other Greeks at their subjugation makes clear that the opposite choice (i.e. of death instead of survival) had been a

---

[48] Fisher and Hoekstra 2017: 374–5. [49] For examples, see Ostwald 1988: 10.

genuine option. These passages show that people have it in themselves to overcome their survival instinct in extraordinary circumstances for the sake of higher aspirations.

Fisher's and Hoekstra's paradigmatic examples for hard necessity are situations in which, to use modern terminology, the mechanical laws of nature determine the outcome of an event: if a ship sinks in a storm, or if a spear is driven through a person's heart, the result is inevitable, and human effort has no leeway to influence the outcome.[50] Now the decisive question is whether Thucydides recognizes any analogous hard necessities in the forces influencing collective human behaviour. Ostwald as well as Fisher and Hoekstra think that, in some passages, ἀνάγκη and related words refer to fixed psychological constraints of human behaviour.[51] Prime examples of hard necessity that weigh on people's actions are the claims, put forward by the Athenian speakers at Sparta and at Melos, that human behaviour is subject to a natural necessity that forces a ubiquitous quest for power on everyone alike (1.76.2, 5.105.2). Due to its 'universality', Ostwald considers the psychological compulsion exerted by the quest for power 'deterministic'.[52] Fisher and Hoekstra find an analogy between this type of compulsion and 'tragic overdetermination', which they describe as 'acting under the compulsion of an external and implacable force'.[53]

Two specific reasons prompt the conclusion that the natural constraint envisaged by the Athenian speakers at Sparta and at Melos amounts to hard necessity. First, the passive phrasing in both passages, putting 'the three greatest things' and 'compulsory nature' in the position of the agent, suggests that people cannot choose their goals, but that these are fixed and given to them. As Fisher and Hoekstra comment with regard to the passive phrasing, 'psychological forces are...depicted as if they

---

[50] Fisher and Hoekstra 2017: 374.
[51] At the same time, Ostwald as well as Fisher and Hoekstra note that in many other passages ἀνάγκη refers to practical necessities in Thucydides (Ostwald 1988: 35–6; Fisher and Hoekstra 2017: 375). De Romilly (1971: 124, 125) and Schneider (1974: 104–10) do not think that hard psychological necessity (unlike practical necessity) has much of a role to play in Thucydides. Finally, it should be noted that Fisher and Hoekstra do not apply the specific term 'hard necessity' to instances of psychological compulsion. They stress, however, that psychological compulsion 'sits awkwardly with the paradigm of practical necessitation' (376).
[52] Ostwald 1988: 42.
[53] Fisher and Hoekstra 2017: 376 and 377. One should note that Ostwald disagrees with Fisher and Hoekstra as to whether Thucydides himself endorses the thesis, put forward by the Athenians at Sparta and Melos, about the hard necessity of the desire for power: Ostwald thinks he does (1988: 38), whereas Fisher and Hoekstra are more inclined to view it as a rhetorical ploy used to further the Athenians' political aims on each respective occasion (2017: 385–6).

were the hardest of necessities'.[54] Instead of human beings selecting what motivation to act on, the relationship is reversed, with the motivating power controlling the apparent agents.

Second, Ostwald as well as Fisher and Hoekstra point out that psychological necessity as depicted by the Athenian ambassadors at Sparta and Melos does not only make itself felt in specific situations, but that it has an unconditioned universality, applying always and to everyone.[55] The natural compulsion to seek, and make use of, power is prior to any specific situation in which agents may find themselves. By contrast, circumstances in which one's life is at stake, so that a certain course of action is 'necessary' (in the sense of being induced by survival instinct), usually have a much narrower scope: necessity arises in a specific situation of extreme danger and disappears when the situation has ceased.

According to Richard Ned Lebow, ancient Greeks (Thucydides being no exception) 'understood people and *poleis* (city states) to be motivated by honor, interest, and fear'.[56] In this way, basic continuity obtains between the psychology of individuals and of cities.[57] In the Mytilenean Debate, Diodotus explicitly draws attention to this connection, observing that the motivating forces that apply to individuals (τινὰ, 3.45.6) exert their influence 'to no lesser degree on cities' (καὶ οὐχ ἧσσον τὰς πόλεις, 3.45.6). In fact, in Diodotus' view, cities succumb even more thoroughly than individuals to predetermined motivational drives. He adduces two reasons for this position: cities are usually confronted with the highest conceivable stakes, 'freedom or dominion over others' (ἐλευθερίας ἢ ἄλλων ἀρχῆς, 3.45.6), and the dynamic of heightened collective states carries everyone along, so that 'each individual, joined by all the rest, irrationally presumes too far' (μετὰ πάντων ἕκαστος ἀλογίστως ἐπὶ πλέον τι αὐτὸν ἐδόξασεν, 3.45.6). It is very difficult to find Thucydidean examples of cities capable of shedding the natural compulsion to strive after power. On this issue, Leo Strauss, followed by Clifford Orwin, observed: 'Thucydides just as his Athenians on Melos

---

[54] Fisher and Hoekstra 2017: 383.
[55] Ostwald 1988: 38; Fisher and Hoekstra 2017: 376.   [56] Lebow 2007: 171.
[57] Visvardi (2015: 46): '[T]he analogy between individual and collective psychology permeates Thucydides' *History* and converts questions of psychology into political and moral dilemmas.' See also Jaffe 2017: 202–3.

did not know of a strong city which failed to rule a weak city when it was to the former's interest to do so, merely for reasons of moderation'.[58]

Complementing the approach focused on ἀνάγκη and similar terms, another group of scholars (whose chief representatives are Adam Parry, Peter Pouncey, and Virginia Hunter) has focused on Thucydides' stress on the necessity of specific processes. They take their cues from passages (such as the two statements about the circular pattern of history) that demonstrate Thucydides' belief in the inevitability of certain events, without necessarily referring to ἀνάγκη. According to these scholars, the combined evidence suggests Thucydides' commitment to the doctrine that the rise and fall of cities proceeds according to a foreordained pattern.

The *Archaeology* provides a blueprint for the conception of an archetypical historical process in Thucydides. Basic human impulses, such as fear and self-interest as well as aggression, incite cities to build up and solidify power.[59] In order to do this, they have to dispose of specific material resources, in particular walls, commerce, communications, and material surplus.[60] The capacity to wield these factors is an indicator for a city's power, which allows it to impose order on the surrounding world.[61] In the course of extending their power and imposing order, cities build empires (ἀρχαί) and turn weaker cities into their subjects. Such an empire has an 'inherent tendency to expansion',[62] a process that leads to the absorption of more and more smaller cities.[63] Due to an inexorable dynamic, the quest for power sooner or later escalates into an ever insatiable desire, which gradually sheds any moral, and even prudential, constraints. In Hunter's words, the result is '*physis* uncontrolled'.[64] Eventually, this release from all restraint, combined with the pressures induced by war, results in

---

[58] Strauss 1964: 192; Orwin 1994: 86. The Spartans, who gladly resign the leadership of the Greek league against Persia to the Athenians, are merely an apparent exception: they have to deal with the helots, a massive internal population of subjects over whom they rule with an iron fist (Strauss 1964: 191–2; Orwin 1994: 85). Similar considerations apply to the Chians. Thucydides acknowledges their prudent moderation, which he considers second only to that of the Spartans (8.24.4). Yet he also notes that the Chians have the largest slave population in all of Greece, again only second to that of the Spartans (8.40.2), the consequence being that in Chios slaves 'are punished more severely if they have committed any misdeeds' than anywhere else in Greece (χαλεπωτέρως ἐν ταῖς ἀδικίαις κολαζόμενοι, 8.40.2).
[59] Pouncey 1980: xi.   [60] Hunter 1982: 20.   [61] Parry 1972: 53–4.
[62] Hunter 1982: 229.   [63] Pouncey 1980: xii.   [64] Hunter 1982: 266.

self-destructive endeavours and civil strife, tendencies that drive even the most powerful cities into ruin.[65] The picture is tragic because the same forces that engender the rise of civilization are responsible for its undoing.[66] All three scholars make emphatically clear that Thucydides regarded this process as inevitable.[67]

0.4 Determinism 'up to a point'

The clear emphasis on necessity, both in terms of collective psychological compulsion and of the inevitable process of self-undoing, raises the question how it can be squared with the narrative stress on chance and contingency. While it seems difficult to uphold the claim that Thucydides was unqualifiedly committed to the contingency of events, it would also be implausible to discard altogether the narrative emphasis on unpredictability.

Scholars concerned with Thucydidean necessity have in fact recognized this tension. According to Martin Ostwald, it is clear that even the hard variant of necessity is not equivalent to the modern notion of causal determinism. This is the view that each event is ineluctably bound to happen as it does, predetermined by the logic of a mechanistic universe in which every single state of affairs inevitably follows from the preceding one. According to Ostwald, Thucydides' position is merely '"deterministic" up to a point'.[68] As Ostwald observes, no antecedent necessity forced the allies to offer the hegemony to the Athenians, so that the various innate necessities of imperialism would not have arisen if the allies had never made that move.[69] Elsewhere he points out that, although the Athenians' original decision in favour of the Sicilian Expedition was probably determined by the innate determinism of imperialism, 'there is no evidence that he [*sc.* Thucydides] regarded each step in the denouement as determined by ἀνάγκη to occur as it did and in the sequence in which it did'.[70] In a similar vein, Pouncey points out: 'Thucydides does not seem to insist on the absolute

---

[65] Pouncey 1980: xii; Hunter 1982: 266. [66] Parry 1972: 55; Pouncey 1980: xiii.
[67] Parry 1972: 55; Pouncey 1980: xii; Hunter 1982: 231, 232, 266. [68] Ostwald 1988: 42.
[69] Ostwald 1988: 42. [70] Ostwald 1988: 52.

determinism of human nature.'[71] Pouncey notices the cases of individuals (namely Pericles, Brasidas, and Hermocrates) who withstand the general drift of destructive forces.[72] Finally, Peter Brunt remarks that it would be wrong to assume that Thucydides did not recognize any 'freedom of choice at all'.[73] Referring to the Thucydidean dictum that during stasis people become subject to 'necessities that leave no room for choice' (ἐς ἀκουσίους ἀνάγκας πίπτειν, 3.82.2), Brunt stresses that this statement has a flipside, namely the implication that at other times human beings must possess some freedom of choice. Acknowledging Thucydides' awareness that people 'could act with more or less passion or circumspection', Brunt summarizes: 'But their choice was always more or less restricted by their own nature, which compelled them to act from self-regarding motives.'[74]

The phrase 'more or less restricted', as well as Ostwald's '"deterministic" up to a point', indicates that Thucydidean necessity apparently comes in degrees. This idea of partial necessity requires elucidation. Is the absolute character of necessity not part and parcel of the concept? Does necessity not imply a 'must' that leaves no room for exceptions?

It follows that the second major task of this book, in addition to the elucidation of the nominal style, will be to come to terms with Thucydidean necessity, in particular the interaction of psychological determination with degrees of more or less unconstrained action. The challenge will be to answer how there can be both necessity and flexibility, both predetermination and contingency, and both compulsion and scope for choice.

---

[71] Pouncey 1980: 35, 173 n. 6.   [72] Pouncey 1980: 35.   [73] Brunt 1993 [1963]: 156.
[74] Brunt 1993 [1963]: 156.

1
Thucydides' Abstract Nominal Style

The Main Features and Differences
from the Plain Style

Dionysius of Halicarnassus was not alone among the ancients in his verdict that Thucydides' style strains the limits of the Greek language. Taking recourse to a rather mild label, Cicero called Thucydides 'at times somewhat obscure' (*interdum subobscuri*, *Brut.* 7.29). Elsewhere he expresses himself more forcefully, remarking that Thucydides' speeches 'contain so many obscure and cryptic sentences that they are hardly understandable' (*ita multas habent obscuras abditasque sententias, vix ut intellegantur*, *Or.* 9.30). Several factors contribute to this impression.[1] While other Greek authors strive for balance, Thucydides is fond of *variatio* and frustrates the expectation of symmetry. He shares with Gorgias a penchant for antithesis but tends to construct his pairs of opposites in such a complicated manner that the nature of the contrast is often obscured. Instead of writing in a periodic style in which the end of the sentence and the end of a sense-unit coincide, he prefers to extend his sentences beyond the natural closure provided by the end of a sense-unit. Finally, there is Thucydides' noteworthy tendency, highlighted in the Introduction, towards abstract nominal phrases. According to Dionysius, the chief reason for Thucydides' obscurity lies in what he considers to be Thucydides' striving for brevity (*Thuc.* 24.363.4–9; see also *Pomp.* 3.239.11–13). This, in turn, is often just another label for Thucydides' tendency to use abstract nominal expressions. For, as we will see in detail below, his fondness for linguistic abstractions enables him to express entire subordinate clauses in one noun phrase.

---

[1] For summaries of the main features of Thucydides' style, see Blass 1887–98: i.205–44; Classen-Steup i. lxxii–lxxxiv; Schmid 1948: 181–204; Dover 1965a: xiii–xvii; Rusten 1989: 21–8.

After providing an overview of various types of abstract nouns in Section 1.1, I will use Section 1.2 to offer a systematic analysis of four principal ways in which Thucydides invests his language with an abstract imprint. Based on this survey, the remainder of the chapter will centre on the excursus on stasis at Corcyra in book 3, also known as the *Pathology* of war. This segment represents the most thoroughgoing example of Thucydides' abstract style: according to both ancients and moderns, no other extended passage in Thucydides' work contains a similar density of abstract nominal expressions.[2] Section 1.3 will compare the excursus on stasis with Thucydides' preceding narrative account of the same events (3.70–81). Through this direct juxtaposition, the stylistic extravagance of the *Pathology* will come to light.

1.1 Abstract Nominal Phrases in Ancient Greek

Commentators agree about the idiosyncratic nature of Thucydides' inclination towards abstraction. The following remark by John Finley sums up the *communis opinio*:

> Thucydides' diction was highly, by Greek standards enormously, abstract ... [H]is pages are studded both with general nouns and, more characteristic still, with infinitives, neuter adjectives and neuter participles doing service for nouns.[3]

Finley mentions a range of distinct abstract nominal forms. Before moving to the various methods by which Thucydides introduces abstraction, it will be profitable to get an overview of the different types of abstract forms that occur in ancient Greek.

---

[2] In Hermogenes' judgment, it is an example of Thucydides' 'nominal style' (λέξις ... ὀνοματική, Hermog. Περὶ ἰδεῶν. 249.12). Finley (1942: 262) writes that the *Pathology*, together with the Corinthians' juxtaposition of the Athenian and Spartan character (1.70), exemplifies 'Thucydides' generalizing manner at its height'. Dover (1997: 32) remarks: 'Thucydides' characterization (iii.82f.) of stasis is one of the passages which most readily spring to mind in response to the stimulus of the words "Thucydidean style".'

[3] Finley 1942: 261–2. See also Classen-Steup i. lxxiii; Denniston 1952: 28.

In his book on abstract nouns in Sophocles, A. A. Long provides the following handy definition of abstract nouns. He distinguishes nouns that refer to physical objects from all other nouns. Abstract nouns make up this second class of nouns: they do not refer to particular objects, but to generalizing classes, and signify concepts, qualities, actions, and the like.[4] Abstract nouns can be subdivided: one branch of abstract nouns is derived from verbs and denotes an action or the result of an action, the other traces itself back to adjectives and signifies properties or qualities.[5]

Keeping these two branches of abstract nouns in mind, we can distinguish four specific types of Greek abstract expressions, all of which are frequently attested in Thucydides:[6]

(1) Abstract nouns, which can be either adjectival (e.g. ἀνδρεία, 'manliness', derived from ἀνδρεῖος, 'manly') or verbal (e.g. μάθημα, 'learning', derived from μανθάνω, 'to learn').[7] Adjectival abstracts are also called *nomina qualitatis*. Verbal abstracts come in two different categories. One class are *nomina actionis* which correspond in sense to the active infinitive, such as ὄψις in the sense, 'seeing' or 'vision'. The other category of verbal abstracts is called *nomina acti*. For the most part, *nomina acti* are synonyms of passive participles: for example, κηρύγματα ('announcements') means the same as the nominalized participle τὰ κεκηρυγμένα ('things that have been announced').[8]

Some abstract nouns, like πόλεμος or τύχη, are very common, but there are others, e.g. many verbal nouns in -σις and -μα, which Thucydides seems to have coined himself.[9]

(2) Articular infinitives. A neuter article combined with an infinitive can be equivalent to a verbal noun.[10] At one point, for instance,

---

[4] Long 1968: 12.
[5] Snell 1952: 152–8; Browning 1958: 61; Denniston 1952: 24; Long 1968: 13–14.
[6] For these four types of abstract expressions, see Denniston 1952: 24–38. Denniston has three groups: (1) abstract substantives, (2) neuter adjectives and participles, (3) articular infinitives. I will treat neuter adjectives and neuter participles as different groups.
[7] The following distinctions are based on Browning 1958: 61 and Long 1968: 13–14.
[8] For an example of τὰ κεκηρυγμένα in this sense, see Th. 4.38.1.
[9] A list of all verbal nouns that occur in Thucydides and are *hapax legomena* can be found in Wolcott 1898: 106–15. See also Sihler 1881: 96–104; Browning 1958: 66–8; Blass 1887–98: i.213; Rusten 1989: 22.
[10] K-G ii. 2–3, 37–43.

Thucydides has the Mytilinean envoys at Olympia use the infinitival form τὸ ἐπιχειρεῖν as a noun to signify 'initiative to attack': ἐπ' ἐκείνοις δὲ ὄντος αἰεὶ τοῦ ἐπιχειρεῖν ('since the initiative to attack is always in their hands', 3.12.3).

(3) Substantivized adjectives. They are created by using a neuter adjective with an article.[11] Such forms are synonymous with *nomina qualitatis*. An illustration of this usage is the employment of τὸ βραδύ in the sense of 'slowness' (βραδυτής) in Archidamus' speech defending the Spartan character (1.84.1). As Classen-Steup observe, the similarity in terms of content of this form to the corresponding abstract noun is illustrated by the fact that, by using this form, Archidamus directly responds to the Corinthian speakers who employ the noun βραδυτής in their critique of the Spartan manner (1.71.4).[12] Denniston emphasizes that this construction is very frequent in Thucydides while in other prose authors it is relatively rare except for the use of very common adjectives such as τὸ καλόν ('the beautiful, beauty') or τὸ δίκαιον ('the just, justice').[13]

(4) Substantivized participles. Like neuter adjectives, a neuter participle can be combined with an article, thus producing the equivalent of an abstract verbal noun: e.g. τὸ μέλλον in the sense of 'dilatoriness' (1.84.1), again in Archidamus' speech and again corresponding to an abstract noun (viz. μέλλησις) previously used by the Corinthians (1.69.4). Unlike the synonymous articular infinitive, substantivized neuter participles used instead of abstract nouns are rarely attested in other authors, but they occur frequently in Thucydides.[14] The construction is so characteristically Thucydidean that philologists termed it *schema Thucydideum*.[15]

Classen-Steup observe that Thucydides' habit of using substantivized neuter participles and adjectives instead of abstract nouns allows him to 'convey a vivid instance of a specific notion (as opposed to an abstract

---

[11] Denniston 1952: 36.   [12] Classen-Steup i. lxxv.   [13] Denniston 1952: 36–7.
[14] K-G i. 267. Classen-Steup (i. lxxv) remark that Thucydides uses substantivized neuter adjectives and participles more frequently than any other Greek author.
[15] The term seems to have been coined by Reiske 1791: 321.

generality) to the reader'.[16] The same applies to many of the substantivized infinitives found in Thucydides.

Thucydides' use of the last three forms is especially conspicuous because he draws on them more frequently than other Greek prose authors.[17] What is more, several abstract verbal nouns seem to be Thucydides' own coinages and should therefore also count as distinctly Thucydidean.[18] This is particularly true of abstract nouns ending in -σις; but, as Wolcott has shown, Thucydides also invents abstract nouns that have other terminations: nouns ending in -μα, -ία, -εια, -μός among others.[19] With regard to all these Thucydidean coinages of abstract nouns, Wolcott remarks 'that the majority of these words occur again only in late writers, or in imitators of Thucydides'.[20]

1.2 Four Stylistic Devices Used by Thucydides to Foster Abstraction

Thucydides adopts four methods by which he gives his style an abstract character. In practice these four procedures sometimes overlap, but for the sake of clarity I will set them out as distinct categories.

Abstract nominal phrases instead of circumstantial participles, subordinate clauses, and personal nouns

Thucydides frequently replaces two other groups of readily available constructions with abstract nominal forms: the first group comprises

---

[16] Classen-Steup i, on 1.36.1.3: 'Der Gebrauch des neutralen Partt. und Adjj.... ist den Th. vorzugsweise eigen, und besonders dadurch wirksam, daß er für die abstrakte Allgemeinheit des Begriffes eine lebendige Anwendung desselben vor die Seele rückt'.
[17] Blass 1887–98: i.214; Classen-Steup i. lxxv; Sm. 2051; Finley 1942: 264; Schmid 1948: 183; Denniston 1952: 28, 36–7; Huart 1968: 23; Pritchett 1975: 92 n. 32; Rusten 1989: 22.
[18] Sihler 1881, 96: 'One of the most striking features of the style of Thucydides is his tendency towards condensation; and this is particularly observable in his use of verbal nouns in -σις. Such nouns occur, roughly speaking, 400 times. A few of them had obtained general currency before the time of this historian, – for example ὄψις, τάξις, sundry compounds of -βασις, πρόφασις, etc. The great majority of them, however, are distinctly Thucydidean.'
[19] Wolcott 1898: 106–15.   [20] Wolcott 1898: 106.

both subordinate clauses and circumstantial participles, the second consists in personal nouns. The peculiarity of some of these expressions becomes apparent if one rephrases them by using less abstract language.

A nice example of Thucydides' habit to replace a subordinate clause, or a circumstantial participle, with an abstract nominal phrase occurs in the speech of the Mytilenean envoys to the Peloponnesians in Olympia early in book 3 (3.10.1):

ἐν γὰρ τῷ διαλλάσσοντι τῆς γνώμης καὶ αἱ διαφοραὶ τῶν ἔργων καθίστανται.

For diversities in action rest on divergence of mentality.

Thucydides could easily have rendered the thought expressed by the nominal phrase 'divergence of mentality' by a genitive absolute: 'when people diverge with regard to their mindset'—ἀνθρώπων τῇ γνώμῃ διαλλασσόντων—'diversities in action arise'. Thucydides, however, uses not a circumstantial participle but a nominal construction, rendering the verbal element as a substantivized neuter participle.

The example also illustrates another feature of Thucydides' fondness for abstract phrasing. Thucydides likes to qualify nominalized participles and adjectives by attributive phrases. According to Dover, he tries to 'assimilate' these neuter formations to regular nouns 'by attaching genitives or possessive adjectives to neuter adjectives and participles'.[21] In our passage, a genitive (τῆς γνώμης) modifies the substantivized participle. Dover cites the following excerpt from a speech by Alcibiades as an example of a nominalized adjective accompanied by a possessive pronoun: τῷ ἐμῷ διαπρεπεῖ τῆς Ὀλυμπίαζε θεωρίας (in Dover's translation: 'the conspicuous distinction of my participation in the Olympic Games', 6.16.2).[22] Similarly, an abstract noun can be accompanied by an extended attributive phrase: τὴν πρὸς ἀλλήλους τῶν καθ' ἡμέραν ἐπιτηδευμάτων ὑποψίαν ('suspicion about each other's daily activities', 2.37.2).[23] In general, Greek prose authors tend to avoid adding attributes to abstract

---

[21] Dover 1997: 34.   [22] Dover 1997: 34.
[23] For further examples, see Rusten 1989: 23.

nouns since the combination can be cumbersome.[24] Thucydides' style runs directly counter to this entrenched habit.

The next example, taken from the speech of the Corinthians at Athens, illustrates Thucydides' tendency to create new abstract nouns (1.41.2):

καὶ ἡ <u>εὐεργεσία</u> αὕτη τε καὶ ἡ ἐς Σαμίους, τὸ δι' ἡμᾶς Πελοποννησίους αὐτοῖς μὴ βοηθῆσαι, παρέσχεν ὑμῖν Αἰγινητῶν μὲν <u>ἐπικράτησιν</u>, Σαμίων δὲ <u>κόλασιν</u>

And both this <u>service</u> and the one rendered to you in connection with the Samians, namely the fact that because of us the Peloponnesians did not help them, afforded you <u>dominance</u> over the Aeginetans on the one hand, and <u>punishment</u> of the Samians on the other.[25]

In this passage, the nouns 'service' (εὐεργεσία), 'dominance' (ἐπικράτησις), and 'punishment' (κόλασις) could, due to their evident verbal root, easily be replaced by verbal constructions featuring εὐεργετέω, ἐπικρατέω, and κολάζω: 'And you have come to prevail over the Aeginetans and have punished the Samians because, each time, we did a service to you, urging the Peloponnesians not to help them' (e.g. καὶ Αἰγινητῶν μὲν ἐπεκρατήσατε, Σαμίους δ' ἐκολάσατε διότι ἑκατεράκις ὑμᾶς ηὐεργετήσαμεν ἀποτραπόντες τοὺς Πελοποννησίους αὐτοῖς μὴ βοηθῆσαι). The fact that both ἐπικράτησις ('predominance') and κόλασις ('punishment') are not attested before Thucydides makes his striving for abstract phrasing in this passage especially conspicuous.[26]

The third example illustrates Thucydides' use of an abstract in place of a personal noun. When the Spartan invading forces begin to ravage the area of Acharnae in book 2, the reaction of the Athenians is described in the following way (2.21.2):

...ἐδόκει τοῖς τε ἄλλοις καὶ μάλιστα <u>τῇ νεότητι</u> ἐπεξιέναι καὶ μὴ περιορᾶν.

...it seemed best to all others and especially to <u>the youth</u> to go out and not to suffer it.

---

[24] Denniston 1952: 35–6.
[25] For the rendition of παρέχω as 'make possible', see Classen-Steup i, on 1.41.2.9.
[26] Wolcott 1898: 107 and 112.

Denniston regards this example as an attempt to use an abstract noun 'wherever its employment is at all possible',[27] pointing out that a more standard Greek idiom would have been readily available: 'the young men' (τοῖς νέοις).[28]

In sum, abstract phrases used in place of circumstantial participles, subordinate clauses, and personal nouns reduce the number of constructions that are unambiguously verbal and personal. In many cases, Thucydides' penchant for abstract constructions goes directly against the marked tendencies that one finds in other Greek prose writers.

Abstract Nouns in Subject Position

Antiphon is the only Greek prose author who uses abstract nouns more frequently in subject position than Thucydides.[29] Thucydides' pronounced tendency towards abstract subjects is especially striking in light of Denniston's observation that '[i]n most Greek prose-writers *abstract substantives are seldom made the subject of verbs*: the normal agents are human beings.'[30]

The placement of abstract nouns in subject position frequently results in personification. Personification is produced by the combination of an abstract subject with a main verb that expresses an activity which, strictly speaking, can only be carried out by a human subject.[31] According to Denniston, this frequently results in 'cases of strikingly vivid, almost allegorical, *personification*'.[32] The following excerpt from the speech of the Corinthians at the gathering of the Peloponnesian allies provides an instructive example (1.122.1):

---

[27] Denniston 1952: 28.   [28] Denniston 1952: 28.
[29] Radford 1901: 5; Denniston 1952: 28. Finley (1967b: 106–7) observes several close parallels between Thucydides' style and a passage from the treatise Περὶ Ὁμονοίας, a work by Antiphon the Sophist, whose identity with the orator remains controversial.
[30] Denniston 1952: 28.
[31] Radford uses the label 'verbs of action' for such verbs and defines them as 'verbs expressing voluntary actions, such as a person is accustomed to perform of his own free will and accord' (1901: 4).
[32] Denniston 1952: 30.

ἥκιστα γὰρ πόλεμος ἐπὶ ῥητοῖς χωρεῖ, αὐτὸς δὲ ἀφ' αὑτοῦ τὰ πολλὰ τεχνᾶται πρὸς τὸ παρατυγχάνον· ἐν ᾧ ὁ μὲν εὐοργήτως αὐτῷ προσομιλήσας βεβαιότερος, ὁ δ' ὀργισθεὶς περὶ αὐτὸν οὐκ ἐλάσσω πταίει.

For war least of all proceeds according to stated terms, but mostly war itself, of its own accord, devises its plans to suit the occasion; under these circumstances, the man who maintains his composure when confronted with it [literally: 'holding intercourse with it', note the personifying connotations] is safer, while he who loses his temper in the face of it does not make less blunders.

War, the subject of the first sentence, is described as if it were a human agent: it does not comply with agreements and it devises startling schemes from its own resources. War comes to resemble a distinct type of human: a plotter and schemer. Although it appears no longer in subject position in the second sentence, the personification continues. People confronted with war have to get along, or might get angry, with it, just as one would with other human beings.

Nominal Periphrasis

The technical term for the third device by which Thucydides fosters abstraction is nominal periphrasis.[33] Nominal periphrasis is a linguistic operation through which the expression of activity, normally the function of the main verb, is taken over by a noun; the main verb is left with the simple function of expressing that the action takes place. The following example, which derives from Thucydides' account of the true cause and the contingent triggers of the Peloponnesian War, will help to clarify the phenomenon (1.23.6):

λύσαντες τὰς σπονδὰς ἐς τὸν πόλεμον κατέστησαν

Dissolving the truce, they got themselves into the war.

Nominal periphrasis takes place in the phrase ἐς τὸν πόλεμον κατέστησαν. Instead of saying 'they began to make war' (ἐπολέμησαν or

---

[33] Porzig 1942: 11-12; Freundlich 1987: 15.

ἤρξαντο πολεμεῖν), Thucydides writes, based on a literal translation, 'they settled themselves into the war'. In periphrasis, a noun (πόλεμος, 'war') is used to express action. As a result, the place of the main verb of the sentence comes to be occupied by what Freundlich calls an *inhaltsarmes Verb*, i.e. a verb that lacks strong semantic content (καθίσταμαι, 'to be set up, settle oneself, come into being'). I will call these verbs 'asthenic' or 'pale' as opposed to 'vivid' verbs. Such asthenic main verbs have merely the function of indicating the actuality, potentiality, or unreality of the action expressed by the noun. Other examples of asthenic main verbs are εἰμί ('to be'), γίγνομαι ('to become'), ἔχω ('to have'), ποιέομαι ('to make'), or ξυμβαίνω ('to happen'). These verbs are often combined with prepositional phrases that contain the noun to which the verbal content has been transferred (ἐς τὸν πόλεμον in the above example).

The rhetorician Alexander draws attention to Thucydides' particular fondness for nominal periphrasis (Alexander Rhetor, *Fig.* 32.15–18):

καὶ ὡς τὸ παρὰ Θουκυδίδῃ, 'οὐ περὶ ὧν ἐδιδάσκομεν ἑκάστοτε τὴν μάθησιν ἐποιεῖσθε' ἀντὶ τοῦ ἐμανθάνετε· πολὺ δὲ τὸ σχῆμα παρὰ τῷ ἀνδρὶ τούτῳ.

And, as in Thucydides, we read 'you did not take note of the things that we kept on reporting on each occasion' instead of 'you noted'; this figure occurs frequently in this author.

While modern languages accommodate nominal periphrasis quite comfortably, Denniston observes that ancient Greek generally made much less use of this construction:

Verbal abstracts...are very much rarer in Greek [*sc.* than in English]. Formal English prose goes out of its way to seek them: 'to suffer loss', 'to feel indignation', 'to bear a grudge', 'to be in such a state', for ζημιοῦσθαι, χαλεπαίνειν, μνησικακεῖν, οὕτως ἔχειν. Such periphrases are far rarer in Greek, and far less varied.[34]

---

[34] Denniston 1952: 24.

Given the relative scarcity of nominal periphrasis in classical Greek, Thucydides' habit of adopting this construction must have contributed considerably to the idiosyncrasy of his prose style.

Agent-less Periphrasis: Impersonal Passive Phrases

Impersonal quasi-passives make up third category of abstract expressions frequently found in Thucydides. Most instances of so-called impersonal passives are formed through a particular kind of nominal periphrasis. Thucydides' comment about the mood among the Athenians at Sicily when they set out for their retreat offers a good example (7.75.5):

> κατήφειά τέ τις ἅμα καὶ κατάμεμψις σφῶν αὐτῶν πολλὴ ἦν
> At the same time, there was much dejection and blaming of themselves.

Thucydides might have written: κατήφησάν θ' οἱ Ἀθηναῖοι ἅμα καὶ πολὺ κατεμέψαντο ἑαυτούς. The proposed verbal rephrasing has 'the Athenians' in subject position whereas in Thucydides' version the function of the subject is fulfilled by the abstract nouns κατήφεια and κατάμεμψις, both of which refer to emotional states. In the alternative version, the reader is left in no doubt about the agent. Thucydides' periphrastic locution, on the other hand, allows him to avoid making the agent explicit. This type of periphrasis is frequent with the verbs εἰμί, καθίσταμαι, and γίγνομαι. The subject position of the verbal component distinguishes this type of nominal periphrasis from cases frequently involving prepositional phrases, classified under the previous category. According to Freundlich, the expressions under consideration strike a passive note:

> In some cases [sc. of nominal periphrasis] the agent of the verb is only vaguely referred to in a general manner so that we are entitled to speak of agent-less periphrasis of the verb (passivum impersonale)... Let us call such cases of periphrasis simply 'agent-less'. In these cases, it is

striking that the verbal content regularly refers to general moods: terror, consternation, etc.[35]

It should be noted that, from a morphological (as opposed to a semantic) point of view, Thucydides' phrase is not passive in the strict sense. Nevertheless, the term 'impersonal passive' is justified, not least because Greek, unlike Latin, only vary rarely features genuine impersonal passive constructions.[36]

1.3 Corcyrean Stasis in Two Stylistic Registers

The idiosyncrasies typical of Thucydides' abstract style are not spread evenly throughout his work. While they tend to cluster in speeches and in authorial excursuses, they recede in those parts of the work in which Thucydides' primary concern is to provide a precise chronicle of military events as they unfold.

This difference between two different types of style did not escape Dionysius of Halicarnassus. Despite his disapproval of the *Pathology*, Dionysius has high praise for Thucydides' foregoing event-based narrative of the internal conflict at Corcyra (3.70–81): 'As long as he represents events in the common and customary stylistic manner, he expresses everything clearly, concisely, and ably' (ἕως μὲν ἐν τῷ κοινῷ καὶ συνήθει τῆς διαλέκτου τρόπῳ τὰ πραχθέντα δηλοῖ, σαφῶς τε καὶ συντόμως καὶ δυνατῶς ἅπαντα εἴρηκεν, *Thuc.* 28.372.9–11). It is worth bearing in mind that both the narrative and the excursus are concerned with the same topic: the escalation of civil war at Corcyra. Given the identical subject matter, the thoroughgoing stylistic shift is all the more noticeable. The role given to abstract language is a major distinguishing feature between these two sections.

---

[35] Freundlich (1987: 19): 'In einigen Fällen schwebt der agentive Träger des Verbalinhaltes nur allgemein vor, so daß man von einer agenslosen Umschreibung des Verbs sprechen darf (passivum impersonale)... Wir dürfen solche Umschreibung einfach als agenslos charakterisieren. Dabei fällt das Vorherrschen von Verbalinhalten auf, die sich auf die allgemeine Stimmung beziehen: Schrecken, Bestürzung und dgl.'

[36] See K-G i. 125 A. 2; Sm. 1746.

The Corcyrean narrative comprises 5.25 *OCT* pages, whereas the *Pathology* amounts to 2.5 *OCT* pages (excluding chapter 84, whose authenticity is dubious). For the sake of simplicity, let us calculate with 5 vs. 2.5 *OCT* pages. In terms of the amount of text, this yields a ratio of 2:1 between narrative and excursus.

The respective number of abstract subjects is one significant benchmark in comparing the style of the two passages. In order to gauge this parameter, it will be necessary to avoid counting abstract nouns that have a natural tendency to appear in subject position: indications of the time of day (e.g. ἡμέρα, νύξ), especially when combined with verbs of motion,[37] and collective nouns (e.g. δῆμος, πόλις). Moreover, I have counted abstract subjects that function, after their initial occurrence, as the implied subject of subsequent verbs just once.[38] It has been my general practice to count only explicitly stated (as opposed to implied) abstract subjects.

With these policies in place, I count thirty genuine abstract nominal phrases in subject position in the *Pathology*.[39] By contrast, the preceding narrative, twice as long, contains ten such subjects.[40] If one takes the relative lengths of the two texts into account, the *Pathology* contains six times as many abstract nouns as the narrative section.[41]

---

[37] See Radford 1901: 5.
[38] Compare the following example: οὕτως ὠμὴ ⟨ἡ⟩ στάσις προυχώρησε, καὶ ἔδοξε μᾶλλον, διότι ἐν τοῖς πρώτη ἐγένετο, 3.82.1. In this passage, I register just one explicitly stated abstract subject, namely στάσις, which also functions as the implied subject of ἔδοξε and ἐγένετο.
[39] ⟨ἡ⟩ στάσις, 3.82.1; τὸ Ἑλληνικόν, 82.1; διαφορῶν, 82.1; αἱ ἐπαγωγαί, 82.1; πολλὰ καὶ χαλεπά, 82.2; ἡ αὐτὴ φύσις, 82.2; ἕκασται αἱ μεταβολαί, 82.2; ὁ ... πόλεμος, 82.2; τὰ τῶν πόλεων, 82.3; τὰ ἐφυστερίζοντα, 82.3; τόλμα ... ἀλόγιστος, 82.4; μέλλησις ... προμηθής, 82.4; τὸ ... σῶφρον, 82.4; τὸ πρὸς ἅπαν ξυνετόν, 82.4; τὸ ... ἐμπλήκτως ὀξύ, 82.4; ἀσφαλείᾳ ... τὸ ἐπιβουλεύσασθαι, 82.4; τὸ ξυγγενές, 82.6; αἱ τοιαῦται ξύνοδοι, 82.6; ἀντιτιμωρήσασθαι ... τινα, 82.7; ὅρκοι, 82.7; ἀρχὴ ἡ διὰ πλεονεξίαν καὶ φιλοτιμίαν, 82.8; τὸ πρόθυμον, 82.8; εὐπρεπείᾳ ... λόγου ... ἐπιφθόνως τι διαπράξασθαι, 82.8; τὰ ... μέσα τῶν πολιτῶν, 82.8; πᾶσα ἰδέα ... κακοτροπίας, 83.1; τὸ εὔηθες, 83.1; τὸ γενναῖον, 83.1; τὸ ... ἀντιτετάχθαι ἀλλήλοις τῇ γνώμῃ ἀπίστως, 83.1; ὁ διαλύσων ... λόγος ἐχυρός, 83.2; [sc. ὁ διαλύσων] ὅρκος φοβερός, 83.2 (on the construal of these last two subjects, see Classen-Steup iii, ad loc.).
[40] στατήρ, 3.70.4; ἐπιστροφή, 71.2; μάχη, 74.1; τῆς τροπῆς, 74.2; ἔφοδος, 74.2; τῆς ... στάσεως, 76.1; κόσμος, 77.2; ἡ ... ναυμαχία, 78.4; χρημάτων, 81.4; ἰδέα, 81.5. Notice that the impersonal subjects of the following phrases should not be counted as abstracts: ὥστε καὶ χρήματα πολλὰ ἐμπόρων κατεκαύθη ('so that also much merchandise of traders was burned', 74.2), τὰ ἐπιτήδεια ἐκεῖσε αὐτοῖς διεπέμπετο ('provisions were being sent to them there', 75.5). In these passages, χρήματα and τὰ ἐπιτήδεια have a concrete sense, denoting objects that can be apprehended with the senses.
[41] The 10 abstract nouns in the narrative section are spread across five *OCT* pages. This yields an average value of 2 abstract noun per *OCT* page. By contrast, the 30 abstract nouns in the excursus occur in the space of merely two and a half *OCT* pages. Converted to an average value, the excursus has 12 abstract nouns per *OCT* page. Thus, the ratio of abstract nouns is 2:12 or 1:6, narrative vs. excursus.

Among the abstract subjects that one finds in the excursus, sixteen belong to the class of substantivized neuter adjectives, participles, and infinitives (including two infinitives used without the article but functioning as subjects). In the narrative section, however, Thucydides does not use any nominalized neuter forms in subject position at all.[42]

In fact, however, these numbers are based on a conservative estimate, which ultimately underplays the scope of the stylistic shift between narrative and excursus. In the narrative section, nearly all the abstract subjects are common nouns drawn from the military, economic, and political sphere (e.g. μάχη, χρήματα, στάσις). All of these nouns function as subjects of commonplace verbs, in most cases of εἰμί or γίγνομαι. In the relevant passages, these verbs are typically not used as copulas but in an existential sense, indicating that 'X was the case' or that 'X occurred'. Finally, these abstract subjects are generally not qualified by further abstract nouns (e.g. in the genitive) or by adjectives. Comparative evidence drawn from Herodotus' *Histories* and Xenophon's *Anabasis* and *Hellenica* shows that abstract subjects featuring these three characteristics are not particularly uncommon.

Consider, by way of example, Thucydides' phrase μάχη...γίγνεται (3.74.1). The relevant combination (μάχη in subject position with a form of existential γίγνομαι or εἰμί) is amply attested in Herodotus and Xenophon: it occurs eighteen times in the *Histories*,[43] and fourteen times in the *Anabasis* and the *Hellenica*.[44] Another example from Thucydides' narrative of events at Corcyra is τῆς...στάσεως ἐν τούτῳ οὔσης (3.76.1). Herodotus' *Histories* have two and Xenophon's *Anabasis* and *Hellenica* three instances of στάσις without an adjectival modifier used as subject of γίγνομαι or εἰμί.[45] The numbers are not quite as high as for μάχη, but this is not surprising in the light of the far lower frequency of the word στάσις. As a third Thucydidean example, one might consider the noun τροπή ('routing'), which occurs in the phrase γενομένης...τῆς τροπῆς (3.74.2). In the relevant military sense, τροπή occurs two times in Herodotus, and four times in the two works

---

[42] The only candidate is τὰ ἐπιτήδεια (3.75.5), but in the relevant context this term has a concrete sense (see n. 40).
[43] Hdt. 1.30.5, 1.39.2, 1.79.1, 1.214.1, 2.63.3, 2.120.3, 4.3.3, 6.136.3, 7.1.1, 7.226.2, 7.230, 7.235.4, 9.16.5, 9.23.1, 9.62.2 (twice), 9.69.1, 9.101.1.
[44] Xen. *An.* 2.1.6, 2.2.21, 5.2.9; *HG* 3.1.2, 3.2.29, 3.4.25, 3.5.19, 4.2.18, 4.2.23, 4.8.29, 6.4.9, 7.5.20, 7.5.26, 7.5.27. Note that I have not included *An.* 2.1.1 because the passage is certainly spurious.
[45] Hdt. 3.82.3, 7.2.1. Xen. *An.* 6.1.29; *HG* 1.1.32, 1.7.35.

of Xenophon. One of Herodotus' two instances of τροπή, and two out of Xenophon's four, occur in subject position, with γίγνομαι as main verb.[46] Thus, every second instance of τροπή in the sense of 'routing' functions as subject of γίγνομαι in these two authors.

Seen against this background, most abstract subjects from the Thucydidean narrative of the civil war at Corcyra are not particularly noteworthy: they refer to military actions and follow the pattern of the examples amply attested in Herodotus and Xenophon.[47] One might object that the phrases thus produced belong to the impersonal passive variety of nominal periphrasis, which has been classified, in Section 1.2, as one of the four methods used by Thucydides to enhance the abstract character of his style. However, such phrases are not very striking if they refer to military events and are used, as is the case in the present passage, to sum up where things stand before the narrative moves to a new stage. The existence of some variants of nominal periphrasis that are common in ancient Greek does not alter the fact that Thucydides' style is marked by an unusually high rate of periphrasis, a fact appropriately stressed by Classen-Steup.[48] This distinctly Thucydidean tendency finds expression in periphrastic phrases that are more unconventional than the above-mentioned commonplace variants, for which Herodotus and Xenophon provide many parallels.

In addition to these nouns denoting military or political events, the narrative section features two further abstract subjects that are unremarkable for similar reasons: terms from the judicial and financial sphere (στατήρ, 3.70.4; χρημάτων, 81.4) used with verbs that refer to legal and economic activity. The assertions that 'a stater was imposed as a fine' (ἐπέκειτο, 3.70.4) and that 'money was owed' (ὀφειλομένων, 3.81.4) are entirely commonplace. After the subtraction of these various run-of-the-mill abstract subjects, merely one passage remains from the chronicle of events: πᾶσα ... ἰδέα κατέστη θανάτου ('every form of death occurred', 3.81.5). Even the evidence of this passage is qualified because it stands in the final chapter of the narrative, at a point of transition from the report of concrete events to the generalizing manner of the *Pathology*.

---

[46] Hdt. 7.167.1. Xen. *An.* 1.8.25, 4.8.21.
[47] These subjects from Thucydides' narrative section are: ἐπιστροφὴ γένηται, 3.71.2; μάχη ... γίγνεται, 74.1; γενομένης ... τῆς τροπῆς, 74.2; ᾗ ἔφοδος, 74.2; τῆς ... στάσεως ... οὔσης, 76.1; ἦν ... κόσμος, 77.2; ἡ ... ναυμαχία ... γενομένη, 78.4.
[48] See Classen-Steup i. lxxiii.

If one applies the same three strictures (standard noun from the military, political, or economic sphere, *without* any adjectival or substantival attribute, *plus* commonplace verb) to the *Pathology*, one must discount three abstract subjects (3.82.1, 82.2, 82.6).[49] Thus, after the exclusion of these nouns, twenty-seven abstract nouns in subject position are distributed over the two and a half *OCT* pages of the *Pathology* whereas the five *OCT* pages of the narrative section feature just one relevant abstract subject. With the different length of the two sections included in the reckoning, this more indicative set of data yields startling numbers: the ratio of genuinely noteworthy abstract nouns in subject position is 54:1, excursus relative to narrative.

Combinations of abstract nominal phrases roughly synonymous to circumstantial participles or subordinate clauses introduced by a conjunction represent another significant point of comparison between the narrative section and the *Pathology*. The relevant nominal phrases are marked by the following two characteristics: first, their principal constituent is an abstract noun (including substantivized infinitives) that either stands in the instrumental dative or is governed by a preposition; second, a further non-personal substantival modifier (including infinitives) is attached so that it depends grammatically on the first.[50] An obvious example, drawn from the excursus on stasis, is πύστει τῶν προγενομένων ('by their learning of the things that had happened before', 3.82.3), which Dionysius of Halicarnassus streamlines by substituting a synonymous circumstantial participle: ἐπιπυνθανόμενοι τὰ γεγενημένα ('learning afterwards of the things that had happened', *Thuc.* 29.374.14). As it happens, during the narrative section, Thucydides does in fact employ the participial form of πυνθάνομαι in the manner exemplified by Dionysius' correction: 'The Athenians had sent off these [*sc.* ships] under the command of Eurymedon, the son of Thucles, when they learned of the

---

[49] διαφορῶν οὐσῶν, 3.82.1; ἕως ἂν ἡ αὐτὴ φύσις ἀνθρώπων ᾖ, 82.2; αἱ τοιαῦται ξύνοδοι [with implied ἐγένοντο], 82.6.

[50] Phrases consisting of a single noun in the instrumental dative are also frequently equivalent to a participial phrase (e.g. τῇ δικαιώσει, 3.82.4). However, I do not count them because, taken by themselves, such single-noun phrases do not represent a glaring deviation from normal Greek usage. Thucydides' idiosyncrasy consists in the combination of such abstract nouns with further nominal forms that depend on them. Cf. Rusten (1989: 23): 'Accompanying the increase in abstract nouns is a preference for lengthy attributive phrases.' The examples cited by Rusten from the Funeral Oration show that what he has in mind is precisely the phenomenon of combined abstract noun phrases.

civil strife' (ἃς [sc. ναῦς] οἱ Ἀθηναῖοι πυνθανόμενοι τὴν στάσιν ... ἀπέστειλαν καὶ Εὐρυμέδοντα τὸν Θουκλέους στρατηγόν, 3.80.2). The phrase shows that the participial construction was anything but inconceivable for Thucydides.

The excursus on stasis contains sixteen combined abstract noun phrases of the type described.[51] By contrast, the narrative section features four such phrases (3.70.5, 74.1, 75.4, 80.2). If one allows for the difference in text length, the ratio is 8:1, *Pathology* to narrative.

These numbers, however, again understate the extent of the stylistic difference between the two passages. Three of the combined abstract noun phrases from the narrative are in fact quite unremarkable: 'because of the amount of the fine' (διὰ πλῆθος τῆς ζημίας, 3.70.5), 'due to the strength of their position' (χωρίων ... ἰσχύι, 3.74.1), and 'until midday [literally: 'until the middle of the day']' (μέχρι μέσου ἡμέρας, 3.80.2). As regards 3.80.2, it is worth pointing out that substantival μέσον with a dependent genitive is a common construction in Xenophon (see Classen-Steup iii, ad loc.). All three phrases are entirely transparent, even in isolation from any context. By contrast, none of the phrases from the *Pathology* is similarly accessible. For the sake of comparison, one might consider this phrase: λογισμῷ ἐς τὸ ἀνέλπιστον τοῦ βεβαίου (3.83.2), which one might translate literally as 'due to their expectation regarding the hopelessness of any reliability'. This example may count as an extreme case, even by the standards of the *Pathology*. Other, less compressed phrases, however, are still much less transparent than the two passages from the narrative. For instance, in the phrase ἔργων φυλακῇ (3.82.7), it is immediately evident that some variant of the instrumental dative governs a genitive. Still, the phrase resists immediate comprehension. For one thing, this has to do with the higher degree of abstractness of ἔργων and φυλακῇ in comparison with the phrases from the narrative. Additionally, the combination of the two nouns defies immediate comprehension, in marked contrast to the

---

[51] Combined nominal phrases in the excursus on stasis: διὰ τὸ μὴ ἐς ἀκουσίους ἀνάγκας πίπτειν, 3.82.2; πύστει τῶν προγενομένων, 82.3; τῶν ... ἐπιχειρήσεων περιτεχνήσει, 82.3; τῶν τιμωριῶν ἀτοπίᾳ, 82.3; διὰ τὸ ἑτοιμότερον εἶναι ἀπροφασίστως τολμᾶν, 82.6; μετὰ τῶν κειμένων νόμων ὠφελίας, 82.6 (I accept the transmitted text, following Stuart Jones' *OCT*, but diverging from Alberti); ἔργων φυλακῇ, 82.7; πλήθους τε ἰσονομίας πολιτικῆς καὶ ἀριστοκρατίας σώφρονος προτιμήσει, 82.8; μέχρι ... τῇ πόλει ξυμφόρου, 82.8; ἐς ... τὸ ἑκατέροις που αἰεὶ ἡδονὴν ἔχον, 82.8; μετὰ ψήφου ἀδίκου καταγνώσεως, 82.8; εὐπρεπείᾳ ... λόγου, 82.8; φθόνῳ τοῦ περιεῖναι, 82.8; λογισμῷ ἐς τὸ ἀνέλπιστον τοῦ βεβαίου, 83.2; τῷ ... δεδιέναι τό τε αὑτῶν ἐνδεὲς καὶ τὸ τῶν ἐναντίων ξυνετόν, 83.3; ἐκ τοῦ πολυτρόπου αὐτῶν τῆς γνώμης, 83.3.

combinations 'the amount of the fine' and 'the strength of the position' found in the narrative section: φυλακή can both be active ('guarding, keeping, preserving') and middle ('precaution') and ἔργα can refer to both impersonal 'events' and 'deeds' of human agents. Understanding the meaning of this phrase ('with caution concerning the actions [sc. of their opponents]') must rely on the context, and it even then requires some reflection.

The narrative in fact features merely one combined abstract noun phrase that bears comparison with the complex structures prevalent in the *Pathology*: τῇ τοῦ μὴ ξυμπλεῖν ἀπιστίᾳ ('due to their distrustful refusal to sail with them', 3.75.4). Thus, a more indicative ratio regarding the distribution of combined abstract noun phrases is 32:1, *Pathology* to narrative.

The following direct juxtaposition of two comparable passages (one from the narrative section, the other from the excursus) will bring the semantic difference between circumstantial participle and combined noun phrase into focus. Both excerpts involve forms of the verb δείδω. The constructions are also similar in that the forms of δείδω appear relatively early in the sentence, indicating an act of reflection that precedes action.[52]

Let us begin by quoting the excerpt from the narrative section (3.74.2):

δείσαντες οἱ ὀλίγοι μὴ αὐτοβοεὶ ὁ δῆμος τοῦ τε νεωρίου κρατήσειεν ἐπελθὼν καὶ σφᾶς διαφθείρειεν, ἐμπιπρᾶσι τὰς οἰκίας τὰς ἐν κύκλῳ τῆς ἀγορᾶς καὶ τὰς ξυνοικίας, ὅπως μὴ ᾖ ἔφοδος...

Fearing that the people might attack and get possession of the dockyard at the first onset and destroy them, the oligarchs set fire to the houses surrounding the market-place and to the tenement-houses, in order that an assault might not take place...

The passage from the *Pathology*, whose main verb has 'men of inferior intellect' (οἱ φαυλότεροι γνώμην) as subject, reads as follows (3.83.3):

τῷ γὰρ δεδιέναι τό τε αὐτῶν ἐνδεὲς καὶ τὸ τῶν ἐναντίων ξυνετόν, μὴ λόγοις τε ἥσσους ὦσι καὶ ἐκ τοῦ πολυτρόπου αὐτῶν τῆς γνώμης φθάσωσι προεπιβουλευόμενοι, τολμηρῶς πρὸς τὰ ἔργα ἐχώρουν.

---

[52] As Huart observes (1968: 337), δείδω, unlike φοβέομαι, usually refers to fear attended by reflection.

For, they [sc. the men of inferior intellect] boldly proceeded to action due to fear of their own inferiority and of the intelligence of their opponents, lest they might be weaker when it came to words, and lest they, because of the versatility of their opponents' intelligence, might become the victims of their plots first.

In both passages the form of δείδω refers to one party's anticipation of their opponents' actions and of the danger that these acts might pose. This anticipation leads, in each case, to purposeful, if perhaps rash, action by human agents, each time captured by the subject of the main verb (ἐμπιπρᾶσι, 3.74.2; πρὸς τὰ ἔργα ἐχώρουν, 83.3). In light of these parallels, one might conclude that the semantic difference between the two constructions is slight.

In fact, however, the two constructions have different implications. The first passage, which contains the circumstantial participle, is clear-cut: it ascribes fear of enemy action to the oligarchs at one particular moment in the conflict at Corcyra. Personal agents (οἱ ὀλίγοι) are the centre of attention and are the originators of the actions that take place. By contrast, the articular infinitive in the second passage has a more general ambit: lying between a purely verbal and a purely nominal phrase, the infinitive describes the mental process of being afraid as a general fact. Kohn, in commenting on Thucydidean articular infinitives, emphasizes that they signify the bare notion of a verb, not limited by reference to a specific subject or a specific time of occurrence.[53] Compared with the circumstantial participle, the infinitive redescribes action as if it were an independent and impersonal occurrence: calculation inspired by fear is presented as a fact that determines what people do rather than as an action controlled by them.

The narrative of events at Corcyra features a total of six participial constructions along the lines of the passage just examined: a participle

---

[53] Kohn (1891: 29–30): 'Infinitivo enim cum generatim atque universe loquimur, ipse agendi motus exprimitur, ubi agi aliquid aliquo tempore consentaneum est, ita ut hoc verbi modo (inf.) eoque cum articulo coniuncto notio tantum actionis significetur et nuda et libera, cui quidem actioni non insunt fines, nisi quod fit aliquo tempore' ('For, when one talks in general and universal terms, the mere operation of acting is expressed through the infinitive. This happens in cases where it is proper <to say> that something is done at some time—it being understood that, by this verbal mood [inf.] and by its combination with the article, merely the notion of bare and unrestricted action is expressed. There are indeed no limits imposed on this action, save only that it happens at some time').

expressing fear (mostly through a form of δείδω), which qualifies a personal subject, comes early in the sentence and is followed by the main verb, which captures the action prompted by the thought process.[54] It is striking that the narrative section does not present a single instance of the roughly synonymous alternative construction that is based on the combined abstract noun phrase. Thucydides must have been aware of the unwieldiness produced by an accumulation of nominal phrases: the construction was ill-suited to the economic exposition of events in a steady narrative flow. By contrast, the format of the excursus, unencumbered by the imperatives of a forward-moving narrative, allows for a different manner of representation: a register that enables Thucydides to uncover the true character of stasis.

The two sections contain a further set of passages whose comparison reveals characteristic differences. At an early point in each section, Thucydides uses imperfect forms of στασιάζω, by which he summarizes the general situation under stasis before explicating it in greater detail. In the narrative, Thucydides writes: 'For the Corcyreans had been engaged in civil strife ever since the captives had returned to them—namely, the men from the naval battles off Epidamnus who had been released by the Corinthians' (οἱ γὰρ Κερκυραῖοι ἐστασίαζον, ἐπειδὴ οἱ αἰχμάλωτοι ἦλθον αὐτοῖς οἱ ἐκ τῶν περὶ Ἐπίδαμνον ναυμαχιῶν ὑπὸ Κορινθίων ἀφεθέντες, 3.70.1). The termination -άζω, found in the verb στασιάζω, usually denotes action in Greek.[55] It follows that, taken literally, the verb captures the Corcyreans' active pursuit of civil strife, as opposed to a more passive and static notion (as, for instance, in τῆς ... στάσεως ἐν τούτῳ οὔσης ['civil strife was at this stage'] at 3.76.1). The entry in Beekes' *Etymological Dictionary of Greek* reflects this active nuance of the verb στασιάζω: 'to form parties, divide, quarrel'.[56] The personal subject used in the quotation matches the active shade of meaning.

---

[54] In addition to 3.74.2, see the following five passages: δείσαντες δὲ ἐκεῖνοι μὴ ... ἀποπεμφθῶσι, καθίζουσιν ..., 3.75.3; ὁ δὲ δῆμος δείσας μή τι νεωτερίσωσιν ἀνίστησι ... αὐτούς ..., 75.5; οἱ δ᾽ Ἀθηναῖοι φοβούμενοι τὸ πλῆθος καὶ τὴν περικύκλωσιν ... οὐ προσέπιπτον, 78.1; δείσαντες μὴ ὅπερ ἐν Ναυπάκτῳ γένοιτο, ἐπιβοηθοῦσι, 78.2; οἱ Κερκυραῖοι δείσαντες μὴ ... οἱ πολέμιοι ἢ τοὺς ἐκ τῆς νήσου ἀναλάβωσιν ἢ καὶ ἄλλο τι νεωτερίσωσι, τούς τε ἐκ τῆς νήσου πάλιν ἐς τὸ Ἥραιον διεκόμισαν, 79.1.

[55] Sm. 866, 6.   [56] Beekes 2010: ii. s.v. στάσις.

In the corresponding passage from the excursus, the same verb is used, but this time with an impersonal subject: 'the affairs of the cities were engaged in civil strife' (ἐστασίαζε... τὰ τῶν πόλεων, 3.82.3). In English, the combination of the impersonal subject with the verb 'to engage (in civil strife)' is jarring, but the literal translation reflects the same clash in Thucydides' Greek. The phrasing suggests that impersonal events, not human agents, are the actual driving forces behind stasis. Thus, by using an abstract nominal phrase as subject of στασιάζω, Thucydides implies that circumstances play the role of the agent in stasis. By contrast, the passage from the narrative section does not prompt this conclusion because it combines a personal subject with the verb στασιάζω. Thus, the comparison between these two passages illustrates nicely what Dionysius has in mind when he observes that a 'common and customary stylistic manner' prevails in the narrative section, and that this type of style differs radically from the more distinctly Thucydidean register that one finds in the *Pathology*.

1.4 Conclusion

The two self-contained sections that Thucydides juxtaposes in his account of the internal upheaval at Corcyra are the archetypes of two fundamental stylistic registers that leave their mark on the *History* as a whole. Thucydides takes recourse to a smooth stylistic register, exemplified by the narrative section on the conflict at Corcyra, when reporting a sequence of events, usually of military nature. This style is unassuming, plain, and matter of fact, featuring personal subjects, active main verbs, and participial phrases. The *Pathology* of the War represents the opposite stylistic register: it abounds in impersonal subjects and favours static nominal phrases over synonymous verbal expressions that emphasize the role of human agents.

The idiosyncrasy of the abstract register raises the question as to why Thucydides was drawn, at least at certain points in his work, to a manner of expression that runs counter to many of the ingrained traits of Greek prose style. The glaring differences with the plain style show that Thucydides was perfectly capable of adopting an accessible, commonplace form of presentation if he wanted to. This strongly suggests that a conscious effort informed his adoption of the abstract style. In order to elucidate the nature of Thucydides' motivation, we will proceed to analyse more systematically the specific implications of his stylistic choices in the *Pathology*, the undisputed *locus classicus* of the abstract nominal register.

2
The Implications of Thucydides' Abstract Style
The *Pathology* (3.82–3)

The time has come to examine the stylistic extravagances of the *Pathology* directly, without the mediation of Thucydides' plain style. The analysis of Thucydides' stylistic choices is meant to offer an explanation as to why Thucydides considered abstract phrases, in the words of Colin Macleod, 'the proper vehicle of his thought'.[1] The implications of Thucydides' stylistic choices can best be assessed if one organizes them into groups according to themes.

2.1 Persons Treated as Things

In the *Second Letter to Ammaeus* and *On Thucydides*, Dionysius of Halicarnassus observes in connection with Thucydides' style that 'things are made to stand in for persons by him' (πράγματα δὲ ἀντὶ σωμάτων ... ὑπ' αὐτοῦ γίνεται, *Amm.* II 14.433.18–19; cf. *Thuc.* 24.362.16–17).[2] The following passage from the excursus on stasis exemplifies this tendency (3.82.4):

---

[1] Macleod 1983e [1979]: 123.
[2] In the *Second Letter to Ammaeus*, Dionysius illustrates this habit by an example drawn from the Corinthians' account of Athenian versus Spartan character: τὸ δὲ ὑμέτερον τῆς τε δυνάμεως ἐνδεᾶ πρᾶξαι τῆς τε γνώμης μηδὲ τοῖς βεβαίοις πιστεῦσαι ('It is your way to accomplish less than your power would afford and to trust not even the most certain insights of your judgment,' 1.70.3). As Dionysius observes, τὸ ὑμέτερον has taken the place of ὑμεῖς, an instance of 'a thing replacing a person' (πρᾶγμα ὑπάρχον ἀντὶ σώματος, *Amm.* II 14.434.12).

Style and Necessity in Thucydides. Tobias Joho, Oxford University Press. © Tobias Joho 2022.
DOI: 10.1093/oso/9780198812043.003.0003

τὸ δὲ σῶφρον [sc. ἐνομίσθη, from the preceding sentence] τοῦ ἀνάνδρου πρόσχημα, καὶ τὸ πρὸς ἅπαν ξυνετὸν ἐπὶ πᾶν ἀργόν.

Moderation [came to be regarded] as a screen for cowardice, and wise consideration of everything as inactiveness in everything.

Replacing impersonal by personal nouns, Dionysius rewrites this passage as follows (*Thuc.* 29.375.18–19):

οἱ δὲ σώφρονες ἄνανδροι, καὶ οἱ συνετοὶ πρὸς ἅπαντα ἐν ἅπασιν ἀργοί.

Moderate men [came to be regarded] as cowardly, and those who wisely gave attention to everything as inactive in everything.

Dionysius' personal nouns replace a construction of which Thucydides is particularly fond: nominalized neuter adjectives. The difference in phrasing reveals a different assessment of the paramount factor in stasis: Dionysius makes personal agents central; Thucydides gives priority to impersonal patterns.

The following passage from the *Pathology* contains three examples of abstract language. Two of these phrases exemplify the use of nominalized neuter adjectives used instead of personal expressions (τὸ ξυγγενές, τὸ ἑταιρικόν), the other that of an articular infinitive in place of a subordinate clause or a circumstantial participle (διὰ τὸ ἑτοιμότερον εἶναι ἀπροφασίστως τολμᾶν). Examining the passage will enable us to gain insight into the implications of Thucydides' substitution of things for persons (3.82.6):

καὶ μὴν καὶ τὸ ξυγγενὲς τοῦ ἑταιρικοῦ ἀλλοτριώτερον ἐγένετο διὰ τὸ ἑτοιμότερον εἶναι ἀπροφασίστως τολμᾶν.

Furthermore, the kindred became more alien than the partisan[3] due to its being more ready to act rashly without hesitation.

In translating this passage, I have kept as closely as possible to Thucydides' Greek in order to preserve the indeterminateness of the

---

[3] I use the adjective 'partisan', as a translation of ἑταιρικός, in the sense of 'relating to an adherent of a party or a political cause'.

nominalized neuter adjectives τὸ ξυγγενές ('the kindred') and τὸ ἑταιρικόν ('the partisan'). Such expressions can have a collective sense ('everything that is kindred', 'everything that relates to being a partisan') and an abstract sense ('kindredness', 'the quality of being kindred' and 'partisanship', 'the quality of being a partisan').[4] In relation to ἀλλοτριώτερον ἐγένετο, τὸ ξυγγενές and τὸ ἑταιρικόν seem to be used in the abstract sense: 'kinship became a less intimate bond than partisanship'.[5]

When 'kinship' becomes 'more alien than partisanship', a major transformation takes place: kinship stands to lose its core meaning. A synonym for τὸ ξυγγενές is τὸ οἰκεῖον, a word that does not only bear the connotations of 'kindred', but also of 'one's own'. If the 'kindred' is equivalent to 'one's own', then being 'alien' (ἀλλότριος) is the negation of kinship. As LSJ point out, οἰκεῖος and ἀλλότριος are in fact used as antonyms in Greek.[6] Because kinship is defined as supreme 'ownness', it is on the verge of disintegration if it becomes 'more alien', i.e. 'less one's own', than other structures of affiliation. A personal expression ('people considered their kinsmen more alien than their partisans') would fail to express that the institution of kinship suffers debasement and that a formerly ingrained type of behaviour loses its grip on people. The verb ἐγένετο, one of the asthenic verbs used in nominal periphrasis, also contributes to this general impression. While Thucydides could easily have written 'people considered kinship more alien than partisanship', he prefers the phrasing 'the kindred became more alien than the partisan'. Instead of focusing on human beings who judge and act, he highlights the emergence of states of affairs.

The abstract sense of the substantivized neuter adjectives ceases to be entirely satisfactory when one moves on to the third abstract phrase: the articular infinitive διὰ τὸ ἑτοιμότερον εἶναι ἀπροφασίστως τολμᾶν. Τὸ ἑταιρικόν serves as the implicit subject of the infinitive τὸ ἑτοιμότερον

---

[4] According to Patzer (1937: 91), nominalization of neuter adjectives has its origin in the attempt to indicate the collectivity of all persons to whom a specific characteristic belongs: 'the kindred' and 'the partisan' originally merely meant 'all the people who are kindred' and 'all the people who are partisan'. From there, the step to the abstract usage is not far: 'Was durchweg allem seiner Art zukommt... und sich an allem durchweg als dasselbe äußert..., das läßt sich von dem, an dem es auftritt, abheben und für sich betrachten' (1937: 91).
[5] Classen-Steup iii, on 3.82.6.36.   [6] LSJ s.v. οἰκεῖος A.II.1.

εἶναι. In rendering the articular infinitive into English, translators usually assume a rapid transition from the abstract to the collective usage and switch their translations from 'partisanship' to 'partisans': 'because partisans were more ready to act rashly without hesitation'. Yet, instead of positing an abrupt shift, it may be worth wondering whether the collective and the abstract usage remain simultaneously in play. As Patzer has shown, in Thucydides both senses often coexist within one and the same phrase.[7] As we will see shortly, blurring the lines between the collective and the abstract usage has its advantages for Thucydides.

Partisanship becomes more important than kinship 'due to its being more ready to act rashly without hesitation' (διὰ τὸ ἑτοιμότερον εἶναι ἀπροφασίστως τολμᾶν). The phrasing prompts the reader to wonder how, given its abstract nuances in what precedes, τὸ ἑταιρικόν can function as the subject of both 'being ready' and of 'acting rashly', verbs that seems to call for a human subject. By blurring the line between abstract and collective use, Thucydides conveys two ideas at once: on one level, a group of individuals, collectively labelled as 'partisans', are willing to display rashness; yet on another level, an impersonal factor acts through them. This force consists in the behavioural patterns that partisanship brings in its wake. This tendency towards rashness is responsible for the increased appreciation of partisanship in comparison with kinship. In the final analysis, this shift in estimation is not caused by personal agents, but by rampant conditions and forces. Thucydides makes this point by transferring the abstract connotations from ἑταιρικόν to the implied subject of the infinitive.

These peculiarities cannot be discounted as occasional and ephemeral. The following passage shows the same tendencies (3.82.8):

τὰ δὲ μέσα τῶν πολιτῶν ὑπ᾽ ἀμφοτέρων ἢ ὅτι οὐ ξυνηγωνίζοντο ἢ φθόνῳ τοῦ περιεῖναι διεφθείροντο.

The middle range of citizens was destroyed by both sides either because they did not take part in the struggle or out of envy that they would survive.

---

[7] Patzer 1937: 92.

Τὰ μέσα τῶν πολιτῶν ('the middle range of citizens') is used instead of 'moderates' or 'neutrals' (e.g. οἱ μέσοι πολῖται[8]). It is not people—'the moderates'—who occupy the subject position in the sentence. Without referring to this particular passage, Jeffrey Rusten has remarked that a locution like τὰ μέσα τῶν πολιτῶν reverses the usual relation between substantive and attribute:[9] instead of speaking of 'moderate citizens', Thucydides makes 'moderate range' the governing substantive and 'citizens' its dependent genitive. The phrase implies that human beings are primarily defined by their affiliation with a specific group, both with regard to their perception by others and their own scope for action. Those who found themselves in the middle were defined by this categorization and, as a result, crushed by the revolutionaries on either side.

What is more, the combined abstract noun phrase φθόνῳ τοῦ περιεῖναι (literally 'out of envy of their [sc. the neutrals'] surviving') expresses in an extremely compressed way the notion that the warring parties begrudged the neutrals their prospect of surviving. Citing this passage as an instance of Thucydidean *variatio*, Ros observes that the dative case corresponds directly to the causal subordinate clause introduced by ὅτι.[10] The construction illustrates Thucydides' tendency to use phrases combining several abstract nouns instead of synonymous subordinate clauses: phrasing that is nominal and impersonal takes precedence over a verbal and personal alternative. In capturing the motivation of the warring factions, Thucydides uses a construction that evokes a general mindset rather than activity: φθόνῳ τοῦ περιεῖναι. In his note on the passage, Krüger quotes two lines from Euripides, which express a similar thought: 'For those who are unfortunate are not well disposed towards the more fortunate, given that they themselves fare poorly' (οἱ δυστυχεῖς γὰρ τοῖσιν εὐτυχεστέροις / αὐτοὶ κακῶς πράξαντες οὐ φρονοῦσιν εὖ, Eur. *IT* 352–3).[11] As these lines show,

---

[8] Thucydides himself uses the phrase μέσος πολίτης (6.54.2) of Aristogeiton. Classen-Steup (vi, on 6.54.2.9) quote a scholiast's observation that the meaning here is 'citizen of the middle class'. In the passage from the *Pathology*, μέσος suggests 'neutral' rather than 'belonging to the middle class' (Classen-Steup iii, on 3.82.8.67). Nevertheless, the passage from book 6 provides evidence that the combination of the noun πολίτης with the adjective μέσος as an attribute was readily available to Thucydides.

[9] Rusten 1989: 22.   [10] Ros 1938: 399.

[11] Krüger i, 2, on 3.82.9. In the *OCT* of Euripides, Diggle discards these lines as an interpolation. Irrespective of whether they are by Euripides, they illustrate how the idea captured by Thucydides might be more easily expressed in standard Greek.

Thucydides' basic idea can easily be expressed in lucid Greek based on verbal and personal phrasing. Nonetheless, Thucydides prefers to pile up abstract verbal nouns, thus producing the strained phrase 'out of envy of surviving'. For all its tangled character, Thucydides' phrasing conveys a nuance that more standard phrasing would not transmit: his phrase, unlike the lines from Euripides, avoid explicit reference to a personal subject. The action of human subjects is not the centre of attention. Instead, general states descend upon human beings and define their actions.

2.2 Impersonal Agents

Dionysius complements his observation that Thucydides tends to treat persons as things by highlighting the opposite tendency: 'things are treated as persons in his work' (πρόσωπα δὲ παρ' αὐτῷ τὰ πράγματα γίνεται, Amm. II 14.433.6; cf. γίγνεται... σώματα ἀντὶ πραγμάτων, Thuc. 24.362.17–18). This may sound as if Thucydides' style featured a further tendency that went directly against the emphasis on the impersonal. Yet Dionysius' example shows that the phenomenon he has in mind is the application of language implying personhood to non-personal phenomena. The passage cited by Dionysius marks the conclusion of the Corinthians' speech at Sparta and is their final appeal to their Spartan audience: 'Endeavour to act as leaders of a Peloponnesus that has not been diminished as compared to when your fathers handed it over to you' (τὴν Πελοπόννησον πειρᾶσθε μὴ ἐλάσσω ἐξηγεῖσθαι ἢ οἱ πατέρες ὑμῖν παρέδοσαν, 1.71.7). The example of 'things treated as persons' is 'the Peloponnesus': the Corinthians refer to a territory in the manner appropriate to human beings when they imagine the Spartans as 'leading forth' the Peloponnesus. In the present context, the Corinthians have to use an impersonal noun because they want to emphasize the Spartans' inheritance from their ancestors. If the Corinthians had used a personal noun instead of 'Peloponnesus', they would have claimed that the Spartans inherited 'the Peloponnesians' from their ancestors, an implication that any Spartan ally surely wanted to avoid. The Peloponnesus stands metonymically for 'the Peloponnesian League' or, as Dionysius thinks, 'the reputation and resources available to it' (τῇ δὲ δόξῃ καὶ τοῖς πράγμασιν τοῖς περὶ αὐτὴν ὑπάρχουσιν, *Amm.* II 14.433.15–16). Yet the action of 'leading forth' makes one think of gathered troops. In this way, Thucydides assimilates resources and military assets to brave allies steadfastly following Spartan leadership. Therefore, the treatment of 'things as persons', just as the treatment of 'persons as things', does not focus attention on personal agents. In fact, it has the opposite effect: the treatment of 'things as persons' challenges the general habit of ascribing personhood to human beings alone. In the final analysis, this type of phrasing raises the impersonal element even further.

Personification is the most forceful manifestation of the general tendency to treat things as persons: it often emphatically attributes agency to impersonal entities. The *Pathology* features the following use of πόλεμος in the role of the 'violent teacher', the most famous example of personification from Thucydides' entire work (3.82.2):

ὁ δὲ πόλεμος ὑφελὼν τὴν εὐπορίαν τοῦ καθ' ἡμέραν βίαιος διδάσκαλος καὶ πρὸς τὰ παρόντα τὰς ὀργὰς τῶν πολλῶν ὁμοιοῖ.

But war, removing daily provisions, is a violent teacher and assimilates most people's temper to their circumstances.

Vivid verbs that one would normally associate with the actions of human agents are combined with the impersonal notion of 'war' as subject of the sentence. Thus, instead of writing that *in war* provisions are taken away from people and that '*in war*, people's tempers are assimilated to their circumstances', Thucydides makes war itself the instigator of both events. Thucydides refers to it as a 'violent teacher' and suggests that it acts 'stealthily', thus imbuing war with characteristics that evoke an agent with a distinct personality. While, as we have seen, neuter abstract subjects challenge the seemingly self-evident assumption that human beings are in charge of events, a new, quasi-personal agent enters the stage: the Peloponnesian War itself.

The personification of war, 'the violent teacher', is reminiscent of another iconic passage from Greek literature: 'War is father of all, and king of all, and he has shown some as gods, but others as men; some he has made slaves, but others free' (Πόλεμος πάντων μὲν πατήρ ἐστι, πάντων δὲ βασιλεύς, καὶ τοὺς μὲν θεοὺς ἔδειξε τοὺς δὲ ἀνθρώπους, τοὺς μὲν δούλους ἐποίησε τοὺς δὲ ἐλευθέρους, DK 22 B 53). In this fragment from Heraclitus, personified War settles the course of human life, just as it determines people's thinking and acting in Thucydides. Charles Kahn has pointed out that, through specific phrases, Heraclitus depicts war in the guise of Zeus, and that the point of the personification is to represent this awesome power as the supreme cosmic principle.[12] Thucydides' personification has similar implications: war moulds people's mentality and governs their actions. As stasis shows, it has turned out to be the principle that governs the world of Greece.

One can trace a series of striking personifications of πόλεμος throughout Thucydides' work.[13] Another example, to be found at 1.122.1, has already been referred to in Section 1.2, as an example of personification. Radford attaches particular importance to this phenomenon:

> Especially noticeable in Thuk. is the frequent personification of πόλεμος, which is treated almost invariably as a personal notion, an unaccountable Power, full of violence and caprice.[14]

Apropos the passage from the excursus on stasis, Macleod explains Thucydides' attribution of personal agency to War in the following way:

> [F]or the historian the real teachers are not persons, but events, the war itself... what is usually more powerful than man, his circumstances or his own nature, governs in syntax as it does in fact.[15]

While war is depicted as an agent, human beings (expressed by a dependent construction, viz. the genitive τῶν πολλῶν) are defined by αἱ ὀργαί and τὰ παρόντα: ὁ... πόλεμος... πρὸς τὰ παρόντα τὰς ὀργὰς τῶν πολλῶν ὁμοιοῖ. By highlighting these states, the passage brings

---

[12] Kahn 1979: 208.
[13] For collections of these occurrences, see Radford 1901: 32; Smith 1918: 241–3.
[14] Radford 1901: 32.   [15] Macleod 1983e [1979]: 125.

THE IMPLICATIONS OF THUCYDIDES' ABSTRACT STYLE 55

impersonal aspects into focus: the factors influenced by the War are primarily collective temperamental states and material circumstances. From a human perspective, one is internal and the other external, but both have the otherness of impersonal powers that exceed the horizon of individual human agents. As Parry writes, 'It is in war... that the forces of things, of external reality, impinge upon men's lives in the most incalculable and overwhelming manner.'[16] The nodal points of the passage are πόλεμος, τὰ παρόντα, and τὰς ὀργάς. The structure of Thucydides' sentence shifts human beings and their agency to a marginal position.

2.3 Reification of Action

Thucydides' emphasis on impersonal subjects is complemented by a tendency to divert attention from the idea of people acting and redescribe action as an impersonal state (3.83.1):

τὸ δὲ ἀντιτετάχθαι ἀλλήλοις τῇ γνώμῃ ἀπίστως ἐπὶ πολὺ διήνεγκεν.
To be distrustfully opposed to each other in one's thinking prevailed far and wide.

The activity that this passage describes (i.e. 'to set oneself against one another') is not expressed by a main verb as one would expect. Instead it is conveyed by a nominalized phrase: an articular infinitive in the position of the grammatical subject. This stylistic choice has two consequences. First, personal agency is removed. Through the conspicuous absence of a personal subject, the impression is avoided that people are ultimately in charge of their acts. Second, the nominalization of 'setting oneself against each other' leads to reification of an activity: what one would ordinarily describe as an action ('they set themselves against each other') is understood as a fact ('the setting-oneself-against-one-another'). Almost all dependent elements, with the sole exception of ἐπὶ πολύ, are grouped around the subject τὸ ἀντιτετάχθαι. This arrangement is a variant of

[16] Parry 1981: 91.

Thucydides' tendency, mentioned in Section 1.1 (pp. 30–31), to encumber abstract nouns by attaching a cluster of dependent phrases to them. The main verb has ceased to be the focal point of syntax and thought. The use of the perfect verbal aspect stresses the static, dispositional quality of the expression; as a result, standing in mutual opposition has the character of a persistent and immutable fact.

The lengthy phrase τὸ ἀντιτετάχθαι ἀλλήλοις τῇ γνώμῃ ἀπίστως is then used as the subject of διαφέρω. In the relevant sense, the verb makes one think of competitors, of whom one outstrips the other.[17] In characteristic fashion, Thucydides does not employ a human being as the subject of this forceful verb, but rather has it governed by an impersonal phrase with static connotations. The active dimension suggests the thrust of external circumstances while the impersonal side refers to the collective forces that overtake human beings.

The following example features an impersonal quasi-passive construction, which has a very similar effect (3.82.8):

ὥστε εὐσεβείᾳ μὲν οὐδέτεροι ἐνόμιζον, εὐπρεπείᾳ δὲ λόγου οἷς ξυμβαίη ἐπιφθόνως τι διαπράξασθαι, ἄμεινον ἤκουον.

As a result, neither side practised piety; yet those for whom it worked out, through the pretence of speech, to achieve their objective with malicious acts enjoyed a better reputation.[18]

---

[17] See LSJ s.v. A.III.4.
[18] Against Classen-Steup and Krüger (but with Poppo-Stahl ii, 1, ad loc., Alberti [given his punctuation of the passage also adopted in my quotation], and the 'many other interpreters' mentioned by Classen-Steup), I am inclined to take εὐπρεπείᾳ λόγου to be part of the relative clause and to depend on διαπράξασθαι, i.e. the infinitive governed by ξυμβαίη. Classen-Steup and Krüger take it with ἄμεινον ἤκουον. It is clear that the assonant words εὐσεβείᾳ and εὐπρεπείᾳ mark an antithesis, a contrast made unmistakable by μέν–δέ. The crucial question is whether the antithesis is between 'practising piety' and '(using the pretence of speech) to achieve an objective with malicious acts' or between 'practising piety' and '(using the pretence of speech) to have a good reputation'. The term 'pretence of speech' refers to Thucydides' preceding observation that the leaders of each party use venerable slogans to promote their self-interested ends, a strategy that they pursue 'with the help of a fair-sounding name' (μετὰ ὀνόματος... εὐπρεποῦς, 3.82.8). The adjective εὐπρεπής clearly looks forward to the cognate noun in the phrase εὐπρεπείᾳ λόγου, thus providing a strong indication that the two phrases refer to the same phenomenon. In adopting 'fair-sounding names', the party-leaders 'made the polity their prize' and 'dared the most dreadful things' (τὰ μὲν κοινὰ... ἆθλα ἐποιοῦντο,... δὲ... ἐτόλμησάν... τὰ δεινότατα). This suggests that the 'pretence of speech' is used by them rather to 'achieve their objective with malicious acts' than 'to enjoy a better reputation'. For this reason, it seems more plausible to construe the phrase in question with the relative clause. Notice that the

The sentence has a passive flavour because the phrase rendered as 'it worked out to achieve something' (ξυμβαίη...τι διαπράξασθαι) is approximately equivalent to 'something is achieved'. By filling the position of the verb with the impersonal ξυμβαίνει, the idea of mere occurrence (as opposed to action) occupies the central hub of the clause. With the exception of the dative object οἷς, all dependent phrases found in this clause are grouped around the infinitive διαπράξασθαι, and none accompany the verb ξυμβαίνει. The infinitive performs the function of the subject in this sentence. As such, it fulfils the function of a substantive, even without an article.[19] In this way, Thucydides organizes the sentence not around the verb but around the subject, whose regular syntactic function is not to express the idea of action. Thus, he systematically undermines the idea that actions, usually expressed by the verb, provide the basis for events. Instead of emphasizing action, Thucydides highlights a condition. The pale verb ξυμβαίνει contributes to the overall effect by suggesting that, paradoxically, actions happen to people rather than flowing from their unencumbered choices.

2.4 Passivity and Settled States

Freundlich points out that the impersonal passive variety of nominal periphrasis, introduced in Section 1.2, is frequently used to capture the force of general emotional states.[20] The chapters on stasis contain a good example of Thucydides' habit of associating passive phrasing with overpowering passions (3.82.8):

---

word order supports this conclusion. In their general survey of Thucydides' style, Classen-Steup draw attention to Thucydides' habit of placing phrases that are part of a relative clause in front of the relative pronoun for the sake of emphasis (see Classen-Steup i. lxxvi, and on 1.5.2.11, where they provide a list of examples). This is just what Thucydides does with εὐπρεπείᾳ λόγου if one construes this phrase with διαπράξασθαι. For the alternative view, see Krüger i, 2, on 3.82.9, and Classen-Steup iii, on 3.82.8.65.

[19] See Sm. 908 ('The function of the substantive may be assumed ... by an infinitive with or without the article'), 1984; Ros 1938: 148–9.

[20] Freundlich 1987: 19.

ἐκ δ' αὐτῶν [sc. πλεονεξίας καὶ φιλοτιμίας] καὶ ἐς τὸ φιλονικεῖν καθισταμένων τὸ πρόθυμον.

And from these sources [i.e. greed and ambition] people's impulsiveness also arose as they were getting caught up in contentiousness.

If one supplies ἐγένετο ('arose') or something similar as main verb with τὸ πρόθυμον, the periphrastic character of the phrase becomes evident: it can be considered as the impersonal variant of 'they became impulsive'. Thucydides uses 'impulsiveness' (τὸ πρόθυμον) as the subject of an implicit verb with the sense of 'happening' or 'arising', thus representing it as an impersonal phenomenon confronting people. The passive implications of the periphrastic phrasing suggest people's exposure to this rampant condition.

The quotation contains a second case of nominal periphrasis: the participial phrase 'getting caught up in contentiousness' (ἐς τὸ φιλονικεῖν καθισταμένων). Using a compound of ἵσταμαι, Thucydides alerts the reader to the fact that people are caught up in a state that determines their actions. This state is expressed by τὸ φιλονικεῖν, another neuter phrase. The passage highlights a constellation of impersonal forces: ἐκ πλεονεξίας καὶ φιλοτιμίας [= αὐτῶν]—ἐς τὸ φιλονικεῖν—τὸ πρόθυμον. These impersonal forces predominate. The only verbal element, apart from the implied ἐγένετο, is the circumstantial participle of καθίσταμαι. This verb does not evoke agency but suggests that people are brought into a certain state. The predominance of impersonal forces is complemented by the vanishing of agency.

Parry draws attention to Thucydides' particular fondness for compounds of ἵστημι. For him, the primary place that exemplifies this tendency is the account of the growth of Greek power in the *Archaeology*:

The nodal points of this development of power are largely indicated by compounds of ἵστημι. These verbs signify the putting into a position of something, or the taking up of a position.[21]

---

[21] Parry 1981: 99.

Parry's observation also sheds light on the chapters on stasis. Apart from the aforementioned phrases (ἐς τὸ φιλονικεῖν καθισταμένων, 3.82.8), forms of καθίσταμαι show up in the following two passages, both of which involve the impersonal passive variety of nominal periphrasis: at the transition between narrative and excursus, πᾶσά τε ἰδέα κατέστη θανάτου, καὶ οἷον φιλεῖ ἐν τῷ τοιούτῳ γίγνεσθαι, οὐδὲν ὅ τι οὐ ξυνέβη καὶ ἔτι περαιτέρω ('Every kind of death occurred, and there was nothing which tends to happen in such a situation, that did not happen—and even worse things', 3.81.5), and, later in the excursus, πᾶσα ἰδέα κατέστη κακοτροπίας... τῷ Ἑλληνικῷ ('every kind of wickedness confronted all that was Greek', 3.83.1). Based on Parry's observation regarding the *Archaeology*, the compounds of ἵστημι emphasize situations into which people are put by the pressure of stasis. Leaving the impersonal passives aside for a moment, one should note that the first passage shows further characteristic features: an accumulation of asthenic verbs suggesting occurrence (γίγνεσθαι—ξυνέβη) and expressions implying patterns (οἷον—φιλεῖ—ἐν τῷ τοιούτῳ—οὐδὲν ὅτι οὐ). By hinting at a deep structure that will recur in other situations and places, these locutions contribute to the generalizing character of Thucydides' language.

The two phrases πᾶσα ἰδέα κατέστη θανάτου (3.81.5) and πᾶσα ἰδέα κατέστη κακοτροπίας (3.83.1) recall a number of other passages in which Thucydides uses similar expressions elsewhere in the *History*: each time, the phrase πᾶσα ἰδέα occurs with a dependent genitive of an abstract noun and with nominal periphrasis, in all but one case involving a form of καθίσταμαι.[22] The nouns that qualify ἰδέα as dependent genitives are: πόλεμοι (1.109.1), θάνατος (3.81.5), κακοτροπία (3.83.1), φυγή (3.98.3, 112.7), and ὄλεθρος (3.98.3, 7.29.5). Lateiner has drawn attention to the fact that in these phrases πᾶσα ἰδέα 'is always restricted by a term involving πάθος [in the sense of "calamitous suffering"].'[23] Thus, the

---

[22] Aside from the two phrases from the *Pathology*, these are: 1.109.1, 3.98.3, 3.112.7, 7.29.5. Except for 3.112.7, all passages involve nominal periphrasis with καθίσταμαι. Even if 3.112.7 does not feature a form of καθίσταμαι, the phrase 'taking recourse to every kind of flight' (ἐς πᾶσαν ἰδέαν χωρήσαντες τῆς φυγῆς) nonetheless represents an instance of nominal periphrasis.

[23] Lateiner 1977: 47 n. 14. For 'calamitous suffering', see 44. Lateiner (47 n. 14) notes two exceptions, namely 2.19.1 and 2.77.2, where 'the phrase does not involve πάθος' and 'refers to

expression πᾶσα ἰδέα appears to be especially suited to reports of uncontrollable and destructive events.

One instance of this phrase is especially remarkable because it appears in another paradigmatic passage: the account of the slaughter at Mycalessus. Thucydides describes the disaster as follows: καί τότε ἄλλη τε ταραχὴ οὐκ ὀλίγη καὶ <u>ἰδέα πᾶσα καθειστήκει ὀλέθρου</u> ('And so at that point, very considerable confusion and, in particular, every form of destruction came to pass', 7.29.5). As Lateiner mentions, events at Mycalessus represent the most intense form of πάθος: the episode features one of three instances of πάθος that 'Thucydides claims... to have been the war's most severe'.[24] By using the construction with πᾶσα ἰδέα and a form of καθίσταμαι in the *Pathology*, Thucydides characterizes wickedness (κακοτροπία) and death (θάνατος) likewise as πάθη, as occurrences reducing people to a passive role. Nominal periphrasis with καθίσταμαι is an especially suitable manner of articulating the onset of πάθος because, instead of expressing agency, it suggests that people find themselves put into a settled condition.

2.5 Convulsions of 'Greekness'

The phrase 'every kind of mischievousness confronted all that was Greek' (πᾶσα ἰδέα κατέστη κακοτροπίας... τῷ Ἑλληνικῷ, 3.83.1) involves a further peculiarity. Τὸ Ἑλληνικόν belongs to the aforementioned neuter phrases that often combine a collective and an abstract sense in Thucydides: 'the Greek world' as well as 'Greekness'. There is something incongruous about the combination of the substantivized neuter with the noun κακοτροπία: 'wickedness' or 'badness of manners' (κακοτροπία) applies more naturally to individuals rather than to 'the Greek world' or 'Greekness'. While, except for Thucydides, κακοτροπία is only attested in much later sources,[25] the LSJ entry on the noun τρόπος shows that in the relevant sense ('ways, habits,

---

military ingenuity'. But in these cases, the phrase does not appear in subject position and is not combined with καθίσταμαι. Therefore, these passages are in fact no exceptions for the purpose of our investigation.

[24] Lateiner 1977: 50.   [25] LSJ s.v. κακοτροπία.

character, temper') this word occurs only in connection with persons.[26] Thucydides could easily have avoided the incongruity by writing that 'every kind of wickedness confronted *the Greeks*'.

The *Pathology* features one further instance of τὸ Ἑλληνικόν, which occurs earlier in the excursus and sheds light on the passage just discussed: πᾶν ὡς εἰπεῖν τὸ Ἑλληνικὸν ἐκινήθη ('just about everything that was Greek was convulsed', 3.82.1). On this occasion, the general phrasing of the passage is consistent with the neuter form: there is nothing odd about the claim that 'the Greek world', or 'Greekness', were shaken. Τὸ Ἑλληνικόν in this passage probably alludes to a famous passage in Herodotus.[27] After the battle of Salamis, the Athenians tell the mistrustful Spartans that Athens will never betray τὸ Ἑλληνικόν (Hdt. 8.144.2). The rest of the Athenians' statement shows that the term does not only suggest 'the Greek nation', but that it also has the abstract sense of 'Greekness'. For, according to the Athenians, τὸ Ἑλληνικόν consists of shared blood relations, a shared language, common religious practices, and likeness of habits (Hdt. 8.144.2): these are the institutions that make Greeks what they are.

All four factors highlighted by the Athenians in Herodotus recur in the Thucydidean *Pathology*, but they disintegrate under stasis. As pointed out above, Thucydides draws attention to the erosion of kinship relations (3.82.6). He also traces the corruption of language, reflected in a new application of words that are evaluative of human behaviour (3.82.4–5). In two passages, Thucydides reports the breakdown of the religious basis for people's actions.[28] Finally, the inherited habits of the Greeks are corrupted under stasis: 'the customary evaluation expressed by words' (τὴν εἰωθυῖαν ἀξίωσιν τῶν ὀνομάτων, 3.82.4) shifts and, as we saw, 'badness of habits' (κακοτροπίας, 3.83.1) becomes rampant.

The implication of Thucydides' neuter phrase at 3.82.1 appears to be that 'Greekness' itself is shaken under stasis: the basic practices and beliefs that define Greek self-understanding. Thucydides combines passive

---

[26] LSJ s.v. τρόπος A.III.2. Most passages refer to individuals, fewer examples to collective character. In either case, the reference is always to persons.

[27] I owe the reference to Hdt. 8.144.2 to Jonathan Hall.

[28] πίστεις οὐ τῷ θείῳ νόμῳ ... ἐκρατύνοντο ('pledges were not ... confirmed by divine law', 3.82.6); εὐσεβείᾳ μὲν οὐδέτεροι ἐνόμιζον ('neither side practised piety', 82.8).

phrasing (ἐκινήθη) and the neuter form to capture this development. By echoing Herodotus' τὸ Ἑλληνικόν, Thucydides seems to suggest that the Greek world has tumbled from the apex of its glory into an abyss: from the appeal to Greek unity after the Panhellenic victory at Salamis to the dissolution of Greekness in the wake of divisions which even tear cities apart—not to speak of the bonds connecting 'all [πᾶν] that is Greek'. Using the neuter τὸ Ἑλληνικόν, Thucydides moves beyond the experience of the specific 'Greeks' living at the time: his point is that, at the deepest level, Greekness itself is caught up in the destructive maelstrom.

This train of thought suggests an answer as to why Thucydides also uses the neuter phrase at 3.83.1, writing that 'every kind of wickedness' confronted τὸ Ἑλληνικόν (instead of οἱ Ἕλληνες). He wants to show that, when people begin to display 'badness of habits' on a large scale, it is a general mentality that acts through them. This is the reason why κακοτροπία confronts 'Greekness': Thucydides wishes to emphasize that, when stasis prevails, depraved acts are primarily due to a general corruption of mentality that conditions people's actions. By contrast, personal agents are not the prime movers.

This interpretation receives additional support from the observation that Thucydides makes next (3.83.1):

οὕτω πᾶσα ἰδέα κατέστη κακοτροπίας διὰ τὰς στάσεις τῷ Ἑλληνικῷ, καὶ τὸ εὔηθες, οὗ τὸ γενναῖον πλεῖστον μετέχει, καταγελασθὲν ἠφανίσθη.

Thus, due to the acts of civil war, every kind of wickedness confronted τὸ Ἑλληνικόν, and so it happened that simplicity, in which noble-mindedness has the greatest share, was derided and disappeared.

In the present passage, καί does not merely suggest addition but conveys a more specific shade of meaning: the element added is represented as a 'nähere Bestimmung' (Kühner-Gerth), i.e. an elaboration in greater detail, of what preceded.[29] Καί indicates that by noticing the disappearance of noble simplicity Thucydides specifies what happens when wickedness affects 'Greekness'. The substantivized neuter adjectives τὸ

[29] K-G ii. 246.

εὔηθες and τὸ γενναῖον dovetail with τὸ Ἑλληνικόν, which directly precedes them: the morphological parallel forges a link between these terms, suggesting that they are of the same type. The phrase involving μετέχω, which expresses what τὸ εὔηθες most fundamentally consists in, proves beyond doubt that these neuters have an abstract sense: they must refer to general dispositions (as opposed to collectives, whose mention would make no sense in the present passage). Thus, the neuters illustrate what it means for τὸ Ἑλληνικόν to be affected by 'badness of habits': noble simplicity, once part and parcel of τὸ Ἑλληνικόν, now vanishes. Then, τὸ Ἑλληνικόν must also, at least predominantly, refer to a general attitude: the Greek way of being.

It is interesting that Thucydides' phrasing implies that the character trait of noble simplicity itself (as opposed to individuals distinguished by it) becomes an object of scorn. One usually laughs at people, not at general dispositions. Yet, for Thucydides, what is significant about this laughter is that it leads to an erosion of general norms of behaviour. It fits into the picture that Thucydides uses passive verb forms: καταγελασθέν and ἠφανίσθη. These passive phrases do not specify any agents. Noting the derision of time-honoured simplicity, Thucydides puts emphasis on a general mentality spreading in the manner of an impersonal force.

2.6 Predominance of General Forces

The phrases featuring πᾶσα ἰδέα with a form of καθίσταμαι also manifest another frequent implication of the nominal style: the generality of recurring patterns. The following passage provides further evidence for this tendency (3.82.8):

> πάντων δ' αὐτῶν αἴτιον ἀρχὴ ἡ διὰ πλεονεξίαν καὶ φιλοτιμίαν.
>
> The cause of all these things [sc. the evils of stasis] was the exercise of power fuelled by greed and ambition.

Thucydides' thought would be much easier to understand had he adopted a verbal expression: 'People did all these things because they were greedy and ambitious and, therefore, sought to exercise power'[30] (e.g. πάντα δ' ἔπραξαν ὅτι φιλοτιμούμενοί τε καὶ πλεονεκτοῦντες ἄρχειν προυθυμήθησαν). However, the abstract expression offers a semantic surplus missing in the alternative verbal and personal phrasing. The abstract phrases lack the specificity of reference implied by our rephrased version, thus imbuing the passage with a generalizing tone. The general perspective enables Thucydides to widen his observation about Corcyra to the Greek world at large. Porzig described this very phenomenon in the following way:

> The locution with *nomen actionis* expresses the event with less definiteness and less specificity, but it embraces a wider range of possibilities. The reason for this is the lack of any personal subject; the agent does not need to be expressed at all.[31]

If we do not limit the scope of an action by associating it with a specific subject, it is less clear *who* acts in the way described. Moreover, as Nicole Loraux has stressed, nouns do not refer to a specific time whereas 'verbs have the disadvantage of implying temporality'.[32] Through the generality of his expression, Thucydides points to underlying patterns that manifest themselves at different times and with different agents.

As Pouncey observes with regard to the excursus on stasis: 'All behavior has been reduced to uniformity.'[33] The impersonal generality highlighted by Pouncey is largely due to the prominence of the abstract style in this passage. The determination of events through a general pattern suggests forces that limit the individual's scope for action.

---

[30] Classen-Steup (iii, on 3.82.8.53) cite the scholiast glossing ἀρχή as ἡ ἐπιθυμία τοῦ βούλεσθαι ἄρχειν ('the desire that consists in wanting to rule'). As I will argue in Chapter 4 (pp. 127–8), the scholiasts' paraphrase in fact misses a crucial implication of the passage, namely Thucydides' attempt to collapse the duality between internal disposition and external situation.
[31] Porzig (1942: 21): 'Die Wendung mit Nomen actionis sagt den Vorgang mit weniger Bestimmtheit, weniger als tatsächlichen aus, dagegen umfaßt sie einen weiteren Kreis von Möglichkeiten. Das geschieht dadurch, daß sie kein personal bestimmtes Subjekt hat; der Agens braucht überhaupt nicht ausgedrückt zu sein.' On the connection between *abstract* style and generality, see also Allison (1997: 247): 'For Thucydides abstraction provided the means by which to engage in semantic ascent from specific events described by singular terms to the more general.'
[32] Loraux 2009 [1986]: 287.   [33] Pouncey 1980: 147.

2.7 Emphasis on Incidents Occurring as Opposed to People Acting

Thucydides highlights the general significance of the phenomena manifesting themselves during stasis, a feature responsible for their eternal validity (3.82.2):

καὶ ἐπέπεσε πολλὰ καὶ χαλεπὰ κατὰ στάσιν ταῖς πόλεσι, γιγνόμενα μὲν καὶ αἰεὶ ἐσόμενα, ἕως ἂν ἡ αὐτὴ φύσις ἀνθρώπων ᾖ, μᾶλλον δὲ καὶ ἡσυχαίτερα καὶ τοῖς εἴδεσι διηλλαγμένα, ὡς ἂν ἕκασται αἱ μεταβολαὶ τῶν ξυντυχιῶν ἐφιστῶνται.

And many grievances fell upon the cities during civil war, things that have happened time after time and will always happen again as long as the same nature of human beings persists, but they will be severer or milder and differing in their forms, depending on how in each case the reversals of circumstances come to pass.

Thucydides draws attention to a pattern marked by impersonal recurrence and highlights the power responsible for it: ἡ φύσις ἀνθρώπων. Noticing parallels between this passage and the Hippocratic treatise Περὶ φύσεως ἀνθρώπου, Rechenauer points out that both works share the idea of φύσις as an unchanging constant with general validity for all human beings: unlike the 'forms' of its manifestation (εἴδεσι), nature does not change in any fundamental way over time and under the impact of other factors such as age, individual characteristics, or climate.[34] Underneath the surface differences, an unchanging reality comes into view.

Thucydides observes that afflictions recurring over time will differ in degree 'depending on how in each case the reversals of circumstances come to pass' (ὡς ἂν ἕκασται αἱ μεταβολαὶ τῶν ξυντυχιῶν ἐφιστῶνται, 3.82.2). The verb ἐφίσταμαι suggests that *something* 'occurs, comes into being', not that *someone* acts. It is another compound of ἵστημι with implications of a settled situation *confronting* people (notice the

---

[34] Rechenauer 1991: 180. On the meaning of εἶδος in the present context, see Swain (1994: 313): 'In this passage *eidos* (in the plural) refers to the shape/form/appearance of *stasis* including its effects on persons.'

prefix ἐπι-).³⁵ Thucydides combines this verb with the subject αἱ μεταβολαὶ τῶν ξυντυχιῶν. This dual nominal phrase ('reversals of circumstances') refers to the imposition of large-scale conditioning factors. These forces ultimately determine the specific shape that events will take. In Thucydides, μεταβολή is often more emphatic than mere 'change': it tends to refer to a 'reversal', in the sense of an unexpected, sudden transformation that leads to disorientation and overthrows people's expectations.³⁶ Thucydides underscores the primacy of occurrence over agency by combining μεταβολαί with a further abstract noun: αἱ μεταβολαὶ τῶν ξυντυχιῶν, literally 'reversals of that which happens to people'.

The accumulation of different words that emphasize the notion of incidents occurring (as opposed to people acting) is not confined to this passage. In a similar way, Thucydides piles up verbs that mean 'to happen' in chapter 23 of book 1. This chapter contains Thucydides' programmatic summary of the unparalleled amount of 'sufferings' that came with the Peloponnesian War: παθήματά τε ξυνηνέχθη γενέσθαι ('it came to pass that sufferings happened', 1.23.1). One should keep in mind that ξυμφέρομαι can also suggest 'to meet, to come together' or, in a hostile sense, 'to meet in battle'.³⁷ If Thucydides had merely written παθήματα ἐγένετο, there would be no suggestion that events set themselves against human beings in the manner of an active force. In a similar way, ἐφίσταμαι is used in the passage from the stasis excursus: in addition to expressing occurrence, the prefix ἐπι- can also suggest 'to stand against', thereby giving the verb (as LSJ remark) a 'hostile sense'.³⁸ Thus, when accumulating expressions which emphasize occurrence rather than agency, Thucydides likes to combine terms that stress the facticity of things happening (([ξυν-]τυχιῶν, [ἐφ-]ἱστῶνται, [ξυν-]ηνέχθη,

---

³⁵ Classen-Steup iii, on 3.82.2.14 compare this passage with Soph. OT 776–7 (πρίν μοι τύχη / τοιάδ᾽ ἐπέστη), and Eur. Med. 331 (ὅπως ἂν ... παραστῶσιν τύχαι).

³⁶ Stahl (2003 [1966]: 67) renders μεταβολή as 'reversal' adding that it signifies 'the complete *disorientation* of those who had at first been so *well oriented*'. The plague at Athens is the Thucydidean μεταβολή par excellence: Thucydides uses this word of the plague itself (2.48.3) and of its effects (2.53.1), and so does Pericles in his last speech (2.61.2). The plague strikes Athens with suddenness and overwhelming force. Both aspects are implied by the term μεταβολή.

³⁷ LSJ s.v. B.I.   ³⁸ LSJ s.v. B.III.2.

γενέσθαι) with language that implies rapid motion (μεταβολαί) and hostile opposition (ξυν-[τυχιῶν], ἐφ-[ιστῶνται], ξυν-[ηνέχθη]).

2.8 Phrases Involving πίπτω

The phrase 'many grievances fell upon the cities' (ἐπέπεσε πολλὰ καὶ χαλεπά...ταῖς πόλεσι, 3.82.2) gives us occasion to return to the comparison with the narrative section about events at Corcyra one more time. The relevant segment from the narrative refers to a naval battle between a Peloponnesian fleet and a combined force of Athenian and Corcyrean ships (3.78.1):

> καὶ οἱ μὲν Κερκυραῖοι κακῶς τε καὶ κατ' ὀλίγας <u>προσπίπτοντες</u> ἐταλαιπώρουν τὸ καθ' αὑτούς· οἱ δ' Ἀθηναῖοι φοβούμενοι τὸ πλῆθος καὶ τὴν περικύκλωσιν ἀθρόαις μὲν οὐ <u>προσέπιπτον</u> οὐδὲ κατὰ μέσον ταῖς ἐφ' ἑαυτοὺς τεταγμέναις, προσβαλόντες δὲ κατὰ κέρας καταδύουσι μίαν ναῦν.

And the Corcyreans, <u>attacking</u> without any order and with few ships at a time, were struggling on their side of the battle. Yet the Athenians, fearing the superior numbers of the enemy and the risk of encirclement, did not <u>attack</u> the ships that were arrayed against them as a whole nor did they attack at the center, but they made an assault on the wing and sank one ship.

Both forms of προσπίπτω in this passage have human subjects. While the Corcyreans fare poorly and the Athenians are more successful in their attacks, the phrasing implies both times that personal agents are in charge of their actions. Contrast this with this excerpt from the *Pathology*: the excursus combines the compound of πίπτω with substantivized neuter adjectives in subject position (πολλὰ καὶ χαλεπά). Impersonal factors descend upon the Greek cities with the vehemence typical of the enemy in battle. Yet the agent behind these ills remains obscure. One can take precautions against human attackers, but it is not at all clear how one is to react to assailants in the guise of impersonal forces.

In Thucydides in general, ἐπιπίπτω occurs most frequently in military contexts, a usage closely resembling that of προσπίπτω in the cited passage from the narrative section.[39] Thucydides also provides evidence for a second systematic usage of ἐπιπίπτω: in three passages, it has the plague as subject and expresses affliction by a rampant disease. This twofold picture corresponds to the prevailing usage of ἐπιπίπτω outside of Thucydides.[40] In both of its chief uses, ἐπιπίπτω runs parallel to the largely synonymous ἐμπίπτω: Connor observes that it is 'normally reserved for physical attacks and grievous physical or psychological states'.[41] Scholars have pointed out that both ἐπιπίπτω and ἐμπίπτω repeatedly occur with the plague as subject, a combination found six times in all.[42]

When ἐπιπίπτω appears in the stasis passage, it is semantically charged by the two contexts in which this verb, as well as its synonymous counterpart, frequently occurs. Loraux observes that, as a result, 'Thucydides... describes *stasis*... as a scourge which attacks cities from outside'.[43] Furthermore, Hornblower stresses the verb's medical resonance, which he illustrates by quoting a phrase featuring ἐπιπίπτω from the Hippocratic treatise *Airs, Waters, Places*.[44] It will be useful to consider this passage in more detail. The author discusses how bodily constitutions that are used to warm climates react when they are unexpectedly confronted with a cold spring (ch. 10: II 46.14–48.3 Littré):

...ὁ ἐγκέφαλος, ὁπηνίκα αὐτὸν ἔδει ἅμα καὶ τῷ ἦρι διαλύεσθαι καὶ καθαίρεσθαι ὑπό τε κορύζης καὶ βράγχων, τηνικαῦτα πήγνυταί τε καὶ ξυνίσταται, ὥστε ἐξαίφνης τοῦ θέρεος ἐπιγενομένου καὶ τοῦ καύματος, καὶ <u>τῆς μεταβολῆς ἐπιγενομένης</u>, ταῦτα τὰ νοσεύματα <u>ἐπιπίπτειν</u>.

...just at the time when the brain ought to have relaxed with the onset of spring and be purged by mucous discharge and hoarseness, it congeals and becomes solid; as a result, with the sudden onset of summer and heat, and with <u>reversal setting in</u>, the above-mentioned diseases <u>befall</u>.

---

[39] The verb occurs nineteen times in Thucydides. In eleven passages, it refers to the attacking party in a situation of military conflict: 1.110.4, 1.117.1, 2.93.4, 3.3.3, 3.112.3, 3.112.5, 4.25.9, 4.72.2, 7.29.3, 7.29.5, 8.84.4.
[40] LSJ s.v. II.1.   [41] Connor 1984: 109 n. 3.
[42] Parry 1969: 116; Swain 1994: 306–7. Ἐπιπίπτω: 2.48.3, 2.49.6, 3.87.1; ἐμπίπτω: 2.49.4, 2.53.4, 2.61.2. In addition, προσπίπτω is also used of the plague at 2.50.1.
[43] Loraux 2009 [1986]: 263.
[44] Hornblower i, on 3.82.2. See also Swain (1994: 306): 'The verb here [*sc.* at 3.82.2] is *epipiptein* which again recalls medical talk.'

In addition to the use of ἐπιπίπτω (highlighted by Hornblower), a further parallel emerges with the stasis excursus. Thucydides' ὡς ἄν... αἱ μεταβολαὶ...ἐφιστῶνται (cited in Section 2.7) recalls the phrase τῆς μεταβολῆς ἐπιγενομένης in the Hippocratic author. Ἐπιγίγνομαι, just like ἐφίσταμαι, is a generally asthenic verb, which can also suggest 'to come upon, assault, attack'.[45] Using this language, the Hippocratic writer describes what happens when a dry and cold spring suddenly supervenes in regions with relatively warm winters: because the body has been warm, the veins and brains have not hardened and disease befalls as a result. The μεταβολή of climatic circumstances, which leads to deterioration in health, consists in an external, meteorological phenomenon. Using very similar language, Thucydides implies that the evils of stasis and the reversals of circumstances likewise refer to impersonal forces beyond the control of individual agents.

In sum, given the two contexts in which ἐπιπίπτω typically occurs, the 'many grievances' of stasis assume the shape of an enemy on the attack and are likened to severe illness, which by implication reduces the city to an organism suffering from an agonizing condition. In either case, impersonal forces prevail and reduce human beings to passivity.

Interspersed throughout the *History*, ἐπιπίπτω and ἐμπίπτω recur in several passages that highlight emblematic events encapsulating the specific character of the Peloponnesian War. As scholars have pointed out, two of these forces are stasis and the plague.[46] A third larger than life-sized impersonal attacker, used as the subject of ἐμπίπτω, is ἔρως, the power collectively afflicting the Athenians and prompting them to undertake the Sicilian Expedition (6.24.3). Finally, Thucydides' account of the atrocity at Mycalessus features three instances of ἐπιπίπτω (7.29.3, twice at 29.5).[47] As Reinhardt has observed, Thucydides' report

---

[45] LSJ s.v. II.2.
[46] On the relationship between the War and the plague, Parry (1969: 115) observes: 'The Plague is a πάθος, like war, and in fact, it is a partner of war.' See also Luginbill 1999: 8. On the link between stasis and the Peloponnesian War, see Connor 1984: 103–4; Loraux 2009 [1986]: 265–6; Price 2001: 73–7 (maintaining, however, that Thucydides highlights the link not between stasis and war in general, but between stasis and *this* exceptional war, in which the boundaries between two phenomena of a different order are blurred, see 67–72).
[47] In the first two passages, the subject of ἐπιπίπτω is personal, each time referring to the assailants. In the third passage, however, the verb has an abstract subject, viz. the 'disaster' (ξυμφορά) that 'fell upon' the town. The close succession of these instances of ἐπιπίπτω suggests

regarding Mycalessus is 'a symptom of the War' as a whole: it sheds light on its distinctive 'physiognomy'.[48]

The idea that the War, as well as its proxies, recall superhuman attackers can also be found in 1.23, the summary account of the distinctive character of the Peloponnesian War. As Thucydides writes, the War, together with the many disasters that happened in its wake, 'attacked' the Greek world (ταῦτα γὰρ πάντα μετὰ τοῦδε τοῦ πολέμου ἅμα ξυνεπέθετο, 1.23.3). The verb ξυνεπιτίθεμαι is reminiscent of the synonymous compounds of πίπτω; in addition, the substantivized neuter subject recalls the 'many grievances' (πολλὰ καὶ χαλεπά, 3.82.2) that Thucydides uses as subject of ἐπέπεσε in the *Pathology*.

All the cited subjects used with ἐμπίπτω, ἐπιπίπτω, and ξυνεπιτίθεμαι refer to conditions that the Greeks called πάθη or παθήματα. According to Erich Auerbach and David Konstan, the terms comprise passions, diseases, and external afflictions, with the notion of suffering being the common denominator.[49] In combination with the compounds of πίπτω, these passive states assume the shape of active assailants. Kallet observes with regard to one specific instance of these compounds: '[W]hat the Athenians were doing, or what was happening to them, was in some sense beyond or out of their entire control, ... they were objects being affected, not the collective agent.'[50] Kallet's comments aptly summarize the implications of all the passages involving compounds of πίπτω. Thucydides suggests that human beings, who (one would have thought) play the role of agents, are in fact exposed to forces beyond their control.

---

that Thucydides wanted the reader to notice the connection between its different uses, i.e. between the more literal meaning of military attack and the more pointedly metaphorical idea of infliction by a severe state.

[48] Reinhardt 1966: 207 and 208. See also Stahl 2003 [1966]: 136; Lateiner 1977: 47.

[49] Auerbach 1967 [1941]: 162; Konstan 2006: 3–4.

[50] Kallet 2001: 134. In making this comment, Kallet refers to the following passage: τῶν ἄλλων ἀναλωμάτων μεγάλων προσπιπτόντων ('the other expenses fell upon them [sc. the Athenians] in great numbers', 7.28.4). One might object that the expenses used as the subject of προσπίπτω do not belong to the emblematic manifestations of the Peloponnesian War. Yet Kallet convincingly argues that the section to which this passage belongs (viz. the excursus on the Athenians' dire financial situation after the establishment of the Spartan fort at Deceleia) must be read in conjunction with the immediately following account of Mycalessus (2001: 140–2). The latter clearly reflects the War's distinctive character. As Kallet observes, the recurring of compounds of πίπτω represent a crucial link by which Thucydides connects the two sections (2001: 141).

It is noteworthy that, when it comes to πίπτω itself (i.e. the *verbum simplex* as opposed to one of its compounds), it is used with (an implied) personal subject (οἱ ἰδιῶται, 3.82.2) in the excursus on stasis. Elaborating on different forms taken by the cyclical pattern of stasis, Thucydides observes that during peace 'cities and individuals have a better cast of mind' (αἵ τε πόλεις καὶ οἱ ἰδιῶται ἀμείνους τὰς γνώμας ἔχουσι, 3.82.2); favourable circumstances lead to a more healthy mentality 'because they [*sc.* cities and individuals] do not lapse into necessities that leave no room for choice' (διὰ τὸ μὴ ἐς ἀκουσίους ἀνάγκας πίπτειν, 3.82.2).[51] Πίπτω captures a passive experience in this passage: individuals and collectives do not make a choice, but 'lapse into' a situation. Thucydides uses an articular infinitive (as opposed to a roughly synonymous circumstantial participle or subordinate clause) to underscore the notion that a condition descends. One might object that διά with an articular infinitive is a relatively common construction in Greek, basically equivalent to a causal clause. Yet, Gildersleeve observes that, prior to Thucydides, the articular infinitive, especially when used after a preposition, was not a particularly common construction in Greek.[52] Gildersleeve points out that the work of Thucydides marks an abrupt shift: 'Instead of a sparing use of prepositions, he indulges in the construction without stint (fifteen different prepositions), and absolutely riots in the use of διὰ τό, which occurs seventy times.'[53] Thus, the evidence suggests that the basic equivalence between a subordinate clause and a corresponding articular infinitive may not have been as much taken for granted by Thucydides' time as it became in later Greek prose.[54]

---

[51] For the translation of ἀκούσιοι ἀνάγκαι, see Classen-Steup iii, on 3.82.2.16: '(eigentlich Nötigungen zu unfreiwilligen Handlungen) "Notstände, zwingende Umstände, in welchen die freie Entschließung aufhört"'.
[52] Gildersleeve 1878: 11–14.   [53] Gildersleeve 1878: 14.
[54] In general, documentation of the orators' use of the articular infinitive shows that it occurs rarely in the early orators and becomes more widespread over the course of the fourth century (Gildersleeve 1878: 15, and 1887: 332; Kosch 2017: 79–80). For statistics of its use after prepositions such as διά, see Wagner 1885: 5 n. and Gildersleeve 1887: 336. Antiphon and Aeschines are exceptions to the general tendencies (the former using more, and the latter less, articular infinitives than the chronological scheme would suggest); but this is unsurprising given their specific stylistic preferences: Antiphon is generally fond of abstract expressions (Denniston 1952: 23 and 31), and Aeschines strives after naturalness (Blass 1887–98: iii, 2. 230–1), thus avoiding a construction that had taken a while to get a firm foothold in Greek usage.

As Heiny has pointed out, a distinctive feature of the articular infinitive is that it binds the words that stand between the article and the infinitive closely together, bracketing them as a tightly integrated unit.[55] In general, it is a characteristic feature of the article in ancient Greek that it stands not too far away from the noun to which it belongs. Due to this tendency, the sequence that runs from the article to the noun is marked off as a unit. In the articular infinitive construction, more words can generally stand between the article and the infinitive than in other nominal phrases. The option of delaying the infinitive to which the article belongs has the effect of evoking the reader's suspense. When the infinitive is finally mentioned, it attracts extra attention due to the delay.[56]

In the present passage, this feature of the articular infinitive has the effect that the emphasis falls heavily on the infinitive: τὸ μή... πίπτειν, 'because of their avoidance of lapsing'. This nominalized verbal state becomes the centre of attention, while everything that stands in between is subsumed in the unifying structure that runs from the article to the infinitive. Thus, the event itself (i.e. the mere fact of the avoidance of this lapse) becomes the focus of attention. In the passage under discussion, part of the construction's effect has to do with the fact that the subjects are merely implied: all emphasis rests on the event expressed by the infinitive. This nuance would be lost if Thucydides had chosen a synonymous construction with a circumstantial participle or a subordinate clause. In that case, the endings of the participle or the verb would refer the reader back to the subject of the main verb (i.e. αἵ τε πόλεις καὶ οἱ ἰδιῶται), thus diverting attention from the bare, general fact that a lapse into necessities takes place. In accordance with the prevailing tone of the excursus, the infinitive represents the prevalence of necessity as an impersonal occurrence.

By implication, it is not up to human beings whether they will suffer this fate or not, but to circumstances beyond their control. Rechenauer stresses the 'reactive' dimension of human nature, both in Thucydides and the medical writers: 'If human nature is exposed to a distinct set of circumstances, it will react, of necessity, in a distinct way; the presence of the same circumstances guarantees the occurrence of the same

---

[55] Heiny 1973: 179.   [56] See Heiny 1973: 179–82.

THE IMPLICATIONS OF THUCYDIDES' ABSTRACT STYLE 73

reaction.'[57] The claim that, if they are exposed to adverse circumstances, people 'lapse into necessities' eloquently expresses this notion. Once these 'necessities' or 'compulsions' (ἀνάγκαι) impose themselves, choices can be made only one way. As a result, they cease to be true choices.

2.9 Conclusion

In contrast to the narrative section about Corcyra, the *Pathology* of the War represents a stylistic register that runs counter to many of the ingrained traits of Greek prose style: it abounds in impersonal subjects, verbs devoid of specific content, passive phrases, and unwieldy clusters of abstract nouns. As a result, actions are redescribed as occurrences happening to people, impersonal entities replace human agents, people are locked into particular states, and events are represented as conforming to patterns. Given these implications, the style that predominates in the *Pathology* can be described as depersonalizing. Taken together, these various aspects tend to de-emphasize personal agents and stress collective dispositions, transpersonal forces, and the impetus of the events themselves.

At this point, it will be useful to recall the distinction, introduced in Section 1.3, between Thucydides' abstract style (epitomized by the *Pathology*) and his plain style (exemplified by the preceding narrative treatment of civil war at Corcyra). Both stylistic modes play a vital role in capturing the phenomenon at hand: the plain style offers a prim reconstruction of the events, thus establishing the concrete factual basis of what has happened, whereas the intractable abstract style provides an analysis of the fundamental forces at play in the situation. In this way, Thucydides uses the *Pathology* to distil the essence of the foregoing description. Whereas the narrative section presents a sequence of events with human beings in the role of agents, now Thucydides gives attention not to a course of action, but to a general state of affairs, marked by a constellation of patterns and occurrences. He

---

[57] Rechenauer (1991: 139): 'Wenn die Menschennatur bestimmten Umständen ausgesetzt ist, reagiert sie mit Notwendigkeit in einer ganz bestimmten Art; dabei ist durch die Gleichheit der Umstände eine Gleichheit der Reaktion garantiert.'

is interested in the array of forces that determine the events recounted in the preceding report. Allison makes a similar observation about the type of passages exemplified by the *Pathology*, pointing out that 'Thucydides... investigates the *forces* behind an action by rehearsing their characteristics in speeches and analyses where the abstract is foremost'.[58]

Notwithstanding their contrasting character, the two opposite modes of exposition also have something crucial in common: they are different manifestations of the same Thucydidean ethos, a posture marked by the uncompromising, serious concentration on the analysis of the Peloponnesian War. In his narrative reconstruction of events, Thucydides makes no concessions to those among his readers who might long for a more varied account, a narrative enriched by details of human interest. By contrast, what matters to Thucydides is the rigorous establishment of the chain of events. As Strasburger observes, Thucydides' narrative largely avoids anecdotal features, emphasis on heroic feats, attention to individual character traits, and consideration of the passions experienced by individuals (as opposed to collective impulses).[59] Adopting this largely impersonal perspective, Thucydides focuses attention on the collectives representing the various sides involved in the Peloponnesian War. By the same token, Thucydides also adopts an uncompromising stance when pursuing his second, complementary goal: his search for the forces ultimately responsible for events. This time, he refrains from the assumptions implied by a smoother and more common Greek idiom, such as the priority of personal subjects, the centrality of action (as opposed to impersonal occurrence), and the primacy of the specific moment over any eternal regularity. In their own way, both registers make no concessions to those desiring an easily digestible account.

---

[58] Allison 1997: 246. Patzer (1937: 97–102) also observes that Thucydides pursues two distinct objectives, of which either one or the other predominates in different sections of the *History*: one is historical (in the modern sense of the word), the other anthropological. These tendencies correlate closely to the two Thucydidean registers analysed in the present chapter as well as Chapter 1. Erbse (1968 [1961]: 617–18) draws attention to the same two modes of Thucydidean historiography: on the one hand, Thucydides is committed to a meticulous reconstruction of events; on the other, his ultimate objective is to illuminate 'the general dimension in particular events' ('das Allgemeine im Einzelereignis', 618).

[59] Strasburger 1982: 784–5, 787–8, and 1966: 60. On the same issue, see also Bruns 1896: 9 and 75 (with the second passage contrasting Thucydides with Herodotus); Bender 1938: 36–37; *HCT* i. 26–8; de Romilly 1958: 50 (commenting on the general effacement of peculiar traces of individuals in Thucydides' account); Gribble 2006: 440–1.

In both registers, Thucydides diverges from widely held assumptions concerning the priority of individual personhood in events. In sections marked by the plain style, Thucydides typically avoids portraits of individuals enriched by anecdotal detail, thus de-emphasizing the influence of personal factors on the course of events. The priority of personal agents is also called into question by the implications of several constructions characteristic of the abstract style. Two distinguished interpreters of Thucydides confirm the impression that in this crucial respect the two registers have similar implications, notwithstanding the evident differences that otherwise separate them in style and purport. According to de Romilly, Thucydides' repression of anecdotal details in narrative sections marked by the plain style reflects his quest for an essentialized narrative, an account reduced to the most basic storyline and characterized by 'an unfailing mechanical rigor'.[60] Connor makes a very similar observation with regard to the abstract style when he writes that '[a]n inexorable, impersonal regularity prevails' in Thucydides' account of stasis.[61] Both scholars highlight Thucydides' emphasis on what one might describe as an impersonal element pervading human affairs. In combination, their observations show that this concern marks both the plain and the abstract style. Of these two stylistic registers, the abstract style brings the reader more directly face to face with the forces ultimately responsible for the course of things.

---

[60] de Romilly 2012 [1956]: 26. De Romilly nicely illustrates the repression of anecdotal detail by comparing Thucydides' narrative of the attempted investment of Syracuse with Plutarch's account of the same events in the *Life of Nicias*: 11–12, 24.
[61] Connor 1984: 104.

3
The Passivity of the Powerful

The emphasis of the *Pathology* on the eternal repetition caused by human nature (3.82.2) implies that personal agents do not have the power to break this cycle. At another prominent place, in the chapter on method, Thucydides makes a very similar observation, in which he hints at an element of inevitability combined with the notion of impersonality. In making this observation, he draws on the abstract nominal idiom familiar from the *Pathology* (1.22.4):

ὅσοι δὲ βουλήσονται τῶν τε γενομένων τὸ σαφὲς σκοπεῖν καὶ τῶν μελλόντων ποτὲ αὖθις κατὰ τὸ ἀνθρώπινον τοιούτων καὶ παραπλησίων ἔσεσθαι, ὠφέλιμα κρίνειν αὐτὰ ἀρκούντως ἕξει.

It will be sufficient that those will judge my work useful who will want to get a clear idea about the things that have happened and at some point will happen again in the same or a similar manner in accordance with the human condition.

Thucydides draws on impersonal phrases (τῶν γενομένων...τῶν μελλόντων...τοιούτων καὶ παραπλησίων) that stress the notion of things happening as opposed to agency. The power that is responsible for the recurring pattern is also captured through an impersonal phrase: τὸ ἀνθρώπινον. Dionysius' remark that Thucydides substitutes 'things for persons' is pertinent once again (*Amm.* II 14.433.18–19, 14.434.12).

The neuter τὸ ἀνθρώπινον includes, as Stahl has emphasized, 'the external circumstances affecting human existence, so that we should precisely translate τὸ ἀνθρώπινον by "that which pertains to man", pointing to the human condition in a comprehensive sense'.[1] Stahl himself mentions chance as belonging to these conditions that confine human existence. In the same spirit, Hornblower underlines that the term 'is broader than "according to human nature"; it means something more like "the human condition" or "situation"'.[2] Similarly, Edmunds renders it as 'the objective limitations set upon human plans and aspirations.'[3] In the stasis section, Thucydides stresses that the impact of circumstances will force the 'nature of human beings' ($\varphi\acute{\upsilon}\sigma\iota\varsigma$ $\grave{\alpha}\nu\theta\rho\acute{\omega}\pi\omega\nu$, 3.82.2) to reveal itself. This emphasis on the exposure of $\varphi\acute{\upsilon}\sigma\iota\varsigma$ to circumstances helps to explain the idea of $\tau\grave{o}$ $\grave{\alpha}\nu\theta\rho\acute{\omega}\pi\iota\nu o\nu$ as 'the human situation'. Human nature should not be understood as consisting in inner qualities that exist in isolation from the encompassing world. Unlike the Olympians in Homer, human beings cannot distance themselves from the upheavals that occur in the external world; these percussions are rather part of what constitutes the human mode of being. This type of being is best characterized by one of Thucydides' neuter phrases, namely $\tau\grave{o}$ $\grave{\alpha}\nu\theta\rho\acute{\omega}\pi\iota\nu o\nu$. From the point of view of language, this phrase belongs to the same category as $\tau\acute{\alpha}$ $\tau\epsilon$ $\gamma\epsilon\nu\acute{o}\mu\epsilon\nu\alpha$ $\kappa\alpha\grave{\iota}$ $\tau\grave{\alpha}$ $\mu\acute{\epsilon}\lambda\lambda o\nu\tau\alpha$ (or $\pi o\lambda\lambda\grave{\alpha}$ $\kappa\alpha\grave{\iota}$ $\chi\alpha\lambda\epsilon\pi\grave{\alpha}\dots\gamma\iota\gamma\nu\acute{o}\mu\epsilon\nu\alpha\dots\kappa\alpha\grave{\iota}$ $\alpha\grave{\iota}\epsilon\grave{\iota}$ $\grave{\epsilon}\sigma\acute{o}\mu\epsilon\nu\alpha$, from the chapters on stasis at 3.82.2). The impersonal phrase suggests the influence of structuring factors, surrounding circumstances, and recurring patterns. Thus, this phrasing hints at the impact of impersonal factors on human action.

This argument faces the objection that, in the same passage, Thucydides expresses his ambition of offering readers a 'useful' ($\grave{\omega}\varphi\acute{\epsilon}\lambda\iota\mu\alpha$, 1.22.4) account. Some scholars have thought that this usefulness must be practical, and that Thucydides' work is supposed to offer a lesson as to how one might avoid the disasters portrayed in the Peloponnesian War.[4] Taking a different line, Adam Parry points out that the usefulness Thucydides has in mind is unlikely to be practical:

---

[1] Stahl 2003 [1966]: 29. De Romilly (1958: 55) takes the same line: '[L']"humain" a un sens plus large [*sc.* than human nature]: il vise aussi une condition matérielle... et tout un ensemble de moyens d'action...; il englobe donc une somme de limitations physiques et morales, de ressources physiques et morales susceptibles de se combiner en situations similaires.'
[2] Hornblower i, on 1.22.1.   [3] Edmunds 1975: 154.
[4] Finley 1942: 309–10; Weidauer 1954: 68–9; Herter 1968a [1950]: 280.

'[T]he "usefulness" was limited to the reader's acquisition of a clear picture.'[5] If Thucydides was aiming at practical utility, this ambition would be hard to reconcile with his ascertainment of a circular pattern, which, one would think, a putative practical effect of his work would need to suspend.[6] What is more, one of Thucydides' remarks in the excursus on the plague provides evidence against the ascription of much of a practical ambition to Thucydides. In the passage in question, Thucydides declares that he will describe the plague's symptoms to facilitate future recognition in case the disease returns (2.48.3). This, however, is all that he aims for: recognition of the plague when it returns. In no way does he envision that his record may help people to be more successful in curing the plague in the future.[7] The same ethos underlies Thucydides' assertion of the 'usefulness' for future readers at 1.22.4.[8]

Thucydides' emphasis on a circular pattern and the implications of the nominal style set us the task of arriving at a clearer understanding of what Thucydidean necessity consists in and what the nominal style contributes to this topic. The goal of this chapter is to provide answers to these two questions. Its starting point will be the exposition provided in the *Archaeology* of the basic forces that drive political action. Based on the analysis carried out in the *Archaeology*, we will turn to the speech of the Athenian ambassadors at Sparta, one of the key passages on necessity in Thucydides (1.73–88). Seeking to justify the Athenian empire in front of a Spartan audience, the Athenians champion the idea that natural

---

[5] Parry 1969: 109. Cf. Kapp 1930: 92–4; *HCT* i, on 1.22.4; de Romilly 1958: 42–8; Stahl 2003 [1966]: 15–18; Ostwald 1988: 63.

[6] Thus, Swain (1994: 320) rightly points out: 'As a constant human nature was not to be changed, its patterns of behavior were unstoppable (cf. 3.45.7), and there was no possibility of practically confronting it or of offering a "cure".'

[7] This point has been made by Pelling in an unpublished paper entitled 'Why read Thucydides?'. See also Parry (1981: 111): 'What is most notable is his [*sc.* Thucydides'] refusal to offer any hope of ever doing anything about such a visitation. As far as practical measures are concerned, Thucydides' mood is entirely fatalistic.'

[8] As Hornblower points out (1987: 134), this does not altogether exclude the possibility that statesmen can learn from Thucydides' work: it teaches them what kinds of events to expect and what the prevalent forces are. But Thucydides does not offer them a blueprint for how they are to respond when they encounter these forces. Moreover, even if one allows for utility in this limited sense, the emphasis of Thucydides' work falls on the quest for understanding as such, with potential usefulness playing an ancillary role.

necessity governs all political behaviour, and that this force ultimately impels the Athenians to strive after ever greater power. In making this point, however, the Athenians are guided by rhetorical aims, with a view to dissuading the Spartans to go to war. Therefore, the Athenians' account cannot be simply taken at face value. As a result, it will be necessary to consider the merits of the Athenians' position in light of Thucydides' own account of the rise of the Athenian empire in the *Pentecontaetia*.

3.1 The Thucydidean Standpoint: The *Archaeology*

In the *Archaeology*, Thucydides gives a rapid account of early Greek history from prehistoric time down to the eve of the Peloponnesian War. His goal is to demonstrate that the Peloponnesian War was more momentous than any earlier event in Greek history (1.1.2). At the same time, this survey serves a further, perhaps even more vital purpose: W. R. Connor has observed that the *Archaeology* 'analyzes forces that have long operated in Greek history and that are likely still to be evident in the great war that he has chosen for his subject'.[9] The section on method, in which Thucydides notes the recurrence of events 'in accordance with the human condition' (1.22.4), stands at the culminating point of the *Archaeology*. The animating forces that Thucydides dissects in the foregoing chapters should provide a prime example of the manifestation of τὸ ἀνθρώπινον in historical events.

Over the course of the *Archaeology*, Thucydides portrays the development of Greece from a miserable early condition, in which Greeks lacked fixed habitations and commerce and were constantly exposed to instability and external threats. An image of extreme disorganization emerges. The chaos of pre-historical Greece is reflected in a thoroughgoing lack of stability and balance. Early Greece is stirred, on the one hand, by excessive movement, which is manifest in constant migrations and a nomadic lifestyle (1.2.3), and on the other, suffers from extreme immobility, due to the lack of mercantile traffic and secure travelling (1.2.2).

[9] Connor 1984: 26.

Thus, oscillating between extremes, the world of early Greece is disrupted by the equally dismal alternatives of incessant flux and paralyzing inaction.

The *Archaeology* traces the development of strategies through which humans, responding to the unbalanced world around them, impose order and stability on the ubiquitous chaos. The account systematically uncovers, as several scholars have stressed, a definite set of material factors that enable the Greeks to impose order: ships, city walls, and wealth.[10] Ships enable the movement necessary to conduct traffic, fortifications lead to the stability required for long-standing fixed habitations, and monetary resources accrue from the mutually balanced employment of the first two factors. Money simultaneously provides a stimulus to refine both the instruments enabling extension and the factors furthering unity.[11] Thus, motion and stability are both indispensable for the rise of a city, but they must be brought into a carefully calibrated balance.[12]

The axis around which all these material factors rotate is the acquisition, maintenance, and expansion of power. Parry has emphasized the insistent use of words meaning 'power' in the *Archaeology* and concludes: 'The historical facts which make up the object of intellection appear primarily as words meaning *power*.'[13] Power, the capacity to do things, enables people to impose order and stability on the chaotic flux of the world. But the *Archaeology* also shows the inherent propulsion of power towards extension and new acquisition. The verbal connotations of δύναμαι are indicative of this tendency: a capacity wants to be actualized and will not rest content with an inactive maintenance of the status quo.[14] This ever self-enhancing striving to extend one's power is traced, on a macroscopic level, by the development recounted in the *Archaeology*

---

[10] De Romilly 2012 [1956]: 157–60; Parry 1972: 53–4; Loraux 2006 [1981]: 365; Hunter 1982: 20–2; Allison 1989: 14.

[11] For the crucial contribution made by financial resources, see Kallet 1993: 35.

[12] On the principle of the Archaeology that civilization requires balance between motion and rest, see further Joho 2021: 18–20.

[13] Parry 1972: 52. Parry counts twenty-three instances of δύναμις, and thirty-five references to power if one includes related terms, such as δυαντός, δύνασθαι, ἰσχύς, βιαζόμενοι, ἐκράτησαν, κρεισσόνων.

[14] Strasburger (1966: 59) comments on the meaning of the term: '*Δύναμις* und das Verb δύνασθαι... bedeuten nicht nur "die Macht" als starren absoluten Tatbestand, sondern vor allem auch ihre Komponenten und Abstufungen: das "Potential".'

as a whole:[15] as Loraux observes, 'the Archaeology culminates in an epiphany of Athenian dynamism'.[16] Indeed, Athens on the eve of the Peloponnesian War possesses an impressive array, heretofore unparalleled, of those factors that constitute the basis of δύναμις: walls, ships, and wealth. As pointed out above, the impersonal term 'the human condition' suggests that material conditions do not represent an accessory aspect, an element extrinsic to the constitution of human beings; instead, part and parcel of what it means to be human is to be exposed to the power exerted by impersonal circumstances.

The account offered in the *Archaeology* also highlights another fundamental aspect of Thucydides' outlook, again alluded to by the neuter form τὸ ἀνθρώπινον. As pointed out at the end of Chapter 2 (p. 74), Strasburger has stressed Thucydides' general avoidance of anecdotal features and domestic scenes and his concomitant disinterest in portraying the character of specific individuals. Strasburger takes this as an indication that *'the scope for individuals' influence* is restricted in his account',[17] a feature that we will examine more extensively in Chapter 6.

The following example, and the comparison with Herodotus, shows the rigour with which Thucydides reduces the room given to individual traits. In recounting the notable fleets of early Greece, Thucydides mentions the Samian tyrant Polycrates. The same man appears also in the third book of Herodotus' *Histories*, where he is likewise singled out for the considerable extent of his power. In addition to stressing the impressive military resources wielded by Polycrates (3.39.3), Herodotus notes that a particular aspect of Polycrates' character contributed to his series of successes: Polycrates was so ruthless that he preyed on friends just as much as on enemies, offering the disarming justification that one

---

[15] De Romilly (2012 [1956]: 173) has identified two major sections of the *Archaeology* (the first dealing with the origins of the Trojan War [1.2–11] and the other with the time since the Trojan War [1.12–19]). While the clear-cut separation may suggest a rupture in the historic continuity, de Romilly in fact highlights various thematic parallels by which both sections are linked (2012 [1956]: 174). In summarizing her results, she writes: 'There is nothing in it [i.e. in Thucydides' style of representation] that suggests starting over, while everything suggests continuity' (2012 [1956]: 174). Thus, the *Archaeology* as a whole traces one continuous development, moments of disruption and regression notwithstanding.

[16] Loraux 2006 [1981]: 365.

[17] Strasburger (1982: 784): 'Zunächst ist bekanntlich das *Wirken der Einzelpersönlichkeit* in seiner Darstellung eingeschränkt.' See also Gribble 2006: 439.

will be dearer to a friend to whom one has returned his goods than to one who has remained entirely unmolested (3.39.4). Herodotus considers this nugget of wisdom worth reporting because it helps to explain Polycrates' success as a tyrant. In Thucydides' *Archaeology*, by contrast, even a colourful figure of the stature of Polycrates is viewed exclusively from the angle of the familiar impersonal forces: 'Polycrates, ruling as a tyrant over Samos in the time of Cambyses, wielded power through his fleet, and he subdued several islands and captured Rhenea in particular and consecrated it to Delian Apollo' (καὶ Πολυκράτης Σάμου τυραννῶν ἐπὶ Καμβύσου ναυτικῷ ἰσχύων ἄλλας τε τῶν νήσων ὑπηκόους ἐποιήσατο καὶ Ῥήνειαν ἑλὼν ἀνέθηκε τῷ Ἀπόλλωνι τῷ Δηλίῳ, 1.13.6). Thucydides uses the figure of Polycrates to highlight the operation of some of the permanent driving forces that shape the course of history: the material assets provided by a high-performance fleet and the innate quest of human beings for greater power; the distinctive traits of the individual Polycrates, despite the richness of available material, is irrelevant for Thucydides' purpose: the disclosure of τὸ ἀνθρώπινον. 'The human' has a generalizing scope and is based on a recurring pattern, aspects that leave little room for the distinctive aspects of a particular human being.

In light of these considerations, it comes as no surprise that the *Archaeology* also introduces the reader to the characteristic features of Thucydides' nominal style. The emphasis of the nominal style on passivity, impersonality, patterns, and occurrence without agency is the analogue to the suppression of any colourful characterization of individuals. To begin with, Adam Parry has noticed that the *Archaeology* features a great number of 'compounds of ἵστημι, usually in the middle voice, which are regularly used to mark significant qualitative changes in the historical situation'.[18] The following example, not mentioned by Parry but drawn from the *Archaeology*, illustrates this employment of ἵστημι compounds: 'As Greece grew more powerful and continued to acquire still more wealth than before, more often than not <u>tyrannies came to be established</u> in the cities since the revenues were growing' (δυνατωτέρας δὲ γιγνομένης τῆς Ἑλλάδος καὶ τῶν χρημάτων τὴν κτῆσιν ἔτι μᾶλλον ἢ πρότερον ποιουμένης τὰ πολλὰ <u>τυραννίδες</u> ἐν ταῖς πόλεσι <u>καθίσταντο</u>, τῶν

[18] Parry 1972: 52.

προσόδων μειζόνων γιγνομένων, 1.13.1). The new phase in the historical process, the rise of tyrannies, is expressed by the notably agent-free compound of ἵστημι. This event is flanked by three sets of genitive absolutes (δυνατωτέρας...γιγνομένης τῆς Ἑλλάδος—[τῆς Ἑλλάδος]... τὴν κτῆσιν...ποιουμένης—τῶν προσόδων μειζόνων γιγνομένων), which express, either through agent-free forms of γίγνομαι or through the generalized impersonal subject 'Greece' with the phrase 'to acquire wealth', the working of those forces that animate the development traced in the *Archaeology*: increase of power and of wealth (δυνατωτέρας—τῶν χρημάτων τὴν κτῆσιν) leads to still greater augmentation of wealth (τῶν προσόδων μειζόνων γιγνομένων). This use of γίγνομαι (capturing the forces that animate the historical process) is, just like the employment of compounds of ἵστημι, a recurrent feature of the *Archaeology*.[19] In addition, it is noticeable that each of the three genitive absolutes features a comparative (δυνατωτέρας—ἔτι μᾶλλον ἢ πρότερον—μειζόνων). In combination with the forms of γίγνομαι, they suggest that Greece has reached a new stage on a developmental spectrum, thus underlining the notion that a process is taking place.

Apart from compounds of ἵστημι and a preference for the semantics of process over those of action, the *Archaeology* provides evidence for another stylistic idiosyncrasy familiar from the analysis provided in Chapters 1 and 2: impersonal neuters. The increase in naval skill, which one might expect to be achieved through the active role of personal agents, is described as an event which simply occurs: 'Those cities that were founded in most recent times, as <u>circumstances had already become more favourable for navigation</u>, had more surplus of money' (τῶν δὲ πόλεων ὅσαι μὲν νεώτατα ᾠκίσθησαν καὶ ἤδη πλωιμωτέρων ὄντων περιουσίας μᾶλλον ἔχουσαι χρημάτων..., 1.7). Due to the neuter form πλωιμώτερα, the increase in naval skill is framed as a process. In addition, comparative phrases (πλωιμωτέρων and μᾶλλον) cluster and underline the processual character of the enhancement of naval skill and wealth. By contrast, purposeful human agency is not emphasized. The neuter form is complemented by two abstract nouns: περιουσία and χρήματα. These nouns describing

---

[19] For further examples, see 1.12.1, 15.1, 15.3, 16.1, 19.

material factors fence in the verb ἔχω, which is lacking in specific content. The actions of cities are to a large degree conditioned by the forces of power, wealth, and navigation.

Another occurrence of the impersonal neuter πλωιμώτερα leads to the same conclusions: 'But when the navy of Minos had been established, circumstances became more favourable for navigation between each other' (καταστάντος δὲ τοῦ Μίνω ναυτικοῦ πλωιμώτερα ἐγένετο παρ' ἀλλήλους, 1.8.2). The neuter stands again in the comparative and is again coupled with a form of γίγνομαι. This phrase and the verb καθίστημι, which (as Parry says) captures a change in the historical situation, combine to convey the notions of an impersonal process channelling the development of Greece. Both phrases are impersonal passives. Thucydides uses these expressions instead of active phrases such as 'when Minos had acquired a fleet' or 'the Greeks began to sail the seas'. It is interesting to note that Thucydides takes recourse to both of these phrases later in the *Archaeology* on the occasion of the Corinthians' crackdown on piracy (ἐπειδή τε οἱ Ἕλληνες μᾶλλον ἔπλῳζον, τὰς ναῦς κτησάμενοι..., 1.13.5). The comparison with the passage about Minos is instructive: Thucydides presents the groundbreaking establishment of seafaring under Minos in depersonalizing language as the emergence of a new constellation of circumstances whereas he sees scope for personal agency later on. These actions, however, cannot but take place against the backdrop of a settled situation. This is the central message of the 'anatomy of power' (to borrow Connor's phrase) that Thucydides has placed programmatically in front of his account of the War proper in order to introduce the reader to the 'way of looking at the past' called for by his material.[20]

3.2 Thucydides and His Speakers

In the remainder of this and some subsequent chapters, we will consider passages from several Thucydidean speeches. The interpretation based on these passages faces the problem of Thucydides' relationship to his speakers. Christopher Pelling states a sensible principle for gauging the motives behind Thucydides' incorporation of a given detail in a speech:

---

[20] For the quotation, see Connor 1984: 26.

[W]e must always be prepared to ask questions about Thucydides as well as about the speaker: not merely why the speaker said it or might be thought to have said something like it, but also what made it interesting enough to Thucydides to survive the selective process and figure in his version.[21]

Roughly speaking, one can distinguish two different, sometimes competing, motivations that Thucydides might have had in selecting material for his speeches.[22] On the one hand, the speakers often advance arguments that are rhetorically convenient, regardless of whether they contain true insights about the situation at hand. Thucydides presumably wants the reader to engage critically with the viewpoint advanced by the speaker. In probing the speaker's claims, the reader has to consider relevant sections of the narrative as well as potential arguments offered by the opposite side. On this view, Thucydides' goal is to show the mentality, the manipulations, and the fallacies that animate political debates, especially under the severe conditions of war.

On the other hand, the speeches give Thucydides the opportunity to let the speakers express important higher-order insights—for instance, about the driving forces behind events.[23] The frequent tendency of Thucydidean speakers to confront the fundamental principles underpinning political events strongly suggests this assumption, especially in view of Thucydides' restraint regarding full-blown systematic explanations in his own voice. Because it is unlikely that these kinds of reflections took up the same proportion of space (if any) in orations actually delivered, a methodical ambition appears to animate Thucydides' selection from a presumably much longer original.[24]

---

[21] Pelling 2000: 120.
[22] On the specific contribution made by Thucydidean speeches (as opposed to discourse in the narrator's voice), see Pelling (2000: 121): 'Direct speech is appropriate for some things, for intricate logical argument, for presenting (and implicitly unmasking) the thought-processes which underlie an action or the disingenuous rationalisations which purport to justify it... It is also appropriate for giving his characters a dramatic voice, with all the immediacy that direct speeches give.'
[23] Strasburger, comparing the function of speeches in Herodotus and Thucydides, puts this issue well: '[The speeches' main function in both historians is to achieve] geistige Transparenz der geschichtlichen Situation, bei *Herodot* oft auch als ein Stück allgemeiner Lebensdeutung, bei *Thukydides* vor allem als Aufdeckung und Analyse der die geschichtliche Aktion treibenden Kräfte' (1972: 39).
[24] One of the thorniest issues in the study of Thucydides concerns the historical basis of the speeches. Scholarly heavyweights have vigorously argued for either of the extreme positions

If a given speaker comments on the principles underlying the course of events, the speaker's analytical ambition as such does not entitle us to conclude that Thucydides agrees with the position put forward.[25] Many times the insight to be gained from a speech takes a somewhat different shape: a speaker's remark often highlights the important issues and offers illuminating parameters for their assessment without containing the whole truth about the situation.[26] The speakers draw attention to the pertinent questions, but in most cases their thoughts do not represent the last word on the subject: they shed light on crucial aspects but pass over or de-emphasize others that do not suit their rhetorical goals.

At the same time, one should also keep in mind that, in some important regards, the inclusion of direct discourse is based on quite different assumptions in modern literature than in ancient Greek texts:

---

available on this issue: at one end of the spectrum are those who argue for quite a high degree of historical accuracy (Gomme 1937: 171–6; Kagan 1975: 76–9; Cogan 1981a: x–xvi; Wilson 1982b: 100–1), at the other stand the proponents of free, or nearly free, invention (Meyer 1899: 385; Schwartz 1919: 25; Egermann 1972: 582). Given what Thucydides himself says in the chapter on method, I consider free invention to be unlikely. After all, Thucydides says that he kept 'as closely as possible to the sense, taken in the aggregate, of what was really said' (ἐχομένῳ ὅτι ἐγγύτατα τῆς ξυμπάσης γνώμης τῶν ἀληθῶς λεχθέντων, 1.22.1). In light of this statement, it seems certain that a Thucydidean speech bears at least some resemblance to its historical prototype and that Thucydides made an effort to stay true to what was said in the original speech. At the same time, Thucydides clearly does not provide verbatim reports. Stylistic continuity among the various speeches suggests that Thucydides is largely responsible for their wording. The act of rewriting surely involved selectivity: Thucydides would only try to record, where this was possible, those points that he thought to have revelatory power with regard to the situation at hand. Moreover, given that on many occasions his only basis for the content of a delivered speech must have been the bitty recollections of eyewitnesses, the resemblance with the original is likely to have been tenuous on several occasions. For a clear statement of the freedom that Thucydides' own declaration leaves for his versions of the speeches, see Wilson 1982b: 103. For a balance struck between the poles of 'the extreme historical accurist and the extreme free compositioner', see Pelling 2000: 117–18.

[25] See Scardino (2007: 461), apropos the speeches: 'Am wichtigsten ist aber ihre Funktion als...Kommentar..., wobei die Positionen der Redner a priori nicht mit der des Historikers übereinstimmen, sondern mit dem Geschehenszusammenhang und den auktorialen Äußerungen in Beziehung gesetzt werden müssen.' See also Strasburger (1968a [1954]: 445): 'Die objektive Wahrheit liegt...sehr oft unausgesprochen, gewissermaßen schwebend, im Schnittpunkt der subjektiven Meinungen, in der Mitte zwischen Rede und Gegenrede, oder gar im Treffpunkt von drei oder von mehr Reden, wozu als weitere Äußerung noch das Wort des Historikers selbst treten kann, einschränkend oder bestätigend, eventuell an einer weit abliegenden Stelle des Werkes.'

[26] Compare Rood's (1998: 286) way of putting the issue: '[T]he perceptions and words of Thucydides' characters suggest frameworks for understanding the narrative: they create a dialogue between the perspectives of characters and the perspectives of readers who know the end to which the narrative looks, or who are at least educated by repeated patterns of mistaken and self-fulfilling perceptions.'

moderns are usually concerned to portray the interaction, and clash, of subjective points of view, whereas an important, though not exhaustive, function of direct discourse in Greek historiography is to record generalizing utterances with a claim to objective truth. Due to these tendencies, Virginia Woolf's claim that 'Greek is the impersonal literature' captures a true insight.[27] The term suggests that Greek literature is not concerned with the representation of personal idiosyncrasy and radical subjectivity, factors that necessarily limit and skew every individual's perspective on the modern view. Instead, the chief concern of Greek literature lies in capturing what is typical, elementary, and characteristic, not in order to arrive at an abstract generality, but to capture a plastic concreteness, undisguised by an overload of psychological complexity. Based on prevalent modern assumptions, every human psyche is infinitely complex and, therefore, radically individual. This presupposition naturally leads to the notion that direct discourse is an expression valid only from the point of view of one isolated subject. The Greeks tended to take a different view. In Homeric epic, for instance, fundamental insights with a general applicability to human affairs are typically expressed not by the narrator, but by a particular character. The thoughts on the fragility of human existence expressed by Achilles to Priam are a case in point (*Il.* 24.525–33). Put into the mouth of the narrator, such thought would have been entirely incommensurate with the ethos of Homeric objectivity. Events are to speak for themselves, and the narrator looks at them with noble restraint, abstaining from sentimental or moralizing comments. This trait of the narrator in epic was recognized and admired by the Greeks of the classical era. In the *Poetics*, Aristotle observes that one of the most praiseworthy features of Homer is his restraint with regard to authorial comment. 'For,' says Aristotle, 'the poet should say very little in his own voice' (αὐτὸν γὰρ δεῖ τὸν ποιητὴν ἐλάχιστα λέγειν, Arist. *Po.* 1460a7).

Greek historiography owes its habit of incorporating extensive, self-contained speeches to the Homeric model, on whose ethos the historians modelled their own style.[28] In addition, Thucydides' sparing use of

---

[27] Woolf 1925: 57. 'Impersonal,' that is, when approached with expectations informed by the reading of modern literature.
[28] See Strasburger 1972: 38. On Thucydides' imitation of Homeric ethos, see Joho 2017: 594–600.

authorial exposition of principles (with the exception of self-contained excursuses) is surely inspired by the comparable restraint exercised by the Homeric narrator, whose exemplary status is attested by Aristotle's commendation. With the form, Thucydides (as well as other historians) also adopted some of the thought patterns familiar from epic. Therefore, one must always reckon with the possibility that in Greek historiography a character's speech rises to a level of objectivity that would seem implausible from a modern standpoint.[29] Such an objective status is especially evident in those passages in Homer, tragedy, or Herodotus in which a *daimon* comes to speak through an individual.[30] When it is possible for divine forces to express their views through human beings, individual characters can plausibly be endowed with a level of insight that would seem jarring in a modern context. While Thucydides dispenses with the religious framework, he maintains some of the presuppositions that come with it.

3.3 Compulsion by 'The Three Greatest Things'

In Thucydides' account, the great debate at Sparta in book 1 marks the moment when the course of events is irreversibly set for war: we witness the dawning of a new iron age. During this debate, the Athenians give a speech, which provides an exception to the general observation made by Thucydides that the 'truest cause' (τὴν μὲν... ἀληθεστάτην πρόφασιν, 1.23.6) for the Peloponnesian War, namely that the Athenians rose in power and that the Spartans became afraid of them, was 'most invisible in what was said' (ἀφανεστάτην δὲ λόγῳ, 1.23.6). The Athenians point out quite clearly that the Spartans consider the Athenian ascendancy as contrary to their own interests, and that they are using justice as a pretext

---

[29] Putting an observation in the mouth of a speaker may in fact heighten the degree of objectivity instead of decreasing it. As Ostwald observes (1988: 32), 'Thucydides has given his own view the aura of objective truth' by recording the recognition of the War's necessity in two different speeches, the first given by the Corinthians and the second by Pericles.' Eduard Meyer (1899: 381) makes the same observation with regard to Archidamus' declaration of the basic practices that sustain the Spartan way of life.

[30] Pelling (2006: 158), mentioning Croesus' remarks on the funeral pyre as well as Cyrus' reaction, provides a nice example from Herodotus: '[T]ruth seems to speak, strangely and even supernaturally, through the participants' remarks in a way that goes beyond their surface relevance.'

to cripple the power of Athens (1.76.2). Therefore, their position shares much common ground with Thucydides' view about the causal nexus that led to the Peloponnesian War. Given this affinity, the Athenians' account of the natural necessity that has driven them to acquire their empire deserves an unprejudiced hearing.

The Athenians claim that their dominion over the allies is nothing that people should make an outcry about because, as they say, acquiring power is a constant necessity that human nature imposes on everyone alike (1.76.2):

> οὕτως οὐδ' ἡμεῖς θαυμαστὸν οὐδὲν πεποιήκαμεν οὐδ' ἀπὸ τοῦ ἀνθρωπείου τρόπου, εἰ ἀρχήν τε διδομένην ἐδεξάμεθα καὶ ταύτην μὴ ἀνεῖμεν ὑπὸ ⟨τριῶν⟩ τῶν μεγίστων νικηθέντες, τιμῆς καὶ δέους καὶ ὠφελίας, οὐδ' αὖ πρῶτοι τοῦ τοιούτου ὑπάρξαντες, ἀλλ' αἰεὶ καθεστῶτος τὸν ἥσσω ὑπὸ τοῦ δυνατωτέρου κατείργεσθαι...
>
> In this way, we have done nothing astonishing at all nor anything that deviates from the human way if we accepted dominion when it was given to us and did not let it go, conquered by the three greatest things, namely honour, fear, and advantage; nor, again, were we the first to do this and led the way in this kind of behavior, but it has always been an established fact that the weaker is kept down by the stronger...

According to the ambassadors, the Athenians cannot possibly let go of the empire because they have been 'conquered by the three greatest things' (ὑπὸ ⟨τριῶν⟩ τῶν μεγίστων νικηθέντες). Conquest typically implies a human subject. Contrary to this expectation, the Athenians ascribe proper agency to the impersonal forces of fear, honour, and advantage inasmuch as these factors occupy the grammatical position of agent in a passive construction.

Mark Fisher and Kinch Hoekstra make two supporting observations about the phrases in question. First, as noted in the Introduction, they point out that the phrase 'being defeated' (νικηθέντες) suggests what they call a case of 'hard necessity'.[31] The Athenians are not just referring to a practical necessity with the implication that, given the circumstances, they had no viable alternative course after weighing all their options. The

---

[31] Fisher and Hoekstra 2017: 382–3.

phrase rather suggests that the forces in question are so strong that they overpower human beings without leaving them much leeway. Second, Fisher and Hoekstra draw attention to the fact that the phrase ὑπὸ ⟨τριῶν⟩ τῶν μεγίστων νικηθέντες precedes the three terms 'honour, fear, and advantage', with τριῶν being an insertion by modern editors. If one reads the phrase in isolation from the apposition and without the addition, it means ' defeated by those who are greatest'. The phrase τῶν μεγίστων appears in the construction that normally indicates the *person* by whom an action is done. For a moment, the reader is given the impression that the Athenians have come face to face with 'the greatest possible conquerors' just as if they were 'forced by the hand of god'.[32] Only after the participle νικηθέντες, the appositional phrase τιμῆς καὶ δέους καὶ ὠφελίας follows and makes clear that τῶν μεγίστων is in fact neuter. The greatest conquerors are not personal agents, whether human or divine, but impersonal motivations.

With the following genitive absolute, the Athenians emphasize that their behaviour is not freely chosen but structurally determined: αἰεὶ καθεστῶτος τὸν ἥσσω ὑπὸ τοῦ δυνατωτέρου κατείργεσθαι ('the fact always having been established that the weaker is kept down by the stronger'). The event of 'the weaker being kept down by the stronger' fills the position of the subject in this phrase. This is another instance of the frequent phenomenon that an activity, by being combined with the perfect participle of καθίσταμαι, is described as a static disposition. De Romilly has drawn attention to other perfect forms used by the Athenians to describe the situation that has come to confront them (τοῖς πολλοῖς ἀπηχθημένους καί τινων καὶ ἤδη ἀποστάντων κατεστραμμένων, 'after it had come to pass that we had become hateful to most [sc. of our allies], and that some of them had already been subdued [sc. by us] after they had even seceded', 1.75.4). De Romilly observes that these forms highlight 'a settled result' ('marquant un résultat acquis'), and that 'the consequences proceeding from it will invariably head, with ever increasing speed, into the same direction'.[33]

Thucydides' fondness for periphrasis with καθίσταμαι, for which we already found evidence in the chapters on stasis (3.81.5, 82.8, 83.1), recalls the Hippocratic notion of κατάστασις. As Pouncey and Swain have pointed out, the term denotes 'constitution' or 'overall condition' in

---

[32] Fisher and Hoekstra 2017: 383.
[33] De Romilly 1971, 114: 'les conséquences qui en découlent vont, en s'accélérant, toujours dans le même sens.'

the medical authors.³⁴ With regard to the use of the term in *Epidemics* books 1 and 3, Langholf observes that, in several passages, the term refers both to the 'state' of a disease and the 'condition' of the weather, a dual usage that springs from 'the underlying medical doctrine of a close interrelation between the weather and the diseases, which both form one "system".'³⁵ The use of κατάστασις in medical terminology clearly shows that vocabulary derived from καθίστημι readily suggests a settled condition that determines, or at least circumscribes, the behaviour of an entity. The Thucydidean passage just cited shows that the Athenian ambassadors draw on the same connotations as the author of the medical treatise: using the perfect participle belonging to καθίσταμαι, they claim that human behaviour is conditioned by a general human constitution, just as the weather situation provides the conditions for certain diseases.

In yet another passage, the Athenians put emphasis on the idea of their own passivity: they were not only 'defeated' by 'the three greatest things', but they were also 'compelled' (κατηναγκάσθημεν, 1.75.3), with fear, honour, and advantage again playing the role of quasi-agents (1.75.3):

ἐξ αὐτοῦ δὲ τοῦ ἔργου [sc. ἡγεμόνας καταστῆναι] κατηναγκάσθημεν τὸ πρῶτον προαγαγεῖν αὐτὴν ἐς τόδε, μάλιστα μὲν ὑπὸ δέους, ἔπειτα καὶ τιμῆς, ὕστερον καὶ ὠφελίας.

As a consequence of this very fact [sc. the Athenians' establishment as leaders] we were first compelled to extend the empire to its present state, chiefly by fear, then also by honour, finally also by advantage.

In this passage, the word ἔργον is best rendered in English by the impersonal 'fact' instead of 'deed'.³⁶ The Athenians' acceptance of leadership over the allies is more a 'fact' than a 'deed' because the Athenians reacted to circumstances, which confronted them. De Romilly parses the phrase ἐξ αὐτοῦ δὲ τοῦ ἔργου as 'ensuing from the affair itself' and remarks: 'Things seem to develop with an inner dynamic... this phrase indicates that henceforth facts themselves play the role of determining factors.'³⁷ Events accumulate a self-sufficient thrust, and the actions of human beings conform to this dynamic.

---

³⁴ Pouncey 1980: 23; Swain 1994: 309.   ³⁵ Langholf 1990: 169-70.
³⁶ On the different sets of connotations, depending on context, of the word ἔργον (activity vs. achievement and fact vs. deed), see Immerwahr 1960: 276.
³⁷ De Romilly (1971: 114): '[L]es choses semblent se développer d'elles-mêmes... *ex autou de tou ergou*, c'est-à-dire "à partir de la chose même": elle [sc. cette expression] indique que les faits eux-mêmes sont dorénavant déterminants.'

The ambassadors' choice of the word καταναγκάζω show how fear, honour, and advantage motivate action. Seth Jaffe compares the impetus emanating from them to 'the Aristotelian good' and points out that this stimulus 'exerts a teleological compulsion or pull. Thucydidean cities and individuals are pulled toward certain ends, if not toward the Socratic goods of the soul'.[38] In a similar vein, Luginbill observes that 'Thucydides' concept of *anangke* is perhaps best described as "pressure" to act'.[39] It is not conceivable that anyone can rid oneself from the pull of these motives: they may assume a different shape in different circumstances, but they will always exert a fundamental influence.

As the Athenian ambassadors claim, they did not acquire their empire by force (ἐλάβομεν οὐ βιασάμενοι, 1.75.2), but in the wake of the Spartans' withdrawal from the leadership and the allies' simultaneous request that the Athenians 'become leaders' (ἡγεμόνας καταστῆναι, 1.75.2). Once this 'fact' has taken shape, consequences arise that have the power of compulsions: actions are dictated by the three greatest things. In experiencing this process, the Athenians claim to 'be subject to human nature' (χρησάμενοι τῇ ἀνθρωπείᾳ φύσει, 1.76.3). Χράομαι in the sense of 'to suffer, to be subject to' is synonymous with πάσχω.[40] According to the ambassadors, passivity, necessity, and the irresistible pull of circumstances are the prevalent notions defining the Athenians' rise to power.

In assessing the speech of the Athenian envoys, one must not overlook their rhetorical objective: they wish to dissuade the Spartans from going to war, a goal emphasized both by Thucydides (1.72.1) and the envoys themselves (1.78.4). The compulsory motivations cited by the Athenians as inevitable causes of their quest for empire make for a viable apology:[41] if the Athenians, just like everyone else, have no way of escaping the 'three greatest things', then it is hardly possible to blame them for the actions induced by these wielders of universal influence. Nevertheless, it would also be wrong to dismiss the envoys' arguments simply because they serve a rhetorical function in a political speech. We must consider whether any other portion of Thucydides' *History* throws some light on

---

[38] Jaffe 2017: 197.   [39] Luginbill 1999: 46.
[40] LSJ s.v. χράομαι (C) C.III.1: 'experience, suffer, be subject to, esp. external events or conditions'.
[41] Raubitschek (1973: 43) observes that the Athenians' claims regarding the three compulsory universal motivations 'certainly convey a note of apology', and Orwin (1994: 48) points out that this part of their argumentation amounts to an 'excuse' for the imperial rule of Athens.

the validity of the Athenians' claims, thus forming the basis for an independent assessment.

3.4 The Process of Imperial Growth in the *Pentecontaetia*

The *Pentecontaetia*, which spans the period between the Persian Wars and the eve of the Peloponnesian War (1.89–118), follows immediately after the debate at Sparta. As Thucydides himself points out, this section is his account of the emergence of the Athenian empire (1.89.1, 118.2). Scholars have observed that the *Pentecontaetia* gives the reader an opportunity to compare the controversial claims made by the Athenians with Thucydides' narrative.[42] Thus, it provides a benchmark ideally suited for a comparison between the Athenians' claims and Thucydides' presentation of the facts.

The *Pentecontaetia* opens with the following assertion (1.89.1):

Οἱ γὰρ Ἀθηναῖοι τρόπῳ τοιῷδε ἦλθον ἐπὶ τὰ πράγματα ἐν οἷς ηὐξήθησαν.

For in the following way the Athenians entered into circumstances in which they rose.

As Allison observes, the phrase τὰ πράγματα has 'definiteness' and 'solidity about it'.[43] In Thucydides, it typically refers to 'circumstances' or 'affairs'.[44] Thus, it has has a similar meaning as, for instance, τὰ ὑπάρχοντα or τὰ παρόντα. In the clash between the powers of human thought and external reality, it belongs to the side of sturdy, impersonal

---

[42] Raubitschek 1973: 40; Orwin 1994: 50.   [43] Allison 1997: 78.
[44] For passages illustrating this use of τὰ πράγματα, see the following (the first quotation comes from Pericles' first speech, the second from the *Pathology*): ἐνδέχεται γὰρ τὰς ξυμφορὰς τῶν πραγμάτων οὐχ ἧσσον ἀμαθῶς χωρῆσαι ἢ καὶ τὰς διανοίας τοῦ ἀνθρώπου ('For it is possible for the vagaries of events to proceed no less ignorantly than the plans of man', 1.140.1); ἐν μὲν γὰρ εἰρήνῃ καὶ ἀγαθοῖς πράγμασιν αἵ τε πόλεις καὶ οἱ ἰδιῶται ἀμείνους τὰς γνώμας ἔχουσι ('For in peace and favourable circumstances cities and private individuals have a better mentality', 3.82.2).

facts.[45] The Athenians find themselves confronted with the factual reality of external circumstances that make demands on them and in dealing with which they begin to 'rise'.

Another formulation in the *Pentecontaetia* has the same implications. According to Thucydides, his narrative 'provides a demonstration of the way in which the empire of the Athenians came into existence' (τῆς ἀρχῆς ἀπόδειξιν ἔχει τῆς τῶν Ἀθηναίων ἐν οἵῳ τρόπῳ κατέστη, 1.97.2). Thucydides chooses a notably impersonal, agent-free locution with his favourite verb καθίσταμαι. The empire does not emerge because the Athenians actively pursue this goal, but it arises out of a specific constellation of circumstances. Without touching on stylistic considerations, Rhodes interprets Thucydides' account of the Athenian rise to power along the same lines. According to Rhodes, Thucydides 'represent[s] Athens' foundation of the Delian League as an innocent matter, the acceptance of an invitation from the eastern Greeks to be their leader in a continuing war against Persia: we need not suppose that Athens had ulterior motives in accepting the invitation, or enforced her will on reluctant allies from the beginning'.[46]

Indeed, based on Thucydides' narrative, the Athenians do not give the impression that they are purposefully plotting the takeover of the leadership over the Greek alliance. Instead, Spartan lack of enthusiasm to continue in this position stands out: after the victory at Mycale, the Spartans and their Peloponnesian allies return to the Peloponnesus whereas the Athenians do not abandon the Ionian Greeks but continue to press the Persians hard by besieging and taking Sestus (1.89.2). What is more, when the allies begin to complain about the haughty and violent conduct of Pausanias, the newly appointed Spartan commander-in-chief, the Spartans recall him (1.95.3) and subsequently agree to have the command and the further conduct of the war transferred to the

---

[45] On this antithesis, see Parry (1981: 6): '[Thucydides] over and over again sees the word in terms of a division between words and things, between thought and actuality.'

[46] Rhodes 1992: 47. Badian (1993: 132) is also alert to the point Thucydides tries to bring home: '[T]he result [sc. the Athenian subjugation of the allies] had been produced without malice aforethought.' It should be noted that Badian differs from Rhodes in considering Thucydides' account apologetic of Athenian aggression.

Athenians (1.95.7). In the meantime, the allies have already urged the Athenians to take over the leadership of the Greek alliance (1.95.1). Thucydides emphasizes that this request is an unconstrained initiative on the part of the allies: 'In this way the Athenians took over the leadership over the allies, who readily willed this due to their hatred of Pausanias' (παραλαβόντες δὲ οἱ Ἀθηναῖοι τὴν ἡγεμονίαν τούτῳ τῷ τρόπῳ ἑκόντων τῶν ξυμμάχων διὰ τὸ Παυσανίου μῖσος, 1.96.1). What raises the Athenians to the position of leadership is not their own pushiness, but Spartan lukewarmness combined with the allies' disaffection with the Spartan commander. Commenting on the passage in question, Raubitschek emphasizes the common ground between the picture that Thucydides gives in the *Pentecontaetia* and the foregoing speech of the Athenian ambassadors: 'There is ... full agreement between Thucydides (1.94–96.1) and the Athenians (1.75.1-2) concerning the manner in which Athens took over the command of the Greeks after the departure of Pausanias: *ou biasamenoi*, "not forcing" (1.75.2) corresponds to *hekontôn*, "willing" (1.96.1).'[47]

As a result of these various decisions, opportunities for the Athenians to expand their power quickly present themselves. These are the πράγματα referred to earlier. When the allies begin to chafe at their required contributions, the Athenians, far from slackening their expectations, make themselves unpopular by 'applying coercive measures' (προσάγοντες τὰς ἀνάγκας, 1.99.1). Moreover, when going on military expeditions, the Athenians cease to treat the allies on an equal footing, and they turn their newly won military might against their own allies if these try to leave the alliance (1.99.2). According to Thucydides, because of the allies' own preference for monetary contributions over military service, 'the allies themselves were responsible for these things' (ὧν αὐτοὶ αἴτιοι ἐγένοντο οἱ ξύμμαχοι, 1.99.2). In a survey of Thucydides' concept of necessity, Peter Brunt comments on this passage: '[I]t is implied that their [*sc.* the allies'] weakness made it *inevitable* [my italics] that Athens should subdue them.'[48] For, as a result of this situation, 'the fleet was increased for the Athenians from the funds which those [*sc.* the allies] contributed' (τοῖς μὲν Ἀθηναίοις ηὔξετο τὸ ναυτικὸν ἀπὸ τῆς δαπάνης ἣν

---

[47] Raubitschek 1973: 40.   [48] Brunt 1993 [1963]: 156.

ἐκεῖνοι ξυμφέροιεν, 1.99.3). Notice, again, the agent-free construction with which Thucydides speaks of the build-up of the Athenian navy: its strength derives from a process rather than a purposeful acquisition. All these phrases provide support of the following observation made by de Romilly: 'He [*sc.* Thucydides] explains the whole formation of the empire of Athens through a mechanism that plays itself out according to its inner logic, ensuing from certain given conditions... Things proceed as if acting of their own accord.'[49]

Thucydides' representation of the emergence of the Athenian empire recalls his previous analysis of the development of early Greece in the *Archaeology*. As the passage just quoted shows, the increase in ships and money, which are two of the three decisive factors singled out in the *Archaeology*, paves the way towards the predominance of Athens over the rest of Greece. The remaining component of the triad familiar from the *Archaeology*, namely the stabilizing effect of walls, likewise figures in the *Pentecontaetia*. The rebuilding of the city walls, made possible by one of Themistocles' ingenious tricks, stands at the beginning of the *Pentecontaetia* and lays the foundation for the subsequent rise of Athens (1.89.3, 90.3, 91.4). As Foster remarks, 'possessing superior weapons, monetary resources, and confidence, the Athenians act as human beings mostly do act, in Thucydides' view, in this situation.'[50]

There is further evidence for the parallelism between the analysis offered in the *Archaeology* and Thucydides' account of the rise of Athenian power. In the *Archaeology*, Thucydides repeatedly captures the development of Greece towards greater power and better material resources through the word αὐξάνω. The word occurs four times in all during the *Archaeology*, and it stands in the aorist passive in three of these passages (passive: 1.2.6, 12.1, 16.1; active: 1.17). The passive of αὐξάνω also appears twice in the *Pentecontaetia*, each time referring to the growth of Athenian power (1.89.2, 99.3). Apart from the occurrences in the *Archaeology* and the *Pentecontaetia*, the word is used merely three more times in the rest of Thucydides' work.

---

[49] De Romilly (1971: 115): '[I]l [*sc.* Thucydides] explique toute la formation de l'empire d'Athènes par une sort de mécanisme jouant de lui-même, à partir de certaines données... Les choses se font donc toutes seules.'
[50] Foster 2010: 112.

All the remaining instances are to be found early in book 6, each of them referring to the growth of Athenian power: namely, twice to its extent at the time of the Sicilian Expedition (6.12.1 [Nicias], 18.4) and once to its growth after the Persian Wars (6.33.6). Therefore, outside of the *Archaeology*, αὐξάνω always refers to the growth of Athenian power and almost always stands, just like in the *Archaeology*, in the passive. The one exception to this latter tendency is Alcibiades' confident prediction during the Sicilian Debate that the Athenians 'will increase' (αὐξήσειν, 6.18.4) their power by undertaking the expedition. The active form is indicative of a characteristic miscalculation on the part of Alcibiades, in line with his general inclination to overestimate Athenian chances at Sicily.[51]

Contrary to what Alcibiades suggests, human beings will find it difficult to remain actively in charge of their affairs when experiencing a massive increase in power. Augmentation of power is usually more likely to come in the guise of a process that follows its own logic.[52] The combination in the *Pentecontaetia* of passive forms of αὐξάνω with the triad of ships, walls, and money signals that the impersonal forces familiar from the *Archaeology* fuel the ascendency of Athenian power after the Persian Wars. As Tsakmakis observes, the set of factors that initially enable the rise of Athens (money, ships, walls) have been transformed into an 'autonomous, uncontrollable mechanism of power'.[53]

At the end of the *Pentecontaetia*, Thucydides offers a summary of the development that he has been tracing. 'During this period,' he writes, 'the Athenians established their rule on a stronger footing and, as concerns themselves, they progressed to a great height of power' (ἐν οἷς οἱ Ἀθηναῖοι τήν τε ἀρχὴν ἐγκρατεστέραν κατεστήσαντο καὶ αὐτοὶ ἐπὶ μέγα ἐχώρησαν δυνάμεως, 1.118.2). The implications of this passage are Janus-faced. In its first half, the Athenians are depicted as actively engaged in

---

[51] Stahl 2003 [1973]: 177 and 178–9; Macleod 1983b [1975]: 78–80.
[52] Themistocles provides an exception to this tendency when he promotes the building of the Athenian navy and of the walls of the Piraeus (1.93.3); for he consciously anticipated that these measures would fuel Athenian power. Yet Thucydides observes that Themistocles' ability to foresee the future with utmost precision was his distinctive gift, a capacity that made him utterly exceptional (1.138.3).
[53] Tsakmakis (1995: 94): 'die Verwandlung dieser Strukturen zu einem autonomen, unkontrollierbaren *Herrschaftsmechanismus*'.

solidifying their power. In contrast with the passages previously considered, the aorist middle of καθίστημι is indirect reflexive, denoting that the Athenians 'established their rule *for themselves* on a stronger footing'. It might seem that the second half (viz. the phrase ἐπὶ μέγα ἐχώρησαν δυνάμεως) strikes a similar note, but this impression would be misleading. The phrase exemplifies a common construction: the combination of a verb of motion with a prepositional phrase involving a neuter adjective or pronoun that governs a partitive genitive. The standard meaning is that 'so and so reached such and such a degree of something'. Other Thucydidean examples of this construction are cited by Kühner-Gerth: 'matters had come to such a degree of necessity' (ξυνέπεσεν ἐς τοῦτο ἀνάγκης, 1.49.7), 'for we have come to such a height of calamity' (ἐς τοῦτο γὰρ δὴ ξυμφορᾶς προκεχωρήκαμεν, 3.57.3), and 'to reach such a height of misfortune' (ἐς τοῦτο δυστυχίας ἀφικέσθαι, 7.86.5).[54] In all these passages, the grammatical subject is not presented as acting, but as passing into a specified condition. Commenting on a passage from Isocrates' *Areopagiticus*, Benseler suitably renders a variant of this type of phrase (εἰς τοῦτο δ᾽ ἀναισθησίας ἥκειν, Isoc. 2.9) as 'in eum stuporem incidere', i.e. 'to descend to such a degree of obtuseness'.[55] These observations are confirmed by the evidence that scholars have gathered from the works of Lysias, Isocrates, and Demosthenes: they mostly use this construction to capture an objective state or a vice (less often a virtue) that has come to affect the grammatical subject to a special degree.[56] The comparative evidence suggests that the Athenians have been exposed to a process (as opposed to being actively in charge), thus experiencing a dynamic that has carried them to the height of power. Thus, the phrasing has implications similar to the aforementioned passive forms of αὐξάνω.

How can this wording be squared with the suggestion of agency in the earlier part of the sentence? The two halves are coordinated by τε and

---

[54] K-G i. 278–9; Sm. 1325 (classifying the genitive as 'genitive of measure').
[55] Benseler 1832: 127.
[56] The following examples are found in K-G i. 279: εἰς τοῦτο τῆς ἡλικίας ἀφῖκται, Lys. 5.3; εἰς τοῦτο δ᾽ ἀναισθησίας ἥκειν, Isocr. 7.9; εἰς τοῦτο γάρ τινες ἀνοίας ἐληλύθασιν, Isocr. 8.31; εἰς τοῦθ᾽ ὕβρεως ἐλήλυθεν, Dem. 4.37; εἰς τοῦθ᾽ ἥκει τὰ πράγματ᾽ αἰσχύνης, Dem. 4.47. For a wealth of further examples from Isocrates, Lysias, and Demosthenes, see Benseler 1832: 127 [on *Isoc.* 2.9]; Frohberger 1868: ii, on Lys. 14.2, and ii. 139 [Anhang]; Rehdantz 1873 ii, 1. 234-5 [Index s.v. Genitiv].

καί: while τε attaches itself to τὴν ἀρχήν, the clause introduced by καί begins with αὐτοί. Thucydides apparently wants to highlight some correspondence between the two terms because the form αὐτοί in the second half of the sentence is not necessary: the subject οἱ Ἀθηναῖοι at the opening would have been sufficient. If Thucydides had dropped αὐτοί, the emphasis in the second clause would have fallen on ἐπὶ μέγα δυνάμεως, a notion that would naturally have corresponded to τὴν ἀρχήν. As things stand, the coordination between τὴν ἀρχήν and αὐτοί suggests that the Athenians' consolidation of their power also has an impact on *themselves*. As Kühner-Gerth observe, the units coordinated by τε and καί often have a causal relationship,[57] a nuance that, combined with the highlighted analogy, might be rendered as follows: 'the Athenians solidified their rule—and *what this meant for themselves was that* they progressed to a great height of power'. As the first half of the sentence shows, the Athenians contribute to this outcome with their deliberate actions. At the same time, however, they have become susceptible to a process.

In the same passage, Thucydides points out that the Spartans did not interfere with the Athenians 'until at last the power of the Athenians was plainly exalting itself and they were beginning to encroach on their alliance' (πρὶν δὴ ἡ δύναμις τῶν Ἀθηναίων σαφῶς ᾔρετο καὶ τῆς ξυμμαχίας αὐτῶν ἥπτοντο, 1.118.2). Once again, Thucydides pictures the increase of Athenian power as a process, with the abstract noun δύναμις occupying the position of the subject and the verb (ᾔρετο) suggesting a progressive development. As in the aforecited passage, Thucydides combines this phrase with a further verb that suggests agency (τῆς ξυμμαχίας αὐτῶν ἥπτοντο). In summing up the *Pentecontaetia*, Thucydides' phrasing does not flatly deny the Athenians agency, but it suggests that their actions are hedged in and subsumed by a process that reflects the innate tendency of power towards growth and expansion.

In their interpretation of the *Pentecontaetia*, Rawlings and Stadter have reached a different conclusion than the one presented here. To their mind, Thucydides' goal in the *Pentecontaetia* was to show that in assuming the leadership over the Delian League the Athenians had the goal of subjugating the allies from the very outset. Rawlings and Stadter advance two chief arguments, each to be considered in turn.

---

[57] K-G ii. 250.

First, as Stadter notes, the Athenians display immense dynamism from the very moment in which they take over the leadership of the alliance.[58] This fact in itself, however, does not presuppose a hidden imperial agenda motivating the Athenian takeover. After the immense resoluteness displayed by the Athenians in the foregoing Persian Wars, everybody could expect that, once in charge, they would move heaven and earth to put pressure on the Persians. This would predictably involve the demand that the allies increase their contributions to the conduct of the operations against Persia.

Second, Rawlings, followed by Stadter,[59] has argued that the Athenians' demand, made directly after their assumption of the leadership, that the allies contribute money or ships, had only feignedly the goal of taking revenge on the Persians. This interpretation rests on Thucydides' claim that the Athenians' motive of retaliation against Persia was a $\pi\rho\delta\sigma\eta\chi\mu\alpha$, 'a screen' or 'pretext' (1.96.1). The natural assumption would be, and here I agree with Rawlings and Stadter, that the Athenians' true goal, which the pretext obfuscated, was to solidify their leadership in pursuit of their own self-interest. This does not, however, mean that the Athenians have planned their steps all along with a view to reducing the allies to subjugation under imperial domination. Instead, the comment must be squared with the features of Thucydides' report that suggest the unfolding of a process rather than conscious plotting. It seems likely that the Athenians expected to increase their wealth and power at the expense of the allies as a result of their assumption of the leadership. However, this does not necessarily imply that they had been plotting to reduce the allies to the status of subjects and to establish an overseas empire. The style of Thucydides' account rather suggests the Athenians' implication in a process in which one thing leads to another.[60]

A passage in Pericles' final speech provides support for this interpretation. Pointing out to the Athenians that they hold the empire 'as a tyranny', Pericles goes on to observe: 'a tyranny, which to have assumed seems to be unjust, but to let go of which fraught with danger'

---

[58] Stadter 1993: 46, 48, 69.   [59] Rawlings 1977: 3–6; Stadter: 1993: 46.

[60] On a related note, Hornblower (i, on 1.96.1) observes that it would be historically implausible to ascribe a distinct imperialist agenda to the Athenians from early on: '[T]his seems to impute too great foresight to the Athenians of 478; and there is non-Thucydidean evidence that the mood at the outset was more idealistic than that (see esp. *Ath. Pol.* 23.5 for the dropping of weights into the sea, a solemn act indicating intended permanence[...]).'

(ἢν λαβεῖν μὲν ἄδικον δοκεῖ εἶναι, ἀφεῖναι δὲ ἐπικίνδυνον, 2.63.2). According to Pericles, it *now* (notice the present tense) seems unjust to *have acquired* the empire, which turned out to be a tyranny: if we are to believe Pericles, it is only from the perspective of hindsight that it becomes apparent what the Athenians got themselves into when they accepted the leadership of the Delian League.

If Thucydides had considered the Athenians' claims at Sparta to be nothing but self-serving rhetoric, the *Pentecontaetia* provided him with the opportunity to draw attention to the problematic aspects of the ambassadors' argumentation. Instead, his account largely corroborates the Athenians' version. Therefore, Ostwald is right to emphasize the programmatic importance of the Athenians' speech, especially their stress on constitutive psychological compulsions inevitably bound up with the nature of imperial rule:

> The ἀνάγκαι Thucydides sees as operating in imperial rule are...first articulated by the Athenian ambassadors at Sparta: the hegemony offered by the allies 'compelled' the Athenians, once they had accepted it, to expand their rule under the impact of the universally human motivating powers of fear, prestige, and self-interest.[61]

On the final analysis, the Athenians are caught up in processes and find themselves confronted with situations and opportunities that make irresistible demands on them.

3.5 The Paradox of Empire: Power and Passivity

A crucial lesson to be learned from Thucydides' account of the rise of the Athenian empire is that the opportunities opened by δύναμις have the inherent tendency to develop into necessities, and that a seemingly handy instrument comes to dictate people's actions. In this connection, it is interesting to consider two quotations from speeches incorporated

---

[61] Ostwald 1988: 38. See Orwin 1994: 44; de Romilly 1963 [1947]: 251.

by Thucydides into his work. They lend further weight to the paradoxical notion that the mighty are ultimately not in charge of their own power. On the contrary, they are in fact controlled by it.

In the Sicilian Debate, Alcibiades has no qualms about promoting the idea that power has its alleged possessor in its grip. According to Alcibiades, the Athenians have no choice but to seek ever further expansion (6.18.3):

καὶ οὐκ ἔστιν ἡμῖν ταμιεύεσθαι ἐς ὅσον βουλόμεθα ἄρχειν, ἀλλ' ἀνάγκη, ἐπειδήπερ ἐν τῷδε καθέσταμεν, τοῖς μὲν ἐπιβουλεύειν, τοὺς δὲ μὴ ἀνιέναι, διὰ τὸ ἀρχθῆναι ἂν ὑφ' ἑτέρων αὐτοῖς κίνδυνον εἶναι, εἰ μὴ αὐτοὶ ἄλλων ἄρχοιμεν.

And it is not possible for us to control how far we want to rule, but it is necessary, since we are placed in this position, to plot against some, and not to let go of others, because there is a danger for ourselves that we might be ruled by others should we not ourselves, rule them instead.

Once again, the stylistic features of the passage are meaningful. The intransitive perfect form of καθίσταμαι (καθέσταμεν) suggests that the Athenians are placed into circumstances that largely determine their course of action. Moreover, the long substantival infinitive to which a plethora of dependent constructions are attached has a peculiar force: διὰ τὸ ἀρχθῆναι ἂν ὑφ' ἑτέρων αὐτοῖς κίνδυνον εἶναι, εἰ μὴ αὐτοὶ ἄλλων ἄρχοιμεν ('because of there being a danger for ourselves that we might be ruled by others should we not ourselves rule them instead'). Made to depend on an articular infinitive, the large number of dependent constructions, which even include a conditional clause, produces clunky phrasing. What is more, the subject of the articular infinitive is not personal, but the impersonal word 'danger'. This heavy nominal construction suggests the pressure of circumstances weighing on the Athenians: it is not the case that the Athenians can choose whether they want to run the risk or not. The risk is an objective fact, and due to the requirements of power and self-preservation the Athenians are compelled (ἀνάγκη) to expand constantly. Macleod has drawn the appropriate conclusion from the implications of the picture presented by

Alcibiades: '[H]e makes aggression seem no less than a necessity for the imperial power.'[62]

There is strong evidence that Alcibiades exaggerates people's impotence vis-à-vis their own power to some extent. Alcibiades seems to imply that the possessors of power are subject to a constant necessity of unlimited expansion. In that case, Pericles' strategy for the Peloponnesian War would seem fundamentally ill-conceived because it requires the Athenians to avoid extending their empire while at war (1.144.1, 2.65.7). The self-restraint advocated by Pericles is incompatible with Alcibiades' notion that power generates an irresistible urge for further expansion. Thucydides praises Pericles' war strategy, pointing out that the Athenians would probably have succeeded in the War if they had abided by the Periclean plan (2.65.6-7). This endorsement of Pericles' strategy by Thucydides severely undermines Alcibiades' claim that power inevitably calls forth the necessity of constant expansion. What is more, the Athenian envoys at Sparta maintain that the compulsion exerted by fear, honour, and advantage leaves some room for moderation (1.76.4, 77.2), a claim that we will consider in Chapter 7 (see pp. 252-4). For the moment, it suffices to note that the Athenians' position provides evidence for a more flexible position than the view propounded by Alcibiades. It matters that Alcibiades' claims form part of his agitation for the Sicilian Expedition. If one accepts Alcibiades' endorsement of the necessity of expansion, war with far off Syracuse no longer looks like a high-risk adventure but seems to be grounded in the inescapable way things are. Thus, a self-interested agenda plays an important role in Alcibiades' argumentation, and a case can made that Alcibiades takes the insight regarding imperial necessity too far. At the same time, it would be wrong to dismiss Alcibiades' claims out of hand.[63] His language, which recalls Thucydides' own account of Athenian predominance in the *Pentecontaetia*, has explanatory power. It shows that the wielders of power, despite their apparent mastery over their own

---

[62] Macleod 1983b [1975]: 83.
[63] See Forde (1989: 91): 'The self-interest Alcibiades has in making these arguments should not blind us to the acuity of his analysis here.'

fortunes, inevitably confront situations that implicate them in a process beyond their control.

The notion that power develops into an independent agent can also be found in the speech of the Corcyrean envoys at Athens in book 1. The Corcyreans use a striking personification to capture the allure of δύναμις (1.33.2):

καὶ σκέψασθε· τίς εὐπραξία σπανιωτέρα ἢ τίς τοῖς πολεμίοις λυπηροτέρα, εἰ ἣν ὑμεῖς ἂν πρὸ πολλῶν χρημάτων καὶ χάριτος ἐτιμήσασθε δύναμιν ὑμῖν προσγενέσθαι, αὕτη πάρεστιν αὐτεπάγγελτος, ἄνευ κινδύνων καὶ δαπάνης διδοῦσα ἑαυτὴν καὶ προσέτι φέρουσα ἐς μὲν τοὺς πολλοὺς ἀρετήν, οἷς δὲ ἐπαμυνεῖτε χάριν, ὑμῖν δ' αὐτοῖς ἰσχύν...

And consider this: what good fortune could be rarer or else more painful to your enemies if this power whose accrual you previously deemed worthy of much money and gratitude, is now ready at hand and offers itself to you of its own accord, giving itself without dangers and expense, and, in addition, bringing you virtue in the eyes of the many, gratitude from those to whose aid you come, and strength for yourselves?

Δύναμις has the air of a seducer in this passage, giving itself to the Athenians along with distinction and gratitude and without requiring any payment in return. Yet Thucydides' subsequent account shows that power in fact does not proffer its attractive gifts at zero cost. In deciding in favour of the alliance, the Athenians acknowledge that necessities are incumbent on them, despite their immense power: 'For they thought that war with the Peloponnesians would anyway come to pass for them' (ἐδόκει γὰρ ὁ πρὸς Πελοποννησίους πόλεμος καὶ ὣς ἔσεσθαι αὐτοῖς, 1.44.2). The phrasing suggests that the War will take place, no matter what people do. At the same time, the Athenians hope that they will be able to stand aloof as long as possible from the conflict between Corinth and Corcyra. Based on this policy of non-interference, the Athenians plan to have the various sea powers undermine each other, 'in order that, if in some way the need arose [sc. to go to war], the Corinthians and the rest of those possessing a fleet would be weaker when they [sc. the Athenians] would get into war with them' (ἵνα ἀσθενεστέροις οὖσιν, ἤν τι δέῃ, Κορινθίοις τε καὶ τοῖς ἄλλοις ναυτικὸν ἔχουσιν ἐς πόλεμον καθιστῶνται, 1.44.2). The phrase featuring καθίσταμαι with a dependent prepositional phrase represents the War as a situation in which the Athenians find themselves. They get into circumstances that bring war upon them. Their choices do not influence the question whether the War will come. The power already in the Athenians' possession, far from being tractable, implicates them in necessities.

On the present occasion, the Athenians do have some room for manoeuvring. It is up to them whether to accept an alliance with Corcyra or not and, if so, what kind of alliance it should be. At the same time, Thucydides' summarizing comments suggest that the Athenians' hegemony ultimately forces the War upon them. These considerations cast an ironic light on the Corcyreans' presentation of power offering itself generously to the Athenians. The Corcyreans are right to imply that power has agency of its own; but this super-agent, far from generously giving presents, will make uncompromising demands in due course. Δύναμις will eventually require the possessor to actualize it and every actualization of its potentials will create new demands for expansion and enhancement.

3.6 Conclusion

According to the Athenian ambassadors at Sparta, everyone, including their Spartan rivals, must act under the constraint of fear, honour, and advantage. The Athenian ambassadors consider this situation an evident fact, a conviction reflected in the self-assured, analytical tone of their speech. There is no hint that the 'greatest things' may spin out of control and wreak havoc. Yet what if, for all his exaggeration, Alcibiades does have a point when he claims that δύναμις instigates its possessor to overstep one boundary after the next? How will it be possible to control this restless and imperious potential?

The Athenians at Sparta claim that the three greatest things have their origin in 'human nature' (τῇ ἀνθρωπείᾳ φύσει, 1.76.3). Human nature is also responsible of the eternal pattern that Thucydides sees reflected in the evils of civil war (3.82.2). In the stasis section, Thucydides writes that the ultimate 'cause' (αἴτιον) of the general havoc was 'the exercise of power fuelled by greed and ambition' (ἀρχὴ ἡ διὰ πλεονεξίαν καὶ φιλοτιμίαν, 3.82.8). Two of the three motivations highlighted by the Athenians bear resemblance to the basic drives that produce stasis: φιλοτιμία is an excessive variant of the striving for τιμή, and πλεονεξία is a perverted form of ὠφελία, the quest for material advantage. Notice in this connection that, according to LSJ, a suitable rendition of πλεονεξία is frequently 'advantage'.[64] The parallel goes further: just as, according to the Athenians, honour and advantage are the urges that incite people to seek ἀρχή (κατηναγκάσθημεν...προαγαγεῖν αὐτήν [sc. ἀρχήν, see 1.75.1], 1.75.3), so ambition and greed make the warring parties long for ἀρχή in the polis when stasis prevails.

Fear, the third impulse highlighted by the Athenians, can also be found in the stasis section. Fear of being outwitted by their opponents prompts people to 'proceed foolhardily to deeds' (τῷ...δεδιέναι... τολμηρῶς πρὸς τὰ ἔργα ἐχώρουν, 3.83.3). The connection with foolhardy action suggests that fear, just as much as greed and ambition, causes people to act in excessive and uncontrolled ways during stasis.

The fact that variants of fear, honour, advantage, and the quest for ἀρχή are prominent in the stasis section undercuts the self-assured tone adopted by the Athenian ambassadors. Read alongside each other, the speech of the Athenians and the excursus on stasis convey the impression of tragic ambiguity. According to the Athenians, the ineluctability of human nature is a hard fact that calls for sober acknowledgement. Rational awareness usually goes along with confidence, which is based on the conviction that mental penetration lays the foundation for mastery over the external world. The self-assured tone of the Athenians conveys just this impression. By contrast, the stasis section highlights the disruptiveness of the three greatest things and thereby puts a different complexion on this issue: the possibility of hedging human nature is nowhere in sight. The Athenians' emphasis on the ineluctable pull

---

[64] LSJ s.v. A.II.1. Examples are the phrase ἐπὶ πλεονεξίᾳ, in the sense of 'with a view to one's own advantage', from Th. 3.84.1 (which is probably spurious), as well as τὰς πλεονεξίας...τὰς ἰδίας...τὰς δημοσίας (in the sense of 'advantages in private' and 'in public') at Xen. Cyn. 13.10.

of human nature bears the stamp of a genuine insight. Yet the bare factuality of this natural constraint raises the question of how much room for effective countermeasures realistically exists. A yawning abyss opens up between thought and action and between theory and practice—the antagonism between λόγος and ἔργον.

4
A World Governed by Neuters
'The Human' as a Substitute for 'The Divine'

The last chapter ended on a sceptical note. The question arose as to whether the detached analysis of the Athenians at Sparta may in fact have misrepresented the motivations intrinsic to human nature in some vital respects. As I argued in the conclusion of Chapter 3 (pp. 105–7), the parallels between the 'three greatest things' and the collective passions rampant during stasis imply that the constraint exerted by the quest for power ultimately sets human action on a self-destructive trajectory. These contrary viewpoints (the Athenians at Sparta vs. the *Pathology*) reflect what Pouncey has described as 'a double track of speculation about human nature, one of tolerance, or even approval, of the will to power when it is consolidated into national unanimity..., but also a pessimistic awareness that the same drive may set itself more immediate goals and destroy a society by *stasis*'.[1] As this chapter will illustrate, the various horrors (described in the chapters on stasis) are not the only indication in Thucydides' work that the impulses governing human nature pose a threat to those subject to them.

The following analysis aims to show that, in general, the views put forth by speakers in the *History* regarding the impact of human nature align with either one or the other of the above two perspectives. Most speakers (with the majority being Athenians) adopt the tone of the envoys at Sparta, considering the quest for power as a necessity based on natural disposition. Speakers taking this view seem to imply that, if one recognizes such a quest as an ineluctable fact, a stable forecast of human behaviour becomes possible. As a result, deliberative bodies can make their decisions in light of this insight. It is not surprising that this perspective predominates in

[1] Pouncey 1980: 37.

speeches; after all, a speaker addressing a political body faces the need to convince his audience that the proposed course of action makes a difference for the better. Nevertheless, in the Mytilenean Debate, Diodotus manages, in a speech rife with hidden meaning, to draw attention to the perilous aspects of the forces that drive human nature: their sudden, domineering, and often cataclysmic character.[2] Diodotus would find it difficult to propagate these sombre insights if he had to deduce them, not from the decisions of the renegade ally Mytilene, but from the acts of his Athenian audience.

Proponents of both perspectives draw upon the depersonalizing linguistic style, but they prioritize different aspects of it. This chapter will go on to show that the depersonalizing style recalls language that other Greek writers use to capture the divine governance of earthly affairs. In the final analysis, the speakers presented by Thucydides seem to suggest that natural necessity has replaced the belief in a divinely sanctioned fate.

4.1 The Mainsprings of Action: Natural Conditions and Impersonal Factors

The position of the Athenians at Sparta resurfaces most notably in three subsequent speeches addressing the theme of necessity. The three passages are linked by close parallels in both thought and style. They are to be found in Cleon's speech during the Mytilenean Debate (3.39.5), in Hermocrates' speech at Gela (4.61.5), and in the Melian Dialogue (5.105.2).

The following two passages are less systematic statements of necessity than the Athenians' speech at Sparta. That said, they draw attention to a new aspect by emphasizing that natural necessity involves a neutral, impersonal element. The first passage is stated by Cleon in the Mytilenean Debate, the second by Hermocrates during his speech at the Conference at Gela:

---

[2] On the ambiguities of Diodotus' speech, see Manuwald 1979: especially 419–21.

110   STYLE AND NECESSITY IN THUCYDIDES

Cleon (3.39.5): πέφυκε γὰρ καὶ ἄλλως ἄνθρωπος τὸ μὲν θεραπεῦον ὑπερφρονεῖν, τὸ δὲ μὴ ὑπεῖκον θαυμάζειν.

For in any case, human beings are naturally disposed to despise that which flatters, and to admire that which does not yield.

Hermocrates (4.61.5): πέφυκε γὰρ τὸ ἀνθρώπειον διὰ παντὸς ἄρχειν μὲν τοῦ εἴκοντος, φυλάσσεσθαι δὲ τὸ ἐπιόν.

For everywhere the human is naturally disposed to rule that which yields, but to guard against that which attacks.

Two features of these passages deserve closer investigation: first, the use of πέφυκε as the main verb; secondly, the high number of nominalized neuter participles in both passages.

In these two passages, all four dependent infinitives ('to despise', 'to admire', 'to rule', and 'to guard against') refer to distinctly human modes of action. By contrast, the main verb πέφυκε does not denote action but suggests a condition that underlies these actions. This idea is conveyed by a combination of form and content: the perfective aspect suggests an enduring state and the lexeme related to φύσις expresses the idea of a constitution governing human behaviour.

The term φύσις played a central role in the writings of the Hippocratic authors, among others. It was their term for the regularities governing the reactions and strivings of the human body, which they tried to understand through close empirical observation.[3] Also frequent in the Hippocratic corpus are phrases built around the perfect πέφυκε. As Burger points out, they usually have the same referent as the noun φύσις, namely the constitution and dispositions of the body and its organs.[4] In 88 per cent of the passages, the Hippocratics use πέφυκε without a dependent infinitive, unlike Thucydides in the two examples above.[5] The term mostly means (with a predicate nominative) 'to be X by nature' (where X refers to some specific characteristic) or (typically with a prepositional phrase) 'to have grown, to have developed out of something or in some place'. If the

---

[3] Patzer 1937: 96–7; Weidauer 1954: 40; Swain 1994: 315–17.   [4] Burger 1925: 61.
[5] Based on a *TLG* search, I found 107 examples of a form of πέφυκε in the Hippocratic Corpus. Dependent infinitives are used in only thirteen cases.

medical writers use the verb with a dependent infinitive, the latter invariably refers to an organ or some bodily phenomenon, suggesting that it is 'disposed by nature' to behave in a certain way or to take a specified course.[6] By contrast, the infinitives in the two Thucydidean passages refer to activities and states of mind distinctive of human beings. Given that the Hippocratics deal with medical subjects, the difference in and of itself may not be surprising. Still, Thucydides draws on the connotations suggested by a form that was widespread throughout the Hippocratic Corpus, while at the same time giving it a different spin. The comparison with two other historians, namely Herodotus and Xenophon, will elucidate that Thucydides' usage is distinctive.

Herodotus' work contains fifteen instances of φύομαι in the perfect stem, but none of them is combined with an infinitive. Only three of them have personal subjects (3.80.4, 7.46.3, 7.153.4), adding up to a fifth of all occurrences in Herodotus. In the various Herodotean passages, the meaning of πέφυκε is invariably the same as what one finds in the medical writers when they employ these forms without the infinitive: 'to have grown' or 'to be X by nature'. It is interesting that two of these passages involve identical phrasing: Herodotus states that some person (first the generic figure of 'the tyrant', second an ancestor of Gelon named Telines) 'is by nature the opposite' (τὸ ὑπεναντίον πέφυκε) of some general disposition (3.80.4, 7.153.4).[7] For Herodotus, the construction involving πέφυκε (which he most frequently employs to indicate the natural growth of trees, hair, or horns)[8] appears to convey such markedly impersonal connotations that, even in combination with personal subjects, he uses neuter predicates that identify the respective persons with generalized dispositions.

---

[6] ἀριθμέεσθαι (*Prognosticon* ch. 20: II 170.2); διογκοῦσθαι (*De diaeta in morbis acutis* ch. 4: II 246.3–4); καταναγκάζεσθαι (*De articulis* ch. 47: IV 206.9); ψύχειν (*De flatibus* ch. 14: VI 112.1); ἐς βυθὸν φέρεσθαι (*De flatibus* ch. 14: VI 112.3); γίγνεσθαι (*De affectionibus* ch. 18: VI 226.5–6); νόσους λάζεσθαι καὶ μᾶλλον πονέειν (*De locis in homine* ch. 1: VI 276 1.4); κάτω χωρέειν (*De locis in homine* ch. 9: VI 292.24); ἀναλῶσαι τὰ ὑπάρχοντα (*De diaeta Bk. 1*, ch. 2: VI 470.2); ἕλκειν (*De diaeta Bk. 2*, ch. 40: VI 538.4); θερμαίνειν (*De diaeta Bk. 2*, ch. 56: VI 568.4); ἐν γαστρὶ λαμβάνειν (*Prorrheticon* Bk. 2, ch. 24: IX 54.6–7); κινεῖν (*Epistulae* 27: IX 418.13). Note that all references are to Littré's ten-volume edition of the Hippocratic Corpus. The references take the following form: chapter of a given Hippocratic work, volume in Littré's edition, page number in that volume, line number.

[7] The general disposition consists in freedom from feeling resentment (τὸ δὲ ὑπεναντίον τούτου ἐς τοὺς πολιήτας πέφυκε, 3.80.4) and in a 'valiant spirit and manly strength' (ὁ δὲ λέγεται ... τὰ ὑπεναντία τούτων πεφυκέναι, 7.153.4).

[8] Trees: 1.193.4, 2.32.6, 2.56.2, 2.91.2, 2.138.4, 4.172.1. Hair: 2.38.2. Horns: 2.74.

Xenophon (including the pseudo-Xenophontic *Constitution of the Athenians*) has thirty-five instances of the perfect stem of φύομαι. Eight are combined with an infinitive and five of these eight phrases have non-human subjects.[9] Thus, almost two thirds of the passages where Xenophon combines perfect stem forms of φύομαι with the infinitive recall the Hippocratic usage: they refer to types of behaviour or developments that are 'natural' to various non-human phenomena.

Thucydides' use of the perfect of φύομαι differs considerably from Herodotus and Xenophon. Such forms occur seven times in Thucydides' work, always in speeches. It is remarkable that all instances of the verb φύω in Thucydides are intransitive perfects. All but one have generalized human subjects,[10] and all, again but one, govern an infinitive.[11] In Herodotus and Xenophon the perfect forms represent merely one usage of φύω among several; the phrases featuring πέφυκε and similar forms have non-human subjects much more frequently than human subjects; and they either do not feature dependent infinitives at all (Herodotus), or do so only in a minority of cases (Xenophon). Thucydides differs from Herodotus and Xenophon in these three regards: he exclusively uses the perfect; human subjects outweigh non-human subjects (by a ratio of 6:1); and instances of πέφυκε (and similar forms) with an infinitive outweigh instances lacking an infinitive (again by a ratio of 6:1).

The three passages in which Xenophon uses perfect forms of φύομαι with the infinitive and with human subjects remain to be considered. At first glance, these passages recall the two Thucydidean phrases in the

---

[9] Three of the five phrases involving non-human subjects refer to the 'natural' behaviour of horses (*Eq.* 5.4, 7.12, 10.14.), one to social conditions 'naturally' conducive for a city to flourish (*Vect.* 5.2.), and one to the natural effects of ἔρως (*Cyr.* 5.1.16).

[10] αὐτοὺς [= τοὺς Ἀθηναίους] ... πεφυκέναι (1.70.9, Corinthians at Sparta); πέφυκε ... ἄνθρωπος (3.39.5, Cleon); πεφύκασί ... ἅπαντες (3.45.3, Diodotus); πεφύκασι [sc. οἱ ἄνθρωποι] (4.19.4, Spartans at Athens); πέφυκε [sc. ἡ Σικελία, used metonymically for 'we Sicilians'] (4.61.3, Hermocrates at Gela); πέφυκε ... τὸ ἀνθρώπειον (4.61.5, Hermocrates). The passage that does not involve a human subject is the following: πάντα γὰρ πέφυκε καὶ ἐλασσοῦσθαι (2.64.3, Pericles).

[11] The passage that lacks an infinitive is: οὐ γὰρ [sc. οἱ Ἀθηναῖοι] τοῖς ἔθνεσιν, ὅτι δίχα πέφυκε [sc. ἡ Σικελία], τοῦ ἑτέρου ἔχθει ἐπίασιν (4.61.3, meaning: 'For it is not that [the Athenians] attack because [Sicily] is naturally divided in two tribes, out of hatred for one of them'). Notice that, in terms of semantics, the use of πέφυκα with adverbial δίχα is equivalent to a construction with the infinitive, perhaps involving an implied γίγνεσθαι, see Classen-Steup iv, on 4.61.3.11, and i, on 1.64.1.5.

speeches of Cleon and Hermocrates: they refer to behaviour that is said to be 'natural' for human beings, in the sense that this behaviour is based on constitutive, universally present characteristics. One passage, which features the passive infinitive κρατεῖσθαι, expresses the notion that humans are 'naturally disposed to be governed' by a set of physical states: hunger, thirst, coldness, and heat (πεφύκασι γὰρ [sc. οἱ ἄνθρωποι] ὑπὸ τούτων κρατεῖσθαι, Cyr. 5.1.11). Therefore, despite the personal subject, this passage in fact belongs with the phrases featuring non-human subjects: physical states (as opposed to human beings) are represented as quasi-agents due to the agent construction following the passive verb. The situation is different in the other two passages, which address activity and behaviour proper to human beings. Both of these other two passages highlight the attachment that is part and parcel of close kinship relations: 'decent' women are naturally disposed to 'care for' (ἐπιμελεῖσθαι) their offspring as well as their possessions rather than to neglect them (Oec. 9.19), and people in general are naturally constituted so as to 'love' (φιλεῖν) their close kin (Hier. 3.9). Thus, in these two passages, Xenophon refers to behaviour induced by natural instinct, suggesting that affection for one's kinsfolk, rather than being a matter of choice, is naturally engrained.

Returning to Thucydides, one finds that the infinitives in the speeches of Cleon and Hermocrates are of a different cast. They refer either to heightened emotions ('to despise' and 'to admire') or to purposeful action ('to rule' or 'to guard oneself'). These infinitives, in contrast with Xenophon's two passages regarding affection for one's kin, evoke a varied range of human behaviour, acts and dispositions not obviously imposed by natural instinct. The context of the passage from Xenophon's *Cyropaedia* shows particularly clearly that the construction involving πέφυκε is usually at odds with the idea of agency. According to Xenophon, human beings are 'naturally disposed to be governed' by visceral, instinctual impulses such as hunger and thirst (πεφύκασι γὰρ ὑπὸ τούτων κρατεῖσθαι), whereas 'being in love is a matter of choice' (τὸ δ' ἐρᾶν ἐθελούσιόν ἐστιν, Cyr. 5.1.11). The contrast of natural disposition with what is voluntary clearly indicates that the perfect of φύομαι expresses a behaviour that is necessary and predetermined. If Xenophon considers even erotic passion to be voluntary, it seems likely that he would be still more inclined to conceive of the acts suggested by Thucydides' infinitives similarly (viz. admiration, disdain, willingness to dominate, and caution). The two speakers in Thucydides, however, depict these acts and mental states as being subject to natural predisposition.

In sum, Thucydides' tendency to join the perfect of φύομαι with dependent infinitives shows that he combines two distinct notions: first, the perfect forms related to φύσις emphasize naturally determined patterns; secondly, the infinitives highlight various types of distinctly human activity. Passivity and activity are combined in these expressions. The phrases under consideration suggest that actions take place due to and in accordance with impersonal dispositions that exert their influence at a more fundamental level.[12]

The passages from the speeches of Cleon and Hermocrates share another stylistic feature: a cluster of nominalized neuter participles ('that which flatters', 'that which does not yield', 'that which yields', and 'that which attacks'). Roughly synonymous personal expressions (e.g. 'those who flatter' or 'those who do not yield') would be suggestive of people and the acts they choose to perform. By contrast, the neuters evoke a world in which personal agents do not play a paramount role in the causation of events. With this in mind, it is worth citing an observation made by Heiny regarding the use of various nominalized neuter participles in a speech that Brasidas delivers just before the battle of Amphipolis (5.9.8):[13]

---

[12] It is worth noting that the passages cited by LSJ to illustrate the use of the perfect and second aorist stem of φύομαι with the infinitive (s.v. φύω B.II.2, 'c. inf., to be formed or disposed by nature to do so and so') come (with the exception of the various Thucydidean passages and one late example from Julian the Apostate) exclusively from Pindar and the tragedians. The infinitives used by these authors recall the Thucydidean passages in that they refer to verbs that highlight human activity. Consider the following example from Sophocles' *Philoctetes*: 'For I am naturally disposed not to do anything based on evil tricks' (ἔφυν γὰρ οὐδὲν ἐκ τέχνης πράσσειν κακῆς, 88). Thus, the Thucydidean phrases involving πέφυκε with an infinitive have their closest contemporary parallels in poetry. This provides further evidence for Thucydides' tendency to diverge from regular prose. Verbal parallels between Thucydides and poetic—in particular, tragic—usage will concern us again in Section 4.4 of this chapter.

[13] The passage cited by Heiny is part of Brasidas' plan for his colleague Clearidas to join the battle only after Brasidas has already made an initial attack. Brasidas justifies this strategy as follows: τὸ γὰρ ἐπιὸν ὕστερον δεινότερον τοῖς πολεμίοις τοῦ παρόντος καὶ μαχομένου ('For whatever attacks at a later stage is more terrifying to the enemy than that which is already present and involved in the battle', 5.9.8).

Brasidas is concerned with justifying his advice by reference to a general law of military science, a law that holds in and of itself, apart from the particular individuals to whom it applies. Hence he uses the *neuter singular which is about as impersonal and objective as anything.* [my emphasis][14]

The neuters used in Brasidas' speech are not meant to qualify human choice, but they nonetheless refer to 'a general law of military science'. Applied to the 'natural' behaviour of human beings, these neuter forms evoke transpersonal dispositions that govern human behaviour. In Hermocrates' speech (4.61.5), even the subject is put into such a neuter form: τὸ ἀνθρώπειον, 'the human', which recalls τὸ ἀνθρώπινον from the chapter on method (1.22.4).

Neuters are also found in the Hippocratic writings. A good example appears in *Airs, Waters, Places*, whereby the author makes the following claim about people inhabiting areas with rough and extreme climates (ch. 24: II 92.6-9):

> τό τε ἐργατικὸν ὀξὺ ἐνεὸν ἐν τῇ φύσει τῇ τοιαύτῃ καὶ τὸ ἄγρυπνον, τά τε ἤθεα καὶ τὰς ὀργὰς αὐθάδεας καὶ ἰδιογνώμονας, τοῦ τε ἀγρίου μᾶλλον μετέχοντας ἢ τοῦ ἡμέρου...
>
> [You would see that] energetic keenness inheres in such a nature and the ability to go without sleep, and that their dispositions of character and temperaments are stubborn and given to holding their own opinions, and that they have a share in wildness rather than tameness...

The nominal phrases point to similarities between Thucydides and the author of the Hippocratic treatise, while also bringing differences into focus. Whereas the nominalizations are all based on adjectives in the Hippocratic text, Cleon's and Hermocrates' nominalizations are mostly based on participles. Because of this, they have a somewhat different effect: Thucydides reifies activity and thus interlocks the idea of disposition with the notion of action.

---

[14] Heiny 1973: 100.

According to Ostwald, the Athenian ambassadors at Melos provide 'the strongest statement on imperial ἀνάγκη in the whole of Thucydides' work'.[15] In advancing this view, the ambassadors draw on several features of the idiom also used by the Athenians at Sparta, Cleon, and Hermocrates (5.105.2):

ἡγούμεθα γὰρ τό τε θεῖον δόξῃ τὸ ἀνθρώπειόν τε σαφῶς διὰ παντὸς ὑπὸ φύσεως ἀναγκαίας, οὗ ἂν κρατῇ, ἄρχειν.[16]

For we think that the divine according to common belief and the human manifestly rule under the compulsory influence of nature wherever they have power.

Τὸ ἀνθρώπειον and τὸ θεῖον, which play the role of grammatical subjects of the verb ἄρχω, are used instead of the personal constructions οἱ ἄνθρωποι and οἱ θεοί. The emphasis does not fall on personal agents and their choices, but on behavioural constants, which in turn are governed by the super-agent φύσις ἀναγκαία in a passive construction.

The phrase φύσις ἀναγκαία invites comparison with a passage from Xenophon's dialogue *Hiero*. It provides clear evidence that the construction of πέφυκε with the infinitive is closely linked with the idea of necessity. The speaker, Sicilian tyrant Hiero, refers to 'those who are naturally disposed by nature [τῶν φύσει πεφυκότων] and at the same time compelled by custom to love [sc. their kinsfolk] in the highest degree' (τῶν φύσει πεφυκότων μάλιστα φιλεῖν καὶ νόμῳ συνηναγκασμένων, 3.9). Natural disposition (τῶν φύσει πεφυκότων) and necessity (συνηναγκασμένων) seamlessly complement each other. This combination recalls the coupling of the noun φύσις with the adjective ἀναγκαῖος in the passage from the Melian Dialogue. Despite this parallel, there is a difference between the two passages. Xenophon applies words related to φύσις and ἀνάγκη to different realms (i.e. nature vs. custom), with each exerting a similar

---

[15] Ostwald 1988: 41.
[16] Alberti prints ἀπὸ φύσεως instead of ὑπὸ φύσεως. The manuscript tradition is unanimous in transmitting ὑπό, whereas ἀπό is found in a papyrus fragment and a quotation of the passage in Dionysius of Halicarnassus (*Thuc.* 40.394.6–7). Ὑπό is much better suited to express the evident meaning of this passage, namely that ἀναγκαία φύσις is 'the decisive cause' in the situation envisaged ('maßgebende Ursache', see Classen-Steup v, on 5.105.2.6).

kind of compulsion. Thucydides, on the other hand, merges the ideas associated with each of these word families by applying words from both lexemes to a sole phenomenon.

According to the Athenian ambassadors, natural necessity has the force of an everlasting law. In making this point, they use language that recalls Thucydides' own observations, in the chapter on method and in the stasis section, of the circular pattern through which history is perpetually bound to move (5.105.2):

καὶ ἡμεῖς οὔτε θέντες τὸν νόμον οὔτε κειμένῳ πρῶτοι χρησάμενοι, ὄντα δὲ παραλαβόντες καὶ ἐσόμενον ἐς αἰεὶ καταλείψοντες χρώμεθα αὐτῷ, εἰδότες καὶ ὑμᾶς ἂν καὶ ἄλλους ἐν τῇ αὐτῇ δυνάμει ἡμῖν γενομένους δρῶντας ἂν ταὐτό.[17]

And we have neither laid down this law nor were we the first to be subject to it once it had been established, but we have received it as something already in existence and we will leave it behind as something that will exist forever; so, we are subject to it, knowing that both you and others would do the same thing if you were to come into the same position of power.

The participles of 'to be' (ὄντα... καὶ ἐσόμενον ἐς αἰεὶ) recall similar forms in Thucydides' authorial statements concerning the permanence of circularity (νόμον... ὄντα... καὶ ἐσόμενον ἐς αἰεί, 5.105.2 ~ τῶν τε γενομένων... καὶ τῶν μελλόντων... ἔσεσθαι, 1.22.4 and γιγνόμενα... καὶ αἰεὶ ἐσόμενα, 3.82.2). Moreover, in the stasis section and in the Melian Dialogue, similar phrases suggest the notion of eternal validity (αἰεὶ ἐσόμενα, 3.82.2; ἐσόμενον ἐς αἰεί, 5.105.2). In expounding upon the law of the stronger, the Athenians at Melos echo at least part of Thucydides' own position (to be gleaned from the two aforementioned authorial

---

[17] Alberti prints καινῷ instead of κειμένῳ. The latter is transmitted by all manuscripts, but the former has been inserted into two manuscripts by a corrector. Yet κειμένῳ alone produces a satisfactory meaning. The Athenians have just stated that they have 'not laid down this law'. It would be redundant for them to continue by saying 'nor are we subject to a new law'; for the relevant idea (i.e. 'we are doing nothing novel') has already been expressed by the Athenians' insistence that they are not the originators of the law of the stronger. It is also easier to explain how κειμένῳ led to καινῷ than the other way around: if the letters -με- mistakenly dropped out in the process of copying, a corrector might easily try to fix κεινῳ by changing it to καινῷ.

statements), namely that fixed, recurring patterns play a considerable role in the causation of human behaviour.

As Ostwald has observed, the three motivations of fear, honour, and advantage, which, according to the Athenians at Sparta, inevitably affect human choices, also induce the Athenians to attempt to conquer Melos.[18] The main difference between the views expressed in the two speeches about natural necessity lies in the claim of the Athenians at Sparta that they have acted with relative justice compared to what others might have done (1.76.3).[19] The Athenians at Melos do not acknowledge any such scope. Macleod draws an apt comparison between their position and the view he ascribes to the Athenians of the Periclean age, whose representatives are the ambassadors at Sparta:[20] 'The Athenians [at Melos] are simply the victims of their own power, there is no attempt to do what Thucydides saw as Pericles' great achievement, to control the natural impulses of the Athenian people and empire.'[21] The extent to which necessity can be reconciled with any moderating influence will be the concern of subsequent chapters. For the moment, it is sufficient to keep in mind that natural necessity may in fact not be quite as rigid as the Athenians at Melos portray. From a rhetorical point of view, it would indeed be highly inconvenient for them to admit any scope when it comes to actualizing the impulse to exert power. Such a concession could give the Melians an opening to urge the Athenians to practise moderation.[22]

---

[18] Ostwald (1988: 41): 'fear that an insurrection of their subjects may overthrow them [cf. 5.91.1, 97], concern that failure to conquer Melos will impair their prestige among their allies and in the Greek world [cf. 5.95, 97, 99], and the advantage to the preservation of the empire that possession of Melos will entail [cf. 5.91.2, 97]'.

[19] This claim will be examined in more detail in Chapter 7 (pp. 252-4).

[20] For parallels between Pericles and the Athenians at Sparta, see Raubitschek 1973: 46 (Pericles' last speech) and 47 (his first speech).

[21] Macleod 1983a [1974]: 62. See also Ostwald (1988: 42): 'The drive to dominate others is here described as a necessary outgrowth of a universal order sanctioned by nature, to which all humans certainly (and the gods probably) are subject, whether they like it or not.' Pelling sees both continuity and difference between the Athenian speeches at Sparta and at Melos: 'These [sc. the claims of the Athenians at Sparta] may be the seeds of the later development for instance the Melian Dialogue, where the question of justice is deflected rather than confronted; but we are not there yet' (2012: 308).

[22] Even Bosworth, who argues convincingly for what he calls, albeit in a limited sense, 'the humanitarian aspect of the Melian Dialogue', intends for this description to cover only the events subsequent to the initial Athenian decision to attack Melos (1993: 31-2 and 43). If, however, this decision itself were open to question, the Athenians would face the challenge of having to justify their line of action, thus confronting a task that would pose serious difficulties.

In terms of our investigation of the depersonalizing style, it is crucial to note the strong idiomatic continuity between the various passages that deal with the necessity of empire. Thucydides' style impresses a set of interconnected notions upon the reader: (1) the passivity of human beings even when they appear to be involved in vigorous activity; (2) the dominance of impersonal behavioural patterns and structures; (3) the parallelism between human behaviour and natural processes; (4) the subjection to ἀνάγκη. These ideas converge in the notion that the quest for power is an inevitable constant in human behaviour.

Holmes comments on the seemingly anthropomorphic language that Hippocratic authors apply to natural phenomena and physical objects:

> Sensing in these instances does not coincide with sentience but describes, rather, physical interaction with the environment. Thus, when these writers claim that vessels or bodies sense winds or changes in temperature, we should see this not as animism but as a kind of anti-anthropomorphism..., an anti-anthropomorphism that redescribes felt, socially embedded experience in terms of physical change.[23]

Thucydides pursues the same strategy from the opposite angle: he depersonalizes action by using substantivized neuter forms and the perfect of φύομαι. His strategy and the procedure ascribed by Holmes to the Hippocratic authors have a similar effect: they imply that human behaviour is, to some extent, subject to the same forces that govern inanimate nature.

In this vein, Marinatos makes a pertinent observation regarding the list of παθήματα (caused by human beings and non-human phenomena alike) that Thucydides considers distinctive of the Peloponnesian War (1.23.1).[24] As Marinatos points out, 'affinity' prevails 'between natural and moral order', a notion 'which shows that, for the ancients, both nature and morality were subject to the same laws'.[25] The neuter phrases and the constructions involving πέφυκα and φύσις support this view. The

---

[23] Holmes 2010: 111–12.
[24] On the implications of Thucydides' emphasis on both natural and man-made disasters in his characterization of the Peloponnesian War, see also Bruzzone 2017: 896–900.
[25] Marinatos 1981: 25.

world conjured up by Thucydides' speakers is ruled by φύσις and impersonal, factual neuters.

It is also worth considering Parry's summary of the perennial Thucydidean antithesis between words categorized as λόγος (e.g., as Parry writes, 'judgment or speech or intention etc.') and ἔργον (e.g., citing Parry again, 'fact, thing, resource, power, etc.'):

> On one side of the constantly repeated and endlessly varied opposition, we find e.g. λόγος, γνώμη, διάνοια, ἀκοή, ὄνομα, ἐλπίς, διδαχή, μέλλοντα; on the other, ἔργον, παρασκευή, μελέτη, δύναμις, βία, ἔρως, φύσις, ὄντα, παρόντα. The point of this whole terminological system is to present history as man's constant attempt to order the world about him by his intelligence.[26]

Human beings, with their rational faculties, appear to belong on the first side of the antithesis, whereas raw material realities and circumstances—suggested by neuters such as παρόντα, ὑπάρχοντα, ἔργα, πράγματα, or παθήματα—belong on the other. However, one wonders whether the neuter term τὸ ἀνθρώπινον suggests that, at least in situations of crisis, human beings are more accurately assigned to the category of 'things' and 'stuff' rather than that of 'spirit' and 'intellect'.

4.2 Human Nature Personified

Diodotus' speech in the Mytilenean Debate also belongs to the group of passages that address the constraints imposed on human behaviour by φύσις. At the same time, Diodotus' speech gives the topic an entirely new spin (3.45.3):[27]

---

[26] Parry 1972: 57.
[27] On the relations between Diodotus' speech and the thesis about the necessity of empire, cf. Orwin (1994: 155): 'Attentive listeners will recognize Diodotus' arguments as variations on the theme of the Athenian thesis [i.e. on the necessity of empire advanced by the ambassadors at Sparta]...If human nature is such that Athens cannot but strive to rule, it is such that her subjects cannot but resist being ruled.'

πεφύκασί τε ἅπαντες καὶ ἰδίᾳ καὶ δημοσίᾳ ἁμαρτάνειν, καὶ οὐκ ἔστι νόμος ὅστις ἀπείρξει τούτου

All people are naturally disposed to do wrong both privately and publicly, and there is no law that will restrain them from this.

The characteristic perfect form of φύομαι, which suggests that human beings are conditioned by φύσις, recalls the phrasing used by speakers in the aforementioned passages when they discuss the necessity imposed by human nature. Unlike these other speakers, however, Diodotus does not talk about human nature in a self-assured manner; instead, he thinks that human nature causes people to commit transgression as well as make self-destructive mistakes, a danger exemplified by the Mytileneans' decision to revolt against Athens.

By using the verb ὁρμάομαι, Diodotus represents the pressure that human nature exercises as a drive or urge (3.45.7):

ἁπλῶς τε ἀδύνατον καὶ πολλῆς εὐηθείας, ὅστις οἴεται τῆς ἀνθρωπείας φύσεως ὁρμωμένης προθύμως τι πρᾶξαι ἀποτροπήν τινα ἔχειν ἢ νόμων ἰσχύι ἢ ἄλλῳ τῳ δεινῷ.

It is simply impossible and a sign of great naivety if anyone believes that, when human nature is eagerly striving to do something, he has the means to prevent it either by the force of law or by some other terror.

Diodotus' stress on human nature's eagerness 'to do something' implies that he treats it as an actor: he regards φύσις, as opposed to personal agents, as the primary instigator of events.

Diodotus gives a vivid account of the various forces that drive human beings to seek expansion and commit transgression (3.45.4–6):

ἀλλ' ἡ μὲν πενία ἀνάγκῃ τὴν τόλμαν παρέχουσα, ἡ δ' ἐξουσία ὕβρει τὴν πλεονεξίαν καὶ φρονήματι, αἱ δ' ἄλλαι ξυντυχίαι ὀργῇ τῶν ἀνθρώπων ὡς ἑκάστη τις κατέχεται ὑπ' ἀνηκέστου τινὸς κρείσσονος ἐξάγουσιν ἐς τοὺς κινδύνους. ἥ τε ἐλπὶς καὶ ὁ ἔρως ἐπὶ παντί, ὁ μὲν ἡγούμενος, ἡ δ' ἐφεπομένη, καὶ ὁ μὲν τὴν ἐπιβουλὴν ἐκφροντίζων, ἡ δὲ τὴν εὐπορίαν τῆς τύχης ὑποτιθεῖσα, πλεῖστα βλάπτουσι, καὶ ὄντα ἀφανῆ κρείσσω ἐστὶ τῶν ὁρωμένων δεινῶν. καὶ ἡ τύχη ἐπ' αὐτοῖς οὐδὲν ἔλασσον ξυμβάλλεται ἐς τὸ ἐπαίρειν· ἀδοκήτως γὰρ ἔστιν ὅτε παρισταμένη καὶ ἐκ τῶν ὑποδεεστέρων κινδυνεύειν τινὰ προάγει.

But poverty, causing daring through necessity, and wealth, causing greed through outrage and arrogance, and the other circumstances of life, as each of them is mastered by something incurable and stronger, drive human beings into dangers through passion. Moreover, hope and desire are everywhere, the latter leading the way, the former following behind, the latter devising the plan, the former suggesting the ease of fortune. They cause the most harm, and since they are invisible, they are stronger than the dangers which one can see. And, besides these, fortune contributes no less to stirring people up. For, now and again, she presents herself unexpectedly and drives them to take risks from insufficient resources.

It becomes apparent that the impulse to seek power involves not only an inevitable urge towards expansion but also an innate tendency towards risk-taking and self-destruction, as Topitsch and Orwin point out.[28] Instead of stressing impersonal regularity, Diodotus highlights intense passions that plunge cities into the abyss.

Every grammatical subject at 3.45.4–6 consists of an abstract noun combined with a verb. Most of these verbs, if taken literally, refer to actions that are more appropriate to human beings: poverty and wealth 'drive people into danger', desire 'leads the way' and 'devises the plan', hope 'follows behind' and 'suggests the ease of fortune', both hope and desire 'cause harm', fortune 'presents herself unexpectedly' and 'drives people to take risks'. Choices of individual agents do not seem to matter; the real agents are collective psychological and external states. Vocabulary suggestive of drives and urges permeates the passage (ἐξάγουσιν, ἡγούμενος, ἐπαίρειν, προάγει). Finally, the impulses recall overwhelmingly powerful, malicious antagonists (κατέχεται ὑπ'

---

[28] Orwin (1994: 157): 'What is elsewhere an assertion of the priority of one's own good to justice becomes in his [sc. Diodotus'] mouth also a general teaching of human weakness or irrationality.' Topitsch (1943–7: 62): '[U]nmißverständlich unterstreicht Th. die Tatsache, daß die Physis, wenn sie in blindem Trieb zur Macht alle Formen des Zusammenlebens zerstört, letztlich sich selbst vernichtet.'

ἀνηκέστου τινὸς κρείσσονος—πλεῖστα βλάπτουσι—κρείσσω ἐστὶ τῶν ὁρωμένων δεινῶν).

Another passage, which also addresses the themes of necessity and human nature, recalls Diodotus' personifications. The Melian Dialogue features a personification of ἐλπίς, a passion that also appears in the passage from Diodotus' speech. Given the vicissitudes of war, the Melians hold fast to the hope that their prospects in a conflict with Athens may not be as dire as it seems. To this, the Athenians respond as follows (5.103.1):[29]

Ἐλπὶς δέ, κινδύνῳ παραμύθιον οὖσα, τοὺς μὲν ἀπὸ περιουσίας χρωμένους αὐτῇ, κἂν βλάψῃ, οὐ καθεῖλεν· τοῖς δ' ἐς ἅπαν τὸ ὑπάρχον ἀναρριπτοῦσι (δάπανος γὰρ φύσει) ἅμα τε γιγνώσκεται σφαλέντων καὶ ἐν ὅτῳ ἔτι φυλάξεταί τις αὐτὴν γνωρισθεῖσαν οὐκ ἐλλείπει.

For sure, hope is a consolation amid danger, and she does not destroy those who become subject to her if they are backed by resources, though she may harm them. But for those who stake their all (for she is by nature prodigal), she only reveals her true colours when they have been overthrown, and she leaves nothing intact based on which people might henceforth guard themselves against her after having recognized her.

Hope has the air of a bewitching seducer, who lures her victims in with attractive projections and leads them to ruin: she offers deceptive consolation; she harms and destroys; her gifts are seemingly abundant, but without any substance. Hope is a sly trickster, only revealing her true colours when it is too late for the victim. The implications of this personification of hope recall the similar presentation of δύναμις in the Corcyreans' speech at Athens (1.33.2).[30] While ἐλπίς is depicted as an agent, persons are used as subjects of verbs that express passivity. In the cited passage, χράομαι and the aorist passive of σφάλλω play this role. Two further phrases with similar implications follow. The Athenians

---

[29] Cornford (1907: 184) highlights the parallels of this passage with a similar personification of hope in lines 616–25 of Sophocles' *Antigone*.
[30] See Chapter 3, pp. 104–5.

caution the Melians not 'to suffer' that which the Athenians have warned them of (ὃ... παθεῖν), i.e. not to be overtaken by hope, and they give the negative example of 'the many', who 'get caught up in invisible [hopes]' (ἐπὶ τὰς ἀφανεῖς καθίστανται, 5.103.2). In terms of semantics, the passage implies that human beings are reduced to passivity, while all strings are pulled by hope, which plays the role of a larger-than-life-sized agent.

The personifications in Diodotus' speech and in the Melian Dialogue represent one basic variant of depersonalizing phrasing in Thucydides. The passages featuring abstract neuter forms (discussed in Section 4.1 above) illustrate another, contrasting variant. In both accounts, collective and individual human agency are subject to natural constraint, but this force takes on a different shape in each case. The passages featuring substantivized neuter adjectives and perfect forms of φύομαι suggest impersonality, the uniformity of patterns, and static containment. By stark contrast, the personifications found in Diodotus' speech and in the Melian Dialogue suggest superhuman agents, unpredictability, explosiveness, and the unleashing of dynamic forces. According to the first approach, personal agents are replaced by impersonal entities that impose constraints on human behaviour. In Diodotus' account, agency takes place, but the role of the real agents is played by passions and circumstances, so that impersonal factors are almost given the status of personal decision-makers. These two sides of the nominal style bring Dionysius' observation to mind, quoted in connection with the chapters on stasis (see Sections 2.1 and 2.2), that Thucydides sometimes treats persons as things, and things as persons (*Thuc.* 24.362.16–18). On either side, the nominal style implies that human agents are not ultimately in charge of events.

4.3 Collapsing the Duality Between Inner and Outer

It is not easy to find a category that accommodates all the forces personified in Diodotus' speech. Some of the terms refer to passions (e.g. daring, hope, desire), others to external circumstances (e.g. poverty, wealth, fortune). The passage thus systematically undercuts the duality between inner and outer, between passions and circumstances. Diodotus regards all these forces as aspects of φύσις. This foundation becomes apparent when Diodotus summarizes the list of dangerous forces by observing that human nature, once unleashed, cannot be contained (3.45.7).

One may initially be tempted to think in terms of stimulus and effect, whereby material circumstances (e.g. πενία and ἐξουσία) trigger psychological states (e.g. τόλμα and πλεονεξία). Yet this concept is not quite applicable in Diodotus' case. This becomes apparent if we consider the two groups of instrumental datives at 3.45.4: ἀνάγκῃ vs. ὕβρει... καὶ φρονήματι. They indicate means: poverty *by means of necessity*, and wealth *by means of outrage and arrogance*, lead to daring and greed, respectively. As Classen-Steup observe, the neat antithesis between outward circumstances and inward emotions does not hold for the two sets of terms placed in the dative: necessity is an external circumstance, but arrogance and confidence are emotions.[31] Despite the qualitative difference between material circumstances and psychic states, the parallelism suggests that they have something vital in common.

The antithesis between inner and outer becomes even more unsatisfactory when applied to the concluding part of 3.45.4: 'the other circumstances of life, as each of them is mastered by something incurable and stronger, drive human beings into dangers through passion' (αἱ δ' ἄλλαι ξυντυχίαι ὀργῇ τῶν ἀνθρώπων ὡς ἑκάστη τις κατέχεται ὑπ' ἀνηκέστου τινὸς κρείσσονος ἐξάγουσιν ἐς τοὺς κινδύνους). The term αἱ ἄλλαι ξυντυχίαι clearly represents a general category, which the preceding specific instances represented by ἡ πενία and ἡ ἐξουσία fall under. The dative ὀργῇ is supposed to fulfil the same function for τόλμαν and πλεονεξίαν. By analogy, 'something incurable and stronger' must function as a general category for ἀνάγκῃ and for the pair ὕβρει καὶ φρονήματι.[32] It follows that passions (like ὕβρις and φρόνημα, with the latter meaning 'arrogance') can be 'something incurable and stronger' and can 'master' a circumstance

---

[31] Classen-Steup iii, on 3.45.4.16ff. [Anhang]: 'die gleichfalls gegenübergestellten nähern Antriebe zu beiden letztern [sc. τόλμα and πελονεξία], ἀνάγκῃ und ὕβρει καὶ φρονήματι, sind freilich nur äußerlich parallel: jener hat seinen Sitz in den äußern Umständen, dieser im verwöhnten Gemüt des Menschen.'

[32] Cf. Classen-Steup iii, on 3.45.4.16ff. [Anhang]: 'den dort [sc. by πενία and ἐξουσία] näher bezeichneten Antrieben der ἀνάγκη und ὕβρις entspricht hier [sc. in the clause starting with αἱ ἄλλαι ξυντυχίαι] das unbestimmte κρεῖσσόν τι, welches in den einzelnen ξυντυχίαι den entscheidenden Einfluß übt...; dazu gehört z. B. die Ehre oder die Rache, welche erstrebt wird, oder, wie im vorliegenden Falle bei den Mytilenäern, die Freiheit und Unabhängigkeit, die sie zu erreichen suchen.'

(ξυντυχία) in the sense that they exercise the decisive influence. It is hard to see what this is supposed to mean if we suppose a scheme where situations (ξυντυχίαι) *trigger* emotional responses (ὕβρις and φρόνημα). Finally, the sequence of ἐλπίς, ἔρως, and τύχη, which concludes Diodotus' account, leads to the same conclusion. As Cornford has observed, Diodotus represents all three factors as being equally great befuddling temptations that lure people into perilous enterprises.[33] Again, passionate impulses (ἔρως and ἐλπίς) and external circumstances (τύχη) fulfil the same function.

Diodotus' language calls into question the clear-cut antithesis, taken for granted by many modern thinkers, between inner and outer, psychic and material. Instead, he implies that passions are inextricably bound up with, and partially constitutive of, situations. It is significant that the Greek words πάθος and πάθημα convey both external and internal states, as David Konstan points out:

> In classical Greek, *pathos* may refer more generally to what befalls a person, often in the negative sense of an accident or misfortune, although it may also bear the neutral significance of a condition or state of affairs... The specific sense of 'emotion' is in part conditioned by this penumbra of connotations: insofar as a *pathos* is a reaction to an impinging event or circumstance, it looks to the outside stimulus to which it responds.[34]

The two senses of πάθος (passion and external condition) are reflected in Diodotus' account. In his conception, the inner and the outer sphere belong together and are presupposed in every human action: for instance, arrogance and wealth are two aspects, one internal and one external, of the same situation. Instead of having an impervious inner sphere, people are plunged simultaneously into circumstances and the passions that come in their wake. Stahl rightly emphasizes that Diodotus is equally concerned with 'the *situations* in which people find themselves' and 'the *emotions* arising from these situations'.[35] The crucial point is that these two spheres are two sides of the same framework that conditions people's choices and actions. Passions, far from being

---

[33] Cornford 1907: 123.   [34] Konstan 2006: 3–4.   [35] Stahl 2003 [1966]: 120.

private internal states, have the otherness of events. By the same token, circumstances do not leave people scope for a judicious reaction, but affect them with the immediacy and directness of an internal experience.[36] As a result, human beings are not shielded from the outside world by an inner citadel. The pressure of φύσις does not give them scope to take a detached stance.

Further passages provide evidence for the idea that inner and outer are not categorically distinct. The Athenian ambassadors at Sparta imply that the 'three greatest things' (i.e. fear, honour, and advantage: 1.75.4, 76.2) belong to the same category. Yet 'fear' refers to an emotion while 'advantage' and 'honour' concern external goods. One might attenuate the jarring effect by rendering ὠφελία as 'desire for advantage' and τιμή as 'desire for honour'. Yet this rendition implies a nuance that is absent from the actual wording. The same applies to Thucydides' observation with regard to the evils of stasis that 'the cause of all these things was power fuelled by greed and ambition' (πάντων δ' αὐτῶν αἴτιον ἀρχὴ ἡ διὰ πλεονεξίαν καὶ φιλοτιμίαν, 3.82.8). The scholiast renders ἀρχή as 'desire that consists in wanting to rule' (ἡ ἐπιθυμία τοῦ βούλεσθαι ἄρχειν),[37] but again Thucydides' original wording does not feature a reference to a 'desire for' something. The scholiast is surely right to think that stasis is marked by a 'desire for power', and his gloss is an attempt to make Thucydides' thought more accessible. Nonetheless, Thucydides simply speaks about ἀρχή as a bare fact. The term is wider than the scholiast's phrase, suggesting the desire for power as well as the exercise of it. It refers to a situation where this concern with power has become an encompassing determinant of human behavior. Ἀρχή is not subjective (as the scholiast suggests), but objective—not a longing, but a natural fact that characterizes humans, to some extent comparable to breathing or sleeping.

---

[36] This analysis is indebted to Heidegger's account of moods and attunement in section 29 of *Being and Time*. This connection is not anachronistic because Heidegger, in developing his ideas about the fundamental role of moods, went back to Greek thought. For Heidegger, moods are not internal states projected on situations by the subject. Instead, they are pervasive dispositional facts that transcend the divide between inner and outer: it is always via moods that human beings are connected with the world and other human beings. Consider the following quote from *Being and Time*: 'Die Stimmung überfällt. Sie kommt weder von "Außen" noch von "Innen", sondern steigt als Weise des In-der-Welt-seins aus diesem selbst auf' (2001: 136). In giving his account of moods, Heidegger singles out Aristotle's treatment of πάθη in the *Rhetoric* as an important predecessor (2001: 138). Diodotus' emphasis on the primordial interconnectedness between inner and outer is a good example of the mode of thought that drew Heidegger to the Greeks.

[37] See Classen-Steup iii, on 3.82.8.53.

People are so strongly committed to the exercise of power because of the immediate pull of intense passions: 'greed' and 'ambition'. Again, external conditions (ἀρχή) and passions (πλεονεξίαν καὶ φιλοτιμίαν), all denoted by feminine abstract nouns, represent different aspects of a single situation.

The personifications employed by Diodotus emphasize the dynamic side of φύσις: passion, unpredictability, suddenness, and striving. However, Diodotus also ascribes monumental proportions to passions and lumps them together with external situational constraints, thus representing human nature not just as limitlessly potent, but also as a permanent disposition. Pouncey observes apropos another passage that 'mercurial, ephemeral things' (i.e. human passions) are 'given permanence or made monolithic' by Thucydides' manner of presentation.[38] Through the simultaneity of static and dynamic aspects, Diodotus suggests that intense, heightened passions like ἔρως and ἐλπίς have a dispositional dimension: they are not just momentary impulses, but tend to determine human behaviour over an extended period of time—if not for the entirety of human existence!

4.4 Divine Visitation and Natural Drives: Affinities Between Euripides and Thucydides

Cornford has stressed the peculiar resonance, in Diodotus' account of human nature, of the phrase 'as each [sc. circumstance] is mastered by something incurable and stronger' (ὡς ἑκάστη τις κατέχεται ὑπ' ἀνηκέστου τινὸς κρείσσονος, 3.45.4). As Cornford remarks, the verb κατέχω is 'regularly used of spiritual occupation of all kinds', and he goes on to observe that 'κρείσσων is associated with the "daemons", who were called "the stronger ones", οἱ κρείσσονες'.[39] Moreover, Diodotus summarizes his account of the impact of ἔρως and ἐλπίς by observing that 'they, being invisible, are stronger than dangers which one can see'

---

[38] Pouncey 1980: 146.
[39] Cornford 1907: 158 n. 2. In support of the latter claim, Cornford cites the following passages: μή τις τῶν κρειττόνων παρὼν αὐτὰ ἐφθέγξατο, Plato, *Euthyd.* 291a4, and Aelian, *V. H.* 4.17, where, as Cornford writes, 'Pythagoras called the noise in his ears φωνὴ τῶν κρειττόνων.'

(καὶ ὄντα ἀφανῆ κρείσσω ἐστὶ τῶν ὁρωμένων δεινῶν, 3.45.5). In the Loeb edition, Smith suitably translates the phrase ὄντα ἀφανῆ as 'unseen phantoms', a phrase that reflects the daemonic resonance of the term κρείσσων. In fact, the reference to 'invisibility' sustains the allusions to the daemonic realm: the invisible sphere tends to be associated with the gods in Thucydides as well as in Greek literature more generally.[40] In addition, the vivid personifications of ἔρως, ἐλπίς, and τύχη as sly and beguiling tempters give the impression of daemonic agents. Diodotus' language is thus reminiscent of the ominous agency of divine powers that features most prominently in Greek tragedy.

In forging this link, Cornford draws primarily on scenes from Aeschylean drama. Yet the parallels with another tragedian are no less pertinent. It is widely known that Euripides achieved unusual mastery in the graphic representation of glaring states of psychological extremes, conditions that the Greeks believed were induced by daemonic powers.[41] Given Diodotus' particular attention to ἔρως (along with ἐλπίς), Euripides' *Hippolytus* provides an especially good point of comparison: its central theme is Phaedra's crazed infatuation with Hippolytus, an obsession induced by the ruthless agency of Aphrodite. As Finley remarks, when Diodotus 'adduces men's proneness to act on their desires in spite of all deterrents (III 45), he touches perhaps the central idea of... the *Hippolytus*'.[42]

Early on in the play, the Chorus and the Nurse analyse the symptoms of Phaedra's possession in a verbal exchange. Phaedra is pining away in a deranged mental state, which is reflected by visible physical distress. Some bodily symptoms have already been mentioned prior to the scene in question (172–5, 198–202). Now the Chorus describes Phaedra's condition as a 'disease' whose nature is 'unclear' to them (ἄσημα... ἡ νόσος, 269). They wonder what the natural origin of her

---

[40] See Joho 2019: 143–8.

[41] Cf. Dodds (1929: 99–100): 'The accuracy with which he observed the symptoms of neurosis and insanity appears from such scenes as Phaedra's first conversation with the Nurse, or the awakening of Agave out of her Dionysiac trance personality, or again in the figure of Heracles, whose insanity is clearly marked as belonging to the manic-depressive type.'

[42] Finley 1967a: 32. Cf. Fisher and Hoekstra (2017: 377): 'In the surviving works of Euripides we find with particular frequency the claim that *erōs*, or lust, acts on humans as a necessitating force.'

sufferings is (ἥτις ἀρχὴ τῶνδε πημάτων ἔφυ, 272), but the Nurse has no answer. The Chorus take their cues for assessing Phaedra's state from her outward appearance: 'How weak and wasted her body is!' (ὡς ἀσθενεῖ τε καὶ κατέξανται δέμας, 274). The Nurse responds to this observation of outward signs by pointing out that Phaedra's state is hardly surprising, considering she has not eaten anything for three days (275). As far as the Chorus can tell, this abstention from eating can be caused by one of two things: either Phaedra is acting under ἄτη, which in this situation means that she is mentally deranged,[43] or she is consciously planning suicide (276).

Taken by itself, this discussion does not convey the impression that Phaedra has suffered an otherworldly visitation; instead, it appears to reflect an intramundane, psychological phenomenon: Phaedra is afflicted by a violent form of love sickness. Only the word ἄτη, with its connotations of 'supernatural interference',[44] suggests that the impact of a divine power might be at play. In this context, one should keep in mind that Greek religion always conceived of the gods as living, natural forces present within the world and manifesting themselves in heightened, but nonetheless 'natural,' experiences.[45] In the *Hippolytus*, the Nurse expresses the ordinariness of divine visitations: '"You have suffered," she says to Phaedra, "nothing extraordinary, nothing unaccountable, but the visitations of the goddess's anger have struck you"' (οὐ γὰρ περισσὸν οὐδὲν οὐδ' ἔξω λόγου / πέπονθας, ὀργαὶ δ' ἐς σ' ἀπέσκηψαν θεᾶς, 437–8). Thus, the natural dimension has its counterpart in an invisible, divine reality. If one cancels the divine side of the equation, the naturalistic complement remains mostly intact. Given this naturalistic bent of Greek religion, the step from the belief in divine interference to the Thucydidean idea of necessity imposed by nature is smaller than one might assume.

---

[43] Barrett 1964, on 276.   [44] Barrett 1964, on 241.

[45] Cornford (1907: 227) describes this view as follows: 'The inexplicable panic which will suddenly run through an army, the infectious spirit of a crowd, the ecstasy produced by intoxicants, the throes of sexual pleasure, the raving of the seer and of the poet – all these are states of mind in which the self appears to be drowned and swept away. By what? There can be but one answer: some spirit, or daemon, has entered the soul and possesses it. This is the very language used by Diodotus.'

Another theme casts light on the point of contact between the natural and the divine: the issue of Phaedra's Cretan ancestry. She refers to this topic at a moment of high tension when the Nurse is on the cusp of getting her to reveal the cause of her grievous condition. In response, Phaedra suddenly utters exclamations of despair, addressing her mother Pasiphae's and her sister Ariadne's sexual transgressions (337 and 339). What she has in mind is Pasiphae's lust for the Cretan bull and Ariadne's betrayal of Dionysus. Phaedra implies that her suffering belongs to the same type (341), and that the origin of her unhappiness lies there, in the distant past (ἐκεῖθεν ἡμεῖς, οὐ νεωστί, δυστυχεῖς, 343). She implies that the longing for illicit sexual experience is in her family's blood, a naturally inherited predisposition. From this standpoint, the gods have not inflicted an entirely random calamity on Phaedra, an affliction that has nothing to do with who she is. Instead, they precipitate disaster by exploiting a pre-existing weak spot in her natural constitution.

It is interesting that Hippolytus' situation is similar. He is not Theseus' legitimate son, but a bastard child, born from an amazon mother. Faced with Theseus' hammering reproaches, Hippolytus calls out to his mother and wishes that none of his friends should ever suffer the fate of a νόθος, i.e. an 'illegitimate child' (1082–3). The reference to the theme of νοθεία is somewhat out of context, but Barrett explains its relevance by referring to Hippolytus' anxiety that, due to his baseborn status, he has received less of a fair hearing than a legitimate son would have. As Barrett goes on to observe, the sudden reference to this theme gives a subtle hint that Hippolytus' 'feeling of inferiority...lies behind his urge to establish himself in compensation as a paragon of virtues that common man cannot share'.[46] Hippolytus is so excessively concerned with virtuous chastity because his status as an illegitimate offspring has predisposed him in that way. Thus, an explanation wholly believable on a naturalistic level suggests itself for the specific quirk that will lead, in combination with Phaedra's illicit lust, to the play's catastrophic outcome. Again, this natural chink in Hippolytus' character affords Aphrodite the opportunity to carry out her plan.

---

[46] Barrett 1964, on 1082–3.

In this way, both Phaedra's and Hippolytus' genealogy have left unwholesome marks on their specific personality: Phaedra's deformation is caused by her biological inheritance, Hippolytus' by the trauma of his inferior descent. The idea that these troublesome conditions have the dire psychological effects portrayed in Euripides' play is not far-fetched. Thus, it would be possible to provide an entirely naturalistic explanation for the behaviour of both characters. Although the divine can be identified with the natural in this way, this conclusion would nonetheless overlook a significant component: Aphrodite is the force responsible for setting the disastrous sequence of events in motion, exploiting the raw material that is there, but she is not reducible to a purely naturalistic phenomenon. She remains a goddess, marked by superhuman grandeur and a specific personality. Nonetheless, the close correspondence with a naturalistic explanation is evident. When Thucydides deals with the impact of ἔρως on people's actions, he replaces the will of Euripides' goddess with natural necessity. In either case, human beings struggle against a compulsory force that ultimately reduces them to passivity.

Specific verbal parallels between Euripides' and Diodotus' account support this argument. Diodotus emphasizes people's natural propensity to 'err' (πεφύκασί τε ἅπαντες ... ἁμαρτάνειν, 3.45.2). The next steps in his train of thought shows that this natural proneness is linked to human nature's outbursts into passions, such as ἔρως and ἐλπίς. In the *Hippolytus*, the frantic passion induced by divine ἔρως likewise leads to actions marked by 'error', for which speakers also use forms of the word ἁμαρτάνω on several occasions (ἔα μ' ἁμαρτεῖν· οὐ γὰρ ἐς σ' ἁμαρτάνω, 323; ἡμαρτηκόσι, 464; ἁμαρτάνειν, 507; ἁμαρτεῖν, 615; ἐξαμαρτάνειν, 1434). Both in Diodotus' speech and in the *Hippolytus*, glaring errors happen because irrational psychological states overtake people.

Another specific parallel is the idea of 'possession'. As pointed out above, Diodotus conveys it with the verb κατέχω (3.45.4). In the prologue of the *Hippolytus*, Aphrodite draws on the same verb to capture Phaedra's possession by ἔρως: 'Phaedra was possessed in her heart by terrible desire' (Φαίδρα καρδίαν κατέσχετο / ἔρωτι δεινῷ, 27–8). In the same passage, Aphrodite flaunts the fact that Phaedra's seizure was due to her "schemes" (τοῖς ἐμοῖς βουλεύμασιν, 28). This phrase is also reminiscent of Diodotus' characterization of ἔρως: ἔρως typically 'concocts the scheme' (ὁ μὲν τὴν ἐπιβουλὴν ἐκφροντίζων, 3.45.5), when cities undertake bold collective enterprises. In both passages, passionate desire is depicted as a cunning agent whose schemes are expressed through vocabulary derived from βουλεύω. Holmes has observed that two parallel datives occur in the line where Aphrodite gloats over her clever scheming: '[Phaedra has been seized] by terrible desire through my devising' (ἔρωτι δεινῷ τοῖς ἐμοῖς βουλεύμασιν, 27). Holmes comments: 'The two datives, which together fill the line, correspond to two modalities of action in the tragedy.'[47] At one level, Phaedra's experience can be accounted for in naturalistic terms, but at another she is the victim of a personalized goddess.

Various scholars have pointed out that the collective mindset prevailing among the Athenians on the eve of the Sicilian Expedition is strongly reminiscent of Diodotus' account of the influence of ἔρως and ἐλπίς.[48] Thucydides describes the moment when the Athenians enthusiastically endorse the expedition with a compound of πίπτω, the type of verb used to encapsulate the onslaught of irresistible forces in which the Peloponnesian War shows its true colours:[49] 'and the desire to sail fell upon them in their entirety, on all alike' (καὶ ἔρως ἐνέπεσε τοῖς πᾶσιν ὁμοίως ἐκπλεῦσαι, 6.24.3). Connor points out that the combination of ἔρως with a compound of πίπτω recalls the identical phrase from Aeschylus' *Agamemnon* and Euripides' *Iphigenia at Aulis*.[50] In both plays, ἔρως befalls the Greek army in the Trojan War, thus affecting a collective mindset comparable to the ἔρως for Sicily of the Athenians: in *Agamemnon* it refers to the heinous desire of sacrilege after the conquest at Troy, and in *Iphigenia at Aulis* it captures the Greeks' eagerness for the Trojan War.[51] Achilles, the speaker in *Iphigenia at Aulis*, considers this visitation the work of the gods (οὐκ ἄνευ θεῶν, 809), and the ubiquitous presence of daemonic forces in the *Agamemnon* likewise provides strong evidence for the ultimate responsibility of superhuman powers.[52] Similar notions, converging in

---

[47] Holmes 2010: 252–3.   [48] Stahl 2003 [1966]: 121; Wohl 2002: 193; Visvardi 2015: 84.
[49] On these phrases see Chapter 2, pp. 67–70.   [50] Connor 1984: 167.
[51] Aesch. *Ag.* 341–2: ἔρως δὲ μή τις πρότερον ἐμπίπτῃ στρατῷ / πορθεῖν ἃ μὴ χρή, κέρδεσιν νικωμένους. Eur. *IA* 808–9: οὕτω δεινὸς ἐμπέπτωκ' ἔρως / τῇδε στρατείας Ἑλλάδ' οὐκ ἄνευ θεῶν.
[52] Cf. Cornford (1907: 157): 'The conquerors of Troy are beset by Eros, the spirit of rapine; but this passion is not conceived as a natural state of mind determined by a previous state – the effect of a normal cause; it is a spirit (δαίμων) which haunts, swoops down, and takes possession of the soul, when reason slumbers and keeps no watch.'

the idea that ἔρως 'assaults' and 'strikes' Phaedra, also recur repeatedly in the *Hippolytus* (38-9, 238, 438, 527, 530-4).

Faced with the assault of Aphrodite's power, Phaedra does not passively submit but offers determined resistance. In an attempt to describe her inner state, Phaedra pictures her reaction to the attack in terms of a struggle: 'I intended to bear this folly nobly by defeating it through sensible self-control' (τὴν ἄνοιαν εὖ φέρειν / τῷ σωφρονεῖν νικῶσα προυνοησάμην, 398-9). The verb νικάω also occurs in the aforementioned wish of the Chorus in Aeschylus' *Agamemnon* that transgressive ἔρως may not befall the Greek army: this impulse would be a 'desire... to ravage what they must not, defeated by gain' (ἔρως ... / πορθεῖν ἃ μὴ χρή, κέρδεσιν νικωμένους, 341-2). Thucydides' work also provides evidence for this use of νικάω. The Athenian ambassadors at Sparta claim that their fellow-countrymen were 'defeated by the three greatest things' (ὑπὸ ⟨τριῶν⟩ τῶν μεγίστων νικηθέντες, 1.76.2). Just as in the two tragic passages, the Athenian imply that human beings struggle with awesome powers. Despite Phaedra's resolve to emerge victorious, this contest usually ends with the victory of the non-human side, as experienced by the Greeks in Aeschylus and the Athenians in Thucydides. Phaedra, too, must realize that her opponent is much more powerful than she is: 'I did not manage to conquer Cypris' (οὐκ ἐξήνυτον / Κύπριν κρατῆσαι, 400-1).

The Nurse also draws on the idea of a contest between two opponents when she warns Phaedra: 'These things are nothing but *hybris* to wish to be stronger than the gods' (οὐ γὰρ ἄλλο πλὴν ὕβρις /τάδ' ἐστί, κρείσσω δαιμόνων εἶναι θέλειν, 474-5). Notice in this passage, the juxtaposition, just around the caesura, of the words κρείσσω and δαιμόνων: it is absurd for human beings to try to be stronger than the daemons, who are κρείσσονες by definition (as pointed out above). While this juxtaposition draws the words κρείσσω and δαιμόνων together, thus highlighting the close semantic connection between the two terms, the caesura separates them, thereby underscoring the notion of a conflict between human beings and δαίμονες. In much the same spirit, Diodotus says that 'something incurable and stronger' (ὑπ' ἀνηκέστου τινὸς κρείσσονος, 3.45.4) holds the upper hand in every situation, and that the invisible powers of ἔρως and ἐλπίς 'are stronger than seen terrors' (κρείσσω ἐστὶ τῶν ὁρωμένων δεινῶν, 3.45.5). He concludes that it is 'a sign of great naivety' (πολλῆς εὐηθείας, 3.45.7) to think that one has the power to suppress these impulses, thus making the same point as the Nurse with her reference to *hybris*: both speakers consider it absurd to oppose the 'stronger ones'.

In the present context, a passage from Euripides' *Alcestis* also deserves attention. The play's Chorus refers to an impersonal force that governs the cosmos: 'I have found nothing stronger than Necessity nor is there any remedy for it in the Thracian tablets' (κρεῖσσον οὐδὲν Ἀνάγκας / ηὗρον οὐδέ τι φάρμακον / Θρήσσαις ἐν σανίσιν, 965–7). The notion that an impersonal force called ἀνάγκη is the 'strongest' power of all bears close resemblance to what we found in Thucydides. Moreover, the Chorus' realization that no 'remedy' (φάρμακον) avails against Necessity recalls Diodotus' phrase 'something incurable and stronger' (3.45.4). The thought that no 'remedy' exists against some evil is tantamount to saying that it is 'incurable'.

In Thucydides, vocabulary denoting passivity regularly captures people's exposure to the driving forces fuelled by human nature. The same phrasing can also be found in *Hippolytus*. The Nurse says that Phaedra 'has suffered' (πέπονθας, 438) the visitation of Eros (cf. ἐρᾷς, 439). During the Sicilian Debate, Nicias employs the same language in his effort to curb ἔρως. Nicias urges the older men to part company with the younger men, who enthusiastically promote the Sicilian Expedition, infecting the city with a mad desire (cf. δυσέρωτας, 6.13.1), a condition, says Nicias, 'which they [i.e. the youngsters] themselves may have suffered' (ὅπερ ἂν αὐτοὶ πάθοιεν, 6.13.1). Turning back to *Hippolytus*, Phaedra responds to the Nurse's claim that being in love means both pleasure and pain: 'I suppose it is the second that I have suffered' (ἡμεῖς ἂν εἶμεν θατέρῳ κεχρημένοι, 349), where the translation 'suffered' stems from a form of χράομαι. The Athenian ambassadors at both Sparta and Melos use χράομαι in the same sense to express people's subjection to human nature and the law of domination (1.76.3, 5.105.2 [twice]). Additionally, the Athenians at Melos use it of people's tendency to succumb to hope (χρωμένους αὐτῇ, 5.103.1), one of the principal motivations induced by human nature.

On several occasions, characters call Phaedra's state a 'disease' (νόσον, 40; νόσος, 269; νόσον, 394; νοσοῦσα δ' εὖ πως τὴν νόσον καταστρέφου, 477).

Phaedra says that ἔρως 'wounded' her (μ' ἔρως ἔτρωσεν, 392). At one point, the Nurse suggests that Phaedra's suffering may be brought to the attention of 'physicians' (ἰατροῖς, 296) During the Sicilian Debate, Thucydides has Nicias similarly call upon the prytanis 'to become a physician of the city' (τῆς δὲ πόλεως κακῶς βουλευσαμένης ἰατρὸς ἂν γενέσθαι, 6.14), thus characterizing the Athenians' feverish state under the influence of ἔρως and ἐλπίς as a disease, through recourse to 'medical language... in the political forum'.[53]

At last, a striking parallel between Euripides' *Trojan Women* and the Melian Dialogue calls for comment. The relevant passage comes directly before the extended dispute between Helen and Hecuba over the issue of whether Helen is really culpable for the Trojan War, given that the gods instilled overpowering ἔρως into her. A few lines before this *agon* begins, Hecuba turns to Zeus with the following address (885–6):

ὅστις ποτ' εἶ σύ, δυστόπαστος εἰδέναι,
Ζεύς, εἴτ' ἀνάγκη φύσεος εἴτε νοῦς βροτῶν...
Whoever you may be, hard for guesswork to know,
Zeus, whether you are the necessity of nature or the mind of mortals...

As Fisher and Hoekstra have pointed out, the phrase ἀνάγκη φύσεος closely recalls the term φύσις ἀναγκαία used by the Athenians at Melos.[54] This parallel highlights just how thin the line is that separates Euripidean gods and Thucydidean naturalism.[55] Hecuba is unsure whether to address Zeus as natural necessity or as the mind of humans, but either alternative would fit the kind of necessity that prevails in Thucydides' *History*. As we have seen, the noun φύσις and related vocabulary feature prominently as designations of necessity, and psychological forces are frequently its

---

[53] Swain 1994: 305. See also Wohl 2002: 189.   [54] Fisher and Hoekstra 2017: 377.
[55] Lefkowitz (2016: 35) thinks that lines from *Trojan Women* do not convey an impersonal notion of divinity that diverges from traditional religion: '[I]t is not the content of Hecuba's prayer that is new-fangled, but the way in which it is expressed.' However, Menelaus' perplexed reaction (noted by Lefkowitz) clearly shows that Hecuba's identification of Zeus with 'the necessity of nature' and 'the mind of mortals' is meant to be startling: 'What is this? How novel the prayers are that you offer to the gods!' (τί δ' ἔστιν; εὐχὰς ὡς ἐκαίνισας θεῶν, 889). Nothing here suggests that the novelty of Hecuba's address to Zeus concerns merely the form (and not also the substance) of her utterance.

transmitters. The close parallels point to a convergence between the tragic and the Thucydidean angle on the theme of necessity: while Euripides' gods manifest themselves in natural experiences that are readily accessible to the human mind (if also caused by superhuman intervention), the innate drives that one finds in Diodotus' speech are reminiscent of daemonic agents.[56] Thus, the apparent extremes marked by naturalistic empiricism and mythological thought point towards each other. In the final analysis, the parallels between Euripides and Thucydides raise the question of whether, in Thucydides' account, human nature and the forces rooted in it have become a substitute for the divine.

4.5 The Juxtaposition of τὸ θεῖον and τὸ ἀνθρώπειον in the Melian Dialogue

The Athenians at Melos make the claim that natural necessity inevitably impels 'the human' (τὸ ἀνθρώπειον) to seek domination. The term τὸ ἀνθρώπειον, in combination with the reference to the 'law that is and will be forever' (5.105.2), recalls the synonymous τὸ ἀνθρώπινον in the chapter on method (1.22.4). In the latter passage, 'the human' is Thucydides' term for the force responsible for the inevitable recurrence 'of things that have happened and will occur again in the same or a similar way' (1.22.4). This background suggests that τὸ ἀνθρώπειον in the Melian Dialogue plays a similar role: the substantivized neuter refers to the specific manifestation of necessity in the realm of human action, in addition to denoting the collective of all humans.

The Athenian ambassadors employ another substantivized neuter alongside τὸ ἀνθρώπειον: τὸ θεῖον (τό... θεῖον δόξῃ τὸ ἀνθρώπειόν τε σαφῶς διὰ παντὸς ὑπὸ φύσεως ἀναγκαίας, οὗ ἂν κρατῇ, ἄρχειν, 5.105.2). Its parallel position and morphological correspondence with τὸ ἀνθρώπειον suggest an analogy between the two terms.

---

[56] The scholarly literature is deeply divided about the issue of Euripides' stance regarding the personal divinities of Greek mythology. Some scholars have drawn the conclusion that the traditional Greek deities have a purely symbolic function: Verrall 1913: 276–7; Dodds 1929: 101; Lesky 1960: 133–4. Others have insisted on the ongoing importance of the traditional personal gods: Rivier 1975: 184; Lloyd-Jones 1983: 149–50; Kovacs 1987: 72–7; Lefkowitz 2016: 203–4. An agnostic position is adopted by Winnington-Ingram (1960: 188).

Τὸ θεῖον, unlike its counterpart, does not occur in other prominent places of the *History*; it clusters, however, in the Melian Dialogue, where it appears six times.[57] In the Melian Dialogue, the term is introduced into the debate by the Melians. They express the belief that their prospects in a military conflict with Athens are not as hopeless as they may seem. They base this estimate on the role of τύχη (εἰ μὴ [sc. ἡ τύχη] ἀπὸ τοῦ ἴσου ἔσται, 5.104). The Melians justify their belief as follows: 'with regard to fortune that comes from the divine, we trust that we will not have the worst of it because we, who are pious men, hold our ground against unjust men' (πιστεύομεν τῇ μὲν τύχῃ ἐκ τοῦ θείου μὴ ἐλασσώσεσθαι, ὅτι ὅσιοι πρὸς οὐ δικαίους ἱστάμεθα, 5.104). This trust in τύχη is quite odd and comes close to a contradiction in terms: after all, chance and unpredictability are constitutive aspects of τύχη.[58] The Melians want to set their hopes on that which by definition defies people's expectations. Be that as it may, the Melians believe that the divine has a decisive influence on the formation of events.

The Athenians give an extended response, which begins as follows: 'Well, as far as kindness in connection with the divine is concerned, we, too, do not believe that we will be lacking in it' (τῆς μὲν τοίνυν πρὸς τὸ θεῖον εὐμενείας οὐδ' ἡμεῖς οἰόμεθα λελείψεσθαι, 5.105.1). As Denniston writes, τοίνυν, when used (as it is here) in dialogue with a logical force, 'represents the answer as springing from the actual words, or general attitude, of the previous speaker'.[59] The particle suggests that the Athenians will only address the topic of τὸ θεῖον because the Melians have brought it up. As far as the Athenians are concerned, they would not have cared to introduce it into the debate. It is implied that the Athenians do not attach much importance to 'the divine' in connection with the issue at hand.

The Athenians claim that they do not 'deviate from people's usual observances regarding the divine' (τῆς ἀνθρωπείας τῶν μὲν ἐς τὸ θεῖον νομίσεως, 5.105.1). The passage juxtaposing τὸ θεῖον and τὸ ἀνθρώπειον follows (5.105.2), with the opening word γάρ signalling that the passage offers a justification for the preceding claim. The divine and the human are both subject to the same natural pattern of domination: it is therefore unreasonable to suppose that the divine will be offended by the

---

[57] This form occurs just once in the rest of Thucydides' work, in an aside about the Spartans advancing on the battlefield of Mantinea (5.70.1).
[58] On the connection of τύχη with the unforeseeable, see Müri 1968 [1947] 139–40; Stahl 2003 [1966]: 16; Schneider 1974: 95–7.
[59] GP 569.

Athenians' procedure against the Melians. As a result, the Athenians conclude: 'And so with regard to the divine, we are not afraid, based on what is probable, that we shall have the worst of it' (καὶ πρὸς μὲν τὸ θεῖον οὕτως ἐκ τοῦ εἰκότος οὐ φοβούμεθα ἐλασσώσεσθαι, 5.105.3).

The Athenians' wording shows that all their claims regarding the divine have an inherently lower epistemic status than their corresponding assertions apropos 'the human'. In addition to the implications of τοίνυν, two other phrases invite this conclusion. The Athenians base their view that 'the divine' seeks to dominate on 'reputation' or 'belief' (δόξῃ, 5.105.2), whereas they think that the same appetite for power 'clearly' (σαφῶς) marks 'the human'. An authorial statement of Thucydides in the chapter on method is instructive for gauging the implications of the Athenians' choice of words. Thucydides points out that his account of the War's ἔργα, for which he claims 'the utmost degree of precision' (ὅσον δυνατὸν ἀκριβείᾳ, 1.22.2), is not based on 'how they [sc. the events of the War] seemed to me' (οὐδ' ὡς ἐμοὶ ἐδόκει, 1.22.2). In this way, Thucydides opposes his extremely accurate report of events to mere δόξα, thus implying that δόξα and accuracy are generally at odds with each other. He goes on to explain that his main concern is to instruct those who strive for 'clarity' (τὸ σαφές, 1.22.4). Thucydides' use of δόξα and σαφής in the chapter on method shows that according to the Athenians at Melos ideas about 'the divine' have a fundamentally different epistemic status than claims about 'the human': the former are based on unsatisfactory guess-work (δόξα) whereas the latter are marked by the lucidity of reliable knowledge (σαφῶς). Their further claims apropos 'the divine' rest on 'what is probable' (τοῦ εἰκότος, 5.105.3), whereas in the preceding sentence they claim to 'know' (εἰδότες, 5.105.2) the regular behaviour of human beings. Taken together, these phrases suggest that claims regarding 'the divine' are inherently less certain than considerations about human affairs. This implies that views based on 'the divine' are of minor importance when it comes to far-reaching political decisions. With the divine thus safely neutralized, the relevant factor that determines what will happen is 'the human': this force, and not the divine, is ultimately responsible for how things turn out. Upon this note, the Athenians think the topic has been dealt with and turn to more pertinent matters.

Yet, to the Athenians' surprise, the divine comes back when the Melians disclose their decision. They refuse to submit to Athens 'trusting in fortune that comes from the divine and has always saved it [sc. the city of Melos] up to now' (τῇ... μέχρι τοῦδε σῳζούσῃ τύχῃ ἐκ τοῦ θείου αὐτὴν... πιστεύοντες, 5.112.2). The Melians remain convinced that 'the divine' takes precedence over other factors in directing events among humans. Their position, and their resulting decision, leave the Athenians flabbergasted.[60]

The downfall of Melos seems to vindicate the Athenians' reaction. Nonetheless, 'the divine' resembles a phantom haunting the Melian Dialogue due to the recurring references to this force. In this connection, it is curious that both the Athenians and the Melians exclusively draw on the impersonal τὸ θεῖον without ever using οἱ θεοί.[61] In other places where references to the superhuman sphere cluster, the speakers always resort to the personal form: for example, one finds several references to 'the gods' in the Plataeans' speech before the Spartan judges (3.58.1, 58.5, 59.2) and in Nicias' encouragement of the Athenians at Sicily (7.69.2, 77.2, 77.3, 77.4). In the Melian dialogue, the pervasive use of the neuter form draws attention to the parallelism with 'the human', which is likewise impersonal. There seems to be a specific motive behind such a usage in the Melian Dialogue. What could this be?

4.6 Neuter Phrases Referring to Divine Powers in Herodotus and Euripides

Abstract neuter phrases are generally much less distinctive of Herodotus' style than of Thucydides'. However, Herodotus quite frequently employs neuter abstract phrases when referring to the divine. The following list shows some examples: τὸ δαιμόνιον (2.120.5, 5.87.2, 6.84.1), τὸ χρεὸν γενέσθαι (7.17.2), τὰ δεῖ [sc. παθεῖν] (7.17.2), ὅ τι δεῖ γενέσθαι ἐκ τοῦ θεοῦ (9.16.4), and τὸ θεῖον (1.32.1, 3.40.2, 3.108.1–2).[62] Herodotus' use of these phrases does not imply his rejection of personal gods: his work also features many personal designations, both for specific gods or for divinity more generally.[63] The coexistence of impersonal and personal

---

[60] Bosworth draws attention to '[t]he exasperation of the Athenians' parting message' (1993: 42).
[61] Cf. Strauss (1974: 8): '[I]n the Melian dialogue "the gods" are not mentioned but only "the divine," which is more general and more vague than "the gods".'
[62] For further examples, see de Ste. Croix 1977 140–1 and 148 n. 16; Fornara 1983: 78 n. 36.
[63] For a list of various labels commonly used by Herodotus (including the personal designations θεοί and δαίμων), see Fornara 1983: 78 n. 36.

designations suggests that Herodotus registers a spectrum of possibilities. Pötscher associates each of the two different types of labels with a distinct notion: the impersonal phrases point to the operation of a divine force, devoid of personal features, that is deducible from the relentless inevitability manifested by the formation of events;[64] the personal designations, on the other hand, are suggestive of the anthropomorphic gods familiar from traditional Greek religion.[65] Herodotus' objective was not doctrinal definiteness. As de Ste. Croix observes, 'Herodotus' religious outlook is ... not at all consistent.'[66] Instead, he chooses one label or the other depending on what seems plausible in each given case: the impact of personal deities, or the influence of a less clearly defined impersonal power, best captured by abstract neuters.[67] The use of τὸ θεῖον in the Melian Dialogue belongs to the same register as the range of neuter phrases in Herodotus.

The coexistence of personal and impersonal labels notwithstanding, Fornara considers the neuter to be especially characteristic of Herodotus' outlook. As a result, he consistently uses τὸ θεῖον in his discussion of divinity in Herodotus, although this specific phrase only occurs three times in the *Histories* (1.32.1, 3.40.2, 3.108.1–2).[68] He proposes 'fate' or 'divine power' as suitable translations for τὸ θεῖον.[69] Myres renders it as 'Godhead', an 'impersonal and immemorial' power that differs from the personal gods of Olympian religion.[70] Fornara's consistent use of the

---

[64] Pötscher 1988 [1958]: 24–5.   [65] Pötscher 1988 [1958]: 25–6.
[66] De Ste. Croix 1977: 139.
[67] As Myres points out (1953: 51), '[t]he relation between actual Greek gods with personal names (θεοί), the nameless gods of the Pelasgians, and an impersonal and immemorial "Godhead" (τὸ θεῖον), was clarified by his [*sc.* Herodotus'] discovery in Egypt that the world was incomparably older than Greek belief conceived (ii.145) ... [T]here had been no god in human form in Egypt for 11,300 years. In comparison, the Greek "golden age" and the Hesiodic "birth of the gods" were but as yesterday.'
[68] Fornara 1990: 39.
[69] Fornara 1983: 78, and 1990: 39. In his earlier work, Fornara (1983: 78 n. 36) observes that '[i]t would be ingenuity misspent to seek for real distinctions within the broad range of his [*sc.* Herodotus'] terminology. He assigns control alternatively to "the divine" (*to theion*), "the gods" (*theoi*), "divine power" (*daimon*), "fate" (*moira*), "destiny" (*moros*), "the fated" ([*moira*] *pepromene*), and "divine fortune" (*theia tyche*).' Fornara may be right that it is hard to explain why Herodotus prefers one of these labels over its alternatives in each individual passage. Nonetheless, the sheer variety of impersonal phrases listed by Fornara points to Herodotus' quest to designate the divine in ways other than solely through the usage of the personal labels inherited by Olympian religion. Myres (1953: 50–1 [cited in n. 61]) provides a plausible explanation for the different connotations implied by impersonal versus personal designations of divine beings.
[70] Myres 1953: 50.

term τὸ θεῖον implies that according to Fornara this term is best suited to capture Herodotus' general conception of divinity.

Two of Herodotus' references to τὸ θεῖον occur at pivotal moments that belong to episodes endowed by Herodotus with an emblematic character. Each time, τὸ θεῖον is said to be responsible for a radical and imminent turning point in the life of a great individual (Croesus and Polycrates). Herodotus consider the fate of these two rulers paradigmatic: it encapsulates the notion that even the grandest of humans are inevitably exposed to forces beyond their control (on this aspect in Herodotus' treatment of Croesus, see Chapter 6, pp. 207–8, with nn. 17 and 18). Before Croesus and Polycrates are engulfed in the abyss, they are each warned by a wise man (Croesus by Solon and Polycrates by Amasis, the king of Egypt) about the dangers that originate from 'the divine'. Both passages feature references to τὸ θεῖον (1.32.1; 3.40.2). Moreover, as scholars have pointed out, in each passage the divine is said to be φθονερόν (i.e. predisposed towards ill-will), and both speakers use the verb ἐπίσταμαι to state that they know this much about the divine: its tendency towards ill-will.[71]

According to Hellmann, τὸ θεῖον stands for 'a featureless neuter, an efficacious power, which manifests itself in the ineluctable concatenation of events'.[72] Fornara parses τὸ θεῖον along similar lines: the term represents 'the overriding nature of fate, a necessity imposed from without that constrains individuals and states to act according to its own laws and plan'.[73] Finally, de Ste. Croix has stressed that, in Herodotus' view, 'man is dominated by powers and circumstances beyond his control', which is an aspect of his thought 'best described by the word Fate. Rarely is there any suggestion (as in 9.16.4) that what happens has been planned by a god; we commonly hear only of *moira, tisis, to peprōmenon, to mellon genesthai*, or we find some such verb as *chrēn* or *dein*'.[74] In sum, the analyses of these scholars show that neuter phrases based on the model of τὸ θεῖον suggest the operation of a divine force that lacks the personalizing features of the Olympian gods. This power can be described by the term 'fate' because it foreordains the course of a person's

---

[71] Pötscher 1988 [1958]: 21; Fornara 1990: 40; Shapiro 1996: 354 n. 32; Harrison 2000: 45–46.
[72] Hellmann 1934: 118 ('ein gestaltloses Neutrum, ein Wirkendes, das sich in der unausweichlichen Aufeinanderfolge der Geschehnisse manifestiert').
[73] Fornara 1990: 45.   [74] De Ste. Croix 1977: 140–1.

life or a city's fortunes. It is marked by much greater aloofness and elusiveness than the personalized gods of Olympian religion. Due to its lack of personal features, it seems unlikely that human beings can appeal to it via sacrifices and prayers, or that they can hope to receive messages from it through oracles. Communication with an impersonal power seems like a contradiction in terms.[75]

In referring to the divine, the Melians introduce the same term that Solon and Amasis use in Herodotus: τὸ θεῖον. In the Melians' view, divinity will be ultimately responsible for the outcome of the affair facing them. When the Athenians juxtapose 'the divine' with 'the human' in a parallel construction, the connotations of the former also affect the latter. In the Melian Dialogue, the term 'the human' reflects the impersonal necessity that governs affairs among mortals, just as the neuter singular in Herodotus is a way of alluding to divine fate.

In Euripides' plays, neuter phrases are also used as designations of the divine sphere. To begin with, it is worth noting that Euripides, unlike Aeschylus and Sophocles, repeatedly uses the neuter singular phrases τὸ θεῖον and τὸ δαιμόνιον to capture divinity. Τὸ θεῖον is found ten times in the surviving plays and fragments of Euripides.[76] By contrast, Sophocles never uses this phrase; Aeschylus has two instances (*Ag.* 1084; *Ch.* 957), but the phrase from the *Agamemnon* ought to be discounted because τὸ θεῖον does not signify 'divinity' in this passage but merely refers to Cassandra's divine gift of prophecy.[77] Τὸ δαιμόνιον occurs three times in Euripides, but never in Aeschylus and Sophocles.[78]

---

[75] This circumstance does not flatly delegitimize oracles. The example of Croesus shows that it is possible for mortals to communicate with personal gods (in this case Apollo) through oracles, and that these gods have an impact on how events play out (see Chapter 7, pp. 242–3). That said, the same story also shows that Croesus does not have any access to 'the Fates' (1.91.2). These elusive powers, apparently set above anthropomorphic gods, have settled the decisive issue of Croesus' downfall (see Chapter 7, pp. 243–4). Croesus has no means of communicating with the Fates directly, but Apollo seems to be able to negotiate with them. Otherwise, it is hard to see how to make sense of his partially successful intercession on Croesus' behalf (1.91.2–3).

[76] Eur. *Supp.* 159; *IT* 911; *Or.* 267; *Or.* 420; *IA* 394a; *Andr.* 1227; *TrGF* 5.62.1; *TrGF* 5.150.2; *TrGF* 5.491.5; *TrGF* 5.584.2. I have not counted *Rh.* 65 (given the unlikelihood of Euripides' authorship) and a fragment whose attribution to Euripides is disputed (*TrGF* 2.623.2 = 5.1130 N.²). Moreover, *Cyc.* 411 has not been included in the list because the phrase ἐσῆλθέ μοί τι θεῖον is best rendered as 'some divinely inspired thought occurred to me'.

[77] See Fraenkel 1950, on 1084; Denniston and Page 1957, ad loc.

[78] Eur. *Ph.* 352; *Ba.* 894; *TrGF* 5.152.1.

Hippolytus again provides a good starting point for an analysis of the specific implications of Euripides' neuter phrases. When Phaedra reveals to the Nurse after much back and forth that she is in love with Hippolytus, the Nurse makes a striking observation about Aphrodite: 'Cypris is not after all a god, but whatever else turns out to be even mightier than a god, she who has destroyed my mistress here, me, and the house' (Κύπρις οὐκ ἄρ' ἦν θεός, / ἀλλ' εἴ τι μεῖζον ἄλλο γίγνεται θεοῦ, / ἣ τήνδε κἀμὲ καὶ δόμους ἀπώλεσεν, 359-61). The Nurse captures Aphrodite's true nature with the substantivized neuter phrase: εἴ τι μεῖζον ἄλλο γίγνεται. The contrast between the two terms θεός and 'whatever else is mightier' highlights the opposition between a personal and an impersonal power: the latter reflects Aphrodite's true nature. In the quoted lines, Dodds sees the emergence of 'a deeper conception of Kypris and Artemis as eternal cosmic powers': they are equated with 'a force unthinking, unpitying, but divine'.[79] Without denying the personal dimension of Aphrodite and Artemis, Bernard Knox also acknowledges that there is another, equally important side to them: '[T]hey are also impersonal, incompatible forces of nature.'[80] It is interesting that the Nurse, when expressing this depersonalizing notion of divinity, takes recourse to the type of nominalized neuter phrase frequently found in discussions of necessity in Thucydides.

Phaedra gives a long speech in which she declares her resolution to die. In the course of her response, the Nurse remarks: 'For Kypris is something that cannot be borne when she comes in full stream' (Κύπρις γὰρ οὐ φορητὸν ἦν πολλὴ ῥυῇ, 443).[81] This phrase combines a personal subject with a neuter predicate. Barrett notes that, in phrases of this kind, the subject 'normally denotes not an individual but a type... but Κύπρις here is no real individual but merely a name for sexual desire'.[82] While it is debatable whether the play in fact represents Aphrodite in exclusively

---

[79] Dodds 1929: 102.   [80] Knox 1979 [1952]: 226.
[81] Notice that φορητόν is a reading transmitted by Stobaeus whereas the manuscripts have the feminine φορητός. Barrett argues persuasively that the neuter is more likely to be correct: the corruption from neuter to feminine is easier to explain than the reverse (Barrett 1964, on 443-6).
[82] Barrett 1964, on 443-6.

naturalistic terms, Barrett's main point is crucial: the combination of a personal subject with a neuter predicate aligns Aphrodite with a general force manifesting itself as sexual passion. Thus, both cited passages show that neuter phrases highlight an impersonal element in the divine powers that govern the lives of mortals.

Euripides' *Helen* features another remarkable instance of impersonal language capturing the sudden emergence of the divine in the world of human action. In remote Egypt, Helen happens, unwittingly, to cross paths with her husband Menelaus, who has suffered shipwreck on his return journey from Troy. The coincidence is too incredible to be innocuous. When it dawns on Helen who the stranger might be, she says in amazement: 'Oh gods! For to recognize one's friends is also a god' (ὦ θεοί· θεὸς γὰρ καὶ τὸ γιγνώσκειν φίλους, 560). The phrasing is pointedly paradoxical: Helen does not describe the incredible coincidence as 'divine' or 'coming from a god'; instead, the staggeringly improbable event itself is a god. The articular infinitive pairs divine powers with the pivotal, amazing event that exceeds the bounds of human comprehension. The word θεός undergoes a process of depersonalization due to its identification with the articular infinitive: the neuter subject identifies godhead with the manifestation of an impersonal, superhuman element that percolates through the formation of events.

Another impersonal designation used by Euripides for the divine is found in the phrases τὰ θεῶν and τὰ τῶν θεῶν. Heitsch has pointed out that these appellations are hardly in use before Euripides, but that they become quite common in his works from the late 420s onwards.[83] According to Smyth, the genitive with the neuter article (whether singular or plural) denotes 'affairs, conditions, power, and the like'. Thus, the phrases noted by Heitsch suggest 'powers that are of the gods' or 'powers resting with gods'.[84]

---

[83] Heitsch (1967: 24): 'Die neutral-unbestimmte Wendung, die vor Euripides so gut wie nicht zu belegen ist, wird von ihm vom Ende der zwanziger Jahre an häufig und in den verschiedensten Schattierungen – Gaben, Wirken, Satzung, Anspruch, Recht, Wille, Macht und Wesen der Götter – verwendet.'

[84] It is worth noting the subtle difference between the phrase τὰ τῶν θεῶν and its variant τὰ θεῶν. When the noun θεοί is used with the article, it denotes 'the gods' understood as a distinct group of divine beings (e.g. the Olympians). By contrast, when used without the article, the term

Let us consider the implications of this phrase in two passages from the prologue of *Iphigenia at Aulis*.

Owing to the doom that hangs over his house, Agamemnon woefully ponders the perennial vulnerability of all humans, but especially the highborn, when faced with the gods' fearsome power: 'At one time, the forces that rest with gods overthrow a life, when they are not favourable; at another, the varied opinions of people, ever hard to please, destroy it' (τοτὲ μὲν τὰ θεῶν οὐκ ὀρθωθέντ' / ἀνέτρεψε βίον, τοτὲ δ' ἀνθρώπων / γνῶμαι πολλαὶ / καὶ δυσάρεστοι διέκναισαν, 24–7). The juxtaposition between τὰ θεῶν and ἀνθρώπων γνῶμαι gives a hint as to how one is to interpret the neuter phrase. The volatile opinions of the multitude are represented as a malignant force (δυσάρεστοι), threatening to ruin men like Agamemnon, the holders of high offices.[85] It would have been easy to use a subject referring to a human collective in this passage, such as 'the multitude'. Instead, Euripides chooses the abstract noun γνῶμαι, thus highlighting a non-personal force that affects collectives. Τὰ θεῶν ('things that rest with gods'), the term that captures the other force threatening human existence, also belongs to the depersonalizing register, an impression reinforced by the parallelism with ἀνθρώπων γνῶμαι. A personal subject (i.e. 'gods') would have been the obvious choice in combination with a verb that denotes agency (e.g. 'gods like to overthrow a life'). Instead, the phrase chosen by Euripides evokes forces that belong to the sphere of the gods, but which are not necessarily identical with them.[86]

In his response, Agamemnon's old servant picks up his master's neuter phrase. He tells Agamemnon that he, the son of Atreus, was not born under a lucky star: 'It is necessary that you experience joy and pain: for you are by nature a mortal. And even if you do not consent, the powers that reside with gods shall be the ones willing it so' (δεῖ δέ σε

---

suggests 'gods' in a more general, less clearly defined sense. The contrast between indefinite θεοί and definite οἱ θεοί is nicely illustrated by a passage from Xenophon, which Kühner-Gerth quote to illustrate the semantic difference between nouns with and without the article (K-G i. 589): '[Socrates], who, far from not believing in gods, evidently worshipped the gods [i.e. those recognized by the city]' (ὃς [sc. Σωκράτης] ἀντὶ μὲν τοῦ μὴ νομίζειν θεούς... φανερὸς ἦν θεραπεύων τοὺς θεούς, *Mem.* 1.2.64).

[85] As Stockert notes (1992: ii, ad loc.), διακναίω literally means 'break up into small pieces', and it is frequently used to express annihilation, both in a physical and a psychological sense.

[86] Cf. Heitsch (1967: 24): 'Was zunächst das Sprachliche angeht, so entzieht sich τὰ θεῶν durchaus einer genaueren Fassung.'

χαίρειν / καὶ λυπεῖσθαι· θνητὸς γὰρ ἔφυς· / κἂν μὴ σὺ θέλῃς, τὰ θεῶν οὕτω / βουλόμεν' ἔσται, 30–4). The impersonal verb δεῖ highlights the necessity weighing on earthly existence and imposed by the divine. Human beings are inevitably subject to this necessity. The power responsible is again τὰ θεῶν: 'the powers that reside with gods'.

In an odd construction, Euripides combines the participle βουλόμεν' ('willing') with the neuter subject.[87] An impersonal being that wills comes close to a contradiction in terms. A further complication arises from Euripides' use of a periphrastic construction (the predicative participle βουλόμεν[α] with ἔσται) instead of the regular future βουλήσεται. According to Kühner-Gerth, the relevant type of periphrasis (combining a participle with a form of εἰμί) enables a speaker to give greater independence and emphasis to the state of affairs expressed by the verb. As Kühner-Gerth observe, the construction is especially common 'when the participle predicates, in the manner of an adjective, a characteristic token, a permanent feature, or an enduring condition of the subject'.[88] Thus, τὰ θεῶν οὕτω βουλόμεν' ἔσται suggests something along the lines of 'the powers that reside with gods will be characterized by such intentions' or 'will evince such intentions'. The regular verb βουλήσεται would suggest a personal agent's act of willing at a particular moment. By contrast, the periphrastic construction expresses a permanent feature: the phrasing does not an act of volition, but a state. Impersonal, non-sentient powers are responsible for the inevitability imposing itself on Agamemnon. In both passages from *Iphigenia at Aulis*, the phrase τὰ θεῶν captures what Heitsch calls either 'the impact' ('Wirken'), 'the will' ('Wille'), or 'the power' ('Macht') of the divine on

---

[87] Commentators disagree about the right way to construe τὰ θεῶν οὕτω βουλόμεν' ἔσται. There are two options. The first is to take τὰ θεῶν βουλόμεν' as a substantivized participle and to render the passage as 'the will of heaven will be thus'. England (1891, ad loc.) and Weil (1930, ad loc.) opt for this interpretation. The other option, which Stockert (1992: ii, on 33) seems to endorse, is to construe βουλόμεν' with ἔσται as a periphrastic future roughly equivalent to βουλήσεται, which produces the following interpretation: 'The forces that reside with the gods will evince such intentions.' Hartung sees insurmountable difficulties with either solution and considers the text corrupt (1852: 186–7). The specific context provides, I think, considerable support for the solution involving the periphrastic future. We have had a verb meaning 'to wish' in the foregoing protasis (κἂν μὴ σὺ θέλῃς). This gives a strong hint that βουλόμεν' in the apodosis also belongs to the verb. In this way, the verbs of both protasis and apodosis express volition, an arrangement that produces semantic symmetry, with the subjects σύ and τὰ θεῶν juxtaposed in a neat antithesis: 'even if you do not wish it, heaven does.'

[88] On this periphrastic construction, see K-G i. 39 [my translation].

human affairs.[89] Nilsson proposes to render the phrase τὰ τῶν θεῶν as 'fortunes' ('die Geschicke').[90] Combining a neuter article and a personal noun, the phrase τὰ θεῶν (or τὰ τῶν θεῶν) is an attempt to unify two contradictory notions: the idea of impersonal powers (fates or fortunes) affecting events, and that of (at least vaguely experienced) personal gods. This combination of conflicting notions reflects the basic tension between rationalism and myth that Cornford highlighted as the distinctive hallmark of Euripides' tragic art.[91]

Another interesting passage, which presents a whole series of impersonal references to the divine, is found in the antistrophe of the third stasimon of Euripides' *Bacchae*. The Chorus, heartened by the recent turn of events, take delight in the expectation that the enemies of Dionysus will be hunted down at long last. They observe that divinity moves slowly, but that its power is irresistible. The Chorus conclude the antistrophe as follows (893–6):

κούφα γὰρ δαπάνα νομί-	For it costs little to believe
ζειν ἰσχὺν τόδ' ἔχειν,	that *this* has strength:
ὅτι ποτ' ἄρα τὸ δαιμόνιον,	whatever it is—the divine:
τό τ' ἐν χρόνῳ μακρῷ νόμιμον	<a power identical with> that
ἀεὶ φύσει τε πεφυκός.	which has always been lawful
	custom in the long-lasting course
	time and grounded in nature.

This passage features three nominalized neuter forms: τὸ δαιμόνιον ('the divine'), τὸ ... νόμιμον ('lawful custom'), and [τὸ] φύσει ... πεφυκός ('that which has been ... grounded in nature'). Since just one article agrees with the last two items, they are fused into a single notion: 'that which is both

---

[89] Heitsch 1967: 24. [90] Nilsson 1967: i. 774.
[91] According to Cornford (1907: 243), the tension crystallizes in the representation of Aphrodite in the *Hippolytus*: 'A brooding power, relentless, inscrutable, waits and watches and smites. There she stands, all through the action, the white, implacable Aphrodite. Is she no more than a marble image, the work of men's hands? Is there no significance in that secret smile, no force behind the beautiful mask, no will looking out of the fixed, watching eyes? And yet, how can there be?...It must be that poetry has forced on reason some strange compromise. We cannot detect the formula of that agreement; but we know that somehow a compact has been made.'

customary and natural' as opposed to '(a) that which is customary and (b) that which is natural'.[92] The relationship between this combined principle of custom and nature and the third neuter (i.e. τὸ δαιμόνιον) is harder to settle. The phrasing of the passage admits of two interpretations: the Chorus either list two separate items (i.e. [a] the divine and [b] the aggregate of custom and nature) or they refer to just one principle (i.e. the divine—which is identical with the aggregate of custom and nature).[93] The translation of the passage given above is based on the second interpretation. In what follows, I will explain why I consider this option more plausible.[94]

The train of thought pursued by the Chorus throughout the antistrophe (882–96) suggests that they are concerned with one basic principle: the divine. The Chorus begin the antistrophe by foregrounding 'divine strength' (τὸ θεῖον / σθένος, 883–4), a force that they say can be relied upon (πιστόν ⟨τι⟩, 883). They proceed to develop the idea that divine forces are slow to move when faced with sacrilege, but that they eventually punish those who have committed a crime. Throughout the antistrophe, the Chorus place the emphasis squarely on the supreme power of divinity.[95]

---

[92] See Rijksbaron 1991: 115–16.

[93] If there are two factors, τε in line 895 provides a connection with what precedes: it forges a link between (a) the divine and (b) the joint force of custom and nature, thus implying that (a) and (b) are separate factors. Rijksbaron (1991: 114–15) follows Roux (1972: ii, on 893–6) in adopting this interpretation. If, by contrast, the passage refers to just one principle, lines 895–6 are appositional, defining 'the divine' more closely. In this case, τε in line 895 does not refer back but looks ahead to the second τε in line 896, thus coordinating τό ... ἐν χρόνῳ μακρῷ νόμιμον ἀεί with [τό] ... φύσει ... πεφυκός. Grégoire's translation of the passage shows that he takes this view of the role of τε (1961: 278; Budé ed.).

[94] Note, however, that the interpretation that follows (viz. that the Chorus identify τὸ δαιμόνιον with the aggregate of custom and nature) does not depend on the view that lines 895-6 stand in apposition. As Ruijgh (1971: 170-1) points out, τε usually coordinates 'deux faits entre lesquels il existe un lien particulièrement stable: les deux faits coïncident dans le temps et sont souvent les deux facettes d'un seul procès, ou le second fait est déjà impliqué dans le premier'. Let us assume for the sake of argument that τε in 895 connects the joint force of custom and nature (895-6) with τὸ δαιμόνιον (894). In that case, one will still conclude in light of Ruijgh's analysis that the coordinated terms 'conceptually belong together' (Rijksbaron 1991: 115).

[95] The following lines might be considered an exception to this tendency: 'For one must never place oneself above the laws in one's thinking and practices' (οὐ / γὰρ κρεῖσσόν ποτε τῶν νόμων / γιγνώσκειν χρὴ καὶ μελετᾶν, 890-2). If one approaches these lines in isolation from their immediate context, one might conclude that the Chorus regard 'the laws' as an authority in and of itself, thus treating them as a power independent of the gods. The context, however, shows that divine forces guarantee the inviolability of the laws. The preceding sentence is: 'They [sc. gods] hunt down the impious man' (θηρῶσιν τὸν ἄσεπτον, 890). According to Bruhn (1891, on 891), the connection with γάρ must be taken to mean: 'They [i.e. gods] are right to punish

Given this trajectory, it would be inappropriate if, at the antistrophe's culminating moment, they suddenly were to champion two principles (viz. 'the divine' and 'that which is lawful and natural'). Moreover, the term ἰσχύς, which appears in the Chorus' summons to acknowledge that '*this* has strength' (ἰσχὺν τόδ' ἔχειν, 893), recalls the synonymous term σθένος from the beginning of the antistrophe. Since in the earlier passage σθένος is a trait of the divine alone, it would be odd if at the antistrophe's conclusion the divine had to share ἰσχύς with the double principle of custom and nature. In Section 4.4 (see p. 136), we discussed a passage from Euripides' *Trojan Women*, in which Hecuba tentatively identifies Zeus with 'the necessity of nature' (ἀνάγκη φύσεος, 886). This passage clearly shows that the identification of divinity with nature was a thought that occupied Euripides. It stands to reason that the Chorus of the *Bacchae* champion a similar idea. Thus, the dual force named τό τ[ε]...νόμιμον...φύσει τε πεφυκός is ultimately a manifestations of the third neuter abstract: τὸ δαιμόνιον.[96]

Neuter phrases begin to abound in the third stasimon just as the Chorus wonder about the right way to address divinity. As Dodds

---

wrongdoers: for (one must never defy the laws...)'. Thus, respect for the laws is guaranteed by the threat that divine powers will seek out the transgressor. Note that the subject of θηρῶσιν must be supplied from the phrase τὰ θεῶν in the foregoing sentence (886), where it functions as object. The plural form of θηρῶσιν suggests that θεοί (as opposed to τὰ θεῶν) should be understood as subject, but this remains implicit. Apart from this implied subject, the antistrophe of the third stasimon does not feature any reference to personal gods.

[96] Two other considerations support this conclusion. (1) As we saw, two factors that are starkly antithetical (viz. νόμος and φύσις) are merged in this passage. This raises the question as to why Euripides chooses a construction that suggests this fusion, thus presenting an idea that was far from self-evident in the fifth century (see Heinimann 1945: 166–7, and Dodds 1960, on 895–6). Let us assume the alternative interpretation for a moment, i.e. the view that the Chorus champion two distinct principles: (a) the divine and (b) the aggregate of νόμος and φύσις. Based on this interpretation, it is hard to see what Euripides gains by amalgamating the realms of customary law and nature. The Chorus might just as well enumerate three principles. If, however, the other interpretation is correct (namely that the phrase τό τ[ε]...νόμιμον... φύσει τε πεφυκός functions as an apposition modifying τὸ δαιμόνιον), it is possible to provide an explanation for the fusion of νόμος and φύσις: the integration of these principles, in defiance of their antithetical status, expresses the idea that the various forces constraining human existence are based on a single principle. If identification goes as far as overcoming the antithesis between νόμος and φύσις, the principle championed by the Chorus must be characterized by supreme universality. A name for this highest overarching principle is not far to seek: the divine. (2) The demonstrative pronoun τόδ' in the phrase '*this* has strength' clearly suggests that the Chorus will present just one supremely powerful principle instead of two. It should be noted, however, that the weight of this argument is limited because τόδ' is an emendation of τ' transmitted by the manuscript tradition. Emendation is necessary because, as transmitted, the text is unmetrical.

notes, the indeterminate phrase ὅτι ποτ' ἄρα τὸ δαιμόνιον belongs to the register of traditional religious language: 'The indeterminate formulation is an expression of religious humility in face of the unknowable'.[97] The parallels quoted by Dodds show that personal variants of this phrase were not uncommon.[98] In the *Bacchae*, however, the Chorus use a neuter phrase, thus aligning divinity with an impersonal force: τὸ δαιμόνιον. Dodds suitably renders this phrase as 'the unknown daemonic'.[99] What seems relatively certain about this mysterious power is that it finds expression in the joint constraint exerted by two general forces that are accessible to experience: lawful custom and nature. By manifesting itself in these spheres, the divine imposes limits on what human beings can do. The Chorus use the same kind of neuter phrasing with regard to both 'the divine' and the aggregate of νόμος and φύσις. This continuity suggests an analogy between 'the unknown daemonic' and empirically observable foundations of human existence. The impersonal register is also sustained by the Chorus' aforementioned phrase *'this* has strength' (ἰσχὺν τόδ' ἔχειν). The general emphasis on neuter forms reinforces the implications of τὸ δαιμόνιον: divinity is wrapped in mystery, but it seems at least possible to assert that it is akin to the insentient, non-personal factors represented by law and nature.

Grégoire draws attention to further neuter phrases that Euripides uses to capture the divine in the *Bacchae*.[100] Thus, in the fourth stasimon, the Chorus refer to divinity by the term 'that which is invincible' (τἀνίκατον, 1001). This characterization of the divine can be added to the aforementioned series of phrases that involve forms of νικάω and its derivatives (see the present Chapter, p. 134). As pointed out above, in the tragedians these phrases designate the insurmountable force of the divine, and in Thucydides the necessity of 'the three greatest things' (discussed by the Athenians at Sparta). Another neuter phrase captures the divine in the scene of Pentheus' encounter with Cadmus and Teiresias dressed in Dionysiac garb. Teiresias warns Pentheus to beware of the might that belongs to divinity: 'For the foremost powers among

---

[97] Dodds 1960, on 893–4.
[98] Ζεύς, ὅστις ποτ' ἐστίν (Aesch. *Ag.* 160); ὅστις ποτ' εἰ σύ, δυστόπαστος εἰδέναι, / Ζεύς... (Eur. *Tr.* 885–6); Ζεὺς δ', ὅστις ὁ Ζεύς,... (Eur. *HF* 1263).
[99] Dodds 1960: 183.   [100] Grégoire 1961: 278 n. 1 (Budé ed).

humans are two in number, my son' (δύο γάρ, ὦ νεανία, / τὰ πρῶτ' ἐν ἀνθρώποισι, 274-5). As will become clear in a moment, the neuter form τὰ πρῶτα refers to Demeter and Dionysus. Teiresias goes on to suggest that Demeter may ultimately be identifiable with a natural element: 'The goddess Demeter—she is the earth, but call her by which of these two names you like' (Δημήτηρ θεά - / γῆ δ' ἐστίν, ὄνομα δ' ὁπότερον βούλῃ κάλει, 275-6). This notion sorts well with Dodds's interpretation of the role of Demeter and Dionysus in Teiresias' account: 'What underlies this passage is... the traditional opposition of the Dry and the Wet (τὸ ξηρόν and τὸ ὑγρόν) as elements of the world's body and of man's body, which goes back to Ionian thought.'[101] Thus, the phrase τὰ πρῶτα provides a further example of neuter phrases that highlight an impersonal element in divinity, an aspect insufficiently captured by the anthropomorphic language of traditional Greek religion.

One final passage from the *Bacchae* deserves closer attention. It belongs to the Chorus' closing statement at the end of the play (1388-9):[102]

πολλαὶ μορφαὶ τῶν δαιμονίων,
πολλὰ δ' ἀέλπτως κραίνουσι θεοί...

There are many shapes of things divine,
and many things gods accomplish against all expectation...

It is noticeable that Chorus do not say 'the gods take many shapes'. The neuter plural 'things divine' evokes an impersonal element. As we know from the third stasimon of the *Bacchae*, the realms of nature and law represent two of the shapes that 'things divine' may assume. The god Dionysus, who visits Greece in anthropomorphic shape (*Ba.* 4), is yet a third. The passage also provides evidence for the direct juxtaposition of personal and impersonal designations of divinity. After the reference to 'things divine', the Chorus choose the personal label θεοί in the next line.

---

[101] Dodds 1960, on 274-85.
[102] Note that these lines (together with the three that follow) also occur at the close of four other Euripidean plays: *Alcestis, Andromache, Helen,* and *Medea* (the latter with minor variations). See Dodds 1960, on 1388-92.

This juxtaposition illustrates Euripides' willingness to allow for the coexistence of these two contrasting conceptions of divinity.[103]

The bold identification of νόμος and φύσις found in the third stasimon of the *Bacchae* recurs in a specific Thucydidean passage. The Athenian ambassadors at Melos combine the terms φύσις and νόμος when they advance the thesis that the quest for power is a universal condition. They claim that the craving for power is induced 'by the compulsory influence of nature' (ὑπὸ φύσεως ἀναγκαίας), and they identify this necessity with a 'law... [that] will be in existence forever' (τὸν νόμον... ἐσόμενον ἐς αἰεί, 5.105.2). The phrasing of the passage from the Melian Dialogue is reminiscent of the wording found in the *Bacchae* in several respects: first, the antithetical terms φύσις and νόμος (or τὸ νόμιμον and [τὸ] φύσει πεφυκός) are combined and refer to a single fact, namely the inescapable necessity that weighs upon human existence; secondly, 'the law' mentioned in both passages is characterized by eternal validity (ἐν χρόνῳ μακρῷ... / ἀεί, *Ba.* 895–6 ~ ἐς αἰεί, Th. 5.105.2); third, both passages combine this emphasis on 'law' and 'nature' with impersonal terminology used to capture 'the divine' (τὸ δαιμόνιον, *Ba.* 894 ~ τὸ θεῖον [twice], Th. 5.105.2–3).

Another parallel between Euripides' impersonal labels of the divine and Thucydides' emphasis on natural necessity is worth noting. The aforementioned statement of the old servant in lines 30–4 from *Iphigenia at Aulis* features a verbal form related to φύσις (θνητὸς γὰρ ἔφυς, 31), and a substantivized neuter subject that captures the forces ultimately in charge of events (τὰ θεῶν οὕτω / βουλόμεν' ἔσται, 33–4). As pointed out in Section 4.1, Thucydides uses similar intransitive active forms of φύομαι to express the natural necessity that constrains human

---

[103] It is noticeable that the different constructions (impersonal vs. personal) align with different vocabulary in this passage: Euripides uses the term δαιμόνιον (i.e. an adjective derived from the noun δαίμων) to capture the impersonal element, but the word θεός for the personal variant. Schadewaldt (1959: 316) notes that in Homer δαίμων and θεός do not capture different classes of gods, but that they tend to imply different ways in which the divine manifests itself: δαίμων and related terms suggest the mysterious involvement of a superhuman force that lacks clearly defined contours, whereas θεός and its derivatives evoke the presence of a distinct personal deity. The juxtaposition of τὰ δαιμόνια and θεοί in the concluding statement of the *Bacchae* suggests that the impersonal notion of divinity corresponds to the daemonic manifestation of the divine, and that the image of personal gods tallies with the more concrete form of appearance that the word θεός tends to convey. It should be noted, however, that Euripides is not consistent in using this terminology.

action. What is more, some of these passages feature neuter phrases that capture the forces in which necessity manifests itself (2.64.3; 3.39.5; 4.61.5—on the last two passages, see the present Chapter, pp. 110–5). If the reference to divinity were removed from the passage in *Iphigenia at Aulis*, one would be left with the Thucydidean picture.

It is important to remember that Euripides, just like Herodotus, uses impersonal phrases alongside personal designations of the gods.[104] The gods of Olympian religion have not disappeared from the works of these two authors. At the same time, both explore the possibility that divinity may not be quite as anthropomorphic as traditional Greek religion assumes. It seems no coincidence that Euripides, unlike the other two tragedians, frequently uses impersonal phrases (e.g. τὸ θεῖον, τὸ δαιμόνιον, τὰ θεῶν, and τὰ τῶν θεῶν) as names for the divine. It is plausible to draw a connection between this tendency and the equally frequent habit of Euripidean characters or Choruses to engage in sceptical speculation about the true nature of divinity. Time and again, these ruminations lead to the claim that divinity may be identifiable with an impersonal force—be it sexual desire, raging passion, one of the cosmic elements, nature as such, 'mind', νόμος, or an unexpected turnaround in the sequence of events.

As we saw, it is possible to find significant parallels in terms of both style and content between Euripides and Thucydides. In particular, speculation about the impersonal side of divinity in Euripides has much in common with the analysis of natural necessity in Thucydides. Euripides' tentative identification of the divine with nature and other impersonal forces is reminiscent of the conviction, which is repeatedly expressed in Thucydides' *History*, that φύσις represents a basic necessity, a general force that conditions people's choices. These parallels suggest that it is not a huge step from Euripides' depersonalizing notion of divinity to the kind of natural necessity that emerges from the work of Thucydides.

In Thucydides, the speakers in the Melian Dialogue are exceptional in that they, unlike many others, use the impersonal register not just to refer

---

[104] On the ongoing importance of the traditional Olympian gods for Euripidean drama, see Lefkowitz 2016: 193.

to natural forces but also to capture divinity. The references to 'the divine' in the Melian Dialogue subtly evoke the power that determines affairs in the view of Greek thinkers other than Thucydides. Herodotus and Euripides are each a case in point. The Melians set their hopes on 'the divine' because they believe it will protect the just. This position, however, has little support in the picture that emerges from the works of Herodotus and Euripides: impersonal neuter designations of the divine typically suggest a fateful necessity in these authors, a relentless power devoid of feeling that crushes human aspirations.[105]

4.7 Conclusion

Over the course of this chapter, several parallels have emerged between the depiction of 'the human' in Thucydides and the representation of divine forces in other Greek authors. These similarities support the interpretation that in Thucydides 'the human' takes the place of 'the divine' as the power that presides over people's lives and actions. Thucydidean speakers and Thucydides himself frequently use substantivized neuter forms to designate this force. These phrases recall various impersonal designations of divine beings that one finds in Herodotus and Euripides. Similar neuter forms also occur in the Hippocratic Corpus (see the present Chapter, p. 115). The parallels with both the Hippocratic Corpus and phrases evoking divine powers in Herodotus and Euripides show that Thucydidean neuter phrases draw two different perspectives together: the Hippocratic analysis of physiological dispositions and the view that divinely ordained fatalism rules the cosmos. As a result, the neuter phrases simultaneously imply that necessity comes in the guise of impersonal naturalism, and that it wields the kind of power that Greek thinkers tend to ascribe to the divine. Euripides provides direct precedent for this approach.

---

[105] This is not to deny that one also finds evidence for a different approach to the problem of divinity in Herodotus, a line of reasoning that tries to find justice in divine interventions. Compare Fornara: '*To theion* could not brook unchanging individual felicity; it was also an avenging power that secured retribution for unjust acts. Such retribution, apparently, was part of the cosmic design, so that justice and equity were always in process of realization' (1990: 45). For various attempts at balancing these two explanatory models, see Lloyd-Jones 1983: 63 and 68–9; de Ste. Croix 1977: 139–41; Harrison 2000: 110–15; Mikalson 2003: 150–2.

The Athenian ambassadors at Melos attach minor importance at best to claims regarding 'the divine'. They emphasize the necessity that rests on φύσις and τὸ ἀνθρώπειον and imply that these forces, not the divine, are the true bedrock of necessity. The Athenians at Melos, just as several other speakers before them, adopt a confident tone when giving their opinion on 'the human'. In this way, they convey the impression that insight into the forces that govern action protects them against the danger of falling victim to them. Their own language, however, should give them pause: the analogies between the phrases τὸ ἀνθρώπειον and τὸ θεῖον imply that these forces have some defining features in common. What if the new ruler of worldly things, named 'the human', is just as hard to manage as 'the divine' (judging by the picture that emerges about 'the divine' in Herodotus and Euripides)? Does the depersonalizing neuter imply that 'the human', just as much as 'the divine', is marked by intractability, a basic imperviousness to people's plans and aspirations?

The confidence of the Athenian ambassadors that their insight into 'the human' furnishes them with the ability to steer events is first undermined when they fail to convince the Melians of what they consider the right course of action. In due course, further events undercut the notion that the dangers inherent in 'the human' can be neutralized by cool reflection. No sooner has Thucydides concluded his report of the fate of Melos than he proceeds to the next major episode:[106] 'During the same winter the Athenians wished to sail again... to Sicily and subdue it' (τοῦ δ' αὐτοῦ χειμῶνος Ἀθηναῖοι ἐβούλοντο αὖθις...ἐπὶ Σικελίαν πλεύσαντες καταστρέψασθαι, 6.1.1). In their eager pursuit of this objective, the Athenians fall prey to exactly those impulses that Diodotus considers the most baneful manifestations of human nature: ἔρως and ἐλπίς (δυσέρωτας, 6.13.1; ἔρως, 24.3; ἐλπίζων, 6.15.2; εὐέλπιδες, 24.3; ἐλπίδος, 30.2; ἐλπίδι, 31.6).[107] In addition, scholars

---

[106] On this juxtaposition, and its ironic implications, see Cornford 1907: 184–5; Gomme 1954: 122–3; Connor 1984: 158.

[107] Cornford 1907: 205; Ehrenberg 1947: 51; Stahl 2003 [1966]: 120–1; Wohl 2002: 193. On the significance of each term, see also Wassermann 1956: 38–9; Euben 1990: 181. Avery (1973: 1–6) has shown that the theme of ἐλπίς is prominent throughout Thucydides' narrative of the Sicilian Expedition and serves as a major structuring device.

have drawn attention to the irony that the Athenians at Melos pontificate about the dangers of hope (5.103.1, 103.2, 111.2, 113), but that their fellow countrymen are curiously insensitive to the same perils on the eve of the Sicilian Expedition.[108]

A similar irony can be detected in Diodotus' speech. As we saw, his account of the determination of human action by baneful impulses overtly applies to the renegade ally Mytilene, whose irrational behaviour Diodotus tries to elucidate. Yet, on closer examination, Diodotus' observations also shed some light on none other than the Athenians themselves. One of the passions singled out by Diodotus is ἐλπίς, the temptation that comes in the wake of wishful thinking. Near the beginning of the long section centred on Mytilene, Thucydides remarks that the Athenians at first refuse to believe 'the charges' about the secession, 'giving priority to their wish that they might not be true' (μεῖζον μέρος νέμοντες τῷ μὴ βούλεσθαι ἀληθῆ εἶναι, 3.3.1). As Lateiner notes, this attitude is a clear instance of the delusional thinking that ἐλπίς inspires.[109] What is more, Thucydides' wording recalls a passage from the parting message of the Athenian ambassadors in the Melian Dialogue: 'You look at invisible things as if they were already taking place, just out of your wish for them' (τὰ δὲ ἀφανῆ τῷ βούλεσθαι ὡς γιγνόμενα ἤδη θεᾶσθε, 5.113). In their concluding statement, which immediately follows, the Athenians explicitly state that the Melians have become the victims of ἐλπίς (5.113). Both the passage from the Melian Dialogue and Thucydides' statement about the Athenians' initial reaction to the secession of Mytilene feature the substantivized infinitive βούλεσθαι in the causal dative, and they both express the idea that wishful thinking inspires fantastic projections that flatly disregard reality. In both passages, Thucydides could have used a circumstantial participle or a causal clause, constructions that would tie the act of wishing much closer to the subject of each sentence. Denniston observes that the articular infinitive is a shade less abstract than the corresponding noun, but that it nonetheless very

---

[108] Cornford 1907: 202 n. 1; Liebeschuetz 1968: 75; Stahl 2003 [1973]: 182–3; Macleod 1983a [1974]: 58 and 67.
[109] Lateiner 2018: 142.

'nearly...approximates' to it.[110] Thus, Thucydides' phrasing suggests that the Athenians and Melians act the way they do 'because of their wishing it' instead of 'because they wished it'. In this way, the substantivized infinitive τῷ βούλεσθαι is a clear example of the distinctively Thucydidean abstract neuter phrases: the act of 'wishing' is not depicted as an intention formed and controlled by a human subject, but as a comparatively independent impulse that confronts people. The wish comes across as a fact about these people as opposed to an act performed by them. The Athenians will hear from Diodotus that Mytilene has become the victim of this delusional attitude. Yet the story of Mytilene begins with a subtle hint that the Athenians are by no means impervious to the same kind of escapism from reality. The replacement of 'the divine' by 'the human' does not alter the fact that the Athenians remain, just as much as everyone else, at the mercy of an awesome force beyond their control.

---

[110] Denniston 1960: 37.

5
Decision-Making Overshadowed by Necessity

'Again and again Thucydides concentrates his narrative upon climactic moments at which men had to make *important collective decisions.*' Thus Geoffrey de Ste. Croix.[1] The time has come to look at some of these decisions and to find out what light they can shed on the themes discussed in the preceding chapters: do they corroborate the general position, taken up by various speakers and by Thucydides himself, that human beings are subject in their decisions to large-scale collective forces best captured by abstract and depersonalizing phrasing?

We will seek answers to this question by giving attention to three key moments in Thucydides' *History*: the original outbreak of the War, the choices made in the wake of the clash between Athenian and Spartan forces at Pylos and Sphacteria, and the Athenian decision to undertake the Sicilian Expedition. Taken together, the first and the third of these decisions initiate the two major phases of the Peloponnesian War: the so-called Archidamian War and the recrudescence of all-out warfare between Athens and Sparta after the tenuous Peace of Nicias. Summarizing previous scholarship, Rood has emphasized that events at Pylos and Sphacteria are no less consequential: in Thucydides' view, the Spartan peace overture and the Athenian rejection mark a fundamental turning point.[2] The impact that the experience of events at Pylos makes on either side sets the tone for the upcoming phase of the War until the Peace of Nicias.[3] What is more, Thucydides implies, as we will see, that the Sicilian Expedition was a long-term consequence of the soaring confidence that the success at

---

[1] De Ste. Croix 1972: 28.   [2] Rood 1998: 25.
[3] As Rood (1998: 39) observes, the Pylos episode, 'in Thucydides' view, turned the course of the war'.

Pylos provoked in the Athenians. While hopefulness is part and parcel of the Athenian spirit, it is in the wake of Pylos that Athenian hope, combined with desire for more, begins to know no limit. The choice to go to war with Syracuse marks the culmination of a general mentality that has seized the Athenians in the wake of the success at Pylos.

5.1 The Outbreak of the War

The most far-reaching decision mentioned by Thucydides obviously concerns the outbreak of the Peloponnesian War. While the original decision to go to war is made by the Peloponnesians (1.125.2), the Athenians readily take up the gauntlet. They hold a formal assembly at which they discuss how to respond to Spartan demands. Following Pericles' advice, they take a vote not to comply, in full awareness that war will be the likely result (1.145, cf. 1.140.4, 141.1, 144.3). While the formal initiation of the War is the work of the Spartans, both sides undertake steps that they know will directly lead to the outbreak of the War.

Thucydides' statement about the ἀληθεστάτη πρόφασις, the 'truest cause', of the Peloponnesian War casts light on the motivational forces prompting this general willingness to face the War (1.23.6):[4]

τὴν μὲν γὰρ ἀληθεστάτην πρόφασιν, ἀφανεστάτην δὲ λόγῳ, τοὺς Ἀθηναίους ἡγοῦμαι μεγάλους γιγνομένους καὶ φόβον παρέχοντας τοῖς Λακεδαιμονίοις ἀναγκάσαι ἐς τὸ πολεμεῖν.

I consider the truest cause [of the Peloponnesian War], though the one least apparent in what was said, that the Athenians' rise to greatness, as well as the fear they thereby induced in the Spartans, made recourse to war necessary.[5]

---

[4] On the meaning of πρόφασις in this passage, see Hornblower i, on 1.23.6 and the literature cited there. The issue of πρόφασις vs. αἰτία will receive further attention in Chapter 7 (pp. 257–63).

[5] Note that I borrow the translation of the phrase ἀναγκάσαι ἐς τὸ πολεμεῖν by 'made recourse to war necessary' from Kallet (1993: 37).

In semantic terms, the two participial phrases (Ἀθηναίους... μεγάλους γιγνομένους καὶ φόβον παρέχοντας τοῖς Λακεδαιμονίοις) are equivalent to an articular infinitive or a verbal noun. It is an instance of the so-called dominant participle, informally also known as the 'ab-urbe-condita construction'.[6] This construction implies that the hub of the phrase is not the noun governing the participial phrase (i.e. τοὺς Ἀθηναίους), but that the main emphasis falls on the circumstantial participle modifying the noun (μεγάλους γιγνομένους καὶ φόβον παρέχοντας τοῖς Λακεδαιμονίοις). In terms of sense, the Athenians' 'growth to greatness' and concomitant 'inducement of fear' in the Spartans are the subject of the sentence. By contrast, the personal noun τοὺς Ἀθηναίους is merely the grammatical, but not the semantic, subject. Thucydides' phrase is thus equivalent to the following articular infinitive: τὸ τοὺς Ἀθηναίους μεγάλους γίγνεσθαι καὶ φόβον παρέχειν τοῖς Λακεδαιμονίοις.[7]

It would be odd for Thucydides to claim at 1.23.6 (as he would if the grammatical subject τοὺς Ἀθηναίους were also the semantic subject) that the Athenians purposefully compelled the Spartans to wage war, and that their rise to greatness would describe the manner in which they achieved this.[8] The great debate at Sparta shows that the goal of the Athenian ambassadors is to dissuade the Spartans from going to war: the Athenians consider the looming decision for war an 'error' (ἁμαρτία, 1.78.4), which they try to prevent by reminding the Spartans of the arbitration clause of the Thirty Years' Peace (1.78.4).

Some examples drawn from Thucydides' text will show the emphatically nominal and impersonal flavour that phrases involving a dominant

---

[6] Cf. K-G ii. 78 A. 1: 'Das *Participium coniunctum* stellt zuweilen wie im Lateinischen (*occisus Caesar aliis pessimum, aliis pulcherrimum facinus videbatur*) den Hauptbegriff der Aussage in der Weise dar, daß es einem verbalen Substantiv oder einem substantivierten Infinitive entspricht.'

[7] Notice that Crawley's translation of the passage shows that he interprets the participial phrase in the same way: 'The growth of the power of Athens, and the alarm which this inspired in Lacedaemon, made war inevitable' (15). Ostwald's paraphrase of the passage suggests that he came to the same conclusion (1988: 4).

[8] Sealey's construal of the passage, in which the dominant participle plays no role, shows that, if one takes (as Sealey does) 'the Athenians' as the semantic subject, ἀναγκάσαι naturally implies intention (the italics in the following quotations are my own): 'the Athenians *took advantage* of this alarm [*sc.* felt by the Spartans] *in order to provoke* the Spartans to fight' (1957: 11; cf. 10: 'the Athenians were *spoiling for* a fight', 'they *sought to* precipitate war'). In what follows, Sealey (1957: 11) notes a tension between 1.23.6 and 1.88 where Thucydides says that the Spartans voted for war out of fear of Athenian power. As Sealey points out (11), the latter passage makes no mention of Athenian warmongering. The inconsistency disappears when one realizes that the personal noun τοὺς Ἀθηναίους is merely the grammatical, but not the semantic, subject of the verb ἀναγκάσαι.

participle seem to have had. The following passage refers to the first disappointment experienced by the Athenians on their way to Sicily: 'This [sc. the insufficient Egestaean funds], as well as the Rhegians' unwillingness to join the expedition, had gone contrary to their wishes at the very start' (αὐτοῖς τοῦτό τε πρῶτον ἀντεκεκρούκει καὶ οἱ Ῥηγῖνοι οὐκ ἐθελήσαντες ξυστρατεύειν, 6.46.2). It is striking that the participial phrase οἱ Ῥηγῖνοι οὐκ ἐθελήσαντες ξυστρατεύειν, whose chief element in terms of grammar is a personal noun, is coordinated with the neuter form τοῦτο. The parallel syntactic ordering shows that Thucydides considers the participial phrase as semantically equivalent to an impersonal phrase referring to an event.

Another example can be found in the account of events at Pylos and Sphacteria: 'But the reason [sc. for the soldiers' holding out on the island] was the announcement made by the Spartans that volunteers should convey ground corn to the island and wine and cheese...' (αἴτιον δὲ ἦν οἱ Λακεδαιμόνιοι προειπόντες ἐς τὴν νῆσον ἐσάγειν σῖτόν τε τὸν βουλόμενον ἀληλεμένον καὶ οἶνον καὶ τυρὸν..., 4.26.5). From a grammatical point of view, the leading element in the participial phrase, and therefore the subject of the entire sentence, is οἱ Λακεδαιμόνιοι. It must be the subject because αἴτιον, due to the lack of an article, can be safely classified as predicate noun.[9] In light of the personal plural subject, it comes as a surprise that the verb of the sentence is singular, and that the predicate is not an adjectival form in the plural. With a plural subject, one might have expected the phrasing αἴτιοι δὲ ἦσαν οἱ Λεκεδαιμόνιοι, 'the Spartans were responsible (since they had made the announcement...)'. The singular of the predicate noun reflects the semantic as opposed to the grammatical subject of the sentence: the Spartans' 'announcement' (not the Spartans themselves) causes the trapped soldiers' perseverance.

In a similar way, Thucydides' phrasing at 1.23.6 emphasizes, not the grammatical subject (which is personal), but the semantic subject (which is abstract). Thucydides suggests that compulsion issues from an impersonal process, whose components are the Athenians' growth and the concomitant inducement of fear in the Spartans. As Ostwald points out, the notion of simultaneity suggested by the two participial phrases is

---

[9] K-G i. 591; Sm. 1150. Αἴτιον is also considered predicate by Classen-Steup iv, on 4.26.5.13.

DECISION-MAKING OVERSHADOWED BY NECESSITY   163

crucial: '[T]he fact that he [*sc.* Thucydides] uses two present participles and connects them with a καί shows that the process of Athenian growth had the development of Lacedaemonian fears as a concomitant, that, in other words, growing Athenian power gave *ipso facto* rise to Spartan apprehension.'[10] Thus, the participial phrases refer to one interconnected process.

Thucydides' statement about the outbreak of the War involves a further complication: the verb ἀναγκάσαι lacks a direct object. Thucydides thus fails to make explicit who exactly was affected by the necessity that led to the War. Most commentators and translators solve the problem by supplying an object (in the form of an implicit αὐτούς) from the preceding participial phrase φόβον παρέχοντας τοῖς Λακεδαιμονίοις: Athenian growth and Spartan fear forced *the Spartans* into waging war. On this view, only the Spartans are subject to the necessity prevailing at the outbreak of the war.

Although in terms of grammar this construal is sound, Ostwald thinks there is good reason to challenge it. As he points out, the omission of an explicit direct object 'makes the emphasis fall heavily on ἀναγκάσαι'.[11] Thus stressing the bare fact of compulsion, Thucydides wants to represent the inevitability as general and unspecific, as a necessity weighing upon both sides at once.

Various arguments support this construal of the passage. For one thing, at 1.23.4–5 the Athenians and the Peloponnesians together are the subject of the verbal forms ἤρξαντο, λύσαντες, and ἔλυσαν, which refer to the αἰτίαι, the 'grievances', the immediate triggers of the War.[12] According to Sealey, the application of the αἰτίαι to both sides makes it unlikely that Thucydides had connected the 'truest cause' (τὴν ... ἀληθεστάτην πρόφασιν) with the Peloponnesians alone, without emphasizing the shift of referent.[13] Therefore, it seems reasonable to suppose that necessity does not weigh on the Spartans alone but also affects the Athenians.

---

[10] Ostwald 1988: 3. In a similar vein, Jaffe (2017: 61) observes that these two aspects are 'the *two* sides of a single coin. It is Thucydidean necessity which binds obverse and reverse together.'
[11] Ostwald 1988: 3.
[12] On the identification of αἰτίαι with 'triggers', see Pelling 2000: 88, and my discussion in Chapter 7, pp. 258–9.
[13] Sealey (1957: 9): '[T]he αἰτίαι and the πρόφασις have a common point of reference, which comprises the Athenians as well as the Peloponnesians.'

Ostwald himself offers a further crucial argument in support of his rendition: in the last two speeches delivered before the outbreak of the War representatives of both camps declare that the War is a necessity.[14] At the congress of the Peloponnesian allies, the Corinthians claim that a point has been reached at which the Peloponnesians 'have come to meet necessity' (ἐς ἀνάγκην ἀφῖχθαι, 1.124.2). On the Athenian side, Pericles draws the same conclusion before the assembly of the people: 'One must realize that going to war has become a necessity' (εἰδέναι... χρὴ ὅτι ἀνάγκη πολεμεῖν, 1.144.3). Given the ensuing votes, a majority on either side seems to be convinced of the inevitability of the War. One would expect this to be reflected in Thucydides' statement about the truest cause. Hence, the phrase ἀναγκάσαι ἐς τὸ πολεμεῖν is most plausibly rendered thus: 'the Athenians' rise to greatness, as well as the fear they thereby induced in the Spartans, made recourse to war necessary.'[15] The ultimate cause for the War rests on a constellation of situational constraints from which neither side can disentangle itself.

Finally, this interpretation of ἀναγκάσαι as general receives significant support from outside Thucydides' text. Dionysius of Halicarnassus seems to have understood the passage just like Ostwald. In the *Second Letter to Ammaeus*, Dionysius cites the relevant excerpt as a prime example of Thucydides' wilfulness and offers an alternative version (*Amm.* II 6.427.12–16):

βούλεται γὰρ δηλοῦν, ὅτι μεγάλοι γιγνόμενοι οἱ Ἀθηναῖοι ἀνάγκην παρέσχον τοῦ πολέμου· πεποίηκεν δὲ ἀντὶ τῆς ἀνάγκης καὶ τοῦ πολέμου ὀνοματικῶν ὄντων ῥηματικὰ τό τε ἀναγκάσαι καὶ τὸ πολεμεῖν.

He [*sc.* Thucydides] wishes to indicate that the Athenians' growth to greatness[16] caused the necessity of war. Yet for 'necessity' and 'war', which are nominal, he has substituted verbal forms: 'to make necessary' and 'to wage war'.

---

[14] Ostwald 1988: 32.
[15] A yet more literal, but awkward, alternative would be: '[Athenian growth and Spartan fear] applied compulsion with a view to waging war.'
[16] Notice that the standard translations of the *Second Letter to Ammaeus* treat the phrase μεγάλοι γιγνόμενοι οἱ Ἀθηναῖοι as involving a dominant participle and consider an abstract noun the nearest English equivalent: Roberts (1901: 141): 'the growth of Athenian power'; Usher (1974: 415) (Loeb ed.): 'growing Athenian power'.

DECISION-MAKING OVERSHADOWED BY NECESSITY 165

Dionysius replaces the infinitive ἀναγκάσαι with the noun ἀνάγκη, used in a periphrastic construction with παρέχω. This substitution suggests that Dionysius recognized Thucydides' failure to provide an object with ἀναγκάσαι, and that he concluded from this omission that Thucydides wished to represent the compulsion as general. By replacing the infinitive with the noun, Dionysius captures this intended idea without any ambiguity: the phrase 'the necessity of war' implies a general fact and does not call for an object, an aspect that distinguishes it from Thucydides' infinitive.

Dionysius' version provides important evidence as to how a native speaker most naturally construed the Thucydidean passage. Here as elsewhere, however, Dionysius' rewriting leaves one wondering what reasons may have prompted Thucydides to phrase the passage as he did. Attention to the second verbal form criticized by Dionysius will provide an answer to this conundrum. Dionysius also replaces the substantival infinitive τὸ πολεμεῖν with another abstract noun: τοῦ πολέμου. If ἀνακάσαι in Thucydides' original had a clearly stated object (e.g. αὐτούς referring to the Spartans), this would naturally have functioned as the subject of the second substantival infinitive: 'Athenian growth and Spartan fear forced them [*sc.* the Spartans] into waging war.' Lacking both an object and a subject, the two infinitives ἀναγκάσαι and πολεμεῖν suggest that compulsion and the waging of war are general and implicate both sides. At this point, Dionysius could say that his version expresses just that, without needlessly confusing the reader.

Nevertheless, this is not the final world on the issue: Thucydides' πολεμεῖν conveys a nuance that is missing from Dionysius' version. In Thucydides, the articular infinitive has both a nominal and a verbal side. Unlike τοῦ πολέμου in Dionysius, it suggests, not just a static fact, but an ongoing and evolving situation, underlined by the present aspect: 'waging of war' as opposed to 'war' *simpliciter*. Thus, the infinitive, unlike the simple noun, implies some degree of action in progress. It is crucial that this verbal notion is not correlated with a distinct subject performing the action. As a result, 'waging war' does not suggest agency, but rather the unfolding of a process. Faced with Thucydides' phrasing, the reader is led to wonder, first, who it is that experiences compulsion and, secondly, who it is that wages war. By first raising the question of agency (through the use of the infinitive) and then withholding an answer, Thucydides implies that an encompassing, general process has implicated both the Spartans and the Athenians. By contrast, Dionysius' decision to substitute nouns for infinitives directs attention neither to the problem of agency nor to the impact of an evolving process.[17] According to Werner Jaeger, the statement concerning the 'truest cause' summarizes Thucydides' view of the War as 'the result of an inexorable, longstanding process conditioned by a higher necessity'.[18] Thucydides' various stylistic choices (the abstract subject implied by the dominant participle, the suppression of a specific personal object with ἀναγκάσαι, and the infinitives lacking explicit subjects) capture this inevitability with meticulous precision.

5.2 Spartan Fear: A Passive Imposition

Although a long-standing necessity weighs on both sides, it is also true that the Spartans are more directly responsible for unleashing the War. The Spartans vote for War (1.88), a decision subsequently endorsed by the Peloponnesians at large (1.125.1), despite the Athenians' willingness to submit to arbitration as stipulated by the Thirty Years' Treaty (1.78.4, 1.85.2, 1.144.2, 7.18.2). In this connection, it is noteworthy that Thucydides describes the Spartans' subsequent unease about their role in unleashing the War with phrases that strike a note of passivity and impersonality.

The Spartans decide to renew their war effort owing to the situation at Sicily (6.93.1–2) and open Athenian breaches of the Peace of Nicias (6.105.1, 7.18.3). Thucydides notes that their confidence is on the rise because they believe in the justice of their course; for, this time around, it

---

[17] Notice that, as mentioned in the Introduction (p. 9 n. 15), Dionysius discusses the passage about the truest πρόφασις in order to illustrate Thucydides' habit of 'turning nouns into verbs' (ὅταν... τὰ ὀνόματα ποιῇ ῥήματα, Amm. II 6.427.7–8). Prima facie, this alleged Thucydidean habit seems to run counter to our general thesis that Thucydides prefers nominal over verbal phrases, and that he prioritizes the occurrence of events over the agency of people. In fact, however, Dionysius' example shows that, even when using 'verbs instead of nouns', Thucydides undermines the primacy of personal agents and highlights the sway of the situation over human beings. What Dionysius seems to have primarily in mind based on his example is Thucydides' tendency to use articular infinitives instead of the corresponding abstract noun.

[18] Jaeger 1934–55: i. 492 [my translation].

has been the Athenians' turn to break the treaty first (7.18.2). The Spartans have come to face the fact that 'in the previous war the transgression had rather happened on their own side' (ἐν γὰρ τῷ προτέρῳ πολέμῳ σφέτερον τὸ παρανόμημα μᾶλλον γενέσθαι, 7.18.2). When coming to this realization, the Spartans are thinking specifically of their refusal to comply with the Athenians' invitation to submit to arbitration (7.18.2). In resuming the war effort, however, the Spartans are more confident because they believe 'that the transgression, a wrong that had previously been committed by them, too, had now in turn shifted over to the Athenians in identical fashion' (τὸ παρανόμημα, ὅπερ καὶ σφίσι πρότερον ἡμάρτητο, αὖθις ἐς τοὺς Ἀθηναίους τὸ αὐτὸ περιεστάναι, 7.18.3).

The impersonal neuter παρανόμημα, which fills the position of subject in both passages, does not suggest an act people commit, but a state that is the actual agent in the present situation. This condition settles itself, as if by an act of its own will, once on the side of the Spartans and once on that of the Athenians. In both passages, Thucydides uses phrasing with passive connotations in the description of the παρανόμημα involved in unleashing the war: 'the transgression happened on their side', and 'the transgression shifted over to the Athenians'. Furthermore, the pluperfect passive ἡμάρτητο strikes a peculiar note. A standard translation of this form, in combination with the dative σφίσι, would be 'a wrong that had been committed by them'. The dative is best categorized as expressing agent, the regular construction after a passive verb in the perfect stem. Taken literally, however, the dative expresses the person (or thing) to whom something happens or for whom something is done. This original significance of the dative is in play due to the static connotations of the pluperfect ἡμάρτητο, which suggests a permanent, settled result. This interpretation receives support from Smyth's explanation of the rationale for the dative of the agent: 'The usual restriction of the dative to tenses of completed action seems to be due to the fact that the agent is represented as *placed in the position of viewing an already completed action in the light of its relation to himself* [my italics] (interest, advantage, possession).'[19] The associated phrases (γενέσθαι and περιεστάναι) point towards the same conclusion: they emphasize that the

[19] Sm. 1489.

transgression 'happened to' the Spartans. In this specific context, the phrase ὅπερ καὶ σφίσι πρότερον ἡμάρτητο might be more accurately translated as 'a wrong that had previously attached itself to them, too'. The Spartans have the sense that the breaking of the treaty occurred to them, affecting them to their own disadvantage. If Thucydides had wanted to avoid the connotations of a state imposing itself, and instead to ascribe agency to the Spartans, he could easily have used an aorist form followed by ὑπό plus genitive instead of the pluperfect. The phrase would then have suggested, without any ambiguity, that 'the wrong had been committed by them'.

What is the point of the passive connotations that mark the phrases about the original transgression that unleashes the Peloponnesian War? In stating the 'truest cause', Thucydides stresses fear as the dominant motive of the Spartans (φόβον, 1.23.6), an assessment that he endorses in his summary of the great debate in Sparta: the Spartans vote for war 'not so much persuaded by the speeches of their allies as out of fear that the Athenians would become too powerful' (οὐ τοσοῦτον τῶν ξυμμάχων πεισθέντες τοῖς λόγοις ὅσον φοβούμενοι τοὺς Ἀθηναίους μὴ ἐπὶ μεῖζον δυνηθῶσιν, 1.88).[20] In both passages, Thucydides uses, not δέος or any of its cognates, but φόβος and φοβέομαι to designate the fear that asserts itself among the Spartans. As scholars have emphasized, δέος and φόβος denote different types of fear.[21] Δέος signifies fear based on reflection: it is usually directed at the future and can often be rendered as 'apprehension'. Φόβος, by contrast, refers to an affective, irrational state, often amounting to sheer terror. The fear felt by the Spartans at the rise of Athenian power is generally captured by this word: in addition to the two passages in the author's own voice, the Corcyreans in their speech at Athens maintain that 'the war will come' (τὸν ... πόλεμον ... ἔσεσθαι, 1.33.3) because 'the Lacedaemonians are longing for war due to fear of you' (τοὺς Λακεδαιμονίους φόβῳ τῷ ὑμετέρῳ πολεμησείοντας, 1.33.3).

When initiating the War, the Spartans act under the influence of what Huart calls a 'psychosis of fear'.[22] As we will see, passions that have collectives

---

[20] For the meaning of the comparative, see Classen-Steup i, on 1.88.5 (along with their note on 1.82.5.23).
[21] De Romilly 1956: 119–20; Huart 1968: 124, 132–3, 138, 337; Desmond 2006: 361.
[22] Huart 1968: 135.

in their grip play a crucial role in all three far-reaching decisions that mark the beginning of each major phase of the Peloponnesian War. Beset by this mental condition, the Spartans take a decision that in retrospect turns out to be a passive imposition, a mistake that attached itself to them rather than an unenforced decision taken by rational agents.

5.3 The Speech of the Spartan Ambassadors at Athens: Passivity of the Doers and the Margin of Choice

The engagement at Pylos, which commences as an episode of minor importance, quickly evolves into a crisis that might have decided the outcome of the entire War. Once the Athenians have successfully blockaded the Spartan hoplites on the island, a truce is concluded, under which the Spartans send ambassadors to Athens to sue for peace.

The Spartans' speech offers the most sustained reflection in Thucydides' entire work on the factors impacting the decisions of those who have experienced unexpected good fortune. This concern with sound decision-making forges a link with the debate at Sparta and the decision that leads to the outbreak of the War[23]: the Spartans' καλῶς βουλεύσασθαι (4.17.3) recalls the dense cluster of references to εὐβουλία in the speeches of the Athenians and of Archidamus.[24] The theme of decision-making and of the respective weights of choice and necessity thus takes centre stage.

According to the Spartans, the Athenians can still make a genuine choice and avoid the fate of those who paradoxically descend to passivity when faced with unwonted success: 'it is possible for you... not to undergo the experience of those who have received an unexpected blessing' (ὑμῖν... ἔξεστι... μὴ παθεῖν ὅπερ οἱ ἀήθως τι ἀγαθὸν λαμβάνοντες τῶν ἀνθρώπων, 4.17.4). The verb ἔξεστι makes clear that,

---

[23] For further parallels between both situations, see Hunter 1973: 77–8; Stahl 2003 [1966] 143.
[24] Athenians: εὖ βουλευομένοις (1.73.3), ἡ εὐβουλία (1.78.4); Archidamus: εὔβουλοι (1.84.3, twice), εὖ βουλευομένους (1.84.4), κράτιστα βουλεύσεσθε (1.85.2). Notice that in the last passage κράτιστα functions as the superlative of εὖ (though, given the antithesis with the coordinated φοβερώτατα, the literal meaning is also in play).

in the Spartans' view, the Athenians still have scope for free manoeuvring at this point. Yet if they do not use this opportunity wisely, they will soon be faced, as the verb παθεῖν suggests, with a situation over which they will no longer have control. Given the implications of παθεῖν, the Spartan envoys imply that success creates a situation in which people succumb to the influence of psychological states triggered by present circumstances. When this situation prevails, choices are more accurately described as passive impositions than as the self-determined action of a human subject.

The Spartans explain the nature of this 'suffering' of those who have been successful beyond expectation (4.17.4):

αἰεὶ γὰρ τοῦ πλέονος ἐλπίδι ὀρέγονται διὰ τὸ καὶ τὰ παρόντα ἀδοκήτως εὐτυχῆσαι.

For out of hope they always yearn for more because of their being unexpectedly fortunate in their present circumstances.

The Spartan envoys restate the thesis put forward by Diodotus, who holds that collective moods and external circumstances dovetail in jointly driving the decisions of cities (3.45.4–5, see Chapter 4, pp. 121–3). Their language recalls the pivotal terms highlighted by Diodotus (ἐλπίδι, 4.17.4 ~ ἐλπίς, 3.45.5; τοῦ πλέονος ... ὀρέγονται, 4.17.4 ~ τὴν πλεονεξίαν, 3.45.4; τὸ ... ἀδοκήτως εὐτυχῆσαι, 4.17.4 ~ τύχη ... ἀδοκήτως, 3.45.6).[25]

It is crucial that Thucydides would have been free to let the Spartans use a circumstantial participle with a personal subject instead of the sprawling substantival infinitive διὰ τὸ καὶ τὰ παρόντα ἀδοκήτως εὐτυχῆσαι. By adopting this construction, the envoys sustain a tone that is largely agent-free, and thus implicitly impersonal. As a result, the Spartans represent good fortune as a condition imposing itself on people, a force that people do not have under control. The power of impersonal factors is also highlighted by the neuter term τὰ παρόντα: it suggests the heavy, factual weight of the ongoing situation. The participle παρόν occurs several times in connection with events at Pylos and their aftermath, in

---

[25] Cornford (1907: 124–5), without pointing out the verbal parallels, notes that the speech of the Spartan envoys recalls the account of human nature put forth by Diodotus.

both its substantival (5.14.3) and its adjectival variant (4.14.3, 17.4, 18.3, 65.4). The word is especially apt to describe the pressure of immediate circumstances, both in a temporal and in a spatial sense. The gloss by Parry on τὰ παρόντα in connection with its occurrence in the stasis section (3.82.2) as '*immediate, going reality*' that 'assumes control of everything'[26] is apposite: what is παρόν has a direct immediacy that leaves people no room to distance themselves from the pressure of circumstances.

Given Thucydides' thoroughgoing emphasis on τύχη in the Pylos episode, events have shown that circumstances tend to reverse themselves in next to no time, an experience that the Athenians and the Spartans have both made in their present engagement.[27] According to the Spartans, awareness of the factors beyond human control is crucial especially for those who will make a decision in the wake of an unexpected turnaround, be it for better or for worse (4.17.5):

οἷς δὲ πλεῖσται μεταβολαὶ ἐπ' ἀμφότερα ξυμβεβήκασι, δίκαιοί εἰσι καὶ ἀπιστότατοι εἶναι ταῖς εὐπραγίαις.

But those to whom reversals for better or for worse have happened in the greatest numbers also have reason to be most distrustful of prosperity.

Stahl has rightly emphasized that Thucydides draws attention to no fewer than five μεταβολαί in his account of Pylos and its aftermath, and that he thereby seeks to highlight that the radical turnaround is a basic pattern of events.[28] The perfect form of ξυμβεβήκασι underlines the notion of sheer occurrence (as opposed to potentially amenable human action). The phrasing combines suddenness, suggested by the term μεταβολή, and the idea of a permanent situational constraint, thus conveying both abrupt occurrence and locked state.

---

[26] Parry 1970: 19.
[27] Scholars have observed that τύχη (along with an emphasis on unexpectedness) is a leitmotiv for the entire episode: Cornford 1907: 88, 92, 97; Stahl 2003 [1966]: 139–42; Hunter 1973: 73; Babut 1986: 74; Rood 1998: 38–9.
[28] Stahl 2003 [1966]: 151.

It follows naturally from the emphasis on μεταβολαί that chance plays an important role in human affairs according to the Spartan ambassadors. Good fortune is necessary if ambitious undertakings are to succeed, but τύχη is always unreliable (4.18.3):

ὥστε οὐκ εἰκὸς ὑμᾶς διὰ τὴν παροῦσαν νῦν ῥώμην πόλεώς τε καὶ τῶν προσγεγενημένων καὶ τὸ τῆς τύχης οἴεσθαι αἰεὶ μεθ' ὑμῶν ἔσεσθαι.

As a result, it is not reasonable for you to believe that, due to the present might of your city and <the strength afforded by> the things that have accrued to you, the realm over which fortune rules will likewise always be on your side.

Impersonality and emphasis on non-human factors mark several phrases in this passage. While the phrase τὴν παροῦσαν ῥώμην highlights the power of present circumstances over people's thinking, τὰ προσγεγενημένα, another instance of the perfect stem of a verb of occurrence, puts emphasis on things happening as opposed to people acting. Finally, the substantival neuter phrase τὸ τῆς τύχης highlights the impersonal character of τύχη, a force that is indifferent to the aspirations of personal agents.

It is thus only logical that the Spartan ambassadors call those people σώφρων who realize that good fortune is doubtful (τἀγαθὰ ἐς ἀμφίβολον ἀσφαλῶς ἔθεντο, 4.18.4). Again, neuter forms prevail in this statement: they evoke powers and factors intransigent to human control. Therefore, prudent men resist the illusion that they can disentangle themselves from a war whenever they want to (4.18.4). This thought provides another link to the speeches given at Sparta on the eve of the Peloponnesian War. Archidamus had warned the Spartans that, once the War had begun, it would be impossible for them to extricate themselves from it while preserving their honour (1.81.5), and that the War would be likely to last for a very long time (1.81.6). Instead of humans controlling the course of events, τύχαι lead and people must follow (ὡς ἂν αἱ τύχαι αὐτῶν ἡγήσωνται, 4.18.4). The personification of chance draws attention to the real centre of agency: it is not located in human beings, but in the impersonal realm of fortune, characterized by intrinsic mutability (indicated by the plural). Using a similar personification, Diodotus had remarked that ἔρως 'leads the way' (ἡγούμενος, 3.45.5), and entire cities follow its lead, just to plunge into disaster.

In view of the influence of factors beyond human control, the Spartans contend that the Athenians should beware of missing the opportunity to end the conflict before irreparable damage has been done to both sides (4.20.1):

Ἡμῖν δὲ καλῶς, εἴπερ ποτέ, ἔχει ἀμφοτέροις ἡ ξυναλλαγή, πρίν τι ἀνήκεστον διὰ μέσου γενόμενον ἡμᾶς καταλαβεῖν, ἐν ᾧ ἀνάγκη ἀίδιον ὑμῖν ἔχθραν πρὸς τῇ κοινῇ καὶ ἰδίαν ἔχειν, ὑμᾶς δὲ στερηθῆναι ὧν νῦν προκαλούμεθα.

For both of us, reconciliation comes now, if ever, under favourable circumstances, before something incurable intervenes and seizes us, in which case the necessity would arise that, in addition to our public hostility, we harbour an eternal and private grudge against you, and that you would be deprived of the things we now offer.

The phrasing suggests that the favourable opportunity, which opens up the margin of choice, is something that presents itself, rather than being brought off by human beings: the opportunity to conclude peace occupies the subject position in nominal periphrasis (καλῶς…ἔχει…ἡ ξυναλλαγή) whereas the Spartans and Athenians appear in the dative (ἡμῖν…ἀμφοτέροις), a construction evocative of the role of receivers as opposed to doers. Favourable circumstances emerge spontaneously. Now it is up to the human agents to make something of them. The Spartans' appeal recalls their previous point that it is still possible (ἔξεστι, 4.17.4) for the Athenians to avoid the condition typical of those who have enjoyed unexpected success.

This set of ideas evokes a similar moment at the end of the speech of the Athenians at Sparta in book 1. On this earlier occasion, the Athenian ambassadors (just like the Spartans now) stressed that the horizon of choice was still open, but would close if their Spartan audience were to reject the proposal to submit to arbitration: 'While good counsel can still be chosen freely by both of us, we call on you not to undo the treaty nor to transgress against the oaths' (ἡμεῖς…λέγομεν ὑμῖν, ἕως ἔτι αὐθαίρετος ἀμφοτέροις ἡ εὐβουλία, σπονδὰς μὴ λύειν μηδὲ παραβαίνειν τοὺς ὅρκους,

1.78.4). Again, εὐβουλία stands in subject position and human beings in a dependent dative: the opportunity has presented itself—now the Spartans are called upon to make something of it. The Athenians also observe that, most of the time, human beings first come to blows and only begin to negotiate when they are 'suffering evil' (κακοπαθοῦντες, 1.78.3). As soon as this is the case, the chance for a lasting settlement has already been squandered. The passive expression κακοπαθοῦντες recalls the similar connotations of the phrase τι ἀνήκεστον διὰ μέσου γενόμενον ('something incurable intervenes', 4.20.1) from the speech of the Spartans. The Athenians at Sparta observe that the current moment provides a favourable opportunity, in contrast to circumstances in which the scope for decision has dwindled: both they and the Spartans 'are not yet implicated in any such mistake' (ἐν οὐδεμιᾷ πω τοιαύτῃ ἁμαρτίᾳ ὄντες, 1.78.4). The phrasing suggests that, once the War has started, both parties will be placed in a situation that erases the ephemeral moment when genuine choices are possible. Yet, just as the Spartans did not listen to the Athenian ambassadors, so now the Athenians do not heed the Spartans. Despite the diametrically opposite characters of the two cities, their stance at the crucial moment of choice is the same.

Stahl has pointed out that the substantival neuter τι ἀνήκεστον in the Spartans' speech recalls another passage from Diodotus' speech, namely his remark that 'each circumstance is mastered by something incurable and stronger' (ἑκάστη τις κατέχεται ὑπ' ἀνηκέστου τινὸς κρείσσονος, 3.45.4). Stahl comments: '[E]very situation has an ἀνήκεστον ("element of 'incurable'", 3.45.4) hidden within it like a thorn that irresistibly pricks people to reach beyond the situation they have currently attained.'[29] The Spartans place this impersonal power in subject position and combine it with two verbal phrases, one of which captures the occurrence of an event (διὰ μέσου γενόμενον) while the other suggests the seizure of human agents (ἡμᾶς καταλαβεῖν, 4.20.1.). Ever since Homer, the verb καταλαμβάνω had tended to be used of death and disasters.[30] The combination of the two verbal phrases underlines the two contrary

---

[29] Stahl 2003 [1966]: 144.
[30] See the list of examples, including the Thucydidean passage in question, provided by LSJ s.v. A.I.2.

aspects of the 'incurable' that restricts human choices: on the one hand, impersonal occurrence, and on the other, the overwhelming momentum of a hostile visitation.

If this situation comes to pass, all room for choice will have disappeared, a scenario forcefully expressed by the term ἀνάγκη: the Spartans will be condemned to eternal hatred of the Athenians, and the Athenians will no longer be able to attain the terms now offered by the Spartans. As usual, form matches content: the word ἀνάγκη is in subject position (4.20.1), and human beings are once again placed in a dative, which conveys their passive exposure to a force beyond their control.

Thucydides provides some insight into the considerations that inform the Athenians' response to the speech of the Spartan ambassadors. Because they have blockaded the Spartans on Sphacteria, the Athenians think that they can make peace whenever they want to (ὁπόταν βούλωνται ποιεῖσθαι πρὸς αὐτούς, 4.21.2). This active expression, involving a verb of volition and suggesting seamless human control over the situation, sharply contrasts with the Spartans' emphasis on passivity. It is clear that the Athenians could hardly care less about the warnings put forth by the Spartans. According to Thucydides, their dismissal comes from the desire for more: τοῦ δὲ πλέονος ὠρέγοντο (4.21.2). As various scholars have observed, this expression closely recalls the phrase used by the Spartan ambassadors to characterize the perilous mindset that affects the beneficiaries of unexpected good fortune: αἰεὶ γὰρ τοῦ πλέονος ἐλπίδι ὀρέγονται ('for out of hope they always long for more', 4.17.4).[31] Scholars have also pointed out that this phrase recurs yet again at the very end of the Pylos narrative when Thucydides reports that the Athenians 'kept on longing for more' in response to the Spartans' ongoing attempts to recover their captured men and reach an agreement (μειζόνων... ὠρέγοντο, 4.41.4).[32] As these echoes show, the Athenians have succumbed to exactly the mindset against which the Spartans have warned them.

---

[31] Gundert 1968 [1940] 119; Herter 1968b [1954]: 390; Stahl 2003 [1966] 143; Hunter 1973: 79–80; Babut 1982: 51 n. 1, and 1986: 69; Rood 1998: 39.

[32] Herter 1968b [1954]: 390; Babut 1982: 51 n. 1; Rood 1998: 39–40. Herter and Babut observe that the phrase makes a final appearance in the speech of Pagondas in front of the Boeotian troops before the battle at Delium (τοῦ πλέονος δὲ ὀρεγόμενος, 4.92.2). Here, too, it refers to the Athenians.

Several commentators have been critical of the merits of the speech given by the Spartan ambassadors.[33] Others, by contrast, have pointed out that Thucydides' recourse to several ideas and key phrases previously used by the Spartans (in particular their references to τύχη, ἐλπίς, and longing for more) shows that he largely agreed with their account of the factors incumbent on collective decisions.[34] If Thucydides accepts the substance of the Spartans' position, he probably also finds value in their emphasis on human passivity, on the priority of occurrence over action, and on the central importance of impersonal factors, whether in human nature or the outside world, over the purposes of personal agents.

5.4 Victors and Losers After Pylos: An Unlikely Similarity

Thucydides provides insight into the moods that prevail among the Athenians and the Spartans after the Athenians' final success at Pylos and the capture of 120 Spartan and 172 Peloponnesian hoplites. These sentiments will shape their general mindset during the ensuing phase of the War. Although drastically contrary states of mind are dominant in each city, nevertheless both sides, victors and losers, turn out to be equally subject to natural inclinations that elude the moderating influence of rational control.

The Spartans have been reduced to a state of wholesale passivity with regard to the War and are in the grips of fear in the face of a potential revolution of the Helots: Thucydides describes them as 'fearing that a revolution affecting the arrangements of their political system might happen to them' (φοβούμενοι μὴ σφίσι νεώτερόν τι γένηται τῶν περὶ τὴν κατάστασιν, 4.55.1). Thus, the Spartans have succumbed again to fear, the mental state that has been crucial in triggering the Peloponnesian War. The phrasing of the passage merits attention: first, Thucydides uses nominal periphrasis involving a verb in the perfect, thus expressing occurrence as opposed to agency (γένηται); secondly, he fills the position of the subject with a phrase that

---

[33] Herter 1968b [1954]: 388; HCT iii, on 4.20.4; Hornblower ii. 170–2 (on 4.17–20).
[34] Cornford 1907: 121; Gundert 1968 [1940] 119; de Romilly 1963 [1947]: 174–5; Stahl 2003 [1966]: 142 and 149–50; Hunter 1973: 73–4 and 79–80; Babut 1982: 50–1, and 1986: 69.

interlocks two substantivized neuter expressions (νεώτερόν τι... τῶν περὶ τὴν κατάστασιν); thirdly, he marginalizes human agency by using a dative to refer to the Spartans (σφίσι), thus suggesting their passive exposure to circumstances.

According to Thucydides, the reason for the state of shock that prevails among the Spartans is as follows: 'the calamity which had befallen them on the island had been great and unexpected' (γεγενημένου μὲν τοῦ ἐν τῇ νήσῳ πάθους ἀνελπίστου καὶ μεγάλου, 4.55.1). Thucydides combines the term πάθος with a perfect participle of γίγνομαι, a combination that expresses maximum passivity. The situation confronting the Spartans is marked by greatness and unexpectedness, the typical characteristics of a μεταβολή. Thucydides systematically avoids phrasing that might suggest human agency. After mentioning the capture of Pylos and Cythera (Πύλου δὲ ἐχομένης καὶ Κυθήρων, 4.55.1), Thucydides uses another genitive absolute: καὶ πανταχόθεν σφᾶς περιεστῶτος πολέμου ταχέος καὶ ἀπροφυλάκτου ('and War, swift and uncontainable by precaution, encircled them from all sides', 4.55.1). Thucydides represents the War as the Spartans' arch nemesis: it 'encircles them', in the guise of an enemy laying siege to his adversary. Used this way, the verb περιίσταμαι usually requires a personal subject.[35] Instead of merely being confronted with a human opponent, however, the Spartans must deal with an impersonal super-agent, the Peloponnesian War itself.

Thucydides' observations at 4.55 about the general mood prevailing at Sparta in the wake of Pylos feature further phrases that convey the Spartans' passivity (4.55.3):

καὶ ἅμα τὰ τῆς τύχης πολλὰ καὶ ἐν ὀλίγῳ ξυμβάντα παρὰ λόγον αὐτοῖς ἔκπληξιν μεγίστην παρεῖχε...

And at the same time the strokes of fortune caused very great consternation, since they had happened to them contrary to expectation in such great numbers and in so short a time...

---

[35] Notice that LSJ speaks of a 'metaphorical' usage when περιίσταμαι in the relevant sense features a non-personal subject: s.v. B.I.2.

Just as in the previous passage, Thucydides does not direct attention to people acting, but emphasizes events happening (ξυμβάντα). The dependence of τύχη in the genitive on a neuter article, which recalls the same construction in the speech of the Spartan ambassadors at Athens (τὸ τῆς τύχης, 4.18.3), underlines the prevalence of impersonal factors that are largely inaccessible to human planning. Under the pressure of the randomness and unexpectedness of events (ξυμβάντα παρὰ λόγον), the Spartans are reduced to utter consternation (ἔκπληξιν μεγίστην παρεῖχε), a situation captured by nominal periphrasis. This state of mind has prevailed among them since the beginning of the Pylos episode (ὑπὸ ... ἐκπλήξεως, 4.14.3). Far from exercising control, people are firmly in the grips of events: καὶ ἐδέδισαν μή ποτε αὖθις ξυμφορά τις αὐτοῖς περιτύχῃ οἵα καὶ ἐν τῇ νήσῳ ('and they feared that at some point some calamity might befall them again, just like the one that had happened on the island', 4.55.3). According to LSJ, the word περιτυγχάνω means 'to light upon, fall in with' and is used almost exclusively of persons. Thus, just as περιίσταμαι in the previous passage, so περιτυγχάνω normally requires a human agent as subject. By contrast, again like at 4.55.1 (περιεστῶτος πολέμου, 4.55.1 ~ ξυμφορά τις ... περιτύχῃ, 55.3), Thucydides uses a noun referring to an incident to fill the subject position. He sustains the notion that events become virtual agents, whereas the influence of people is submerged.

Finally, Thucydides explains why the Spartans have come to forecast failure in every undertaking: διὰ τὸ τὴν γνώμην ἀνεχέγγυον γεγενῆσθαι ἐκ τῆς πρὶν ἀηθείας τοῦ κακοπραγεῖν ('because of the affection of their collective mindset with despondency as a result of their previous unfamiliarity with suffering misfortune', 4.55.4). This phrase illustrates Thucydides' fondness for clusters of nominal phrases: he lumps together three separate abstract noun phrases in an unwieldy syntactic construct (τὸ τὴν γνώμην ἀνεχέγγυον γεγενῆσθαι—ἐκ τῆς πρὶν ἀηθείας—τοῦ κακοπραγεῖν). The first abstract noun phrase consists of an articular infinitive that features a form of γίγνομαι in the perfect and suggests a situational constraint. Furthermore, the perfect infinitive γεγενῆσθαι implies that the collective mindset is not decided upon, but rather passively imposed upon the very people that one would expect to be agents. The second abstract noun phrase evokes the idea of a reversal, whereas the third again suggests passivity with regard to circumstances.

All three notions are locked together in a single articular infinitive construction that suggests that the Spartans are subjected to an impersonal, static determinant of their behaviour.

The collective mood that prevails at Athens stands in stark opposition to the crushing despondency of the Spartans: the Athenians are in higher spirits than ever, experiencing exuberant hope and confidence. Yet attention to Thucydides' language reveals that the Athenians have in fact more in common with the Spartans than one might initially think.

When the Athenian fleet returns from Sicily (where they went after concluding their business at Sphacteria and then Corcyra), the demos fines and exiles the generals who had been in command. The Athenians allege that the generals could have subdued Sicily but instead chose to return to Athens due to bribery (4.65.3). The people take recourse to such measures even though their original instruction was merely that the generals ought to end the war in Sicily (3.115.4), a point duly stressed by Stahl.[36] The explanation offered by Thucydides is significant (4.65.4):

οὕτω τῇ γε παρούσῃ εὐτυχίᾳ χρώμενοι ἠξίουν σφίσι μηδὲν ἐναντιοῦσθαι.

In such a way, because they experienced present good fortune, did they expect that nothing would stand in their way.

As scholars have observed, the phrase τῇ παρούσῃ εὐτυχίᾳ recalls phrases that occur in the speech of the Spartans at Athens (εὐτυχίαν τὴν παροῦσαν and τὸ καὶ τὰ παρόντα... εὐτυχῆσαι, both at 4.17.4).[37] In capturing the general mood prevailing among the Athenians, Thucydides uses the verb χράομαι in the sense of 'experience, suffer, be subject to', thus availing himself of the same passive register that the Spartan envoys had employed and that he himself just used to capture the general despondency among the Spartans. The power to which the Athenians have become subject is their 'present good fortune'. Through the participle παροῦσα, Thucydides links the auspicious notion of εὐτυχία with the idea of hardened present circumstances. Thucydides'

---

[36] Stahl 2003 [1966]: 150.
[37] Stahl 2003 [1966]: 150; Hunter 1973: 80; Rood 1998: 39–40.

phrasing belies the Athenians' trust in their ability to control the external world at will.

Stahl and Hunter have observed that Thucydides' depiction of the Athenians' collective mindset recalls Cleon's speech in the Mytilenean Debate.[38] Cleon's exhortation that the Athenians ought to make an important decision in the grips of passionate anger does not epitomize political prudence (3.38.1). Nevertheless, the following remark evidently sheds light on the situation at Athens in the wake of Pylos (3.39.4):[39]

εἴωθε δὲ τῶν πόλεων αἷς ἂν μάλιστα καὶ δι' ἐλαχίστου ἀπροσδόκητος εὐπραξία ἔλθῃ, ἐς ὕβριν τρέπειν.

Prosperity tends to turn those cities to insolence to which it comes most consumedly and most suddenly and contrary to expectation.

Cleon's account of the effects of unexpected prosperity is a precise description of the collective attitude prevalent at Athens after Pylos. In the eyes of the Greeks, Pylos was a complete surprise: 'Of all the incidents in this war this event happened most emphatically contrary to the expectation of the Greeks' (παρὰ γνώμην τε δὴ μάλιστα τῶν κατὰ τὸν πόλεμον τοῦτο τοῖς Ἕλλησιν ἐγένετο, 4.40.1). In the end, the outcome was a surprise for the Athenians themselves, because their campaign had been increasingly beset with difficulties after their rejection of the peace overture made by the Spartans (4.26.4). In the passage from the Mytilenean Debate, Cleon refers to prosperity, a term recalling Thucydides' comment about the Athenians' εὐτυχία at Pylos (4.65.4): it 'comes to cities unexpectedly', in the fashion of a daemonic force, and it 'turns them to insolence'. In this way, Cleon presents prosperity via personification, a figure also used in other Thucydidean passages to represent the overpowering forces that impact people's decisions (see Chapters 2, pp. 53–5; 3, pp. 104–5; and 4, pp. 122–3). After Pylos, the Athenians believe that they will achieve whatever objective they decide upon (4.65.4). This expectation certainly smacks of arrogance, a notion evoked

---

[38] Stahl 2003 [1966]: 150; Hunter 1973: 79–80.
[39] For the translation, see Poppo-Stahl ii, 1, on 3.39.4.

by Cleon's reference to ὕβρις. Contrary to the Athenians' confidence, the wording used by Cleon emphasizes the importance of factors that elude human control. It is a deep irony, worthy of tragic drama, that Cleon clearly sees the disastrous impact of sudden good fortune on the Mytileneans, but that he will later encourage the same mentality at Athens. When the Athenians reject the peace negotiations proposed by the Spartan envoys, Thucydides notes: 'Cleon, son of Cleaenetus, most of all urged them to adopt this course' (μάλιστα δὲ αὐτοὺς ἐνῆγε Κλέων ὁ Κλεαινέτου, 4.21.3).

Thucydides leaves no doubt as to what has caused the Athenians to succumb to this overly ambitious state of mind (4.65.4):

αἰτία δ' ἦν ἡ παρὰ λόγον τῶν πλεόνων εὐπραγία αὐτοῖς ὑποτιθεῖσα ἰσχὺν τῆς ἐλπίδος.

The reason was that their unexpected success in most undertakings prompted them to believe in a strength that was based on hope.[40]

The key terms of this passage are familiar from the speech of the Spartans: the word εὐπραγία, denoting a constellation of favourable circumstances, recalls εὐτυχίαν and τὸ...εὐτυχῆσαι (both at 4.17.4) as well as ταῖς εὐπραγίαις (4.17.5); the notion of things happening contrary to expectation (παρὰ λόγον) is reminiscent of the Spartans' emphasis on what comes unexpectedly (ἀδοκήτως, 4.17.4; πλεῖσται μεταβολαί, 17.5; ἀμφίβολον, 18.4); finally, the power of ἐλπίς over people's projections is stressed by the Spartans in a similar way (τοῦ πλέονος ἐλπίδι ὀρέγονται, 4.17.4). The Athenians have thus succumbed to the state of mind that the Spartans have warned them about.[41] There is also a close parallel between this passage and the account of ἐλπίς in the speech of Diodotus: ἡ δὲ τὴν εὐπορίαν τῆς τύχης ὑποτιθεῖσα ('It [sc. hope] suggests the easy provision of

---

[40] See the translation proposed by Classen-Steup (iv, on 4.65.4.17): '(der Umstand,) dass das unerwartete Glück in den meisten Fällen ihnen eine so übermächtige Hoffnung (eig. eine Macht der Hoffnung) einflösste.'
[41] See Hunter (1973: 80): 'We must conclude then that the envoys' remarks on unexpected good fortune represent Thucydides' own considered judgment.' See also Huart 1968: 147.

chance', 3.45.5).[42] In Diodotus' speech, hope is personified and functions as a counsellor (ὑποτιθεῖσα) by suggesting that τύχη will be favourable (τὴν εὐπορίαν). In Thucydides' comment about the cause of the Athenians' confidence (4.65.4), favourable circumstances (εὐπραγία) play the role of the counsellor (ὑποτιθεῖσα) and inspire hope (ἰσχὺν τῆς ἐλπίδος). The terms are nearly the same in both passages, arranged in a slightly different order.

Cornford has noticed a third link between Thucydides' assessment of the prevailing mood at Athens and another passage: Hermocrates' speech at the conference at Gela, when he persuades the Sicilians to keep Athens out of their affairs.[43] This speech comes immediately before the report of the return of the Athenian fleet from Sicily and is, therefore, fresh in the reader's mind when Thucydides assesses the prevailing mood at Athens. Again, it is interesting to consider the stylistic implications of the passage from Hermocrates' speech.

Hermocrates appeals to those Sicilians who expect that the Athenian intervention will settle inner-Sicilian discord in their favour. Instead of indulging in hope, says Hermocrates, the Sicilians should take heed of unforeseen consequences. The parallel pointed out by Cornford appears in the following passage (4.62.4):

τιμωρία γὰρ οὐκ εὐτυχεῖ δικαίως, ὅτι καὶ ἀδικεῖται· οὐδὲ ἰσχὺς βέβαιον, διότι καὶ εὔελπι.

For revenge does not attain success, as justice would require, simply because an injustice has been committed. Nor is strength a secure resource merely because it is full of hope.

While the themes of putative justice and revenge do not bear on the situation at Athens, Hermocrates' use of εὐτυχέω and his reference to strength (ἰσχύς) based on hope (ἐλπίς) recurs just two pages later (Alberti's edition providing the benchmark): Thucydides draws on the

---

[42] Without emphasizing stylistic points, Cornford (1907: 167) observes on a general level that Thucydides puts Diodotus' account of the dangerous cooperation between chance and collective hope (3.45.5–6) in the reader's mind by emphasizing both τύχη and Athenian hope in the wake of Pylos.

[43] Cornford 1907: 169–70.

precise terms used by Hermocrates in his authorial comment about the overconfident Athenian mentality (τῇ... εὐτχυίᾳ and ἰσχὺν τῆς ἐλπίδος, both at 4.65.4). Hermocrates makes clear that a factor other than the elusive strength built on hope is decisive. He captures it by a personified neuter abstract in subject position: 'The instability of the future rules far and wide' (τὸ δὲ ἀστάθμητον τοῦ μέλλοντος ὡς ἐπὶ πλεῖστον κρατεῖ, 4.62.4). Rule, and thus control, belongs not to human beings and their presumed strength, but to a power that implies the very opposite of stability: τὸ ἀστάθμητον, literally 'that which is not firmly set'. The use of this term as subject of the verb κρατέω smacks of wilful paradox. Instead of humans governing events, this power is in charge. Applied to the situation at Athens, the reign of τὸ ἀστάθμητον suggests that, after Pylos just as much as before, the Athenians cannot presume that they have a firm grip on the course of the War.

Another neuter phrase, used by Hermocrates a little earlier, also merits attention (4.62.3):

καὶ εἴ τις βεβαίως τι ἢ τῷ δικαίῳ ἢ βίᾳ πράξειν οἴεται, τῷ παρ' ἐλπίδα μὴ χαλεπῶς σφαλλέσθω.

And if anyone thinks that he will securely achieve anything, either due to the justice of his course or through force, let him not be painfully overthrown by that which proceeds contrary to hope.

Hermocrates points out that those who consider their own agency all-decisive (βεβαίως τι...πράξειν) may soon be reduced to passivity (σφαλλέσθω). He uses another substantivized neuter to highlight the factor that overthrows those who consider themselves invincible, thus resembling an adversarial agent: τῷ παρ' ἐλπίδα. Here as elsewhere, the impersonal phrase suggests a force that is largely inaccessible to human intervention. The impersonal and passive phrasing in the apodosis (τῷ παρ' ἐλπίδα... σφαλλέσθω) forms a stark contrast to the active language used in the protasis (βεβαίως τι... πράξειν). The dichotomy suggests that people easily overestimate what human agency can achieve.

In sum, the passage in which Thucydides highlights the Athenians' belief in the irresistibleness of their power stands at the centre of a network of references: the speeches of both Cleon and Diodotus in the Mytilenean Debate, the speech of the Spartan ambassadors at Athens, and the speech of Hermocrates at Gela. All the passages to which Thucydides alludes feature abstract and impersonal phrasing and converge in one basic idea when applied to the situation of the Athenians after Pylos: as a result of their success, the Athenians have become passive in the face of an irrational mindset induced by the vagaries of circumstances.

Four years later, with the benefit of hindsight, the Athenians come to realize that they were wrong not to conclude peace when their victory at Pylos provided a favourable opportunity (5.14.2).[44] It is a great Thucydidean irony that the successful Athenians just as much as the demoralized Spartans are in the grip of forces beyond their control.[45] The effects of the Spartans' κακοπραγεῖν (4.55.4) paradoxically resemble those of the Athenians' εὐπραγία (4.65.4).

5.5 Athenian Desire for Sicily: A Force Beyond Human Control

The immediate catalyst that causes open war between Athens and Sparta to rekindle to the full extent is the Athenian attack on Sicily. As observed in Section 4.7, two passions in particular, ἔρως and ἐλπίς, stand out as major driving forces that propel the Athenians to attack Sicily (ἔρως: 6.13.1, 24.3; ἐλπίς: 6.15.2, 24.3, 30.2, 31.6). As pointed out above, the rampancy of these passions evokes major themes found in the speech of Diodotus and the Melian Dialogue. It is an eerie irony that the Athenians fall prey to these impulses, after Athenian speakers had

---

[44] Stahl (2003 [1966]: 152) comments: 'The fact that a similar (or even a better) peace was possible years earlier already (after Pylos), but that this opportunity was blindly gambled away twice [sc. at 4.22.3 and 41.3–4] (and without the responsible side's having anything to show for it) is perhaps – aside from the decision to go to war in 431 – the most tragic *discovery* made in the process.'

[45] Compare the following remarks by Herter (1968b [1954]: 390) regarding the question whether a peace settlement after Pylos might have led to a more permanent agreement than the unstable Peace of Nicias was to offer four years later: '[D]ie psychologischen Voraussetzungen waren dafür nicht mehr gegeben: das πλέονος ὀρέγεσθαι, vor dem sie [sc. the Athenians] gewarnt wurden (IV 17, 4), beherrschte sie unwiderstehlich.'

clairvoyantly analysed their pernicious effects on previous occasions. The daemonic aspect of human nature, its capacity to overpower even those who should be aware of its temptations, becomes manifest. One finds the same interaction of clairvoyance and blindness that we observed in connection with Cleon's speech in the Mytilenean Debate and the mentality at Athens after Pylos (see Section 5.4).

Further specific parallels link the situation at Athens on the eve of the Sicilian Expedition with the mentality that the Athenians display in response to events at Pylos. The chief motives inducing overconfidence in the Athenians during and after Pylos were 'hope' (ἐλπίς: 4.17.4, 65.4) and 'longing for more' (ὀρέγομαι: 4.17.4, 21.2, 41.4). In connection with the desire for Sicily, phrases featuring the verb ὀρέγομαι occur twice in the debate between Nicias and Alcibiades: Nicias uses one of these phrases to capture the Athenians' desire for another empire (ὀρέγεσθαι, 6.10.5), and Alcibiades draws on the same term to capture his own desire for fame, which he hopes to attain by conquering Sicily (ὀρεγόμενος, 6.16.6). On the eve of the Sicilian Expedition, the collective Athenian mindset that arose in the wake of Pylos still prevails.[46]

Not only the emphasis on these passions is reminiscent of the mentality induced in the wake of events at Pylos. Passive and impersonal phrases also recur at the moment when the majority of the Athenians commit themselves to the expedition. After Nicias' second speech, whose declared goal has been to avert the Sicilian adventure, Thucydides describes the effect on the Athenians as follows: 'They were not stripped by the burdensomeness of the preparations of whatever it was within themselves that was desirous of the journey' (οἱ δὲ τὸ μὲν ἐπιθυμοῦν τοῦ πλοῦ οὐκ ἐξῃρέθησαν ὑπὸ τοῦ ὀχλώδους τῆς παρασκευῆς, 6.24.2). According to Heiny, Thucydides uses the neuter participle to capture 'some aspect of the Athenians that is desirous of making the voyage to

---

[46] See Macleod (1983f: 142–3): 'Nor is the connection between the two series of events [sc. Pylos and the Sicilian Expedition] merely an odd coincidence. It was overconfidence, caused precisely by unusual and unforeseen success, which led the Athenians to "want more"... and reject the Spartans' appeal for a peace. The same spirit of pride and greed is one motive for the Sicilian expedition.'

Sicily'.[47] As Heiny observes, 'the participle can be interpreted as modifying an unrealized noun, "the aspect desirous of sailing"', a phrase that 'does "beg the question"' of the agent responsible of this action.[48] Thus, the neuter participle conspicuously withholds an agent of the Athenians' desire. It implies that a condition has come to prevail: a mysterious force within the Athenians, best described by impersonal phrasing, is the subject of desire. This condition confronts the Athenians as if it were a factor not controlled by them: Thucydides does not describe it as an inward state, but as an independent force in charge of the desire for Sicily.

Thucydides observes that 'the Athenians were not stripped' of this disposition after listening to Nicias' speech. The verb ἐξαιρέω literally means 'to take out', implying that the Athenians need to be freed from a power that has surreptitiously infiltrated them. This verb is used in the passive with the Athenians as subject: they themselves seem unable to rid themselves of the state that afflicts them. The passive verb is accompanied by the regular construction used of the agent after a passive verb. Yet the role of the agent supposed to strip the Athenians of 'that which desires' is not played by Nicias. Instead, another nominalized neuter phrase fills the position of the agent: 'the burdensomeness of the equipment' (ὑπὸ τοῦ ὀχλώδους τῆς παρασκευῆς, 6.24.2). An impersonal factor (if anything at all) might be the only thing able to overcome the desirous disposition that has taken possession of the Athenians.

After pointing out that the Athenians were not stripped of τὸ ἐπιθυμοῦν, Thucydides continues to summarize the effect of Nicias' second speech: 'but they were much more eager for it [sc. the journey], and so the opposite [of what Nicias had expected] had come to pass for him' (πολὺ δὲ μᾶλλον ὥρμηντο, καὶ τοὐναντίον περιέστη αὐτῷ, 6.24.2). Due to the aspect of the pluperfect, which refers to a fixed state, the medio-passive verb ὥρμηντο ('were eager') suggests a settled condition. Moreover, Thucydides' language reveals that, in his opposition to the expedition, Nicias is up against forces that are too powerful for him:

---

[47] Heiny 1973: 101. See also the following observation made by Huart (1968: 401) with regard to this passage: 'neutre substantivé caractéristique,... où le participe présent suggère, mieux que le substantif, l'attitude de gens qui se mettent en état de réaliser leurs désirs'.

[48] Heiny 1973: 102.

while he tries to redirect the course of events, the momentum of the situation reduces him to passivity. This aspect is captured by a compound of ἵστημι: καὶ τοὐναντίον περιέστη αὐτῷ ('the opposite befell him', 6.24.2). Edmunds has observed that the verb περιίσταμαι 'is used elsewhere of reversals of expectation and of tyche...and more often metaphorically, of war, fear, danger, or suspicion,...than literally'.[49] Thus, it refers regularly to forces over which human beings have no control, a fact reflected in its repeated occurrence in connection with events at Pylos (4.10.1, 12.3, 34.3, 55.1). As noted previously, it also refers to the 'shift' from the Spartans to the Athenians of the unlawful willingness to unleash war (περιεστάναι, 7.18.3). The Athenians' eagerness that confronts Nicias has something in common with all these events: it is a force utterly beyond his, or anyone's, control. In fact, Nicias is reduced to a passive role: as noted above, Thucydides does not refer to Nicias as an agent when this would have been possible; he now refers to him in a dative construction that expresses his exposure to the reversal suggested by περιέστη.

In his first speech, Nicias had already appealed to the older men not to acquiesce in the expedition under pressure of eager and ambitious youths. He appeals to the elders 'not to be madly in love with absent things, which is what they [sc. these youths] may have suffered' (μηδ', ὅπερ ἂν αὐτοὶ πάθοιεν, δυσέρωτας εἶναι τῶν ἀπόντων, 6.13.1). Commenting on the adjective δυσέρως, Victoria Wohl points out that the prefix δυσ- evokes a range of associations: 'Excess, passion, delusion: the prefix *dus-* (bad, diseased, ill-fated) emphasizes the element of pathology.'[50] The use of a form of πάσχω, suggestive of suffering and passivity, matches the connotations of sickness and derangement. Nicias presents the mad infatuation with Sicily as a pathological state that has already infected the Athenian youths and is about to beset the elders as well. Note that, in the narrative of events at Pylos and their aftermath, vocabulary derived from πάσχω refers to the experience of the warring parties on several occasions (πάθει, 4.14.2; παθεῖν, 17.4; πάθους, 55.1).

After the conclusion of Nicias' second speech, a wave of desire sweeps over the Athenians with the force of a daemonic agent: 'And the desire to sail fell upon them in their entirety, on all alike' (καὶ ἔρως ἐνέπεσε τοῖς

---

[49] Edmunds 1975: 129.   [50] Wohl 2002: 189.

πᾶσιν ὁμοίως ἐκπλεῦσαι, 6.24.3). Thucydides uses his favourite device to capture the overwhelming forces innate in the Peloponnesian War: he combines a compound of πίπτω, which suggests onslaught and affliction, with the abstract noun ἔρως in subject position. Euben explains ἔρως to be 'the love of action combined with the desire to get or increase our power over other men or things'.[51] As a subject of ἐμπίπτω, this forceful passion is thus made to resonate with the other quintessential manifestations of the Peloponnesian War (see Chapter 2, pp. 67–70): the 'many evils of stasis', the plague, and the massacre at Mycalessus.

Drawing on the phrase ἔρως ἐνέπεσε, Thucydides makes a specific point about the Athenians' decision. As Kallet observes, 'the expedition itself becomes something out of their full control. The Athenians become not agents but, in a sense, victims as they plan to invade Sicily.'[52] Kallet's observation aptly summarizes not just the Athenians' decision in favour of the Sicilian Expedition, but also Thucydides' general account of the forces that prevail in decisions of paramount importance.

5.6 National Character and Human Nature

Thucydides traces the contrast between Sparta and Athens throughout his work.[53] He states that the two opponents were 'very different in character' (διάφοροι γὰρ πλεῖστον ὄντες τὸν τρόπον, 8.96.5) and that this opposition worked to the Athenians' advantage (8.96.5). In their speech at Sparta, the Corinthians famously flesh out the antithesis that Thucydides invoked in his comments in book 8: Athenian quickness is set against Spartan slowness,[54] and the Athenians' enterprising spirit is contrasted with Spartan faintheartedness.[55] Whereas Sparta's difference

---

[51] Euben 1990: 181.   [52] Kallet 2001: 135.
[53] On the theme of the Spartan vs. the Athenian character, see Gundert 1968 [1940]: 115–32; Strauss 1964: 146–9 and 209–17; Edmunds 1975: 89–93; Rood: 1998: 43–6; Luginbill 1999: 87–96; Jaffe 2017: 202–6.
[54] οἱ μὲν ὀξεῖς, οἱ δὲ βραδεῖς, 8.96.5 ~ ἄοκνοι πρὸς ὑμᾶς μελλητάς, 1.70.4; cf. ἐπινοῆσαι ὀξεῖς, 1.70.2 (about the Athenians) vs. ὑμῶν ἡ βραδυτής, 1.71.4 (about the Spartans).
[55] οἱ μὲν [sc. the Athenians] ἐπιχειρηταί, οἱ δὲ [sc. the Spartans] ἄτολμοι, 8.96.5 ~ (about the Athenians) παρὰ δύναμιν τολμηταί, 1.70.3 and ἐπιχείρησιν ποιεῖσθαι, 1.70.7 vs. (about the Spartans) μηδὲ τοῖς βεβαίοις πιστεῦσαι τῶν τε δεινῶν μηδέποτε οἴεσθαι ἀπολυθήσεσθαι, 1.70.3.

from Athens is a disadvantage, the similarity between the Syracusan and the Athenian character (ὁμοιότροποι, 8.96.5) proves to be crucial for the Syracusans' success. Thus, it is evident that Thucydides regarded national character as having some explanatory value. In terms of the factors that lead to major decisions, the prevalence of fear at Sparta, as well as of hope and desire at Athens, reflects this basic structural antithesis between the Spartan and Athenian characters. As a result, the question arises whether it is still correct to locate the forces that motivate decisions in general human nature as opposed to national character.

Thucydidean speakers do in fact single out each of these contrary sets of motivations (one exemplified by Sparta, the other by Athens) as general human tendencies (fear and defensiveness: 1.75.3, 1.76.2, 3.39.5, 4.61.5; hope and desire: 3.45.5; hope alone: 5.103.1 and 2) rather than as specific national characteristics. In light of these statements, the prevailing picture appears to be that distinctive cities call forth distinctive aspects of human nature, and that they fall prey more easily to those dispositions that correspond to their way of life: the defensive and disciplined Spartans succumb to fear, whereas the free and enterprising Athenians are carried away by hope and desire.

This scheme easily obscures the fact that, both at Athens and at Sparta, the basic human dispositions that are less typical of the city's character also play a role, even if less conspicuously. Despite the prevalence of ἔρως and ἐλπίς at Athens, several speakers highlight fear of the imperial rival Syracuse as a motivation for the Sicilian Expedition.[56] The critics of the expedition disagree with its proponents as to whether this fear is φόβος or δέος. If it is the former, it is panicky and affective, excludes reflection, and is directed at the unknown; if the latter, it elicits deliberation and takes its bearings from what is factual. For Nicias, the Athenians are affected by φόβος (ἐκφοβοῦσιν, 6.11.2). According to Euphemus' speech at Camarina, they feel δέος (6.83.4). Given the Athenians' impending lapse into collective fear and hysteria in response to the mutilation of the Herms

---

[56] Notice that Wohl (2017: 456) observes apropos the inclusion of fear among the three primary motivational forces singled out by the Athenian ambassadors at Sparta that this argument 'suggests an alternate psychology of empire, in which the tragedy of Sicily is propelled not by the endemic affective imbalance of democracy, or by innate Athenian *erōs* and *elpis*, but by a fear inherent to human nature as a whole'.

and the alleged profanation of the Mysteries, it may well be the case that Nicias is correct. This supposition is supported by the fact that Nicias is generally alert to the risks and adverse aspects of the expedition.[57] In any event, both speakers' emphasis on fear directs the reader's attention to this factor, regardless of the fact that rhetorical considerations are at play on both occasions. Moreover, Nicias' and Alcibiades' contention about where the real danger lies for Athens (whether in sitting still or in undertaking the expedition while surrounded by enemies at home) also implies latent fear, which is highlighted by both speakers' conspicuous references to κίνδυνος and related vocabulary (Nicias: 6.9.3, 10.5, 12.2, 13.1; Alcibiades: 6.18.2, 18.3).

The role of fear as a motivating force of Athenian expansion is already apparent in the Melian Dialogue: the Athenian envoys cite concern with their own 'security' (τὸ ἀσφαλές, 5.97) as the chief reason for why the Athenians want to incorporate Melos into their empire. This theme recurs in the Sicilian Debate when Alcibiades argues somewhat perversely that the expedition, far from jeopardizing the fortunes of the city, will promote Athenian 'safety' (ἀσφαλέστατα, 6.18.7). Thus, fear and concerns for security continuously crop up beneath the dominating impulses of hope and desire. The repeated references to these motives indicate that they do have some explanatory value.[58]

The role played by fear at Athens has a parallel at Sparta: despite the Spartans' generally defensive orientation, hope about their prospects in the War plays a considerable role in their decision recounted in book 1. Archidamus twice warns the Spartans to refrain from the deluded hope that they will hold all the aces in the War with the Athenians (1.81.6, 84.4). In the assessment of the Spartans' motive for concluding the Peace

---

[57] Stahl 2003 [1973] 179.

[58] Desmond (2006: 368) thinks that 'scare tactics' are put to the use of 'imperialistic ends' in these passages. This phrasing implies the interpretation that the advocates of the expedition use fear as a respectable, but feigned, motive for their aggressive agenda. Yet Thucydides' general insistence on universal human nature suggests that fear is a genuine motive, which is merely subordinate to more aggressive impulses in the specific Athenian setting. Further passages show that the Athenians themselves think of fear as a motive that prompts some of their political actions. For one thing, the Athenian ambassadors at Sparta include δέος among the 'three greatest things' that motivated the Athenians first to acquire, and then to hold on to, the empire (1.75.3, 76.2). Moreover, Pericles tells the Athenians in his last speech that 'letting go of' the empire would be 'fraught with danger' (ἀφεῖναι δὲ ἐπικίνδυνον, 2.63.2), a warning that implies fear of the consequent risks.

of Nicias, Thucydides himself implicitly indicates that, contrary to Archidamus' warning, the Spartans had been confident of their success in the War: they were willing to conclude peace 'because the War had turned out contrary to expectation for them' (παρὰ γνώμην... ἀποβαίνοντος σφίσι τοῦ πολέμου, 5.14.3). Moreover, the recklessness with which the Corinthians, in their second speech in book 1, take mere possibilities as certainties (1.121.3) and are emboldened by the essential unpredictability of the War (1.122.1) is symptomatic of the befuddling impact of ἐλπίς, even if the word itself does not occur. This is the only speech that Thucydides records from the congress of the Peloponnesian allies. Directly after its conclusion, the Peloponnesians vote for war. Thucydides implies that it struck a chord with its audience.

The most important passage showing the fundamental similarity between Spartans and Athenians occurs at the beginning of book 8, when Thucydides describes the general atmosphere at Sparta in the wake of the Athenian disaster at Sicily. 'Being hopeful' (εὐέλπιδες ὄντες, 8.2.4) the Spartans are described as wholeheartedly committed to press ahead with the War. The exact phrase used by Thucydides occurs on one other occasion in the *History*: when the ἔρως for the Sicilian Expedition strikes, Thucydides describes those Athenians who are in their prime as 'being hopeful' (εὐέλπιδες ὄντες, 6.24.3). Yet the parallel does not end here.

Thucydides proceeds to highlight the Spartans' expectation 'that, after having put those [*sc.* the Athenians] down, they themselves would now securely rule Greece in its entirety' (καθελόντες ἐκείνους αὐτοὶ τῆς πάσης Ἑλλάδος ἤδη ἀσφαλῶς ἡγήσεσθαι, 8.2.4). The ambition to rule over a territory 'in its entirety' is a leitmotiv of the Athenians' infatuation with the conquest of Sicily. Thucydides makes unmistakably clear that this is the Athenians' main objective: distinguishing the ἀληθεστάτη πρόφασις of the Sicilian Expedition from sham justifications, he points out that, 'to name the truest cause, they desired to rule over [Sicily] in its entirety' (ἐφιέμενοι μὲν τῇ ἀληθεστάτῃ προφάσει τῆς πάσης ἄρξαι, 6.6.1). In introducing Nicias' speech, Thucydides reiterates this point, drawing attention to Nicias' awareness that 'they longed for all of Sicily, which was a great undertaking' (τῆς Σικελίας ἁπάσης, μεγάλου ἔργου, ἐφίεσθαι, 6.8.4). The Athenian concern with dominion of Sicily in its entirety thus receives marked emphasis. This theme has already been sounded on the occasion of the Athenians' first attempted interference with affairs at Sicily: during his speech at Gela, Hermocrates puts the emphasis squarely on the Athenians' concern with the conquest of the 'entirety' of Sicily (τὴν πᾶσαν Σικελίαν, 4.60.1; τάδε πάντα, 60.2; οἱ ἔνοικοι ξύμπαντες, 61.1; τὴν πᾶσαν Σικελίαν, 61.2). Alcibiades, who is always at least one step ahead of everyone else, takes this ambition to the next level. As he says in the Sicilian Debate, he thinks that the Athenians are likely to acquire rule over *all of* Hellas if they succeed at Sicily (τῆς Ἑλλάδος ... πάσης ... ἄρξομεν, 6.18.4). In his speech at Sparta, he makes the same point, claiming that the Athenians aim at 'ruling Hellenic civilization in its entirety' (τοῦ ξύμπαντος Ἑλληνικοῦ ἄρξειν, 6.90.3). No sooner do the Athenians, incited by hope, fail disastrously to subject Sicily, and then Greece, in their *entirety* than the Spartans, likewise urged on by hope, begin to think that it is high time for them to rule Greece in its *entirety*. The impression is fixed on the reader's mind that an objective force has leapt to its next victim. Despite eye-catching surface differences, the Spartans are not as different from the Athenians as it may seem.

Athens and Sparta stand for different basic possibilities in which human nature can manifest itself.[59] Even if the dominant drives are different in each city, the basic structure to which humans are subject is the same:[60] larger-than-life impulses and external constellations drive the decisions of the Athenians and Spartans. This interpretation dovetails with Cogan's view that τὸ ἀνθρώπινον is 'something constant rather than something regularly recurrent. It is this constant, this manner of acting in all circumstances, which both causes all events and is revealed in a history of them.'[61] One crucial aspect of this ingrained 'manner of

---

[59] Jaffe (2017: 197) provides a similar account of the interaction between underlying natural predisposition and its manifestation in specific cities: 'Thucydidean cities and individuals are pulled toward certain ends ... All communities ... seek advantage, but they conceive of it differently and pursue it more or less effectively ... These conceptions of advantage also vary within a natural range; for they are not infinitely plastic.'

[60] Note that Pelling (2019: 145) observes with regard to Homer's *Iliad* and Herodotus: 'National nature may be one thing, and it matters; human nature is something bigger. Thucydides would have agreed.' See also p. 212: 'Thucydides will be more explicit than Herodotus in his focus on the ways in which human nature works in everyone, however different they remain.'

[61] Cogan 1981a: 234.

acting', reflected in the neuter τὸ ἀνθρώπινον, is the universal tendency of even the greatest cities to be dominated by awesome impersonal forces finding expression in collective passions interlocked with external conditions. These factors play the role of irresistible motive forces inherent in the dynamic of events. This exposure to factors beyond anyone's control is an inevitable fact about human beings, a characteristic anchored in their constitution and part and parcel of their φύσις. For this reason, the opposite character traits displayed by Athens and Sparta do not belong to the deepest level of analysis.

5.7 Conclusion

The argument presented in this chapter does not imply that Thucydides presents the choices made by people at major moments of decision exclusively through language suggestive of occurrence and passivity. For instance, when Thucydides records the Athenians' vote in favour of the Sicilian Expedition, he does not employ any impersonal or passive phrasing: 'On hearing this, the Athenians voted straightaway that the generals should possess full powers, concerning both the magnitude of the armament and the entire expedition, to act in whatever way would seem best to them for the Athenians'" (ἀκούσαντες δ' οἱ Ἀθηναῖοι ἐψηφίσαντο εὐθὺς αὐτοκράτορας εἶναι καὶ περὶ στρατιᾶς πλήθους καὶ περὶ τοῦ παντὸς πλοῦ τοὺς στρατηγοὺς πράσσειν ᾗ ἂν αὐτοῖς δοκῇ ἄριστα εἶναι Ἀθηναίοις, 6.26.1). Similar passages can easily be adduced from the accounts of the other two decisions. To give just once example, despite his emphasis on the Spartans' passivity in the wake of Pylos, Thucydides writes in active language that the Spartans 'continued to send envoys to them [sc. the Athenians] and tried to recover Pylos and their men' (ἐπρεσβεύοντο παρ' αὐτοὺς καὶ ἐπειρῶντο τήν τε Πύλον καὶ τοὺς ἄνδρας κομίζεσθαι, 4.41.3).

The occurrence of active phrases with personal subjects does not invalidate the passages that stress passivity and prioritize depersonalizing forces over personal agents. The combination of these two stylistic levels provides a further example of the interaction between the plain and the abstract depersonalizing style analysed in Chapters 1 and 2. In a similar way, the fact that human beings are presented as acting and making choices in Homer, Herodotus, and the tragedians does not exclude the view that the gods and fate have a decisive influence on events. Otherwise, it would, for instance, be illegitimate for Herodotus to say that Croesus decided to make war on Cyrus because, strictly speaking, this decision was fated to take place and, therefore, the divine had a hand in inducing Croesus' choice (1.13.2, 91.1–2). Herodotus will take this superhuman aspect into consideration, but, as scholars have stressed, this does not prevent him from providing a narrative centered on events happening on the plane of human motivation and action.[62]

The difference between passages stressing human agency and others emphasizing superhuman forces is one of perspective: while, for much of the time, Greek writers content themselves with recording the way things look to a direct observer by highlighting personal actions and choices, they also like to probe into the fundamental forces at work in a situation. When the latter concern takes centre stage, they traditionally draw attention to superhuman powers that impinge on the actions people perform. In a similar vein, Thucydides regularly takes recourse to emphatically passive and impersonal phrasing when probing the deepest causes of major decisions. Thucydides finds that transpersonal factors such as fear and hope ultimately precipitate the great political decisions on which the fate of cities, and even of Greek civilization as a whole, depends. While a perspective that prioritizes personhood and deliberate agency does not offer the whole picture, it remains valid because it provides the only framework by which it is possible to give a narrative account of *what* happened—and this factual basis must precede any attempt to probe *why* something happened.

---

[62] Meier 1980: 339–40; Pelling 2019: 152–3.

6

Dual Motivation

The Interaction of Necessity and Individual Choice

The preliminary conclusion of Chapter 5, namely that the major decisions recorded by Thucydides show the impact of suprapersonal factors trumping human choices, must be squared with evidence to the contrary. Thucydides' account of the resolution in favour of the Sicilian Expedition does not only show the impact of forces that constrain the decision-making process; it also provides incontestable evidence that individual agents exert considerable influence on the formation of events. The issue of personal agency crystallizes around Alcibiades, whose presentation in Thucydides is 'strikingly personal throughout'.[1] Thus, the section on the Athenians' decision combines a focus on Thucydides' most eye-catching individual with a sustained emphasis, investigated in Chapter 5, on the impact of general human nature in the guise of ἔρως and ἐλπίς. Given the presence of these two levels, this episode is ideally suited for an analysis of the intertwining of individual character and general forces in the formation of decisions.

Thucydides leaves no doubt that Alcibiades' advocacy of the Sicilian Expedition makes a powerful impression on the Athenians (6.19.1). At the same time, the reader is faced with the nagging question whether an opponent of a more impressive calibre than Nicias might have been able to offer more effective resistance to the rampant enthusiasm for the Sicilian adventure. As Macleod observes, Alcibiades and Nicias each impersonate fundamental conflicting inclinations, energy vs. restraint, whereas Pericles was able to unify these antithetical tendencies.[2] The all-encompassing interaction, achieved by Pericles, of contrary dispositions has disintegrated. What, however, if Pericles, or another man bearing his

---

[1] Westlake 1968: 259.   [2] Macleod 1983b [1975]: 86.

(admittedly rare) stamp, had been in Nicias' place? Might he not have been more effective than Nicias in cautioning the Athenians against the campaign against Syracuse, by channelling their inexhaustible enthusiasm for action while restraining them from the lure of irrational impulses? In the so-called valedictory passage on Pericles, Thucydides implies that the inadequacy of Athenian politicians after Pericles' death was responsible for plunging the city into many wayward enterprises that eventually proved fatal for Athenian prospects of success in the War (2.65.11). The interference with Sicily seems to rank among these ill-conceived projects. In sum, it seems plausible to conclude that the political personnel available at a specific occasion matters greatly for how events play out. Hence, in addition to the strand of necessity, the element of personal agents also has some impact, which varies depending on the specific situation and the personnel involved. In this chapter, I will attempt to explain how the opposite strands of individual involvement and necessity interact. The angle of necessity will serve as a starting point.

6.1 The Decision in Favour of the Sicilian Expedition (I): the Paragon of Necessity

In Chapter 5, we saw that desire and hope, the factors singled out by Diodotus, chiefly propel the Athenians to undertake the Sicilian Expedition. Thucydides suggests that these general collective impulses assume a concrete human shape in one specific individual: Alcibiades. In his character sketch of Alcibiades, Thucydides attributes the two passions in one breath to Alcibiades, observing that he was 'desirous to be general' and 'hopeful to conquer Sicily and Carthage' ($\sigma\tau\rho\alpha\tau\eta\gamma\hat{\eta}\sigma\alpha\acute{\iota}\ \tau\epsilon$ $\dot{\epsilon}\pi\iota\theta\upsilon\mu\hat{\omega}\nu\ \kappa\alpha\grave{\iota}\ \dot{\epsilon}\lambda\pi\acute{\iota}\zeta\omega\nu\ \Sigma\iota\kappa\epsilon\lambda\acute{\iota}\alpha\nu\ \tau\epsilon\ldots\kappa\alpha\grave{\iota}\ K\alpha\rho\chi\eta\delta\acute{o}\nu\alpha\ \lambda\acute{\eta}\psi\epsilon\sigma\theta\alpha\iota$, 6.15.2). Both hope and desire are connected with exercising rule or command. The drive to exercise power, on the one hand, and hope and desire, on the other, converge in Alcibiades, thus bearing out the Thucydidean analysis of $\varphi\acute{\upsilon}\sigma\iota\varsigma\ \dot{\alpha}\nu\theta\rho\acute{\omega}\pi\omega\nu$.

It has often been observed that Alcibiades embodies the distinctive mentality of the Athenians in a heightened fashion: their adventurousness, their boldness, their passionate longing, their get-up-and-go.³ A crucial role in forging this link is played by Thucydides' presentation of the general mood at Athens on the eve the Sicilian Expedition. Thucydides uses a wide range of words that suggest 'desire', 'eagerness', and 'urgency' to convey the impression that longing for Sicily is everywhere and spreads in Athens like an external, atmospheric force. Several of the words used to this effect also refer to Alcibiades. In this way, Thucydides systematically sustains the notion that Alcibiades personifies the general forces rampant among the Athenians on the eve of the Sicilian Expedition.

Thucydides himself (6.24.2, 24.4) or Nicias (6.10.1, 13.1) repeatedly use words with the stem of ἐπιθυμέω to refer to the Athenians. Hermocrates also captures the Athenian interest in Sicily by a form of ἐπιθυμία (6.33.2) in his speech, which is full of true insights, at the discussion in Syracuse that functions as a companion piece to the debate in Athens.⁴ In two passages, Thucydides uses words from this group specifically of Alcibiades (6.15.3, 15.4). The same relationship of correspondence between Alcibiades and the Athenians is suggested by forms of ὀρέγομαι: Alcibiades himself mentions his 'longing for fame', using a form of ὀρέγομαι (6.16.6), while Nicias captures the Athenians' general longing 'for another empire' by the same word (6.10.5).

Further phrases underscore the mutually reflective relationship between the Athenians and Alcibiades. Προθυμέομαι refers to each trierarch's eagerness for his ship to excel in the armament against Sicily (6.31.3). Moreover, the Egestaean envoys tell the Athenians enticing (ἐπαγωγά), but untrue things about the situation at Sicily (6.8.2). Ἐπαγωγός, deriving from the verb ἄγω, suggests the idea of urging someone on. Alcibiades is again the one individual in whom this collective mood finds a focused expression. Thucydides uses a phrase about him that combines a word related to προθυμέομαι with a compound of ἄγω: ἐνῆγε δὲ προθυμότατα τὴν στρατείαν ('but he kept on urging the

---

³ Bender 1938: 73; Ehrenberg 1947: 50–1; Westlake 1968: 259–60; Forde 1989: 201–2 (noting parallels and divergences); Orwin 1994: 123; Gribble 1999: 209; Wohl 2002: 191–2, 196–7.
⁴ On the accuracy, proven by subsequent events, of Hermocrates' insights, see Stahl 2003 [1966] 121–2 and [1973] 187; Hunter 1973: 153–66; Bloedow 1993: 124.

expedition most zealously', 6.15.2). In Alcibiades, the urges driving the expedition become, as it were, embodied. He emerges as a condensed concretization of the forces inherent in human nature out of the general atmosphere of desire.

Complementing the parallelism between collective and individual, a host of specific parallels shows that the Athenian infatuation with Sicily is modelled, with considerable precision, on the general mindset described by Diodotus.[5] Cornford has drawn attention to two parallels. First, Diodotus' claim that ἔρως 'leads the way' (ἡγούμενος, 3.45.5) evokes Alcibiades' leadership of the expedition: with Alcibiades at the helm, ἔρως personified indeed does function as the Athenians' leader on their bold Sicilian campaign.[6] Moreover, as Cornford also observes, Diodotus' point that ἔρως 'thinks out the scheme' (τὴν ἐπιβουλὴν ἐκφροντίζων, 3.45.5) evokes two passages relevant to the Athenians' concern with Sicily: one appears in the speech of Alcibiades (ἀνάγκη... τοῖς μὲν ἐπιβουλεύειν, 6.18.3), the other in Hermocrates' speech at the conference of Gela (ἐπιβουλευομένην τὴν πᾶσαν Σικελίαν... ὑπ' Ἀθηναίων, 4.60.1).[7]

Close inspection of Thucydides' text reveals further parallels over and above the echoes noted by Cornford. Diodotus stresses that ἐλπίς typically 'suggests the ease of fortune' (τὴν εὐπορίαν τῆς τύχης ὑποτιθεῖσα, 3.45.5). Alcibiades, the personification of desire and hope, tells the Athenians that the situation in Sicily will in fact 'still be easier to deal with' (ἔτι εὐπορώτερα ἔσται, 6.17.6) than the picture he has just sketched as part of an exceedingly optimistic forecast (6.17.2–5). Alcibiades' wording recalls the phrase used by Diodotus, with the adjective εὐπορώτερα echoing Diodotus' τὴν εὐπορίαν.

Diodotus sounds the theme of invisibility in a statement that refers to ἔρως and ἐλπίς jointly: 'being invisible they are stronger than seen terrors' (ὄντα ἀφανῆ κρείσσω ἐστὶ τῶν ὁρωμένων δεινῶν, 3.45.5). The

---

[5] On the parallel between Diodotus' speech and the Athenian decision to invade Sicily, see Stahl 2003 [1966]: 120–1.

[6] Cornford 1907: 219.

[7] Cornford 1907: 211 n. 4. Cornford remarks that this passage comes immediately after an even closer parallel with Diodotus' speech: οὐδείς... φόβῳ, ἢν οἴηταί τι πλέον σχήσειν, ἀποτρέπεται [sc. from making war] (4.59.2), which evokes ἁπλῶς... ἀδύνατον..., ὅστις οἴεται τῆς ἀνθρωπείας φύσεως ὁρμωμένης προθύμως τι πρᾶξαι ἀποτροπήν τινα ἔχειν ἢ νόμων ἰσχύι ἢ ἄλλῳ τῳ δεινῷ (3.45.7).

perils that beset the invisible realm also feature in Nicias' first speech: he urges the Athenians 'not to endanger available possessions on account of invisible and future things' (μὴ τοῖς ἑτοίμοις περὶ τῶν ἀφανῶν καὶ μελλόντων κινδυνεύειν, 6.9.3). In both passages, the invisible has an alluring attractiveness, a pull that the mundane sphere of things 'seen' and 'available' cannot exert. In addition, both passages involve the idea that the invisible realm induces irresponsible risk-taking: Diodotus thinks that the invisible forces thrust aside 'seen terrors' (τῶν ὁρωμένων δεινῶν), and Nicias sees the Athenians 'endangering' (κινδυνεύειν) their present possessions out of an infatuation with the invisible.

Summarizing his account of human nature, Diodotus highlights the impossibility of effectively resisting irrational collective impulses 'when human nature is zealously eager to achieve something' (τῆς ἀνθρωπείας φύσεως ὁρμωμένης προθύμως τι πρᾶξαι, 3.45.7). Diodotus' phrase of human nature 'being zealously eager' (ὁρμωμένης προθύμως) resurfaces in the account of the Athenian decision in favour of the Sicilian Expedition. As pointed out previously, Thucydides writes that Alcibiades 'kept on urging the expedition most zealously' (ἐνῆγε δὲ προθυμότατα τὴν στρατείαν, 6.15.2). As a result of his speech, 'the Athenians were much more eager to undertake the expedition' (πολλῷ μᾶλλον...ὥρμηντο στρατεύειν, 6.19.1). This notion is underscored by Nicias at the opening of his second speech: 'I see that you, Athenians, have become altogether eager to undertake the expedition' (πάντως ὁρῶ ὑμᾶς, ὦ Ἀθηναῖοι, ὡρμημένους στρατεύειν, 6.20.1). In two further passages, Thucydides captures the Athenians' obsession with Sicily by forms of ὁρμάομαι (ὥρμηντο, 6.6.1; ὥρμηντο, 24.2). Finally, a phrase used by Thucydides to describe the Egestaean envoys' nagging advocacy of the expedition is of special interest: 'Most of all the Egestaeans' envoys, who were present and were invoking their help ever more zealously, urged them on' (μάλιστα δ' αὐτοὺς ἐξώρμησαν Ἐγεσταίων [τε] πρέσβεις παρόντες καὶ προθυμότερον ἐπικαλούμενοι, 6.6.2). The verb ἐξορμάω recalls Diodotus' ὁρμάομαι and the adverb προθυμότερον his προθύμως. The situation on the eve of the Sicilian Expedition is a paragon of 'human nature striving zealously to achieve something', with the Egestaeans and Alcibiades impersonating the urges that instigate the Athenians.

According to Diodotus, it is futile to find 'some means of averting' (ἀποτροπήν τινα, 3.45.7) human nature when it has become fixated on some objective in the wake of hope and desire. It is hardly a coincidence that Thucydides, and Alcibiades in his speech, repeatedly highlight Nicias' attempt to do the very thing that Diodotus considers pointless. Thucydides remarks that Nicias addresses the Athenians in connection with the projected expedition because 'he wished to avert it' (ἀποτρέψαι ἐβούλετο, 6.8.4). In his rejoinder, Alcibiades urges the Athenians not to let Nicias' divisive promotion of a policy of non-involvement 'avert' them (μὴ ὑμᾶς ... ἀποτρέψῃ, 6.18.6). Faced with the Athenians' enthusiasm about Alcibiades' speech, Nicias realizes 'that he would no longer avert them by drawing on the same arguments [*sc.* that he used before]' (ὅτι ἀπὸ μὲν τῶν αὐτῶν λόγων οὐκ ἂν ἔτι ἀποτρέψειε, 6.19.2). As a result, Nicias gives a second speech, which will have the exact opposite effect of what he has in view: Thucydides, summarizing Nicias' speech, observes that he intended 'to avert the Athenians by the sheer magnitude of troublesome business' (τοὺς Ἀθηναίους τῷ πλήθει τῶν πραγμάτων ... ἀποτρέψειν, 6.24.1). In each of these four passages, a form of ἀποτρέπω refers to Nicias' desire to 'avert' the Athenians from undertaking the expedition. The noun ἀποτροπή, used by Diodotus, is derived from the same verb.

In sum, specific parallels link the account of the Sicilian Debate with Diodotus' speech. These echoes show that the passions rampant among the Athenians are not transient motivations, and they are not merely specific to the situation at Athens on this particular occasion. In light of the parallels with Diodotus' account, ἔρως and ἐλπίς have the character of monolithic, eternal forces carved out of the hard, endurable marble that provides the stuff of human nature. These essentially unchanging, transpersonal forces are at the bottom of the Athenians' eager wish to conquer Sicily.

Thucydides' manner of presentation invites the conclusion that ἔρως and ἐλπίς have much in common with the force exerted, for instance, by Aphrodite in Euripides' *Hippolytus*. To judge by this play, erotic passion is not an inward feeling, fundamentally specific to the delicately drawn features of Phaedra's unique personality. Instead, it comes across as an objective state that attaches itself to Phaedra from without. On this view,

Phaedra's passion for Hippolytus is at bottom the same as, for instance, that of Paris for Helen, notwithstanding some individual variation of the characters' response (Phaedra evidently tries to resist whereas Paris is usually not depicted as particularly stiff-necked when Aphrodite visits him). The permanent features of the experience matter more than attention to the aspects pertaining to a unique individual. Based on the modern assumption that each individual has a uniquely personal perspective, one might expect the experience of an intense passion such as ἔρως to differ fundamentally from one person to another. By contrast, Thucydides' account conveys the same impression as Euripides' *Hippolytus*: what is permanent matters more than the individual response to the force of ἔρως and ἐλπίς. Thus, it makes no essential difference whether these passions stir Alcibiades or the Athenian demos or the Mytileneans. The emphasis on what is permanent and unchanging shows that both Alcibiades and the Athenians, taken as a collective, act under the influence of the innate natural necessity described by Diodotus.

6.2 The Decision in Favour of the Sicilian Expedition (II): the Strand of Individualism

Notwithstanding the impact of necessity, Alcibiades is depicted, more than any other actor in Thucydides, as a person with distinctive character traits. At least some of these character traits are too strongly evocative of Alcibiades' colourful personality to be easily deducible to a general, transpersonal force.

The first example of a markedly individualized feature is Alcibiades' adoption of a conciliatory posture towards his rival Nicias, a stance that complements his disparagement elsewhere (6.18.5–6), which in any case is merely indirect.[8] Nicias does not mention Alcibiades by name during his first speech, but it is blatantly obvious that he has none other than Alcibiades in mind when he criticizes the perilous demagogy of an unnamed youth who delights in his command and plans to finance his

---

[8] On the obliqueness of Alcibiades' polemic against Nicias, see Macleod 1983b [1975]: 84–5.

extravagant lifestyle by the riches to be gained from the expedition (6.12.2). Although Thucydides notes that Alcibiades takes offence at this jab (6.15.2), it is remarkable that, at least on the surface, Alcibiades does not pay Nicias back in kind. Instead, he urges the Athenians to let both Nicias and Alcibiades himself contribute their distinctive qualities to the expedition: 'As long as I am still in the prime that comes with it [*sc.* youth] and Nicias has the reputation of good luck, avail yourselves to the full of the usefulness of each of us' (ἕως ἐγώ τε ἔτι ἀκμάζω μετ' αὐτῆς καὶ ὁ Νικίας εὐτυχὴς δοκεῖ εἶναι, ἀποχρήσασθε τῇ ἑκατέρου ἡμῶν ὠφελίᾳ, 6.17.1). The reference to Nicias' 'reputation for good luck' (as opposed to 'good luck' itself) may well be an oblique jibe, but the fact remains that Alcibiades, rather than trying to oust Nicias, proposes that they cooperate.

Alcibiades is more openly hostile towards Nicias when warning the Athenians of his 'inactivity and divisiveness' (ἀπραγμοσύνη καὶ διάστασις, 6.18.6), but he immediately strikes a conciliatory note when calling for the cooperation of young and old (νέοι γεραιτέροις βουλεύοντες and νεότητα... καὶ γῆρας ἄνευ ἀλλήλων μηδὲν δύνασθαι, 6.18.6), a unity that will find visible expression in the joint command of the two rivals. It turns out that young and attractive Alcibiades courts the favour of old curmudgeons such as Nicias. Alcibiades certainly has ulterior motives in adopting this posture of goodwill, not least the calculation that this demeanour will look much more attractive than the divisiveness of Nicias. He may also think that it will be best to drag his rival into the expedition, rather than having him obstruct Alcibiades' leadership from back home. Nonetheless, joint command will require cooperation between the generals. As a result, Alcibiades' willingness to get along with a man who has just attacked him strikes a relatively affable note.

It is interesting that Plato's *Symposium* provides evidence of the same character trait in Alcibiades. A recurrent theme of Alcibiades' speech in praise of Socrates is his desire to win the favour of Socrates, who, however, never quite succumbs to his charms (217a2–e1, 218a2–7, 219b3–e5, 222a8–c3). Plato plays on the irony that Alcibiades, who epitomizes youth, beauty, and success, courts none other than Socrates—the second Silenus, with his quintessential features of old age and ugliness. In a more subdued way, Thucydides alludes to the same inverse relationship and the light it casts on Alcibiades' wooing of those who are far less attractive than he is. It may well be that this feature of Alcibiades belongs to his close association with ἔρως. Nevertheless, it refers to a very specific manifestation of ἔρως in this particular individual, a facet not to be found in Diodotus' forbidding depiction of the principal urges that animate human nature.

Another distinctive feature of Alcibiades' personality concerns his ability to radiate a kind of cheerful impudence, a character trait particularly visible when he turns venerable principles, staunchly upheld by everyone else, on their heads. In his speech at the Sicilian Debate, he tells the egalitarian Athenians that 'it is not at all unjust [*sc.* for a man who has benefited his city] to take pride in himself and not to be on equal terms with the rest' (οὐδέ γε ἄδικον ἐφ' ἑαυτῷ μέγα φρονοῦντα μὴ ἴσον εἶναι, 6.16.4). Alcibiades' disarming argument for this claim is that, if people were honest in their demand for equality, they should also be willing to share the equal lot of those who fare poorly (6.16.4). The thought seems to be that average citizens insist on the equality of those more gifted and successful, but that they do not want to be the equal of people worse off than they are. According to Alcibiades, those who sniff at people in evil plight ought to be consistent: 'But just as people won't talk to us when we suffer misfortune, so everyone must also endure to be despised by those who have achieved great success' (ἀλλ' ὥσπερ δυστυχοῦντες οὐ προσαγορευόμεθα, ἐν τῷ ὁμοίῳ τις ἀνεχέσθω καὶ ὑπὸ τῶν εὐπραγούντων ὑπερφρονούμενος, 6.16.4). Alcibiades suggests that average citizens want to have no business with a luckless individual; accordingly, they should also accept that those who are extraordinarily fortunate want to have no business with them. Thus, he who has 'big thoughts' (μέγα φρονοῦντα, 6.16.4) is also entitled 'to place himself above [*sc.* the rest] in his thoughts' (ὑπερφρονῶν, 6.16.4). Put plainly, this means that ordinary Athenians should accept that Alcibiades disdains them. Under normal circumstances, an Athenian audience would make short shrift of any speaker airing this idea. Not so, however, in the case of Alcibiades. The Athenians in fact greet his speech with great enthusiasm: after listening to Alcibiades' speech, they 'were far more eager than before to undertake the expedition' (πολλῷ μᾶλλον ἢ πρότερον ὥρμηντο στρατεύειν, 6.19.1).

The same disarming audacity recurs in Alcibiades' speech at Sparta, which he delivers after his condemnation *in absentia* by the Athenians due to his alleged involvement in the mutilation of the Herms and the profanation of the Eleusinian Mysteries. He tells the Spartans, people who surely hold strong views on the topic of patriotism, that it is wrong to think of Alcibiades' attack on his own country as an unpatriotic act: 'And a patriot in the proper sense is not someone who, after having lost his country contrary to justice, does not attack it, but someone who tries to get it back in every manner due to his desire for it' (καὶ φιλόπολις οὗτος ὀρθῶς, οὐχ ὃς ἂν τὴν ἑαυτοῦ ἀδίκως ἀπολέσας μὴ ἐπίῃ, ἀλλ' ὃς ἂν ἐκ παντὸς τρόπου διὰ τὸ ἐπιθυμεῖν πειραθῇ αὐτὴν ἀναλαβεῖν, 6.92.4). 'In every manner' seems to cover far-reaching strategic advice to the home country's arch-nemesis. It would be interesting to know what the Spartans would have said if one of their outlawed royal dignitaries, the regent Pausanias or King Demaratus, had urged the same argument. Yet, faced with Alcibiades' speech, the Spartans 'were much more encouraged after he had explained each of these various things' (πολλῷ μᾶλλον ἐπερρώσθησαν διδάξαντος ταῦτα ἕκαστα αὐτοῦ, 6.93.1). The phrasing closely recalls Thucydides' aforementioned characterization at 6.19.1 of the Athenians' response to Alcibiades' speech, especially due to the occurrence of the phrase 'much more' (πολλῷ μᾶλλον) in each passage. Alcibiades simply gets away with things that would spell instant doom for everyone else.

For all Alcibiades' slyness, there is something amusingly naive about his evident conviction that his audience will accept his blatantly sophistic reinterpretation of cherished Athenian and Spartan principles. In Thucydides' account, these triumphant moments of Alcibiadean nonchalance coexist with instances of disastrous hysteria that his extravagance also elicits. It is true that, sooner or later, doom catches up with Alcibiades, and it does not seem far-fetched to suppose that in retrospect, when the spell of Alcibiades' personality has faded, people tend to have second thoughts about the kinds of things said by him. At the same time, however, Thucydides' presentation also reflects people's willingness to make exceptions for Alcibiades. In this connection, a further interesting parallel with the *Symposium* is worth citing. The members of the sober drinking party held at the house of Agathon have agreed to refrain, for once, from heavy drinking (176e1–3). Yet Alcibiades, exuding Dionysian intoxication, has scarcely entered when they enthusiastically jettison all their good intentions (213a1–4). High-minded principles stand no chance when confronted with Alcibiades' buoyancy.

Gribble remarks, and rightly so, that, when confronted with an actor in Thucydides' *History*, 'we do not get a sense of what kind of person he was, as an "individual"'.[9] Alcibiades, however, is an exception. Thucydides brings out the above-mentioned nuances of Alcibiades' personality through subtle touches. If one approaches Thucydides with modern assumptions, one will still note that he does not display an infinitely complex and varied personality—an expectation encouraged by specifically modern ideas about individualism.[10] Nonetheless, Thucydides directs attention to quite delicate features of Alcibiades' personality that convey the impression of a living, captivating individual. These aspects make Alcibiades a figure that is 'arresting, not intriguing', an opposition used by Pelling to mark out a distinction between ancient and modern individualism.[11] Thus, Alcibiades is marked by plasticity and fullness of life, rather than inexhaustible depth and complexity. At the same time, the highlighted character traits of Alcibiades are not devoid of complexity and involve some degree of tension: the element of the uncanny seducer and the agitator infecting the whole city with hope and desire coexists alongside a more playful frivolity that is reflected in Alcibiades' bold redefinitions, and his reconciliatory spirit. These nuances are not readily reducible to the idea that individuals are possessed by collective forces. In sum, it would be wrong to think that human nature, despite its evident impact, has preprogrammed Alcibiades to act out an impersonal role exhaustively prefigured by Diodotus' general scheme.

The lively personal touches that mark the depiction of Alcibiades are all the more remarkable against the background of the impersonal mode that generally prevails in Thucydides' presentation of individuals. According to Gribble, Thucydides aimed at 'a *deliberate* exclusion of the personal, the private, the individual's life outside the city, a generic

---

[9] Gribble 2006: 446.
[10] On the specifically modern character of this expectation, see Pelling 1990a: 251–3; Gribble 2006: 446.
[11] Pelling 1990a: 237. Pelling uses the phrase in connection with Plutarch's portrayal of individuals.

decision, tied to Thucydides' attempt to create a military-political historiography founded on non-personal causation – cities and armies and money, not people'.[12] In light of these strictures, Thucydides usually not only elides any information concerning the private life of his protagonists (a tendency to which Alcibiades would provide no exception); it also entails a depersonalized presentation of the various characters themselves, a style that focuses exclusively on actions in the political and military arena, but provides hardly any information on the sentiments, preferences, and personal dispositions that may underlie these acts. Alcibiades and Nicias (and arguably, to some extent, Brasidas) are the noticeable exceptions to this very marked tendency.[13] They stand out even by the standards of the latter half of Thucydides' work, which attaches greater importance to the influence exerted by individuals (as opposed to impersonal forces) on the course of events.[14] It is remarkable that Hermocrates' character remains quite aloof, although his ingenuity in manipulating and outwitting his opponents would have offered the opportunity of introducing some more personal traits. It is even more surprising to find that Demosthenes does not receive a more vivid portrayal because his agility and enthusiasm for action would have lent themselves to a more individualized treatment of his character. In connection with Hermocrates and Demosthenes, this lack of individual characterization is especially remarkable because, as Westlake observes, Thucydides was evidently well informed about both of them; in addition,

---

[12] Gribble 2006: 441. See also Bruns 1896: 3 ('Parteiführer, Redner, Gesandte, Feldherren treten auf, sie reden sachgemäss, sie handeln vernünftig; wir begreifen sie intellectuell, aber wir sehen sie nicht vor uns als Wesen von Fleisch und Blut mit den bestimmten Falten und Zügen, die das Individuum ausmachen'); Reinhardt 1966: 192–3; Westlake 1968: 308; Strasburger 1982: 784–6.

[13] In the case of Nicias and Alcibiades, this tendency towards characterization is even reflected, as Tompkins has shown, in the style of their speeches. According to Tompkins, Nicias' frequent use of hypotaxis is an expression of his self-involved character (1972: 200, 204). By contrast, Alcibiades uses sweeping paratactic constructions calculated to gloss over the difficulties that might beset the expedition (1972: 210). Granted, this type of syntactic idiosyncrasy may not be quite the same as the minute assimilation, down to very subtle nuances, between style and a character's infinitely complex personality, which can be found in some modern literature. In the case of Nicias and Alcibiades, the stylistic differences rather concern readily accessible, architectonic characteristics that contribute to a large-scale, systematic antithesis between both speakers. Nevertheless, they throw light on the specific ways that mark these two characters.

[14] See Westlake 1968: 319; Hornblower 1987: 145–6.

Thucydides was able to complement, in the case of Demosthenes, whatever intelligence he received from his sources by his own direct experience of the man who had been his colleague on the board of generals in the year 424/423.[15] In light of all this, it is very striking that Thucydides chooses to highlight much more recognizably personal traits in his presentation of Alcibiades, and that he does so on the occasion of his most detailed presentation of a decision for which Diodotus' analysis of the necessity of transpersonal drives offers the blueprint.

It turns out that Thucydides' presentation of the Athenian decision contains two strands: one strikingly personal and the other emphatically suprapersonal. What is more, these two strands closely intertwine: Alcibiades' intimate association with ἔρως simultaneously belongs both to the individual and to the generalizing register. The question arises how the interaction of these two contradictory strands is to be accounted for.

6.3 Croesus in Herodotus (I): Immanent Motivation Alongside Divine Interference

The interaction of two different planes in motivation (one individual and the other suprapersonal) is not unfamiliar in light of the history of ancient Greek thought prior to Thucydides. Homer, Herodotus, and the Greek tragedians offer examples of a model of dual motivation that combines interconnected strands of human and divine causation. The story of Croesus as recounted by Herodotus lends itself particularly well for an examination of the interaction of individual action and divinely ordained fatalism. It has often been noted that the story of the Lydian king Croesus has paradigmatic significance in Herodotus.[16] Against the backdrop of the dual motivation model in Herodotus, it

---

[15] See Westlake 1958: 265 (on Hermocrates), and 1968: 97 (on Demosthenes).
[16] Marg 1965 [1953]: 290 ('Musterfall'); Lloyd-Jones 1983: 62–3 ('paradeigmatic function'); Visser 2000: 11 ('geschichtsphilosophische Aussage'); Pelling 2006: 172 ('paradigmatic role', 'prototype'); Sewell-Rutter 2007: 4 ('programmatic').

will ultimately be possible to clarify the picture that has emerged from Thucydides' account.

In the first book of Herodotus' *Histories*, Solon famously asserts that the divine inescapably meddles in human affairs (1.32.1). According to Thomas Harrison, it is hard to overestimate the importance of Solon's doctrine for Herodotus' thought: 'The *Histories*, it seems, are founded on the principle of the instability of human fortune...Every reversal... is...an illustration of the force of the divine to disturb human affairs.'[17] If the divine has this crucial impact on events on earth, the question arises whether Herodotus sees scope for personal agency and flexibility in the formation of events. The part of Herodotus' account concerned with the downfall of the Lydian empire lends itself especially well to an exploration of the interpenetration of the human and divine spheres.

The spectre of predestination already overshadows Croesus' life five generations before he is born. After his ancestor Gyges, the founding father of the Mermnadae dynasty, killed the legitimate Heraclidae king of Lydia and usurped the kingship, the Delphic oracle confirms Gyges as king. At the same time, however, it predicts that 'revenge' ($\tau i\sigma \iota s$, 1.13.2) will strike the Mermnadae in the fifth generation. With the accession of Croesus, this fifth generation has mounted the throne. Thus, it is inevitable from the outset that Croesus will suffer doom.[18] Moreover, given that whatever happens to him must be an adequate compensation for the violent end of the Heraclidae, it is safe to assume that Croesus' foreordained doom will involve his loss of royal power. Beyond these broad but important parameters, the oracle does not specify in any greater detail what will happen.

The critical sequence of events begins when Croesus learns of the rise of the Persian empire in the wake of Cyrus' usurpation of the throne. At this point, Croesus is utterly dejected due to his son's death and has spent two years in mourning, apparently having abstained from any activity.

---

[17] Harrison 2000: 63. Many scholars have stressed the foundational significance of Herodotus' belief in divine interference: Hellmann 1934: 117–18; Immerwahr 1966: 312–13; Lloyd-Jones 1983: 62; de Ste. Croix 1977: 142–3; Pötscher 1988 [1958]: 27; Fornara 1990: 37.

[18] See Hellmann 1934: 32; Immerwahr 1954: 36; Stahl 1975: 4; Fornara 1990: 37; Harrison 2000: 224; Gagné 2013: 327.

No sooner has the idea of challenging the Persians entered Croesus' mind than he sheds all apathy: his former go-getting self is revived. His first step is to send out messengers 'instantaneously' (αὐτίκα, 1.46.2) to test various oracles. Whereas the reader just learned that Croesus has been vegetating for two years, he now seems electrified by the challenge. Croesus' excitement is in keeping with the character of a great conqueror, a role that Croesus played up until his son's death. Thus, a natural enough motive initiates the sequence of events that will result in Croesus' predestined downfall.

At this point, Herodotus has not made explicit that the ill-fated fifth generation has assumed the throne with Croesus' accession, as Sewell-Rutter points out: 'Herodotus concentrates on the human and humanly intelligible road to ruin that Croesus treads.'[19] Herodotus has merely dropped a subtle hint to this effect: the fact that Croesus embodies the doomed fifth generation is implicit in Herodotus' survey of the successive Mermnadae rulers of Lydia (1.15–26.1). This circumstance, however, will only be noted by a reader who unaidedly keeps count of the successive Lydian rulers, since Herodotus does not spell out which numerical position belongs to each new king in the generational scheme. This emphasis on the human plane marks Herodotus' presentation of Croesus' fated downfall throughout and matters greatly for the proposed analogy with Thucydides.

After cooking a tortoise in a bronze cauldron, Croesus wants to find out whether any of the well-known oracles have awareness of this rather eccentric act. If they do, Croesus will trust in the oracle's knowledge and reliability. He simply assumes that the former goes hand in hand with the latter: the possibility of divine deception does not cross his mind. The oracles of Apollo at Delphi and of Amphiareus pass Croesus' test. When Croesus hears the Delphic response, 'he immediately worshipped and accepted it' (αὐτίκα προσεύχετό τε καὶ προσεδέξατο, 1.48.1). The word αὐτίκα, which had already marked Croesus' reaction to the news about Persia two chapters earlier, underscores the immediacy of his response. Through the repetition, the reader is given a subtle hint that Croesus' reaction may be a bit too eager.

---

[19] Sewell-Rutter 2007: 7.

Croesus pays no attention to the first two lines of the oracle, which read as follows (1.47.3):

οἶδα δ' ἐγὼ ψάμμου τ' ἀριθμὸν καὶ μέτρα θαλάσσης,
καὶ κωφοῦ συνίημι καὶ οὐ φωνεῦντος ἀκούω.

I know the number of the grains of sand and the measures of the sea,
and I understand the dumb and hear him who does not speak.

As Julia Kindt points out, these lines contain an insight that Croesus would do well to consider: 'It [sc. the oracle] is meant to hint to Croesus that Apollo can see more than he, and that things can turn out to be different than they appear at first sight.'[20] The oracle's words thus contain an implicit warning that Croesus ought not to overestimate the scope of human insight: unlike the divine perspective, human understanding can never be total. As we will see in due course, Croesus, in fact, assumes that the oracle makes the future completely transparent to him. The reason for Croesus' inattentiveness to this important part of the oracle seems clear and reflects a familiar feature of human psychology: because these lines do not suit his preconceived scheme, they fail to attract his attention.

Croesus lavishes gifts on the Delphic oracle 'expecting that, due to them, he would win over the god still more' (ἐλπίζων τὸν θεὸν μᾶλλόν τι τούτοισι ἀνακτήσεσθαι, 1.50.1). Two leitmotivs are sounded here for the first time. One is Croesus' conviction that abundant gifts directly lead to divine benevolence. Yet Croesus overlooks that a mortal, while being free to try to win the favour of the divine, should never assume to have a god in his pocket. This ultimate elusiveness of the rapport between human beings and gods does not enter at all into Croesus' scheme.[21]

The second theme that will recur throughout the story of Croesus' downfall hinges on the word ἐλπίζω. Hellmann observes that Herodotus

---

[20] Kindt 2006: 38.
[21] In this connection, note also Gagné's observation (2013: 329) that divine and human χάρις are essentially different: 'The perenniality of the monuments [i.e. the gifts due to gods] is matched by the immortal life of the god who will receive and keep them. The short existence of the mortal, on the other hand, can hold on to the gifts of the gods only for a limited duration, and as long as the divinity wills it...gift and counter-gift operate on a fundamentally different plane.'

refers to Croesus' habit of forming an expectation about what the future will bring fifteen times between chapters 46 and 85, and that Herodotus uses a form of ἐλπίζω in seven of these passages.[22] As Lateiner writes, Croesus is 'Herodotos' "poster boy" for *elpis*, a paradigm of hoping gone bad, and repeatedly shot down for it'.[23] The repetition of the same word suggests that Croesus' confident anticipation of the course of the campaign has become habitual. If he had listened to Solon, Croesus might have realized that no two days in a man's life are exactly the same, and that chance is at the heart of human existence (1.32.4). This position implies the essential inscrutability of the future. By contrast, Croesus' conviction that he knows what the future will bring does not convey an impression of prudence.

In the second round of consultation, Croesus asks the oracles of Delphic Apollo and of Amphiareus whether he should undertake a campaign against the Persians. From both oracles, he receives the notoriously ambiguous reply that he will bring down a great empire if he makes war on Persia (1.53.3). Herodotus writes that Croesus 'was overjoyed' (ὑπερήσθη, 1.54.1) in reaction to this prophecy, and that he was 'very much expecting that he would destroy the kingdom of Cyrus' (πάγχυ ... ἐλπίσας καταλύσειν τὴν Κύρου βασιληίην, 1.54.1). Croesus' joy reinforces the initial impression that Croesus is bent on undertaking this campaign from the outset: as Walter Marg has noted, his delight is inspired by the oracle's apparent validation of his preconceived plan.[24] Croesus' eagerness is also underscored by his formation of another 'expectation' (cf. ἐλπίσας), even more confident and likewise mistaken, about the future.

In due course, Croesus presents a third question to Apollo's oracle. Herodotus remarks that Croesus 'made excessive use of it' (ἐνεφορέετο αὐτοῦ, 1.55.1). The emphasis on excess recalls the verb ὑπερήδομαι ('be overjoyed'). Pelling remarks that Croesus gets carried away 'by one of the oddest things of all: by that craze for Greek oracular wisdom'.[25]

---

[22] Hellmann 1934: 73-7. In addition to 1.50.1, the following passages feature references to ἐλπίζω: 1.54.1 (Croesus' expectation that he will overturn Cyrus' empire), 56.1 (a mule will never become king of the Medes), 71.1 (same expectation as 54.1), 75.2 (expectation that oracle is on Croesus' side), 77.4 (expectation that Cyrus will not march immediately on Sardes), 80.5 (Croesus' ἐλπίς is destroyed due to the elimination of the Lydian cavalry).
[23] Lateiner 2018: 134.   [24] Marg 1965 [1953]: 293.   [25] Pelling 2019: 116.

In this third round of oracle consultation, Croesus asks whether his rule will last for a long time. The response is that he should run when a mule becomes king of the Medes (1.55.2). Croesus' reaction marks the culmination of the patterns observed: 'About these words, when they reached him, Croesus <u>was by far the most pleased of them all</u>, because he <u>expected</u> that a mule would never rule the Medes instead of a man, and that, therefore, neither he himself nor his descendants would ever lose their empire' (τούτοισι ἐλθοῦσι τοῖσι ἔπεσι ὁ Κροῖσος πολλόν τι μάλιστα πάντων ἤσθη, ἐλπίζων ἡμίονον οὐδαμὰ ἀντ' ἀνδρὸς βασιλεύσειν Μήδων, οὐδ' ὦν αὐτὸς οὐδ' οἱ ἐξ αὐτοῦ παύσεσθαί κοτε τῆς ἀρχῆς, 1.56.1). The patterns of excessive joy (πολλόν τι μάλιστα πάντων ἤσθη) and confident expectation (ἐλπίζων) converge precisely at the moment when Croesus reacts to an oracle that in fact predicts his doom.[26]

The consultation of the oracles shows how Croesus decides to challenge the Persians. This decision functions as the precondition of his fated downfall. Croesus' approach fully accords with the personality of the affluent potentate and irresistible conqueror whose military campaigns have met with nothing but success (1.28–29.1). Despite the foreordained outcome, Herodotus' account does not suggest that divine powers manipulate Croesus to commit acts that are out of character or that could not have originated from his own self. Just as Alcibiades acts on a natural necessity that closely responds to his specific personality, so Croesus performs the steps that will open the door for fate to run its course in perfect harmony with his natural habits.

Herodotus twice takes note of the reasons that lead Croesus to go to war with Persia. All the reasons adduced operate on a human level and do not require the postulation of supernatural agency. When Croesus first hears of the overthrow of his brother-in-law, the Mede Astyages, and the consequent rise of the Persian empire under Cyrus, he follows a rather defensive impulse, considering 'whether he might in any way be able, before the Persians become great, to check the increase of their power'

---

[26] In this way, the series of ever more confident expectations perfectly encapsulates Lateiner's summary (2018: 136) of the generally harmful role of ἐλπίς in Herodotus, no matter whether it suggests 'expectation' or 'hope': '*Elpis* describes either inadequate supposition or a fallback, deceptive comfort…Herodotos observes that results almost always discomfit human calculations.'

(εἴ κως δύναιτο, πρὶν μεγάλους γενέσθαι τοὺς Πέρσας, καταλαβεῖν αὐτῶν αὐξανομένην τὴν δύναμιν, 1.46.1). Then, in a later passage, Herodotus adduces three quite different motives for the campaign (1.73.1): desire for land (γῆς ἱμέρῳ), 'most of all' trust in Apollo's oracle (μάλιστα τῷ χρηστηρίῳ πίσυνος ἐών), and the wish to take revenge on behalf of Astyages (τείσασθαι θέλων ὑπὲρ Ἀστυάγεος, 1.73.2). In particular the first and the third of these new motives represent a swing towards a more offensive orientation.[27] Given his appetite for conquest, it would in fact be surprising if Croesus had not cherished hopes of aggrandizement from the outset when he was faced with the prospect of a large-scale campaign. The depiction of the Persian challenge as a wake-up call supports this view. None of the motives named by Herodotus depend on the supernatural as an explanatory category.

Despite this apparent self-sufficiency of the human level, it is unadvisable to adopt the conclusion, drawn by some scholars, that the divine has no influence on Croesus' decisions at all, and that the notion of a fatalistic strand in events is false.[28] As pointed out above, Croesus was fated to lose his dominion as compensation for his ancestor Gyges' murder of Candaules (1.13.2). After Croesus' defeat by Cyrus, Apollo's oracle harks back to this prediction and confirms the fateful connection between Gyges' deed and Croesus' downfall (1.91.1). A further indication of divine involvement is that it is precisely Croesus' preventive measures that pave the way for his doom. Croesus' repeated consultation of the oracles is meant to keep him out of harm's way. Instead, the oracles set

---

[27] According to some scholars, this change of outlook results from Croesus' increasing encouragement through the seemingly auspicious oracles and his conclusion of an alliance with Sparta (1.70.1 with 56.1): Marg 1965 [1953]: 292; Stahl 1975: 10. Yet, as Pelling (2006: 153 n. 46) points out, this developmental account is probably off the mark since 'explanations in Herodotus work more "paratactically", with later explanations supplementing earlier ones rather than replacing them'. On the compatibility of the two sets of explanations, see Lateiner 1989: 207; Pelling 2019: 103.

[28] This position has been advocated by various scholars: Stahl 1975: 18 ('[A]ll acts and motives..., although fulfilling the conditions of destiny..., do not depend on any supranatural impulses and causations, but can be accounted for by empirical psychology alone' – they can be, but that does not mean that nothing more is going on: cf. Pelling 1991: 139–40); Visser 2000: 26 ('Die Gefahr liegt nicht in einem vom Denken des Menschen nicht beeinflußbaren Regelkreislauf, sondern im Menschen selbst: es ist die Gefahr, irgendwann einem Realitätsverlust anheimzufallen'); Schmitt 2013: 313 ('"Das was sein mußte" war realiter durchweg von Kroisos selbst verantwortet [and is therefore, in Schmitt's view, in no way predestined by fate]').

the stage for a campaign that will engulf Croesus in the abyss.[29] Thus, Williams's observation about divinely ordained fatalism in Greek tragedy also applies to the story of Croesus: '[I]f efforts to avoid the outcome helped in fact to bring it about, this is a reliable sign, after the event, that the supernatural has been at work.'[30]

In addition to the higher-order strictures of fate, some specific features of Croesus' behaviour also provide subtle indications of divine involvement. When Croesus is seized by sudden interest in the rise of Persia, it is likely that his eagerness is boosted by a god in a way analogous to the instances of divine propulsion familiar from Homer.[31] Croesus' enthusiasm about the fateful campaign comes across as too sudden and too frantically excited to seem entirely sound. However, such an impetus merely reinforces dispositions that Croesus already bears within himself, an aspect that also recalls the model of dual motivation in Homer.[32] Another indication of subtle superhuman influence is Croesus' curious appetite for ever further oracular pronouncements, which seems a bit too obsessive to be entirely innocent. Taken by itself, however, the consultation of the oracles is far from abnormal. Instead, it comes across as a reasonable procedure, with Croesus trying to find out what his chances are before undertaking a large-scale campaign. Thus, the consultation itself, as opposed to the specific undertones attached to it, does not suggest derangement but an attitude that befits a circumspect leader. Once again, divine interference proceeds from behaviour that seems plausible on a purely human plane.

---

[29] For a similar parallel with the fatalist strand in Greek tragedy, compare Lévy's (1995: 26) comments on Croesus' attempt to save his son after a portentous dream: '[P]ar une ironie tragique, qu'on retrouvera chez Sophocle, les efforts pour échapper au destin ne font qu'en faciliter l'action.'

[30] Williams 1993: 141.

[31] Such superhuman influence would take the form of added divine emphasis (or 'Nachdrücken', as Lesky [1961: 28] calls it), a factor that sometimes undergirds pre-existing human motivations or dispositions in Homeric epic, as Lesky has shown (1961: 28): 'Im ersten Gesange der Odyssee steigert Athene das Wesen des Telemachos in jeder Weise. Sie gibt ihm μένος und θάρσος und läßt ihn seines Vaters gedenken μᾶλλον ἔτ' ἢ τὸ πάροιθεν (322). Also nicht ein neuer Impuls nimmt hier seinen Ausgang von der Gottheit, sondern Vorhandenes wird durch ihre Einwirkung gesteigert.'

[32] See Gundert's (1940: 229) remarks about the ἄτη befalling Agamemnon during the quarrel with Achilles: '[S]o ist es auch für Homer kein Zweifel, daß wirklich Zeus den Agamemnon in dieses Verhängnis hineingetrieben hat. Aber das Unglück kommt darum doch nicht willkürlich wie von außen über ihn, sondern es ist zutiefst in seinem eigenen Wesen begründet.'

Croesus' sudden transformation from apathy to excitement for action is just one of several indications of divine influence. According to Lloyd-Jones, Croesus had 'Ate working on his mind'[33] when making the decisions in response to the oracles: 'since Croesus was bound to pay for his ancestor's offence, it was inevitable that, to use the Homeric expression, a god should take away his wits.'[34] Lloyd-Jones takes this view without citing specific evidence, but his position has strong textual support. When Croesus is asked by Cyrus for his motives for attacking Persia, he considers his own decision unaccountable in retrospect: 'For nobody is so foolish to choose war over peace' (οὐδεὶς γὰρ οὕτω ἀνόητός ἐστι ὅστις πόλεμον πρὸ εἰρήνης αἱρέεται, 1.87.4). Croesus in fact thinks that Apollo bears the responsibility for his decision to challenge the Persians because nobody in his right mind would have acted as Croesus did (1.87.3)—an assessment that we will revisit in the next section. It is a frequent and strong indication of affliction by ἄτη, as Stallmach points out, when an agent finds actions that he had previously carried out with great conviction utterly incomprehensible in retrospect.[35] The cause célèbre is when Agamemnon could no longer understand his prior decision to take away Briseis and thereby offend Achilles (*Il.* 19.86–9). Another common symptom of ἄτη is the heedless dismissal of wise adviser figures.[36] Again, Croesus is a case in point: the Lydian wise man Sandanis, whose widely admired discretion Herodotus emphasizes (1.71.2), tries to caution Croesus against challenging Persia, but his premonitions are to no avail (1.71.4). Further, Croesus uses the aorist participle of the verb ἐπαίρω in three passages (twice in direct, once in indirect discourse) when looking back on his dealings with Apollo after his downfall: Croesus claims that Apollo 'incited' him to undertake the campaign, specifying in two passages the oracles as Apollo's means to achieve this effect (ἐπάρας ἐμὲ στρατεύεσθαι, 1.87.3; ἐπαρθεὶς τῷ μαντηίῳ ἐστρατεύσατο ἐπὶ Πέρσας, 90.3; τοῖσι μαντηίοισι ἐπάρας Κροῖσον στρατεύεσθαι ἐπὶ Πέρσας, 90.4). Avery has drawn attention to a frequent connotation of ἐπαίρω that Herodotus borrows from Greek poetry, which can be summarized as 'to raise one up to a very high state, but

---

[33] Lloyd-Jones 1983: 62. [34] Lloyd-Jones 1983: 61. [35] Stallmach 1968: 80.
[36] See Stallmach 1968: 80–1.

with the further implication that such an elevation is certain to be followed, indeed must be followed, by a precipitous and disastrous fall'.[37] Ἄτη is, of course, the ancient Greek word for such mistaken elation that paves the way for disaster. Finally, the story of Croesus also exemplifies Stallmach's observation that an agent befallen by ἄτη often has a distinct expectation regarding the future and organizes his actions accordingly, only to find that the exact opposite of what he has anticipated comes to pass.[38] Portraying this specific attitude, Herodotus systematically emphasizes, through the above-mentioned repeated use of ἐλπίζω, Croesus' all too confident expectation that his campaign against Persia will meet with success. Hellmann considers this erroneous outlook a clear indication of Croesus' affection by ἄτη in the sense of clouded state of mind.[39] It is important to note that the mental aberration labelled as ἄτη is never entirely this-worldly but has its origin in the divine, a point stressed by various scholars.[40] Thus, the wealth of hints at Croesus' affection by ἄτη imply that divine forces have beset him with this baneful state of mind.[41]

The oracles are another divine element in the formation of events. Apollo's unlimited knowledge is stated as fact in the first two lines of the first oracular response (1.47.3). Knowing what kind of man Croesus is, Apollo will have anticipated how Croesus was to construe the import of the oracles. In Herodotus, personal character tends

---

[37] Avery 1979: 2. On the passages referring to Croesus, see Avery 1979: 3–4.
[38] Stallmach 1968: 45.
[39] Hellmann (1934: 74): 'Herodot läßt den Leser bei diesem In-die-Irre-Gehen des Kroisos die Umdunklung des menschlichen Verstandes miterleben, wenn ein Schicksalsvollzug sich vorbereitet.'
[40] Dodds 1951: 7; Stallmach 1968: 84–5; Doyle 1984: 146–7.
[41] It is worth emphasizing that the derangement captured by ἄτη may, but need not, imply a sinful state of mind smacking of ὕβρις; see Stallmach (1968: 102): 'das menschliche Handeln, das durch *Verblendung, Betörung* **oder** [!] *Frevelmut* fehlgehend,... sich selbst am Handelnden rächt' [my emphasis]. See also Dodds (1951: 38): '[A]te is often, **though not always**, moralised, by being represented as a punishment' [my emphasis], and Pelling 2006: 150 with n. 34. For a detailed argument why ὕβρις does not apply to Croesus, see Fisher 1992: 358–60. In Croesus' case, ἄτη suggests an intellectual failure, equivalent to mental 'blindness' or 'delusion', but there are no hints of sacrilegious haughtiness. Several aspects preclude the ascription of ὕβρις to Croesus: his honest concern with consulting the oracles and winning Apollo's favour, his reputation of piety (1.86.2), and the divine help (by way of the miraculous rain shower) that rescues him from the funeral pyre (1.87.2). Herodotus notes that Cyrus concludes from this last event 'that Croesus was a man both dear to the gods and excellent' (ὡς εἴη ὁ Κροῖσος καὶ θεοφιλὴς καὶ ἀνὴρ ἀγαθός, 1.87.2). It is hard to see how this evaluation of Croesus could coexist with his putative descent into ὕβρις.

to provide divine powers with a means for bringing a foreordained outcome to pass, a point duly stressed by Roettig.[42] Thus, there transpires an external as well as an internal strand of divine influence on Croesus' actions. The former, chiefly represented by oracles, is conspicuous and openly acknowledged, whereas the latter has a more subdued cast and must be inferred from Croesus' specific conduct and the manner in which the events play out.

Although a fatalistic strand is at work in the actions that lead to Croesus' downfall, Herodotus nonetheless foregrounds the human level of causation: Croesus' actions are based, despite his affliction by ἄτη, on comprehensible motives that dovetail with the personality that Croesus has displayed throughout his career. An oft-cited observation made by Easterling about Aeschylus sums up the Herodotean picture nicely: '[A] divine explanation... is a *diagnosis of something actually observed in human behaviour*, and not a piece of mumbo-jumbo independent of observed phenomena.'[43] In this way, Herodotus pursues a dual strategy, combining respect for empirical plausibility with the inference that, at decisive junctures and at a higher level, the influence of superhuman forces percolates through the raw data of observable facts. It is crucial that the overarching fatalism fulfils itself and assumes living shape in events that fit in seamlessly with natural characteristics of the agents involved. The parallel with Thucydides is clear: while necessity imposes limits that define the sphere of action, these limitations are not uniform and abstract but take concrete shape in individual agents and in the character of specific cities.

A modern reader may wonder whether the divine or the human level is prior, but this concern derives largely from the emphasis on pure and unencumbered autonomy, a priority that results from a characteristically modern version of extreme voluntarism.[44] Yet the issue of unaffected free

---

[42] Roettig 2010: 77.   [43] Easterling 1973: 5–6.
[44] Vernant draws attention to this distinction between Greek and modern ways of thinking: 'It is only for our modern selves that the problem is posed in terms of a choice between free will on the one hand and constraint in various forms on the other' (1988 [1972]: 75; cf.: 49–50). See also Cornford (1907: 154–5) (apropos Aeschylean tragedy): '[W]e require a theory of human motives which will allow of our conceiving them, simultaneously, both as supernatural causes coming from without, and also as integral parts in the working of the agent's mind. Modern psychology is, of course, not equal to the task of this reconciliation.'

will was not of the same urgency to the Greeks,[45] who considered both levels to be, for the most part, simultaneous, even if that coincidence may have struck them as uncanny and mysterious. According to Vernant, part of the power of tragedy consists in the acknowledgement of this mind-boggling simultaneity.[46] Nevertheless, it seems puzzling that Greek writers were not more explicitly bothered by this tension. The next section will aim to answer why this was so.

6.4 Croesus in Herodotus (II): Who Is αἴτιος—Man or God?

After Croesus' defeat by Cyrus, Herodotus reports the episode of Croesus' placement on a funeral pyre and his miraculous rescue by an abrupt downpour out of a clear sky. Following this wondrous event, Cyrus asks Croesus who it was that put the idea of attacking the Persians into his head. Croesus answers that the responsibility lies with Apollo: 'The god of the Greeks was to blame [or 'was responsible']'[47] for these things because he incited me to undertake the campaign' (αἴτιος δὲ τούτων ἐγένετο ὁ Ἑλλήνων θεὸς ἐπάρας ἐμὲ στρατεύεσθαι, 1.87.3). Nobody is so foolish to prefer war over peace (1.87.4), a fact that leads Croesus to conclude: 'However, it was apparently pleasing to some gods that these things happened this way' (ἀλλὰ ταῦτα δαίμοσί κου φίλον ἦν οὕτω γενέσθαι, 1.87.4).[48]

Soon, however, Croesus experiences a complete change of opinion: he discards his initial view that Apollo is to blame in favour of the opposite.

---

[45] Sewell-Rutter (2007: 171) notes that Greek tragedy, despite its thoroughgoing concern with decision, does not raise the 'problem of freedom in the relevant sense [i.e. in the sense of 'free will' – see Sewell-Rutter 2007: 151]. We have found instead a subtle and nuanced interest in the creation and appropriation of necessity by doomed characters.'

[46] Vernant 1988 [1972]: 37 and 81.

[47] On the rendition of αἴτιος, see Pelling (2019: 6): 'Normally...with humans the adjective *aitios* is used of the person held responsible, and the element of moral blame is more strongly felt [sc. than in passages where αἴτιος refers to an impersonal entity, such as a physical phenomenon].'

[48] Wilson prints the singular (i.e. δαίμονί) in his OCT. Both the singular and the plural are transmitted by the manuscript tradition. I prefer the plural because the corruption from plural to singular seems readily explicable: a scribe was misled by the preceding thoughts uttered by Croesus, in which he has been talking about just one god (namely Apollo). It is also worth stressing that the plural form is transmitted by the best manuscript of Herodotus (commonly designated as A in critical editions).

Cyrus grants Croesus permission to question the Delphic oracle about Apollo's alleged betrayal (1.90.4). The Pythia replies that, because Croesus interpreted the oracle poorly, the mistake is all his own, and so he should blame himself and not the god (1.91.4–5)—which is just what Croesus proceeds to do without further grumbling (1.91.6).

Croesus' outright acceptance of the Pythia's response is surprising because it is far from clear that Croesus' interpretation of the critical oracle (viz. the prophecy that Croesus would destroy a great empire) was in fact as misguided as the Pythia suggests. Herodotus describes the oracle as κίβδηλος: 'deceitful' (1.75.2).[49] Since this attribute implies that Apollo's oracle was meant to trick Croesus, one would think that he is exonerated to a considerable degree. On the other hand, Herodotus writes that Croesus 'got the oracle wrong' (ἁμαρτὼν τοῦ χρησμοῦ, 1.71.1). Moreover, after the Pythia's reply, he states that Croesus himself 'acknowledged that the mistake was his own and not the god's' (συνέγνω ἑωυτοῦ εἶναι τὴν ἁμαρτάδα καὶ οὐ τοῦ θεοῦ, 1.91.1). Yet even this straightforward acknowledgement of Croesus' responsibility involves a twist. As Gagné has pointed out,[50] the word ἁμαρτάς refers back to a passage from the Pythia's response, which Herodotus has just reported: 'Croesus paid the full penalty for the mistake of his ancestor in the fifth generation' (Κροῖσος δὲ πέμπτου γονέος ἁμαρτάδα ἐξέπλησε, 1.91.5). Croesus, according to a literal translation, 'fulfils the mistake' of Gyges by making his own 'mistake' in connection with the oracles, thus also 'fulfilling' the destiny that has been awaiting him. From this it follows that Croesus is bound to make his mistake because it has been fated that he will offset his ancestor's mistake. Human responsibility and divine foreordainment are closely interwoven.

Some inkling on Croesus' part that Apollo's oracle was hinting at the downfall of the Lydian empire does not seem to be an unreasonable expectation. If this were not the case, Apollo could hardly tell Croesus

---

[49] On the meaning, both here and elsewhere, of the term κίβδηλος, see Ellis 2016: 77.
[50] Gagné 2013: 337. Note, however, that Gagné interprets the implication of the verbal echo differently: on his view, it highlights Croesus' own sinful actions, thus suggesting that Croesus' 'crime completes the crime of Gyges, and his punishment meets the fault of his ancestor' (337). Yet there is strong evidence that Herodotus does not imply that Croesus is beset by wickedness when deciding to make war on Persia; see above n. 42.

that he should have taken note of the ambiguity and asked which empire the god meant (1.91.4). Nevertheless, Apollo's divine knowledge must have enabled him to foretell that Croesus, given his personality, would interpret the oracle to suit his wishes. In this way, Apollo's oracle is deceitful: it is not beyond the general scope of human reason to realize that one should inquire further, but for this particular man, on this specific occasion, it was beyond his powers.

Why then does Croesus accept Apollo's reply that he himself, and not the god, is 'to blame' and 'responsible', with both senses suggested by the double meaning of αἴτιος? The solution to this conundrum lies in the irresolvable intertwinement of fate and character: despite the various degrees of superhuman influence, Croesus' decisions were also a manifestation of his personal character. The reader experiences this human dimension of Croesus' choices through the orientation of Herodotus' immanent account, which emphasizes decisions and motivations explicable by self-contained human psychology. Another force, however, is also present in Croesus' choices: his personal fate in the guise of his δαίμων. In a seminal paper on tragic decision scenes, Jean-Pierre Vernant draws attention to the simultaneity of the human and the divine element in such situations: '[T]he resolution arrived at by the hero emanates from himself, is in keeping with his own personal character. At the same time ... it is a manifestation, at the heart of human life, of the intervention of supernatural powers.'[51] Immerwahr has stressed that this type of parallel running motivation is applicable to Herodotus: '[T]he majority of the historical actions in Herodotus are accompanied by some kind of divine causation, which parallels human motivation, but on a higher plane.'[52] In this way, both Herodotus and the tragic poets are, as Sewell-Rutter writes, 'quite capable of presenting something as simultaneously a terrible happening, a calamitous element of the universe, and also an

---

[51] Vernant 1988 [1972]: 76. Marinatos also stresses this interplay between character and divine intervention in Herodotus (1982: 264). It does, however, appear from Marinatos's analysis of the story of Polycrates that she does not view these two poles as fully coinciding, and that she regards character to be prior (1982: 260–1). As opposed to this, Vernant maintains the notion of paradoxical simultaneity: see Vernant's application of Heraclitus' maxim ἦθος ἀνθρώπῳ δαίμων (DK 22 B 119) to tragic decisions (1988 [1972]: 37).

[52] Immerwahr 1966: 312. See also Immerwahr 1954: 40–1, and 1956: 257, as well as the following observation by Dodds (1951: 30–1): 'For Herodotus, history is overdetermined: while it is overtly the outcome of human purposes, the penetrating eye can detect everywhere the covert working of *phthonos* [i.e. the influence of a superhuman, fateful power].'

intelligible deed, something that arises for comprehensible reasons from the human motivations and concerns of the agent'.[53] These two strands ultimately cannot be disentangled: the interaction of the divine and the human leads to a genuine, if paradoxical, co-presence. The point made by Pelling about Xerxes' invasion of Greece also applies to Croesus: '[T]he demonic and the naturalistic clearly co-exist very tightly, and the themes are heard in close counterpoint; they are evidently not independent of one another; but it would also be a great mistake to try to reduce either to the other.'[54]

It bears mentioning that Croesus himself does not consider his own responsibility incompatible with divine foreordainment. This is suggested by several passages showing Croesus' continued conviction that his downfall was divinely willed. In his face-to-face encounter with Cyrus immediately after his rescue, Croesus expresses the opinion that his downfall was 'pleasing to some gods' (ἀλλὰ ταῦτα δαίμοσί κου φίλον ἦν οὕτω γενέσθαι, 1.87.4). A little later he again implies that gods precipitated his downfall: 'Since gods have given me to you as a slave...' (ἐπείτε με θεοὶ ἔδωκαν δοῦλόν σοί..., 1.89.1). Taken by themselves, these passages have limited explanatory value because Croesus makes both of these assertions before he receives the reply from Delphi. Yet, on a much later occasion, the war with the Massagetae, Croesus reiterates the same idea with close verbal echoes as part of his counsel to Cyrus: 'since Zeus has given me to you' (ἐπεί με Ζεὺς ἔδωκέ τοι..., 1.207.1). Additionally, Croesus thinks that his own experience provides proof of Solon's wisdom. One of Solon's central tenets is the belief that the divine interferes in human life and throws it into turmoil (1.32.1, 32.9). So, Croesus' undoing, and consequent servitude to Cyrus, remains, to a significant extent, the work of the divine. This equivocation, between 'I am αἴτιος' and 'Zeus has given me to you' only ceases to be blatantly self-contradictory if one accepts the simultaneity of the divine and the human level of causation. Croesus is 'responsible' for his disaster, although it was predestined to happen. These two positions can coexist

---

[53] Sewell-Rutter 2007: 136, see also 150. In these passages, Sewell-Rutter's immediate concern is with tragedy, but he ascribes the same double scheme to Herodotus elsewhere (10–11).
[54] Pelling 1991: 139.

because the actions by which Croesus enables fate to run its course are entirely in tune with his personality.

6.5 Conclusion: Two Motivational Strands in Thucydides

Thucydides' account of the decision in favour of the Sicilian Expedition leaves us, as demonstrated in Sections 6.1 and 6.2, with two simultaneous impressions. On the one hand, Alcibiades acts as an individualized person with a distinctive character. On the other hand, a permanent, objective collective force acts through both Alcibiades and the Athenians at large, and this force reflects a basic necessity that is inherent in human nature. The parallelism between this picture and the notion that divine and human levels interact is readily apparent, as this observation made by Cornford shows: 'Eros, for instance, is in its higher aspect a supernatural "cause", an agency from God, ministering to the divine purpose. But when Eros takes possession of me, it is also *my* passion, an internal spring of action; and I become responsible ($αἴτιος$) for the results that come of it.'[55] According to Cornford, Diodotus' account of the rampancy of $ἔρως$ and $ἐλπίς$ bears close analogy to this construal of the simultaneity of divine and human motivation.[56] Viewed in this light, Alcibiades and the Athenians are, no less than Croesus, 'responsible' for their decision to invade Sicily, although in making this decision they are subject to the dictates of human nature.

In Herodotus, necessity does not cancel out individual responsibility because the fated event (the downfall of the Mermnadae and the Lydian empire) arises in a way that reflects, and even brings most fully to the fore, the character traits of the central individual agent. In challenging the Persians, Croesus shows himself as the man he essentially is. He realizes the personal traits that befit the great conqueror and potentate, a man eager for ambitious undertakings but also spoiled by success and, therefore, unable to refrain from an idea that has come to obsess him. The same situation applies to Alcibiades. Acting out the innate

[55] Cornford 1907: 159.   [56] Cornford 1907: 158–9, 236–7.

necessities of nature, he realizes the dispositions at the heart of his personality: the erotic man, desirous for conquest and worldly goods, who also displays a considerable degree of good-natured, glamorous attractiveness and infatuates the masses with his alluring personality. Thus, Croesus and Alcibiades realize their personalities to the fullest when they execute the inevitable. In this way, the interaction between individual agents and natural necessity in Thucydides resembles the intertwining of character and the course of fate in Herodotus. Another point, to be investigated more thoroughly in Chapter 7, is closely related: the schematism implanted by necessity merely concerns the outlines of what happens, while leaving room for individual traits that cannot be reduced to an all-pervasive mechanism.

This interconnection between individual traits and general principles, as well as between agency and necessity, reflects a general trend that is characteristic of the depiction of human beings in Greek literature and art. It can be summarized as the union of two polar opposites: the natural and the ideal. On this view, Greek literature tends to represent lifelike human beings while at the same time concentrating on those features that reflect an ideal type. For instance, many Homeric characters are the seamless embodiments of a recognizable type (Odysseus is crafty intelligence, Ajax the quintessential warrior, Diomedes the up-and-coming youngster, Nestor wisdom of old age), but they never come across as the mere symbols of a preconceived, abstract idea; instead, their personalities radiate the liveliness, naturalness, and concreteness that comes from close observation and genuine experience. It is striking how fully and uncompromisingly these characters are what they are. As a result, each of these heroes is saliently and memorably recognizable. This feature, in turn, belongs to the core notions usually associated with individuality. In this way, Greek literature tends to avoid two extremes: on the whole, human beings appear neither as quirky characters exhibiting singular idiosyncrasies of outlook and behaviour (one of the hallmarks of modern ideas about individuality)[57] nor as lifeless abstractions detached from

---

[57] See Pelling 1990a: 253 (commenting on the expectations with which a late-twentieth-century audience approaches Greek tragedy): 'We do indeed expect our characters to be much more idiosyncratic, and share Wilamowitz's expectations of complexity and contradictions...

living phenomena (a tendency that one often finds, for instance, in some expressly allegorical art forms). This unification of opposite tendencies has the effect that each side reinforces its counterpart: the individual features are enhanced because they impersonate an ideal norm while the typical comes to life because it manifests itself in features based on close, concrete observation.[58]

Thucydides' version of dual motivation is a variant of this model. Alcibiades comes across as a recognizable individual, but he also embodies a fundamental general fact about human nature (the indomitability and irresistibleness of ἔρως unleashed). In this interaction between individuality and an ideal type, even the noted aspects that mark Alcibiades' recognizably specific personality are integrated into the vivid manifestation of the norm: it fits into the picture that the quintessentially erotic character turns out to be an irresistible charmer, and that this kind of self-infatuated person also displays a certain degree of disarmingly naive impudence.[59] On the other hand, these features are

---

This hankering for the idiosyncratic is a strange and recent prejudice.' Along similar lines, Lesky (1964: 116) observes with regard to Sophoclean tragedy that the protagonists are not 'Charaktere im Sinne des modernen Seelendramas mit seinen bis ins Pathologische differenzierten Individualitäten'. Instead, as Lesky goes on to observe, '[d]iese Gestalten sind alle Träger einer Schickung, die aus der Mitte ihrer Physis kommt und sie aus entscheidenden Wesenszügen heraus der Welt und dem Göttlichen begegnen läßt.'

[58] For a vivid statement of this position, with specific application to Plato's portrayal of characters, see Liegle (1923: 4): 'Man kann dieses allmähliche Herausbilden grosser Urformen des Lebens mit keinem treffenderen Vergleich bezeichnen als dem, den Platon selbst gebraucht hat: dem Schaffen des Bildhauers, der in unablässiger Mühe seine Figuren aus dem Stein herausarbeitet, in denen noch manch unmittelbarer Zug des Lebens erscheint, die aber erhoben sind in die Sphaere der Idee, bei aller lebendigen Kraft und Fülle einer höheren Realität angehörend.' An application of the same model to Thucydides (though here expressed in general terms) can be found in Bender's observation (1938: 36): 'Die Eigentümlichkeit des Griechen, für jede Lebenserscheinung eine absolute Norm anzunehmen, seine Abneigung, die Einzelindividualität und ihre innerliche, persönliche Stellungnahme zu sehr zu betonen... bewirken eine von modernen Gewohnheiten abweichende Gestaltung einer "Persönlichkeit." Daher schwebt dem griechischen Autor im allgemeinen ein Eidos vor Augen, nach dem er seine Gestalten formt.' Collingwood's account of Thucydides provides evidence of the same view, although Collingwood's primary concern is with Thucydides' presentation of events, not with the portrayal of individuals: '[W]hat chiefly interests Thucydides is the laws according to which they [sc. events] happen. But these laws are precisely such eternal and unchanging forms as, according to the main trend of Greek thought, are the only knowable things' (1946: 30).

[59] Pelling (1990a: 254) uses the term '"integrated" character' for this phenomenon, thus highlighting the habit of Greek authors to portray 'traits which group naturally, and do not furnish any paradoxical or unique combinations'.

so well observed and full of life that they cannot be written off as immediate derivations of a general pattern (unlike Alcibiades' desire for conquest and self-enrichment). Commenting on the junction of transpersonal norm and particular event in Thucydides, Pelling gets to the heart of the issue: '[T]he normative does not exclude the singular, but interweaves with it.'[60]

The specific interaction of individual character and transpersonal force has something in common with Phaedra's passion for Hippolytus in Euripides' play: Aphrodite has imposed a crazed desire on Phaedra, an overmastering force has seized her from without, but Phaedra nonetheless must respond to this visitation. She is recognizably the grand character that she was before Aphrodite struck her. As Knox observes, 'Phaedra's purpose and way of life can be summed up in one word, the word which is so often on her lips: $εὐκλεής$, "honorable"... From first to last this is Phaedra's dominant motive, except for the fatal moment when she surrenders her initiative to the Nurse.'[61] Yet, even a character who values dignified behaviour so highly stands no chance when faced with the onslaught of Aphrodite. While Phaedra's self-torment, as well as her eventual decision to die, reflect her characteristic outlook on life, she has no way of emancipating herself from the divine force that affects her. As a result, doom is inescapable. Natural necessity in Thucydides plays an analogous role: specific individuals, and (as we saw in Chapter 5, pp. 192–3) various cities with their particular characteristics, put their own spin on the underlying natural necessity, but they cannot put it aside.[62] Although Alcibiades differs from Phaedra in welcoming $ἔρως$ instead of resisting it, both characters show that the superior force of $ἔρως$ always expresses itself by interaction with the specific character involved.

It is remarkable that, in the Sicilian Debate, an emphasis on individuality in the depiction of the primary actors, unparalleled elsewhere in Thucydides, coincides with a singularly detailed application of Diodotus' general scheme of motivation through transpersonal forces to a specific

---

[60] Pelling 1990a: 259.   [61] Knox 1979 [1952]: 217. See also Griffin 1990: 133.
[62] On the level of individuals, one finds a small number of rare exceptions to this general fact, most notably Pericles. See Chapter 8 and the book's Conclusion.

decision. The same congruence of human and divine involvement applies to Herodotus, again with each side at its peak, as Pelling notes: '[D]ivine explanations and human explanations intertwine, and when one is at its most intense, we tend also to find the other.'[63] One finds the same phenomenon in Thucydides: the more openly individuality manifests itself, the more clearly the pull of necessity comes to the fore. The two opposite poles, far from excluding each other, are so closely connected that a glaring manifestation of one side implicates an equally stark expression of its opposite. The actions of individuals as well as their specific character play the role of the medium through which necessity asserts itself.

---

[63] Pelling 2019: 156.

7
Necessity and Leeway for Choice
Homer, Herodotus, Thucydides

The dual motivation model described in Chapter 6 implies that responsibility is not cancelled out by necessity, but that personal motivation coexists with foreordainment, whether divine or natural. This picture suggests that necessity does not flatly cancel scope for human choice but coexists with it. In that case, it seems reasonable to suppose that necessity in Thucydides is not characterized by absoluteness, but that it leaves at least some room for more or less effective agency. As a matter of fact, it would be patently perverse to claim without qualification that agency has no role to play in Thucydides. Instances of individual agents who triumph over allegedly irresistible natural impulses can be readily cited: Pericles and Diodotus prevail against ὀργή, which has taken hold of the Athenian demos in each case (Pericles: τὸ ὀργιζόμενον, 2.59.3; τὰ τῆς ὀργῆς, 60.1. Diodotus: ὑπὸ ὀργῆς, 3.36.2; ὀργήν, 42.1). On other occasions, important decisions are the result of a close vote. When faced with the issue of an alliance with Corcyra, the Athenians first favour rejection, but accept a modified version of the proposed alliance only at a second meeting of the assembly (1.44.1). The Spartans, faced with the question of whether Athens has broken the Thirty Years treaty, at first seem almost evenly divided about the issue: their usual procedure of voting with a shout does not yield a clear result. As a consequence, they must divide up into two groups, supporters versus rejecters of the war, to determine the majority (1.87.2). With the new system in place, the larger part of the Spartans votes in favour of the war (1.87.3). However, the reader is left with the impression that group pressure, inevitably exerted by the modified procedure, has impacted the result. A third example is the outcome of the Mytilenean Debate: Thucydides notes that the number of votes on either side were almost even (3.49.1). These passages convey the impression that the outcome of the issue at stake might easily have been different. The question arises as to how one is to reconcile this aspect of Thucydides' presentation with the emphasis on necessity.

Attention to the work of two eminent predecessors of Thucydides will pave the way towards answering this question: Homer and Herodotus. Although these authors are clearly committed to the notion of divine foreordainment, they do not give a picture of an all-encompassing compulsion that predetermines every event and action. Instead, what emerges is the notion that necessity, while manifesting itself in climactic events of far-reaching significance, leaves many other aspects open. These include, for instance, the manner in which fated events come to pass. In Sections 7.4 and 7.5 below, Thucydides will be considered in light of these findings: in fact, he adopts an outlook closely analogous to Homer and Herodotus on the formation of events, combining the necessity of major, often catastrophic, events with flexibility regarding the manner in which they come about.

7.1 Can Necessity Be Malleable?

At one of the dramatic highpoints of the *History*, the Athenian demos shows that decisions do not always proceed according to the script of natural necessity. The Athenians decide to revise an earlier extremely harsh decree, which they had passed in a fit of anger about the renegade ally Mytilene. The willingness of the Athenians to reopen discussion suggests that it is not impossible to moderate the influence exerted by natural impulses, notwithstanding the frequent emphasis on the inevitable pull of these forces. With their anger cooled down, the Athenians consider the former decree 'harsh and excessive' (ὠμὸν... καὶ μέγα, 3.36.4). Thucydides states what aspect of the decree now seemed inappropriate: 'to destroy the whole city rather than those who were guilty' (πόλιν ὅλην διαφθεῖραι μᾶλλον ἢ οὐ τοὺς αἰτίους, 3.36.4). This concern with the question of responsibility and guilt, as opposed to considerations of self-interest alone, suggests that the Athenians wish to give the Mytileneans their due.[1] The principle of justice has some bearing on them.

---

[1] As Orwin (1994: 143) puts it: '[W]hen the Athenians awaken the next day with a massive moral hangover, what troubles them about their decision is not its expediency... The way is open to a reconsideration of the justice of the decree.'

It is true that Diodotus, not least in reaction to Cleon's preceding intervention, takes a hard line of self-interest in the speech that ultimately convinces a close majority of the Athenians to retract the earlier decision (3.44.2).[2] However, this does not alter the fact that their crucial initial impulse springs from a lingering concern with appropriate treatment. Furthermore, the juxtaposition of the Mytilenean Debate with the immediately preceding pendant at Plataea highlights the relative moderation of the Athenians. Scholars have noted that the similarity between both situations is hard to miss: each time, one of the two superpowers passes judgment on a former friend, who, after turning into an opponent, is forced by a siege to surrender.[3] The qualms of the Athenians contrast quite favourably with the Spartans' cold-bloodedness.

Twice near the beginning of his speech, Diodotus observes that, faced with the issue of Mytilene, the Athenians deliberate about 'the greatest things' (περὶ τῶν μεγίστων, 3.42.1; πρὸς τὰ μέγιστα, 43.4). Diodotus' reference to τὰ μέγιστα recalls the use of the same term in the Athenians' speech at Sparta (1.76.2). Yet, in the two cited passages, Diodotus does not clarify exactly what he means by the term. This, however, is not the whole picture: he uses the phrase on yet a third occasion, when offering his thoughts on the general forces governing human behaviour. This time he makes explicit what the τὰ μέγιστα refers to: he unpacks them as 'freedom or dominion over others' (περὶ τῶν μεγίστων..., ἐλευθερίας ἢ ἄλλων ἀρχῆς, 3.45.6). Since Diodotus' account of human nature is meant to shed light on the reasons for the Mytileneans' secession, the passage has more do with the Mytileneans than the Athenians at first glance. However, as is often the case in Thucydides, the less immediate frame of reference is of at least equal importance: 'dominion over others' evidently pertains to the Athenians, not least because the term describes their relationship with the Mytileneans, thus referring to the stake that the Athenians have in the present situation. The two previous passages, in which the term τὰ

---

[2] Wassermann 1956: 35–6; Winnington-Ingram 1965: 78; Manuwald 1979: 415–16; Pouncey 1980: 86; Cogan 1981b: 9; Cohen 1984: 50–3; Connor 1984: 85; Euben 1990: 180–2; Orwin 1994: 146–7; Yunis 1996: 94–5. Given the general ascendancy of Cleon and his setting the tone of the debate, Diodotus' apparent tough-mindedness may in fact be a posture, cleverly assumed in order to help justice prevail. On this point, see Strauss 1964: 233–4; Manuwald 1979: 420–1.

[3] See HCT ii. 354; Macleod 1983d [1977]: 118–19; Cohen 1984: 53; Hornblower i. 462–3.

μέγιστα unambiguously refers to the Athenians, are likely to have the same meaning. The verbal parallel aside, this is the case because Diodotus emphatically maintains that his sole reason for wanting the issue regarding Mytilene to be reopened is the advantage of Athens (3.44.1, 44.2, 44.4). He goes on to explain that the advantage sought by him is based solely on the safety of the empire (3.46–7). This concern is identified with 'dominion over others' in the passage at 3.45.6 where Diodotus defines the meaning of τὰ μέγιστα. Therefore, it stands to reason that Diodotus' motive for telling the Athenians that they are concerned with τὰ μέγιστα is that the question regarding Mytilene concerns the vital basis of their empire.

The Athenians at Sparta likewise hold that 'the three greatest things' commit the Athenians to adherence to the empire (1.76.1–2 with 75.3). Thus, in both speeches the term τὰ μέγιστα ultimately refers to the same thing: the fact that for the Athenians the most vital issues of self-preservation have become bound up with the empire. Moreover, both speeches proceed to point out that the 'greatest things' subject human beings to the compulsion brought about by human nature when making their decisions (1.76.3, 3.45.7). As Macleod observes with regard to Diodotus, 'his detailed argument...reveals that empire is necessarily oppressive and revolt inevitable'.[4]

Yet Diodotus' emphasis on necessity is not the whole picture. His respective weighting of τὰ μέγιστα and free choice is double-edged. Referring to the Mytileneans, he suggests that 'the greatest things' leave no choice: the Mytileneans could not help but act as they did due to the compulsory pull of human nature (3.45.3, 45.7). Diodotus' rhetorical situation influences his tendency to minimize any leeway at this point: the offence committed by the Mytileneans will seem less glaring if it can be traced to inevitable traits of human behaviour.[5] However, when considering the significance of τὰ μέγιστα for the Athenians, Diodotus puts the emphasis squarely on their need to make a far-sighted decision. It is true that the Athenians, just like everyone else, are hardwired to

---

[4] Macleod 1983c [1978]: 101.
[5] Macleod (1983c [1978]: 99): '[H]e [sc. Diodotus] undermines a position based on legality or morality by recourse to what men are really like. This is the more effective because Cleon himself had introduced that notion in condemning the Mytileneans (39.5 πέφυκε).'

attend to the vital concern of self-preservation, which depends on the continued existence of their empire. Nonetheless, each time Diodotus stresses that the Athenians have come face to face with τὰ μέγιστα, he makes the point that, because the stakes are so high, careful, provident deliberation is in order (πολλάκις...βουλεύεσθαι, 3.42.1; περαιτέρω προνοοῦντας, 43.4). Diodotus' call for deliberation presupposes that this basic necessity leaves scope for a considered response to be made. What is more, Diodotus' success in the debate proves beyond doubt that moderation and reasoned reflection are possible, even when one is faced with τὰ μέγιστα. By contrast, the Athenians' original harsh decree shows the potential of a short circuit between natural predisposition and ensuing action: people's susceptibility (also highlighted by Diodotus at 3.45.6) to irrational forces in moments when τὰ μέγιστα are at stake. In this case, the impact of necessity is all-determining, and there is no opportunity for reasoned deliberation to intervene.

Cleon's speech shows just how close the Athenians have come to giving in to this direct link between natural predisposition and ensuing action. On his view, decisions ought to proceed according to a chain reaction fuelled by anger (3.38.1):

ὁ γὰρ παθὼν τῷ δράσαντι ἀμβλυτέρᾳ τῇ ὀργῇ ἐπεξέρχεται, ἀμύνασθαι δὲ τῷ παθεῖν ὅτι ἐγγυτάτω κείμενον ἀντίπαλον ὂν μάλιστα τὴν τιμωρίαν ἀναλαμβάνει.

For [sc. if the punishment of an offence is delayed] the victim proceeds with less keen rage against the perpetrator; yet vengeance that follows on the heels of suffering is best suited to exact punishment because it is equally matched.

The two halves of Cleon's statement are marked by contrary stylistic choices: whereas, in the first half, the response of those whose anger has cooled down is captured by personal nouns, the automatism championed by Cleon in the second half is expressed by substantivized infinitives. In the latter segment, the infinitive ἀμύνασθαι functions as subject with the verbal phrase 'to exact punishment' (τὴν τιμωρίαν ἀναλαμβάνει): not a personal agent, but the mechanism of instantaneous vengeance plays the role of decision-maker. The ensuing neuter participial phrases heighten (at least if the transmitted text is accepted) the impersonal flavour of the passage (ὅτι ἐγγυτάτω κείμενον and ἀντίπαλον ὄν).[6] Additionally, as a scholiast points out and as Classen-Steup corroborate, the participial phrase ὅτι ἐγγυτάτω κείμενον functions as the perfect passive of τίθημι.[7] The implication is that vengeance is not an act carried out by a personal subject, but a state that has imposed itself. Cleon's phrasing suggests that, if undiminished anger prevails, impersonal states will dictate the decision without leaving room for other influences to intervene.

When taking the second vote about Mytilene, the Athenians avoid by a hair's breadth self-surrender to the impersonal mechanism approved by Cleon. Since the Athenians' original decree was instigated by a fit of anger (ὑπὸ ὀργῆς, 3.36.2; ὁρμῆς, 36.2), it provides a paragon of the automatism envisioned by Cleon (cf. τῇ ὀργῇ, 3.38.1). Notice that the word ὀργή and a form of the verb ὁρμάομαι are also found in Diodotus' account of the domineering natural impulses (3.45.4, 45.7). By reversing their earlier resolution, the Athenians preserve some degree of the ever-embattled freedom of choice. Yet this turnaround flies in the face of Diodotus' own doctrine about the overwhelming urges that govern human nature (3.45.3–7). It is due not least to the one-time intervention of an otherwise unknown speaker, a man called, as Bruell notes, 'Gift of Zeus'.[8] No

---

[6] The translation given above is based on the transmitted text, printed by Stuart Jones in the OCT and by Alberti. However, most commentators construe the passage differently. They delete ὄν, taking it as a wrong explanatory gloss that intruded into the text, and construe ἀντίπαλον μάλιστα as predicative adjective with τὴν τιμωρίαν; see Poppo-Stahl ii, 1, ad loc.; Boehme-Widmann iii, ad loc.; Classen-Steup iii, ad loc. (along with the Anhang ad loc.); HCT ii, ad loc. Krüger (i,2, ad loc.) puts ὄν in square brackets, but his comment on ἀντίπαλον ὄν implies that he is inclined to keep the transmitted text. With ὄν excised, the passage translates as follows: 'Vengeance that follows on the heels of suffering exacts punishment that is most nearly matched.' On this interpretation, the superlatives 'as closely as possible' (rendered as 'on the heels of' in our translation of the passage: ἀμύνασθαι... ὅτι ἐγγυτάτω κείμενον) and 'most nearly matched' (ἀντίπαλον μάλιστα τὴν τιμωρίαν) tidily correspond to each other. In light of the unanimity of the manuscript tradition, however, the deletion of ὄν seems extreme, especially because it is chiefly based on an argument in favour of stylistic balance. Yet Thucydides actively defies symmetry in many phrases, a fact stressed in every summary of his style (see, for instance, Denniston 1952: 73–4). Indeed, the symmetry produced by the deletion of ὄν is so neat that it is hard to see why anyone should have misunderstood the Greek and have felt the need to provide ὄν as a wrong explanatory gloss.

[7] Classen-Steup iii, on 3.38.1.5 (citing the explanation of the scholiast: εἰ τὸ ἀμύνεσθαι τῷ παθεῖν ἐγγὺς τεθείη).

[8] Bruell 1974: 16.

further mention is ever made of Diodotus.[9] Zeus' gift of prudent second thoughts comes out of nowhere and disappears again.

Diodotus' speech encapsulates the paradox of Thucydidean necessity. As pointed out in Chapter 6, the prominence of ἔρως and ἐλπίς at Athens on the eve of the Sicilian Expedition suggests that the Athenians' own mindset reflects Diodotus' idea of human nature: his doctrine that natural forces inevitably drive cities towards the irrational when τὰ μέγιστα are at stake. In this way, Thucydides' own narrative confirms what Diodotus says about the destructive necessities that weigh on human action. Yet, at the same time, Diodotus' call for prudent decision-making in the face of τὰ μέγιστα does not fall on deaf ears when the Athenians pass judgment on Mytilene. It follows that specific events appear to lend credence to each of Diodotus' two mutually contradictory claims about τὰ μέγιστα: they simultaneously back up and undermine the possibility of prudent decision-making. Thucydides' account of events implies that each of Diodotus' two contrary assertions have some truth behind them.

7.2 The Homecoming of Odysseus: Predestination with Blank Spots

Right from its beginning, Greek thought was concerned with the intricate interplay of personal agency and necessity. The tensions affecting τὰ μέγιστα in Diodotus' speech are a variant of this theme. The origins of this issue can be traced back as far as Homeric epic. In this section, I will consider Homer's engagement with the problem of choice versus foreordainment. This investigation, when complemented by an analysis of similar issues in Herodotus (in Section 7.3 below), will pave the way for explaining how Diodotus (as well as Thucydides) could plausibly

---

[9] *HCT* ii, on 3.41; Hornblower i, on 3.41. The so-called 'Cup of Pericles' discovered at Athens in 2014 has the name of a Diodotus inscribed on it as one of the seven symposiasts (alongside the names of Pericles and his brother Arriphron). It is conceivable that the man whose name has been preserved on the cup is identical with Thucydides' Diodotus. See Matthaiou 2016: 63; Simonton 2018: 221 n. 2. Ostwald (1979: 7–13) attempts to reconstruct Diodotus' specific persona and political role (viz. that he held a public office at the time of the debate) from the tiny bits of information that he gleans from Diodotus' speech in Thucydides.

endorse two seemingly contradictory positions on the topic of agency versus necessity.

In Homeric epic, momentous events are fated to happen and are frequently anticipated by predictions. For instance, the *Iliad* forecasts the fall of Troy and the deaths of Achilles and Hector in this way, and the *Odyssey* the homecoming of Odysseus and the destruction of the suitors.[10] The anticipated events are the highpoints that the action of the epic poems leads up to: the death of a valiant warrior, the fall of a city, the homecoming of a great hero, or the punishment of villains.[11] Scholars have concluded that divine foreordainment does not amount to pervasive determinism, by which every single event is predestined to happen in exactly the way it does, but that it especially concerns the most important and far-reaching events.[12] Thus, considerable scope remains for the relevant actors to influence the course of events within the ambit circumscribed by fate and the will of the gods.

A close examination of one of these predestined events, the homecoming of Odysseus, will reveal the specific implications of the Homeric variant of fatalism. From the point of view of story time (i.e. in terms of the realistic sequence of events as opposed to their ordering in the narrative), the predestination of the homecoming of Odysseus is first addressed during the episode with Polyphemus. After Odysseus has escaped from Polyphemus' cave, he cannot resist taunting the blinded ogre from across the sea. Enraged by the hero's recklessness, Polyphemus addresses his father Poseidon in prayer, asking him to take revenge for his blinding by preventing the hero's homecoming (*Od.* 9.530). Yet Polyphemus has the inkling that the question of a hero's return home may be important enough to be foreordained by fate. He therefore supplements his first request with a second one (9.532–5):

---

[10] The relevant passages are collected by Duckworth 1933: 30–1 (fall of Troy); 28–9 (death of Achilles); 60–1 (death of Hector); 18 and 55–6 (homecoming of Odysseus); 18, 56, and 61–2 (destruction of the suitors).
[11] Adkins 1960: 17–18; Strauss Clay 1983: 154–5.
[12] Otto 1987 [1934]: 357; Schadewaldt 1959: 310–11; Adkins 1960: 11–12 and 21–2; Strauss Clay 1983: 155; Griffin 2004 [1987]: 77.

ἀλλ' εἴ οἱ μοῖρ' ἐστὶ φίλους τ' ἰδέειν καὶ ἱκέσθαι
οἶκον ἐϋκτίμενον καὶ ἑὴν ἐς πατρίδα γαῖαν,
ὀψὲ κακῶς ἔλθοι, ὀλέσας ἄπο πάντας ἑταίρους,
νηὸς ἐπ' ἀλλοτρίης, εὕροι δ' ἐν πήματα οἴκῳ.

But if it is fate for him to see his friends and to come
to his well-built house and his fatherland,
then let him arrive late and in sorry plight, after he has lost all his companions,
on a ship that belongs to strangers, and let him find sufferings in his house.

Poseidon will do his utmost to fulfil the supplementary part of Polyphemus' request, making life as difficult for Odysseus as he possibly can. This appears to warrant the conclusion that it is indeed Odysseus' μοῖρα 'to see his friends and come to his well-built house and his fatherland'; otherwise, Poseidon would make sure that Odysseus never returns home.

In several further passages, various divinities acknowledge, or imply, the predestination of Odysseus' return home (see 5.41-2 [Zeus], 5.288-90 [Poseidon], 5.345 [Leucothea]). The clearest evidence is provided by the terms in which Hermes couches his message to Calypso that Zeus has resolved Odysseus' homecoming (5.113-15):

οὐ γάρ οἱ τῇδ' αἶσα φίλων ἀπονόσφιν ὀλέσθαι,
ἀλλ' ἔτι οἱ μοῖρ' ἐστὶ φίλους τ' ἰδέειν καὶ ἱκέσθαι
οἶκον ἐς ὑψόροφον καὶ ἑὴν ἐς πατρίδα γαῖαν.

For it is not his fate to perish here far from his friends,
but it is still his lot to see his friends and come
to his high-roofed house and his fatherland.

The last two lines are nearly a verbatim repetition of the instructions given by Zeus to Hermes (5.41-2). Yet the first two words spoken by Hermes in these lines (ἀλλ' ἔτι) contain important information not found in Zeus' original wording. Stressing that 'it is still' Odysseus' μοῖρα to return home, Hermes reminds Calypso of something that she had always known, thus making clear to her that she was never entitled to expect anything other than an eventual separation from Odysseus. It follows that Odysseus' homecoming had been preordained already before his arrival at Ogygia. The natural conclusion from Hermes' wording is that the return home has been part of Odysseus' assigned portion from time immemorial.

The foreordainment of Odysseus' homecoming does not mean that the course of his life is predestined in all its facets. It does not even imply that the specific circumstances of his return are set in stone. Noticing the conditional clause in which Polyphemus couches his prayer (9.532–3), A. W. H. Adkins writes: 'If Polyphemus can pray in these terms, he must believe that even if it is *moira* for Odysseus to return, it need not be *moira* for him to return at a particular time or in a particular condition.'[13] It is worth adding that the wretched circumstances of Odysseus' homecoming have always been part of his destiny to a greater or lesser extent, in addition to the return itself. When Odysseus departed for Troy, he had already been warned by the Ithacan seer Halitherses about several aspects of his personal fortune, which are then reinforced by Polyphemus' prayer. Before the assembly of Ithacans in book 2, Halitherses recollects his prophecy to Odysseus: 'I said that, after suffering many things and losing all his companions, he would return home in the twentieth year, unknown to all. By now, all these things are being fulfilled' (φῆν κακὰ πολλὰ παθόντ', ὀλέσαντ' ἄπο πάντας ἑταίρους, / ἄγνωστον πάντεσσιν ἐεικοστῷ ἐνιαυτῷ / οἴκαδ' ἐλεύσεσθαι· τὰ δὲ δὴ νῦν πάντα τελεῖται, 2.174–6). This would suggest that the sufferings attached to Odysseus as a result of Polyphemus' prayer had already been part of his fated lot. However, the seer, just like Polyphemus, does not spell out the specific circumstances that will lead to the companions' ruin and Odysseus' late homecoming.

When the gods are finally moved by Athena to provide for Odysseus' homecoming, Odysseus has suffered the first two hardships that Polyphemus requested: as a result of his various trials, he has lost all his companions, and has now been trapped on the island of Calypso for seven years (7.259). Ultimately, Poseidon is responsible for these specific sufferings (1.68–70, 74–5). Now, however, the gods resolve that it is time

[13] Adkins 1960: 18.

to bring Odysseus home. Significantly, the gods plan Odysseus' homecoming while Poseidon is absent feasting with the Aethiopians on the fringes of the world (1.22-7). This circumstance seems to imply that, if Poseidon had not been away from the deliberations on Olympus, he would have opposed the homecoming of Odysseus, who, in that case, might have returned even later than he does.

Then, in book 5, Zeus commissions Hermes to inform Calypso that she must let Odysseus go (5.30-4):

νύμφῃ ἐϋπλοκάμῳ εἰπεῖν νημερτέα βουλήν,
νόστον Ὀδυσσῆος ταλασίφρονος, ὥς κε νέηται,
οὔτε θεῶν πομπῇ οὔτε θνητῶν ἀνθρώπων·
ἀλλ' ὅ γ' ἐπὶ σχεδίης πολυδέσμου πήματα πάσχων
ἤματι εἰκοστῷ Σχερίην ἐρίβωλον ἵκοιτο...

Tell the fair-tressed nymph our unerring plan,
the return of stout-hearted Odysseus, that he may return
conducted by neither gods nor mortal men;
however, on a strong-bonded raft suffering woes,
let him reach Scheria of the strong clots on the twentieth day...

Zeus' reference to the 'unerring plan' (νημερτέα βουλήν) is reminiscent of the 'plan of Zeus' mentioned in the proem of the *Iliad* (Διὸς...βουλή, 1.5). As Calypso will soon acknowledge (*Od.* 5.137-8), once the highest god has firmly decreed that a specific event will come to pass, nothing can prevent it.[14] Therefore, the plan laid down by Zeus in his instruction to Hermes will from now on be an inescapable component of Odysseus' fate. While, as pointed out above, it is part of Odysseus' fate that his wanderings will end on the island of Scheria (5.288-9, 345), the further specifications made by Zeus seem to be genuine additions, which flesh out the manner of Odysseus' arrival.

By adding these qualifications, Zeus imposes further trials on Odysseus before his return to Ithaca, especially during the journey from Ogygia to Scheria. Zeus' additional clauses partially reinforce the

---

[14] On the supremacy of the will of Zeus, see Krause 1949: 23; Dietrich 1965: 221.

parameters set by Poseidon in response to Polyphemus' request, especially that he will arrive 'late and in sorry plight' (ὀψὲ κακῶς ἔλθοι, 9.534). Floating on a raft exposed to Poseidon's meteorological inferno, Odysseus will experience yet again 'sorry plight'. His arrival on the 'twentieth day' (the twenty days being a mirroring of the twenty years he has been away from home) amounts to another delay because Odysseus would have reached the island of the Phaeacians on the eighteenth day under normal circumstances (5.279). His raft having been shattered by Poseidon, Odysseus floats on the sea 'for two nights and two days', clasping onto a plank (5.388-9). Compared to the seven years on Calypso's island, the further delay may seem negligible. Yet, the realist standpoint implied by this objection misses the point of Zeus' clause: by inflicting two more days amid frightful hardship on Odysseus, Zeus takes heed of Poseidon's will that Odysseus must come home as late as possible.

To sum up, predestination in Homer, instead of amounting to pervasive determinism, operates by drawing boundaries: events must keep within their ambit, but the specific details are largely left open. General initial provisions settle the most momentous events, and some further significant parameters are spelled out by subsequent divine dispensations. In this manner, the contours of Odysseus' fate become increasingly more specific: starting with the fated homecoming, Poseidon adds a first lot of foreordinations in response to Polyphemus' prayer, and Zeus subsequently supplements these provisions by yet further, more detailed specifications.

The question remains as to how much scope the narrowing confines imposed by fate and the gods leave for Odysseus' own agency. To begin with, it is worth noting that Calypso, after her encounter with Hermes, does not tell Odysseus about the gods' resolve; instead, she gives Odysseus the choice to stay or leave, stressing that the latter possibility will involve grievous hardship for him (5.203-10). As a result, when Odysseus decides that he will make the trip, he is not simply executing the will of the gods, but he makes his own free choice to go home. According to Schadewaldt, Odysseus' homecoming is decided on two levels: the divine resolution is matched by Odysseus' own decision, with the former underpinning, but in no way predetermining, the latter.[15] There is no indication that a god interferes with Odysseus' mind and manipulates him to make the required decision. Given, however, who Odysseus is, there can be doubt as to how he will decide. Ἦθος ἀνθρώπῳ δαίμων, as Heraclitus would say (DK 22 B 119). In sum, divine resolve does not annul human initiative, but it is complemented by it, at least when the important decisions of great heroes are involved. It is not a matter of course that humans are given scope for making up their mind in this way. Power of choice is not a faculty enjoyed by everyone alike in equal measure, but it comes in degrees. Great heroes wield more considerable power of choice. Yet the vital outcome always remains in the hands of the gods.

The exact circumstances of Odysseus' arrival on Scheria allow one to assess Odysseus' own contribution to his predestined arrival. When Poseidon's tempest has reduced Odysseus' raft to a wreck, the goddess Leucothea appears in the guise of a sea mew. She advises Odysseus to get rid of his clothes, which are heavy because they are soaked with water, and to reach the land of the Phaeacians by swimming (5.342–5). The goddess gives him an 'immortal' veil, which he is to tie under his breast to protect him from drowning (5.346–50).

Faced with Leucothea's advice, Odysseus does not instantaneously act upon it, but warily ponders what he should do, suspecting that the gods might have set another trap for him (5.356–7). Since the land is far off, it seems difficult to reach by swimming, so Odysseus decides, for the time being, to refrain from following the advice of the goddess, telling himself that he will only let go of his raft when it is so shattered that he has no other choice but to swim (5.358–64). Soon enough, the raft breaks apart, at which point Odysseus climbs a plank and does as Leucothea advised (5.370–5). It is plausible to assume that this way of executing the divine instruction is Odysseus' own contribution to the situation. This conclusion is suggested by the two clearly demarcated stages: the goddess giving advice and Odysseus following it only when he sees fit. If the poet had not wanted to convey this impression, the emphasis on Odysseus' hesitation and his declared intention not to swim before his raft breaks apart would be quite misleading.

[15] Schadewaldt 1970a [1958]: 51.

When the raft is smashed, it is time for Athena to get involved: she calms the opposing winds and rouses the North Wind, who is to carry Odysseus to the Phaeacians (5.382–7). After Odysseus has been tossed about by the waves for two days, the twentieth day arrives on which he is destined to reach the island of the Phaeacians due to the conditions stipulated by Zeus (5.34). Indeed, calm sets in (5.391–2), and we may conclude that the quieting is due to the will of the gods. Now Odysseus realizes that the shore is within reach, and he starts swimming. The initiative is wholly on the side of Odysseus, and the poet does not say that a god helped him at this moment. The poet's reticence at this point has some weight because he soon chooses to make a divine intervention explicit. Odysseus is hurled by the surging waves against the cliffs of the shore. At this moment, Odysseus would have been crushed (5.426) if Athena had not put the good idea into his mind to seize one of the cliffs and hold on to it (5.427–8). Even so, the danger is not averted, and here we come across one of Homer's well-known 'almosts': 'Then indeed unfortunate Odysseus would have perished beyond his fate if bright-eyed Athena had not given him presence of mind' (ἔνθα κε δὴ δύστηνος ὑπὲρ μόρον ὦλετ' Ὀδυσσεύς, / εἰ μὴ ἐπιφροσύνην δῶκε γλαυκῶπις Ἀθήνη, 5.436–7). Odysseus lets go of the cliff at the right moment, emerges from the surging wave, gets out of the area where the waves break, and finally reaches the mouth of the river that will convey him to the shore. The scope for free range granted to the course of events has threatened to disrupt the boundaries set by fate. At this point, Athena must readjust the course of action in order to prevent fate from being defied. If the course set by fate amounted to all-encompassing predestination, such readjustments, which occur relatively frequently, would hardly be necessary.[16]

As noted by Lesky, Homer depicts a wide spectrum of interactions between human and divine motivation: they range from entirely independent human action to the simultaneity of human and divine impetus and, finally, to impulses wholly induced by the gods.[17] The decision to set

---

[16] On the possibility of events occurring ὑπὲρ μόρον and the implications that this aspect has for the Homeric notion of fate, see Otto 1987 [1934]: 353–7; Adkins 1960: 19–20; Schein 1984: 63–4.

[17] Lesky 1961: 32–3, 38.

off towards the coast seems to exemplify the first possibility, whereas the presence of mind inspired by Athena amid the cliffs and surging waves the last. However, as Jasper Griffin points out, Athena's help does not reduce Odysseus to a passive instrument: '[Athena's] favour means success, and it is no less true to say that she favours Odysseus because he is a winner, than to say that he wins because of her favour.'[18] Athena helps Odysseus because the clever idea she offers corresponds with a disposition for insight already present in Odysseus himself. The situation is similar when Leucothea prefaces her advice to Odysseus with the following words: 'However, do just as I say, for you seem to me not to lack understanding' (ἀλλὰ μάλ' ὧδ' ἔρξαι, δοκέεις δέ μοι οὐκ ἀπινύσσειν, 5.342). The particle δέ in the second half of the statement is an instance of so-called δέ for γάρ.[19] Thus, it indicates a causal or explanatory relationship: Leucothea advises Odysseus to follow her advice, (sc. and she has reason to believe that he will in fact follow it) *because Odysseus has a general capacity for understanding*.[20] It is implied that the goddess would not help an obtuse person, who would probably not even know what to do with her advice. Moreover, divine involvement does not tend to proceed via a magical suspension of the natural: the gods do not lift Odysseus out of the raging sea and carry him in mid-air to the shore. The natural parameters of the situation, and the humanly possible, are respected, an aspect that recalls Herodotus' emphasis on the natural formation of events on the human level despite divine foreordainment (see Chapter 6, pp. 212–3). Pelling observes, echoing Strasburger: '[T]he possibility of divine help makes it more believable, not less, that Odysseus could have survived that journey on his raft.'[21]

---

[18] Griffin 2004 [1987]: 77. Compare the following remarks by Gundert about the relationship between character and fate in Homer: '[D]och führt jeder [sc. Homeric hero] das Verhängnis, zu dem er bestimmt ist, nach dem Gesetz seines Charakters selbst herbei. Darum trägt auch jeder die Folgen als sein Teil... So bewirken die Fügungen der Götter nichts anderes, als was diese Menschen aus sich selber heraus leisten und zu leisten vermögen, und die Frage, ob sie "gebunden" seien oder "frei", trifft sie darum nicht' (1940: 237).
[19] GP 169.
[20] For γάρ meaning 'I say this because,' see GP 60–1. Since δέ is used for γάρ in the present passage, it can convey the same connotations.
[21] Pelling 2019: 149. See Strasburger (1972: 22–3): '[D]er Bericht über göttliche Hilfe ist es im Einzelfall oft gerade, was Unglaubliches glaublich macht; kein Grieche würde hinnehmen, daß

In sum, Homeric fate signifies the foreordainment of pivotal events and vital outcomes of long sequences of action, but within the contours thus defined, considerable scope remains: the specific circumstances are left open, as well as, sometimes at least, at what time the fated events are to occur. In the world described by Homer, where the interference of the gods is often explicitly acknowledged, superhuman forces tend to be involved in filling out the blanks left open by fate or by Zeus' plan. But the superhuman strand does not amount to anything like predetermination: first, because the gods are numerous and hardly ever unanimous in their love or hatred of a mortal; secondly, because the ideas and impulses that they induce must typically correspond to some predisposition already present in the character of the particular person involved; and thirdly, because individuals are frequently given scope to contribute to the course of events as long as this does not lead to the event overshooting the boundaries drawn by fate or the gods.

7.3 Herodotus on Divine and Human Action in Relation to Fate: Apollo's Intervention and Croesus' Contribution

The downfall of Croesus in Herodotus sheds some further light on the specific interplay of an overriding paramount force (such as the will of Zeus or fate) and the influence of various subordinate factors (whether lower-ranking deities or human beings). At 1.91, Herodotus reports the oracle by which Apollo replies to Croesus' complaint that the god has been unfaithful by encouraging Croesus to go to war with Persia (1.90.4). This response, put into the mouth of the Pythia, sheds some light on the specific interaction between fate and Apollo's influence.

Apollo points out that Croesus was destined to pay for the sin of his ancestor Gyges (1.91.1), a necessity against which the god is powerless: 'it is impossible even for a god to escape the appointed fate' (τὴν πεπρωμένην μοῖραν ἀδύνατά ἐστι ἀποφυγεῖν καὶ θεῷ, 1.91.1). Fate is

---

Odysseus im tobenden Meer nicht ertrinkt, vernähme er nicht, daß da gleich zwei Göttinnen geholfen haben. Kurz, auch die Götterhandlung verstärkt in ihrer Weise mehr die quasi-*realen* als die märchenhaften Stimmungselemente.'

prior: it lays down certain incontrovertible strictures for Croesus' personal destiny. Yet this foreordainment does not lead to a deterministic universe. Instead, in a manner known from Homer, it sets a frame within which many details remain open. Apollo says he would have liked to deflect the fall of Sardes upon Croesus' children, but that 'he was unable to divert the Fates from their course' (οὐκ οἷός τε ἐγένετο παραγαγεῖν Μοίρας, 1.91.2). 'If the agency of the god,' writes Gagné, 'is limited by the boundaries of the Moirai, it is still able to exercise its will within this framework of allotments.'[22] As a result, Apollo does achieve some significant mitigation for Croesus: Sardes is captured three years later than has originally been predestined, and he saves Croesus from the funeral pyre (1.91.3). It follows that there is some flexibility concerning the exact date of Croesus' downfall, and that the question of his survival, as opposed to his loss of power, is left open by the fatal portion assigned to him.

Throughout his exchange with Cyrus, Croesus refers to the divine by personal designations alone (1.87.3, 89.1, 89.3, 90.2, 90.3, 90.4). It is in character for Croesus to conceive of the divine primarily as a personal being, a counterpart with whom he can have dealings. This has been his approach throughout, and it does win him some favour with Apollo. Yet he does not realize that other forces may be at play, divine agencies less amenable to interpersonal negotiation. The Pythia takes recourse to the impersonal label ἡ πεπρωμένη μοῖρα when referring to the force that is even stronger than a god. Apropos this passage and others featuring the term μοῖρα, Myres observes that, taken by itself, the term suggests 'sheer mechanistic fatalism',[23] and Sewell-Rutter notes 'the role of μοῖρα ("fate") as an impersonal and implacable force'.[24] To be sure, a few lines below the Pythia implies a more personal notion, referring to Apollo's intervention with 'the Moirai'. While failing 'to divert the Moirai' (παραγαγεῖν Μοίρας, 1.91.2), Apollo at least got them to 'grant' (ἐνέδωκαν, 1.91.3) that the fated downfall would take place three years later than originally planned. As these phrases suggest, the Fates are to some degree conceived of as personal entities with whom Apollo can negotiate. On the other hand, the Pythia's testimony implies that it is

[22] Gagné 2013: 328.   [23] Myres 1953: 48.   [24] Sewell-Rutter 2007: 10.

impossible for humans to come into direct contact with the Moirai: otherwise, it is hard to understand why Apollo must appear as Croesus' spokesman before them. Hence, the Fates, even in their personal variant, belong to a secluded sphere, a realm entirely impermeable to human attempts of establishing communication. As Dietrich has shown, the coexistence of personal and impersonal variants of $μοῖρα$ can already be found in Homeric epic.[25] Given this Homeric picture, it seems best not to reduce one aspect of $μοῖρα$ to the other in the Herodotean passage. Moreover, it is evident from the Pythia's phrasing that the Moirai do not play the role of one branch of gods alongside others (such as the Olympians), but that they are different in kind: when the Pythia says that 'even a god' is powerless before $μοῖρα$, it is implied that Moira, whether in the singular or plural, belongs to a different category than the personal designation $θεός$. All this suggests that the Moirai mentioned by the Pythia are conceived as less human-like, and therefore less personal, than the Olympian gods. The crucial point to be gleaned from the Pythia's reply is that ineluctable forces embodying the principle of necessity have determined Croesus' downfall. As a result, Croesus' attempt to influence Apollo, though not entirely ineffectual, cannot have any effect on the vital outcome: the downfall of the Lydian empire has been foreordained by fate. As Myres writes, 'like Homer's "Purpose of Zeus" ($βουλὴ\ Διός$), Fate and Chance, for Herodotus, are above the gods.'[26]

Divine and human elements are crucially combined when Croesus is rescued from imminent death after the fall of Sardes. Cyrus' decision to set Croesus on a funeral pyre and to burn him alive prompts Herodotus to speculate about Cyrus' motives. The last of the three reasons he adduces is that Cyrus wants to see whether 'any of the gods' ($τις\ldots δαιμόνων$) may help Croesus, of whom Cyrus has heard that he is a pious man (1.86.2). This anticipation directs the reader's attention to the possibility of divine interference. The following events supply confirmation that it in fact takes place.

As Croesus sits on the funeral pyre, he suddenly recalls Solon's dictum that one must not consider anybody blessed before death: 'although he was in such great plight, the word of Solon came to Croesus' mind: how it

---

[25] Dietrich 1965: 327–31.   [26] Myres 1953: 52.

had been said by him as by divine inspiration that "no one among the living is blessed"' (τῷ δὲ Κροίσῳ... ἐσελθεῖν, καίπερ ἐν κακῷ ἐόντι τοσούτῳ, τὸ τοῦ Σόλωνος, ὥς οἱ εἴη σὺν θεῷ εἰρημένον, τὸ 'μηδένα εἶναι τῶν ζωόντων ὄλβιον', 1.86.3). As a result of the sudden recollection, Croesus cries out the name of Solon. This exclamation arouses Cyrus' interest. He wants to know who Solon is, whereupon Croesus reports Solon's insights into the human condition. Prompted by this account, Cyrus begins to reflect on the humanity shared by himself and Croesus, and he eventually orders his attendants to take Croesus off the pyre. Yet, this impulse turns out to be insufficient to save Croesus: it is too late to quench the fire. At that point, Croesus calls to Apollo for help, and out of a clear sky a heavy rain shower miraculously extinguishes the fire (1.87.2): an unmistakable instance of the intervention of superhuman forces. This conclusion is also drawn by Cyrus: 'In this way, it is said that Cyrus learned that Croesus was a man both dear to the gods and excellent' (οὕτω δὴ μαθόντα τὸν Κῦρον ὡς εἴη ὁ Κροῖσος καὶ θεοφιλὴς καὶ ἀνὴρ ἀγαθός, 1.87.2).

The need to send the shower suggests that the exact course of action is not firmly established. Otherwise, it is hard to account for the extreme crisis that events reach before Croesus is rescued in the nick of time. In addition, Croesus' appeal for Apollo's help amounts to an important contribution since Apollo would probably not have stirred had Croesus not called for him. It is unlikely that Apollo inspires Croesus to call for the god's help since it would be absurd if a god honoured an individual's act of piety after causing it in the first place. Moreover, Segal points out that Apollo abstains from interference until Croesus has undergone his inward turnaround that crystallizes around his recognition of Solonian wisdom.[27] Thus, Croesus' insight, achieved by human means of experience and reflection, is the precondition of Apollo's rescue mission. Even if Apollo wishes Croesus to be saved, Croesus has to contribute his share.[28] What transpires is the notion that the gods help those who

---

[27] See Segal 1971: 46.
[28] On this point, see Pelling (2019: 152–3): 'The extreme situations are the ones that most clearly reveal the elements at play, and those elements can be both human and supernatural... [H]is [*sc.* Croesus'] insight into Solon's human wisdom and the kings' human interaction were crucial in the scene where Apollo's intervention was also at its most irreducible.'

deserve it. Later in the *Histories*, Themistocles espouses this principle, pointing out that the god usually fosters the endeavours of those people who have planned well (8.60γ).[29] The inference that Cyrus reportedly draws from Croesus' rescue puts the point in a nutshell: 'both dear to the gods and excellent' (1.87.2) are two sides of the same coin.

The following image used by Hans-Peter Stahl encapsulates Herodotus' conception of fatalism, as it transpires in the story of Croesus:

> The involuntary crime [i.e. the one committed by Gyges] and its late vengeance form the immovable foundation that limits the architect's freedom, or, one may say, they are the skeleton which bears the living flesh of Herodotus' story.[30]

Within the framework thus established, Apollo laid down some further restrictions, thus setting up a narrower frame within the bigger one imposed by the Fates. Due to Apollo's initiative, apart from fixing the time of the fall of Sardes, a path is carved out to make Croesus' survival possible. However, Croesus' own contribution is indispensable: if, for instance, he had not, out of his own initiative, sought Apollo's favour through his pious gifts, he would not have been rescued.[31]

In sum, as Maddalena notes, some events—and we might add, with Pelling, that these are usually the biggest ones[32]—are fated to happen, whereas others are not, and so various routes are open and various outcomes are possible in these latter cases.[33] Divine influence typically makes itself felt at decisive junctures, but it does not affect every human act. Herodotean fatalism is compatible with considerable scope for

---

[29] After stressing the importance of fate in Herodotus, de Ste. Croix rightly observes (1977: 141): 'It would be a very serious mistake to suppose that Herodotus habitually thought of man as the helpless prisoner of Fate or of circumstances or of divine purposes (or machinations)... Herodotean man does to a considerable extent make his own destiny, by his own choice.'

[30] Stahl 1975: 17. See also Harrison (2000: 227): 'Fate, it appears, is a plot with a number of alternative endings, one that allows for (a limited number of) different contingencies, for human error and for human choice, as well as divine intervention.'

[31] According to Gagné (2013: 329), Apollo's interventions on Croesus' behalf 'are a form of *charis*, a gift that reflects a certain kind of reciprocity'.

[32] Pelling 2019: 149.   [33] Maddalena 1950: 81–2.

human agency and initiative.[34] Even if human beings have no power to prevent what has been predestined from happening, they have influence over the manner in which a fated event eventually comes to pass.

7.4 Causality Ancient and Modern: Interaction between Entities Versus Deterministic Laws of Nature

The time has come to return to Thucydides. We will now turn to the question of whether Thucydides, just like Homer and Herodotus, might have adopted a variant of necessity that left room for personal initiative. A thought experiment envisioned by Cornford provides a suitable entry point. He illustrates how the Greeks conceived of causation by reference to the Iroquois term *orenda*. The word signifies the endowment of a specific entity with a characteristic, innate power that enables it to have a distinctive impact on other things: for instance, the *orenda* of a knife enables it to cut well, and that of a spearman to hit his target with precision.[35] In light of this notion, Cornford explains (quoting a paper by Edwin Sidney Hartland) that a warrior who strikes down his enemy with a spear will not consider the two events (the hit of the spear and the enemy's death) 'as *cause* and *effect*':

> His view is "that his own *orenda* felt in his passion, his will, his effort, and displayed in his acts and words, the *orenda* of the spear, either inherent in itself, conceived as a personal being, or conferred by its maker and manifested in the keenness of its point, the precision and the force with which it flies to its work and inflicts the deadly wound – these would be to him the true causes of his enemy's fall. His *orenda* is mightier than his enemy's and overcomes it."[36]

In the wake of the rise of natural science, the terms *cause* and *effect*, which Cornford says distinguish the modern conception from that held by the Iroquois and the Greeks, have a specific meaning. In this modern

---
[34] See de Ste. Croix (1977: 143): '[W]ithin the limits set by the gods and Fate and so forth, Herodotus' men do have a very wide power of deciding their own destinies.'
[35] Cornford 1907: 228.   [36] Cornford 1907: 229.

view, causes are 'merely inactive nodes in the chain of events, rather than active originators of a change'.[37] The pertinent notion was formed in the early Enlightenment and represents the bedrock of modern natural science: every event is caused by an anterior set of states and the influence of these antecedent factors does not manifest itself with any flexibility, but according to hard and fast laws of nature. These are operative independent of the specific entities involved in a given situation. If one possesses a set of data—for instance, the mass of a spear and the force with which it is struck—it is possible to predict accurately how far it will fly and what impact it will have on another object. In making this prediction, one appeals to physical laws stated in mathematical equations, in which the spear with its physical properties figures merely as numerical data, and not as an entity with inherent qualities that constitute the substance of spears and by which spears are distinguished from other entities with other specific innate qualities.[38]

By labelling causes 'inactive nodes', Hulswit's point is that the modern notion of causation does not locate efficient causal power in the inherent qualities of objects. Far from acting, these objects are purely passive with respect to the forces formalized in the laws of mechanics. Hulswit writes: '*[A]ccording to the Aristotelian conception, causes are conceived as the active originators of a change that is brought about for the sake of some end... Probably the most radical change in the meaning of cause happened during the seventeenth century, in which there emerged a strong tendency to understand causal relations as instances of deterministic laws. Causes were no longer seen as the active initiators of change, but as inactive nodes in a law-like implication chain.*'[39] By contrast, the

---

[37] See Hulswit 2002: 15.

[38] See Frede (2011: 15): '[The ancients] had a very different conception from ours of what constitutes a cause or explanation. Perhaps the most crucial difference is that nobody in antiquity had the notion of laws of nature, meaning a body of laws which govern and explain the behavior of all objects, irrespective of their kind.'

[39] Hulswit 2002: 41-2. I take the term 'Aristotelian conception', used by Hulswit in the foregoing quotation, to be representative of the commonsensical view in the classical era of Greece, certainly prior to the advent of the Stoics. This is not meant to imply that Thucydides, or any other Greek writer, had teased out the distinctions eventually made by Aristotle. However, just as in our age people do not need to possess specific scientific or philosophical expertise in order to have an intuitive understanding of the function of deterministic laws of nature, so the commonsensical view in Greece was that causation consisted in objects inflicting change upon each other. Aristotle buttressed and refined this common assumption by providing it with a philosophical basis that rests on his substance ontology.

Greeks believed that when a spear hits its target, the inherent qualities distinctive to the spear actively affect those of the other object, and that one set of qualities ultimately asserts itself over the other. This view implies some important differences from the notion of determinism that has become common currency in modernity. Richard Sorabji observes that even Aristotle 'does not firmly stick to the view that every effect of an efficient cause is necessitated',[40] and Hulswitt points out that he associates efficient causes 'with what happens for the most part'.[41] By contrast, in the modern view 'causation and determinism became virtually equivalent'.[42] The Greeks assume interaction between two antagonists, whereas the moderns think of causation as mechanical, as an event that recalls the flipping of a switch.

Of course, the Greeks no less than their modern counterparts realized that even the strongest warrior will fare poorly when hit by a spear or overrun by a chariot. In these cases, the outcome of the struggle is inevitable because the entities involved are unevenly matched to the extreme. Yet, the distribution of power may be more evenly balanced in other situations, and these are the cases in which the divergence between the ancient Greek and the modern outlook leads to different conclusions.

One important result of the different views regarding causation is that the Greeks conceived differently from the moderns of the natural regularity governing the behaviour of an entity. In modernity, the laws of mechanics are thought to regulate motion with exceptionless necessity, and it is inconceivable that they play themselves out with greater or lesser force, depending on the object affected. By contrast, the Greeks tend to think of the determination imposed by φύσις in less rigid and all-encompassing terms. Gregory Vlastos defines φύσις in the following way:

> [T]he *physis* of any given thing is that cluster of stable characteristics by which we can recognize that thing and can anticipate the limits within which it can act upon other things or be acted upon by them...
> [P]*hysis* fixes the limits of the possible for everything *except* the supernatural.[43]

---

[40] Sorabji 1980: 56.   [41] Hulswit 2002: 5.   [42] See Hulswit 2002: 42.
[43] Vlastos 1975: 19.

Φύσις imposes limits that define the range within which a given entity can behave, but it does not necessarily preordain every aspect of behaviour that takes place within the set limits.

The limits that φύσις imposes on many entities are quite narrow so that the scope for variety of behaviour is extremely limited. Examples are plants or stones or bodily organs. However, the matter is different when it comes to human beings as Michael Frede observes: 'Quite generally, the nature of an object is such that, given certain specifiable conditions, it cannot but behave in a certain identifiable way. It is only when we come to more complex animals and, of course, to human beings that the behavior is not entirely determined by the nature of the object and the circumstances or conditions the object finds itself in.'[44] In an analysis of the notion of φύσις in Thucydides, Topitsch rightly points out that the term refers to a 'predisposition' ('Veranlagung'),[45] a view consistent with the definition of φύσις provided by Vlastos and Frede. According to the Athenians at Sparta, for example, human beings will never, under any circumstances, cease to strive for power and cease to be motivated by fear, honour, and advantage. But while these parameters are firmly established, no necessity determines *every single action* that takes place within these boundaries.

A cluster of recurrent phrases provides linguistic evidence that Thucydides indeed conceived of the impact of natural necessity according to the principle of contest and interaction between different entities. Thucydides tends to represent the motivational constraints rooted in human nature, not as a deterministic mechanism, but as an active force that seeks to dominate human beings.[46] Some of the relevant phrases have already been examined in Chapter 4, in connection with the comparison between divine interference in Euripides and natural necessity in Thucydides (see pp. 134–5). The Athenians at Sparta say that they have been 'defeated by the greatest things' (ὑπὸ ⟨τριῶν⟩ τῶν μεγίστων νικηθέντες, 1.76.2). They view human nature in analogy with an

---

[44] Frede 2011: 15–16. [45] Topitsch 1943: 47–50.
[46] Holmes (2010: 137) draws attention to similar language, which combines the ideas of struggle and impersonality, in the medical writers: '[T]he *sōma* has a fundamentally agonal relationship to the world around it: every encounter is a high-stakes struggle for power. If, for example, the liver cannot resist the power of the wind, it cannot *not* suffer harm or escape pains.'

anthropomorphic opponent, adopting the language of conquest and defeat used by Euripides' Phaedra as she plans to 'defeat' the erotic impulse sent by Aphrodite (νικῶσα, *Hipp.* 399). Furthermore, Diodotus uses language that recalls the designation of the δαίμονες as 'the stronger ones': he considers the invisible forces of ἔρως and ἐλπίς 'stronger' than what is seen (κρείσσω, 3.45.5), and he thinks that 'something incurable and stronger' is the decisive element in the formation of every event (ὑπ' ἀνηκέστου τινὸς κρείσσονος, 3.45.4). This use of κρείσσων is also reminiscent of Euripides' *Hippolytus* (475).

These phrases involving the notions of conquest and 'being stronger' recall a conception of divine interference that crystallizes in a passage spoken by Aphrodite in the prologue of the *Hippolytus*. The goddess congratulates herself on the steps already taken with a view to ensuring the downfall of the protagonists: 'Having prepared most of the way long-since, I do not require much further toil' (τὰ πολλὰ δὲ / πάλαι προκόψασ', οὐ πόνου πολλοῦ με δεῖ, 22-3). The gods do not effortlessly preprogramme all events, but they have to expend at least some 'toil' to precipitate the course desired by them. While they will ultimately prove 'stronger', Aphrodite's reference to her πόνος shows that they need to overcome contrary forces. This notion of a contest between opponents (however unevenly matched) is also at the basis of Thucydides' notion of natural necessity.

Another striking instance of phrasing that suggests the idea of 'being stronger' occurs in the last chapter of the *Pathology*, the authenticity of which is, however, disputed:[47] 'human nature' (ἡ ἀνθρωπεία φύσις, 3.84.2) itself is said to be 'stronger than the just' (κρείσσων ... τοῦ δικαίου, 3.84.2). The notion that one thing 'is stronger' than another also occurs in two passages that deal with the plague. Thucydides writes that 'the character of the plague was stronger than λόγος' (κρεῖσσον λόγου τὸ εἶδος τῆς νόσου, 2.50.1); furthermore, Pericles states that 'of all the things that occurred' the plague is the 'only event that happened stronger than expectation' (πρᾶγμα μόνον δὴ τῶν πάντων ἐλπίδος κρεῖσσον γεγενημένον, 2.64.1). Parry remarks that the plague qua quintessential

---

[47] For the reasons that militate against the chapter's authenticity, see Classen-Steup iii, on 3.84 [Anhang].

πάθος is 'equated with the War' and is a 'partner of war'.[48] The plague (just like stasis in Corcyra, the other lookalike of the War) causes the latent necessities of human nature to come to the fore. Its 'being stronger' recalls the impact of divine powers in tragedy, a fact reflected in Pericles' dictum that the plague is to be counted among τὰ δαιμόνια ('things divine', 2.64.2). In the excursus on the plague, Thucydides observes that people even stopped making lamentation for their kin, 'defeated by the mighty evil' (ὑπὸ τοῦ πολλοῦ κακοῦ νικώμενοι, 2.51.5). The neglect of lamentation marks the breakdown of a fundamental institution of Greek civilization. In capturing this situation, Thucydides combines a passive participle of νικάω with the typical agent construction after passive verbs (ὑπό with the genitive). He fills the position of the agent with the neuter term, 'the mighty evil'. In this way, he highlights the idea of struggle and eventual defeat at the hands of an impersonal visitation. The Athenian ambassadors at Sparta express the same idea via the same verb and the same construction when they point out that the Athenians have been 'defeated by the three greatest things' (1.76.2).

Another type of phrase suggests similar conclusions regarding necessity's principle of operation in Thucydides. As we saw in Chapter 3 (pp. 89–92), the Athenian ambassadors at Sparta consider their city's commitment to the empire a necessity due to the compulsory force of the 'three greatest things' (1.75.3, 76.2). While natural necessity thus induces the Athenians to build and maintain their empire, the ambassadors nonetheless hold that the pressure exerted by necessity can be moderated (1.76.3):

ἐπαινεῖσθαί τε ἄξιοι οἵτινες χρησάμενοι τῇ ἀνθρωπείᾳ φύσει ὥστε ἑτέρων ἄρχειν δικαιότεροι ἢ κατὰ τὴν ὑπάρχουσαν δύναμιν γένωνται.

And those deserve to be praised who, while subject to human nature and ruling others as a result, have been more just than they needed to be in light of the power available to them.

The ambassadors claim that the Athenians were 'more just' than others would be in their position, and they consider this relative justice a

---

[48] Parry 1969: 115.

considerable achievement for which they deserve praise (ἐπαινεῖσθαι ἄξιοι). The Athenians consider themselves entitled to acclaim because they have wrested a certain degree of justice from the pressure exercised by natural necessity. Pelling has rightly drawn attention to this fact: 'It is clear how much the Athenians do concede about their motivation, but we should also stress how much they claim.'[49]

The Athenians capture the force whose impact they have moderated with the familiar phrasing suggestive of passivity and impersonal factors. To start with, the phrase χρησάμενοι τῇ ἀνθρωπείᾳ φύσει suggests, here as in some other passages, the passivity of human beings in the face of a condition that besets them or is imposed on them (see Chapter 3, p. 92, Chapter 4, p. 135, and Chapter 5, pp. 179–80).[50] It suggests that people can never rid themselves entirely of the necessity rooted in human nature. Moreover, the participle ὑπάρχουσαν combined with the noun δύναμιν draws attention to the impact of the present situation on people. It is another example of Thucydides' emphasis, which has been noted in previous chapters, on the impact of τὰ πράγματα, τὰ παρόντα, and τὰ ὑπάρχοντα. Far from being passive objects at the agents' free disposal, δύναμις and the available resources exercise sway over their possessors and demand that they actualize the potentials inherent in these factors. In light of these phrases, it is worth recalling Jaffe's observation (mentioned in Chapter 3, p. 92) that necessity in Thucydides bears resemblance to a central aspect of Aristotle's conception of the good: it 'exerts a teleological compulsion or pull' towards advantage, ultimately based on the quest for self-preservation.[51] Without denying the sway of this force, the Athenians imply that human agents enjoy some leeway that makes it possible, not to overcome, but to moderate the inescapable pull. To be sure, despite this possibility, the pressure exerted by the quest for self-preservation and power has the strong tendency to become all-encompassing, at which point it quickly tips over into irrationality (see Chapter 4, pp. 108–9). Hence, according to the Athenians, justice will

---

[49] Pelling 2012: 308.
[50] See, e.g., ἀμαθίᾳ δὲ πλέονι πρὸς τὰ ἔξω πράγματα χρῆσθε, 1.68.1; καὶ ἡμεῖς οὔτε θέντες τὸν νόμον οὔτε κειμένῳ πρῶτοι χρησάμενοι, ὄντα δὲ παραλαβόντες καὶ ἐσόμενον ἐς αἰεὶ καταλείψοντες χρώμεθα αὐτῷ, 5.105.2; ταῖς ἐπιθυμίαις μείζοσιν... ἐχρῆτο, 6.15.3.
[51] Jaffe 2017: 197.

never be the most basic motivation on which people act; nevertheless, it can exercise a mitigating influence on decisions. The Athenians call this attenuating factor moderation (μετριάζομεν, 1.76.4; μετρίοις οὖσι, 77.2). Through the comparative δικαιότεροι, they indicate a degree of freedom that is not absolute but relative to the force exerted by human nature.[52]

In connection with the Athenians' claim to 'be more just' than others, it is interesting to consider an aspect highlighted by Pelling and exemplified by two passages from the Sicilian narrative: Thucydides repeatedly uses phrases involving comparative notions in passages that dissect the specific causes precipitating an event.[53] If one examines these passages, one finds that motives identified elsewhere with the necessities imposed by human nature take precedence, but that they are supplemented by more noble-minded considerations, with these latter factors clearly playing a secondary role.

Thucydides explains the Athenians' eagerness for the Sicilian Expedition as follows: 'the Athenians were eager to undertake the campaign, desiring, to name the truest cause, to rule it [sc. Sicily] in its entirety, but at the same time wanting, in a way that would look good, to help their kinsmen and the allies that had attached themselves to them' (οἱ Ἀθηναῖοι στρατεύειν ὥρμηντο, ἐφιέμενοι μὲν τῇ ἀληθεστάτῃ προφάσει τῆς πάσης ἄρξαι, βοηθεῖν δὲ ἅμα εὐπρεπῶς βουλόμενοι τοῖς ἑαυτῶν ξυγγενέσι καὶ τοῖς προσγεγενημένοις ξυμμάχοις, 6.6.1).[54] The syntactic coordination of the two participial clauses underscored by the adverb ἅμα suggests that the wish to help the allies was not entirely bogus, even if it chiefly derives from the desire to make the expedition seem respectable. As Pelling observes apropos the implications of 'in a way that would look good': '[A]t the very least, it suggests that the desire to look good is itself an additional, even if secondary, cause.'[55] One cause is truest and most fundamental: it is the longing for conquest, fuelled by the natural force of ἔρως. However, the notion of a 'truest cause' implies

---

[52] The form δικαιότεροι is a good example of Strasburger's observation that Thucydides' style reflects his constant search of the right degree and nuance. Strasburger calls this 'eine dauernde peinliche Bemühung um nuancierte Feststellung der Gradualität' (1966: 59).
[53] Pelling 2000: 87.
[54] The manuscript tradition is split between προσγεγενημένοις and προγεγενημένοις. Alberti prints the latter, but (based on Pelling 2021a ad loc.) I am inclined to adopt the former.
[55] Pelling 2000: 87.

that other causes are also involved: their being 'less true' does not mean that they are 'false' but rather that they are less vital. The Athenians' wish to help their allies would not have sufficed to prompt them to undertake the expedition; at the same time, it is a motive present in the constellation of considerations that dispose the Athenians to embark on the Sicilian campaign.

The other passage involving comparative phrasing is Thucydides' mention of the reasons that prompt the various allies to join either of the two warring parties at Sicily. They choose sides, writes Thucydides, 'not based in some way primarily on justice or kinship, but depending on the circumstances confronting each of them, either according to advantage or out of necessity' (οὐ κατὰ δίκην τι μᾶλλον οὐδὲ κατὰ ξυγγένειαν..., ἀλλ' ὡς ἑκάστοις τῆς ξυντυχίας ἢ κατὰ τὸ ξυμφέρον ἢ ἀνάγκῃ ἔσχεν, 7.57.1).[56] The antithesis between 'not primarily by X, but by Y' suggests that the higher-ranking motives are provided by advantage or necessity, which arise out of the circumstances confronting the cities (τῆς ξυντυχίας). The factors mentioned have previously surfaced in the accounts of human nature provided by Diodotus (ἀνάγκῃ, 3.45.4; ξυντυχίαι, 45.4) and the Athenians at Sparta (κατηναγκάσθημεν, 1.75.3; τὰ ξυμφέροντα, 75.5). At the same time, the comparative nuance in μᾶλλον (translated as 'primarily') implies that justice and kinship make a secondary

[56] The genitive τῆς ξυντυχίας depends on ὡς qua adverb of manner. The construction is used most commonly, as it is here, with intransitive ἔχω or ἥκω, see K-G i. 382–3; Sm. 1441. Thus, on a literal translation, the phrase ὡς ἑκάστοις τῆς ξυντυχίας... ἔσχεν means 'in what manner of circumstance things stood for each of them'. As far as the text is concerned, Alberti prints ὡς ἕκαστοι τῆς ξυντυχίας... ἔσχον, whereas the wording adopted by me reproduces Stuart Jones's OCT. The specific combination ἕκαστοι... ἔσχον is not transmitted by any manuscript. However, ἕκαστοι can be found in the Vatican manuscript of Thucydides (with the corrector writing ἑκάστοις in the line above; cf. Alberti's apparatus) and ἔσχον in two of the more recent manuscripts. The latter generally do not count as principal witnesses, but they nonetheless sometimes transmit important readings. Alberti's text is defended by most commentators ad loc.: Poppo-Stahl, Boehme-Widmann, Classen-Steup, HCT, and Dover 1965b. Their principal argument is that impersonal ἔχω is not attested elsewhere in Thucydides. For personal variants of this construction, see 1.22.3, 2.90.4, 6.97.3, and 7.2.1 (variously cited in their notes on 7.57.1 by Boehme-Widmann, Dover, and Pelling 2021b). Nevertheless, based on the principle of the lectio difficilior, it seems less problematic to assume that the more obscure impersonal phrasing suffered corruption through replacement by the personal variant than vice versa. Impersonal ἔχω combined with an adverb of manner and a dependent genitive is not an impossible construction (see τοῖσι οὕτω εἶχε ὅρμου, Hdt. 7.188.3, pointed out by Boehme-Widmann). It also matters that the important papyrus Oxy. 1376 (abbreviated as Π^{18} by Alberti), which dates from the second or third century AD, has ἑκάστοις (due to damage, it provides no evidence for the question of ἔσχεν vs. ἔσχον).

contribution. Otherwise, a simple antithesis would have been in order: 'in no way due justice and kinship, but out of advantage or necessity'. Although the natural selfish pull is always primary, Thucydides leaves room for some degree of modification by more high-minded sentiments.

In characterizing collective human nature as a powerful opponent, Thucydides allows for the possibility that one can modify its pull or even struggle with it: it may be 'stronger' than most people, but the competitive relationship leaves open the possibility that an individual or a city can resist to a greater or lesser extent. It is another question how often people are likely to achieve a degree of modification that make a noticeable difference. The supplementary motives mentioned in the two passages from the Sicilian narrative have a limited influence at most: the decisions made on these occasions would not have taken a noticeably different shape if the sole motives had been the inevitable pull of self-interest as well as, in the case of the Athenians, the quest of power. Nonetheless, Thucydides' conception leaves room for the possibility that agents can exercise some moderation vis-à-vis the pull of necessity. In this connection, a parallel with Euripides' *Hippolytus* is illuminating. Although sexual passion imposes itself as a divine force and may thus seem wholly deterministic in this play, Fisher and Hoekstra point out that this is not the whole story:

> Euripides nonetheless depicts characters who struggle against this simultaneously psychological and supernatural necessity.... Phaedra's lust looks to be a case of hard necessity, imposed as it is by an implacable goddess. Yet... Phaedra valiantly resists acting on her urges, holing up in the palace and trying to starve herself to death.[57]

This situation bears close resemblance to what one finds in Thucydides. On the one hand, human beings cannot escape the necessities imposed on them: Phaedra cannot overcome the lust that Aphrodite has induced, and the catastrophic end that Aphrodite announces at the play's beginning is unavoidable (41–50). Against this background of the inevitable, however, the characters have some scope that allows them to struggle

---

[57] Fisher and Hoekstra 2017: 377.

with the supernatural forces confronting them. Thus, they can behave more or less nobly in the face of necessity. In Thucydides, human nature has been substituted for Euripides' Aphrodite.

7.5 Causation of the Greatest Events: Necessity Intertwined with Contingency

The account given thus far may invite the objection that the type of constraint ascribed to Thucydides hardly merits the label of necessity. If the supposed necessity consists in a predisposition that is open to moderating influence, then it should be possible that human beings can learn to take appropriate countermeasures and thus defer the outbreak of the destructive disposition ad infinitum. In that case, none of the events and developments analysed in Chapter 5 would have had to happen: neither the Peloponnesian War nor the phase of Athenian overconfidence and Spartan despair nor the Sicilian Expedition.

Yet, here again, one must be wary of the typically modern all-or-nothing opposition between mechanistic determinism and a completely open horizon of possibilities. Because of our familiarity with the modern variety of causation, we instinctively tend to equate the idea of historical necessity with a deterministic view of history.[58] Yet, due to the different presuppositions about causation, the ancients conceived of more flexible varieties of fatalism, which, despite their relative elasticity, do not look at the future as an entirely open realm.

Thucydides' statement on the causes of the Peloponnesian War provides a suitable reference point to gauge the respective weight of necessity and openness (1.23.6). In this passage, Thucydides observes the interaction between a foundational and a contingent element of causation: the famous distinction between ἀληθεστάτη πρόφασις and αἰτία, that is

---

[58] On the modern tendency to parse necessity in the realm of history as causal determinism, see Berlin 2002 [1954]: 103. E. H. Carr identifies determinism with 'the belief that everything that happens has a cause or causes, and could not have happened differently unless something in the cause or causes had also been different' (1986: 87). Carr goes on to argue that the endorsement of determinism does not necessarily commit historians to belief in the inevitability of events (89–92).

between the War's 'truest', i.e. essential, 'cause' and the 'reasons' or 'grounds'[59] functioning as prompting occasion.[60] Pelling has observed that Thucydides tends to analyse the causal nexus behind events through

---

[59] Following Hornblower, I will render αἰτία as 'reason' when the word is contrasted with πρόφασις in the meaning of 'cause': see Hornblower i, on 1.23.6. An alternative rendition of αἰτίαι would be 'grievances or accusations' (Pearson 1952: 221). At least in Herodotus, it is indeed the case that the word usually involves 'an element of "blame" or "grievance" or "criticism"' (see Pelling 2019: 7). The undertones suggested by 'grievance' are certainly in play in the Thucydidean passage, too. Nevertheless, this translation seems too narrow in the context of 1.23.6 because it does not sit comfortably with some of Thucydides' phrasing, which suggests that he thinks of the αἰτίαι primarily as part of the interplay of causal factors that lead to the Peloponnesian War. On this point, see Heubeck 1980: 231 (arguing that the causal sense of αἰτίαι is prior to the meaning of 'grievance' at 1.23.6): '[D]ie Formulierung in I 23 selbst: δι' ὅ τι δ' ἔλυσαν, τὰς αἰτίας besagt nichts anderes als ein: δι' ἃς αἰτίας ἔλυσαν, und mit ἐξ ὅτου... κατέστη verweist Thukydides implizit darauf, daß er zuerst dargelegt habe, ἐξ ὧν αἰτιῶν (καὶ διαφορῶν) der Krieg entstanden sei.'

[60] Hornblower i, on 1.23.6: '*Prophasis* here... must mean "underlying cause" as opposed to the "reasons openly given out at the time"... The word ἀληθεστάτη, "true" [sic], makes the causal sense absolutely clear.' See also *HCT* i, ad loc.; Schuller 1956: 976; Sealey 1957: 9; Kagan 1969: 364; Heubeck 1980: 233–4; Pelling 2000: 87–8. Another viable translation of πρόφασις in the relevant sense is 'explanation'. Several scholars have objected that the term 'cause' should not be applied to Thucydides because it implies, in the wake of modern natural science, a deterministic link between cause and effect, which was unfamiliar to Thucydides: Cornford 1907: 68; Lohmann 1952: 28; Pearson 1972: 383; Rawlings 1975: 78. The available evidence suggests that Thucydides uses the word πρόφασις to highlight the factors that are, in the final analysis and with objective validity, responsible for the occurrence of the Peloponnesian War. This notion seems best rendered by the term 'cause' ('cause' reflects more accurately than 'truest explanation' the factor most vitally responsible for the outbreak of the War). On the implications of the word 'cause' that I think make it a suitable translation of πρόφασις, see Pelling 2019: 13 (who, however, prefers to render πρόφασις as 'explanation'). While 'cause' seems best suited to capture the connotations of πρόφασις at 1.23.6, it is true that 'explanation' possesses the advantage of being a more literal translation of πρόφασις: Pearson 1952: 206, and 1972: 381–2; Sealey 1957: 3; Schäublin 1971: 135, and 1989: 1472; Pelling 2000: 268 n. 9, and 2019: 13. In the main, two meanings other than 'cause' (or 'explanation') have been proposed in connection with 1.23.6. First, scholars have argued that πρόφασις refers to the Spartans' subjective 'motive' for going to war, 'the most important factor in the minds of the Spartans': Pearson 1952: 219–21; Kirkwood 1952: 47 and 51; Schäublin 1971: 139–40. A cogent account of why 'cause' fits 1.23.6 better than 'motive' is provided by Heubeck 1980: 230–3. Secondly, Rawlings thought that, under the influence of medical usage, the term means a 'pre-appearance' (1975: 46) or 'antecedent condition' (1975: 81), in which an event (such as a disease or the Peloponnesian War) announces itself (1975: 46–47). Ἀληθεστάτη would then mean that this state was 'most significant, the prerequisite "Vorerscheinung" of the war' (1975: 80). For precursors of this view, see Lohmann 1952: 28; von Fritz 1967, 1: 627–8. Convincing arguments as to why the rendition of πρόφασις at 1.23.6 as 'antecedent condition' is unsuitable have been provided by Schäublin 1979: 12; Heubeck 1980: 232; Hunter 1982: 328; Pelling 2000: 268 n. 9. As far as the other alternative meaning (viz. 'motive') is concerned, it is worth adding the following considerations to Heubeck's above-mentioned account. 'Motive' would be suitable if Thucydides had written that the truest πρόφασις was the Athenians' rise to power and the Spartans' fear (both of which evidently qualify as 'motives' for going to war). However, Thucydides actually says that the truest πρόφασις was the *compulsion* to go to war exerted by Athenian power and Spartan fear. Notice that compulsion is the principal

'league-tables of causal hierarchy' in a manner analogous to the Hippocratic doctors.[61] The medical writers see, for instance, two factors at play in epilepsy: 'a disposition, that bodily state which ensures that an epileptic attack will happen some time, and also a trigger, explaining why it happens now'.[62] This dispositional side interacts with the trigger provided by specific events and individual agents. As Pelling shows, these considerations are relevant to the interpretation of the 'truest cause' of the War, namely the increase of Athenian power and the fear thus instilled in the Spartans: this is the level of underlying disposition. By contrast, the prompting occasions, which Thucydides calls αἰτίαι (1.23.6) are the triggers, i.e. the quarrels about Corcyra and Potidaea. Pelling comments: 'The "truest explanation" makes it clear why there was a war waiting to happen; the "grounds and elements of rift" explain why it happened in 431 rather than 435 or 427.'[63]

The model of disposition and trigger dovetails with Hunter's account of Thucydides' mode of historical explanation. As Hunter observes, Thucydides is committed to the idea that events follow an intrinsic logic according to a recurrent pattern that obtains at all times.[64] In contrast to modern historical writing, Thucydides does not think that the primary task of historical explanation is to seek the specific causal antecedents (e.g. political, military, economic, mentality-wise), operative at one particular point in time alone, whose unique constellation leads to

---

component of the 'truest πρόφασις': in terms of syntax, ἀναγκάσαι is obligatory after ἀληθεστάτην πρόφασιν ἡγοῦμαι, but the two participial phrases (μεγάλους γιγνομένους and φόβον παρέχοντας τοῖς Λακεδαιμονίοις) are merely optional. The crucial point is that compulsion towards war, unlike the increase of a rival's power and fear, does not actually represent a 'motive': it is rather the *effect* of the two motives expressed. By contrast, it makes perfect sense to say that compulsion, produced by Athenian expansion and Spartan fear, was the chief 'cause' of the Peloponnesian War. Furthermore, the aorist aspect of the infinitive ἀναγκάσαι distinguishes it from the present aspect of the participles (γιγνομένους, παρέχοντας): the participles referring to motivational factors are thereby distinguished in kind from the fact of compulsion. It is appropriate to represent motives as ongoing and evolving. If Thucydides had regarded the compulsion also as a motive, he would have been likely to use ἀναγκάζειν. Instead, Thucydides uses a complexive aorist that oversees the compulsion from beginning to end and thus represents it as a fact without stressing its extension in time (see von Fritz 1967, 2: 285 n. 13). Against the background of the present participles, this shift in aspect suggests that Thucydides regards the compulsion not as an evolving motive, but as an impersonal, objective fact. Again, this factual dimension is best captured by the term 'cause'.

[61] Pelling 2000: 87.
[62] Pelling 2000: 88.   [63] Pelling 2000: 88.   [64] Hunter 1982: 156–7.

a particular event.[65] Instead, Thucydides proceeds from the idea of an unchanging general constitution (φύσις), consisting of various psychological forces that interact with external circumstances; when a factor capable of unleashing this innate condition presents itself (τύχη), a process (such as the Peloponnesian War) is launched and unfolds with inexorable necessity.[66] This paradigm, which describes a process endemic to ἀρχή, applies at all times and represents a structure that underlies the multiplicity of specific events.[67] Applying Hunter's model to 1.23.6, one finds that Athenian power and Spartan fear refer to the unchangeable constitution that will ultimately produce the inexorable process (ἀναγκάσαι ἐς τὸ πολεμεῖν). The term πόφασις refers to this level of explanation: the underlying condition that amounts to a necessity. On the other hand, the quarrels regarding Corcyra and Potidaea, which Thucydides calls αἰτίαι, provide the catalyst that releases this foundational predicament. Thus, the level of πρόφασις reflects an inevitable disposition, while that of αἰτία refers to contingent factors. As Ostwald observes, 'in Thucydides' eyes, it is the way the human animal is constituted that made the outbreak of the Peloponnesian War an inevitable necessity.'[68] One cannot know, Thucydides would say, when and exactly how the inevitable is going to happen. But one can know *that* it will happen.

It is striking that, on a stylistic level, the language of chapter 23 reflects the interaction of πρόφασις and αἰτία. In describing the onset of the war, Thucydides systematically combines two sets of phrases with different implications: active diction and language that suggests the onset of a condition. The following is the first passage (1.23.5):

δι' ὅ τι δ' ἔλυσαν, τὰς αἰτίας προύγραψα πρῶτον καὶ τὰς διαφοράς, τοῦ μὴ τινα ζητῆσαί ποτε ἐξ ὅτου τοσοῦτος πόλεμος τοῖς Ἕλλησι κατέστη.

I have first set down the reasons why they undid [the Thirty Years Peace] as well as their disagreements, in order that no one may ever

---

[65] Note that the linearity assumed by modern historical writing implies uniqueness: no point in time is a repetition of what came before but arises from its own singularly specific set of antecedents (Hunter 1982: 163, cf. 142–3). By contrast, Thucydides thinks that a common, eternally valid paradigm underlies the apparent variety of different events (see Hunter 1982: 159).
[66] Hunter 1982: 234–5.
[67] On the innate dynamic besetting ἀρχή, see Hunter 1982: 137.   [68] Ostwald 1988: 32.

have to investigate again as a result of what circumstances such a great war came to pass for the Greeks.

When addressing the triggering occasions (αἰτίας)—the complaints and attributions of responsibility—Thucydides uses the active verb λύω: at this level, the actors do have an impact on the specific course of events that lead to the outbreak of the War. These issues—the quarrels about Corcyra and Poteidaea—represent the 'out of which' (ἐξ ὅτου): the immediate releasing occasion for the War. However, the onset of the War itself is expressed by a compound of καθίσταμαι: the phrase represents the War in the subject position as a condition that arises and entrenches itself once the triggers are in place.

Next comes the famous statement of the truest πρόφασις, discussed in Chapter 5 (pp. 160–6): Athenian growth and its inducement of fear in the Spartans 'made recourse to war necessary' (ἀναγκάσαι ἐς τὸ πολεμεῖν, 1.23.6). This claim is directly followed by Thucydides' announcement that he will now proceed to unpack the openly alleged αἰτίαι (1.23.6):

αἱ δ' ἐς τὸ φανερὸν λεγόμεναι αἰτίαι αἵδ' ἦσαν ἑκατέρων, ἀφ' ὧν λύσαντες τὰς σπονδὰς ἐς τὸν πόλεμον κατέστησαν.

But the reasons openly expressed on both sides, because of which they undid the truce and then got themselves into war were as follows.

Again, Thucydides' reference to the immediate occasion, the 'from which' (ἀφ' ὧν) of the War, features an active form of λύω, and he again employs another form of καθίσταμαι when referring to what happens in the wake of this act: the coming of the War. As a result of the undoing of the treaty, a condition prevails that causes the Greeks to be 'settled into' a state of war. The passages at 1.23.5 and 23.6 resemble each other in using the same specific phrasing to distinguish the two different stages in the causal nexus that leads to the War. The part about the immediate triggering causes features the following components: the term αἱ αἰτίαι, a relative clause introduced by a preposition that identifies the αἰτίαι with an antecedent prompt (the 'out of' or 'from which'), and an active form of the verb λύω. What results from this instigation is expressed, again in both passages, by a form of καθίσταμαι. Parry uses the passage at 1.23.6

as evidence for his aforementioned claim (see Chapter 2, p. 58) that Thucydides likes to use compounds of ἵστημι to indicate an enduring shift in historical circumstances: in Parry's view the passage marks 'the point where the growth of power in Athens, and the fear of it in Lacedaemon, work the great change in the external situation, and there is war'.[69] The αἰτίαι, which result from specific acts, provide the occasion for the onset of a situation that has been waiting to prevail, and which pre-exists no matter what the contingent actions of the two sides will be.

At the opening of book 2, Thucydides uses yet another form of καθίσταμαι to capture the outbreak of the Peloponnesian War. He indicates the beginning of the War proper as follows: 'At this point now, the War of the Athenians and Peloponnesians and the allies of each side begins, during which... they fought continuously after they had passed into it' (ἄρχεται δὲ ὁ πόλεμος ἐνθένδε ἤδη Ἀθηναίων καὶ Πελοποννησίων καὶ τῶν ἑκατέροις ξυμμάχων, ἐν ᾧ... καταστάντες... ξυνεχῶς ἐπολέμουν, 2.1). Thucydides does not write that 'the Athenians and Peloponnesian begin the War'[70], but that 'the War begins', a phrase that one might also use to describe the onset of a condition. Thucydides continues by using the participle καταστάντες, which suggests a state in which the warring parties have been caught up. Thucydides also uses the active verb ἐπολέμουν at the end of the sentence, but the agency at which this phrase hints concerns the fighting that takes place *after* the condition of war has arisen: actions, carried out by personal agents, take place, but they are subordinate to the anterior onset of a condition, highlighted by ἄρχεται with the impersonal subject ὁ πόλεμος and the participle of καθίσταμαι.

It cannot be coincidental that Thucydides again juxtaposes, just as he does at 1.23.5 and 23.6, an active form of λύω with passive phrasing and a form of καθίσταμαι when he anticipates the recrudescence of the War after listing the terms of the Peace of Nicias (5.25.3):

ἔπειτα μέντοι καὶ ἀναγκασθέντες λῦσαι τὰς μετὰ τὰ δέκα ἔτη σπονδὰς αὖθις ἐς πόλεμον φανερὸν κατέστησαν.

---

[69] Parry 1981: 99–100.
[70] Suitable phrases would be ἅπτομαι πολέμου (e.g. Th. 5.61.2), αἴρομαι πολέμου (e.g. Hdt. 7.132.2, Th. 4.60.2, Xen. *Cyr.* 1.6.54, Dem. D. 5.5) or ἄρχομαι πολέμου (e.g. Xen. *HG* 6.3.6).

At last, however, they [sc. the Athenians and Lacedaemonians] were in fact compelled to undo the treaty that had been concluded after the first ten years and again passed into open war.

Three phrases recall the wording that we found in chapter 23 of book 1: the verb ἀναγκάζω, the phrase λῦσαι τὰς σπονδάς, and the expression ἐς πόλεμον κατέστησαν. Just like the original onset of the war (1.23.6), its recrudescence is a necessity, captured by the form of ἀναγκάζω. Moreover, the breaking of the treaty is expressed by an active form of λύω, which Thucydides also uses at 1.23.5 and 6. This verb, however, is qualified by the aorist passive participle ἀναγκασθέντες. The weight of necessity reduces humans to a passive role and induces the actions that result in the breaking of the treaty. The passage is rounded off (the third parallel with book 1—see, again, 1.23.5 and 6) by a form of καθίσταμαι, with the War in a prepositional phrase: the warring parties pass over into a renewed state of war.

The identical phrasing in the synopses of the first and the second beginning of the War reflects a fundamental point. The forms of λύω suggest that agency has some influential power at the level of αἰτία. However, these active verbs are systematically counterbalanced by phrasing which highlights that a condition imposes itself at a more basic level. When released by the triggers, the War comes to prevail in the manner characteristic of a κατάστασις (on this term, see Chapter 3, pp. 90–1): a condition arises and entrenches itself, a state that will henceforth constrain the behaviour of the entire Greek world. The ἀληθεστάτη πρόφασις of the Peloponnesian War concerns this layer of causation, a foundational level where necessity prevails.

7.6 Conclusion: Flexible Necessity

Thucydides considers momentous long-term events, such as the outbreak of the Peloponnesian War, inevitable. At the same time, however, we saw in section 7.1 that agency is not a chimerical notion in Thucydides, but that it can make a real difference to the course of events, at least on occasion. The coexistence of necessity and choice commits Thucydides to a qualified version of fatalism. According to Williams, a model of fatalism thus understood can be found in Greek tragedy, which often presupposes a kind of necessity that does not involve the predetermination of every single action: 'Fatalism, in this sense of long-term or deferred fatalism, does not require the belief that no action ever has any effect... It is not that people's thoughts and decisions never make a difference, but that, with regard to the vital outcome, they make no difference in the long run, although one might have expected them to do so.'[71] This notion also fits what one finds in Thucydides: history is not entirely open, but lies under a fatalistic influence because firmly established predispositions grounded in human nature (a quest for power combined with a susceptibility to irrational passions) are ultimately stronger than collective discipline and the initiatives of provident individuals. Because the natural disposition persists, the point will come at which its potential will be unleashed. This is the reason why it is correct to ascribe to Thucydides the view that certain momentous events are predestined to happen.

Thucydides' thought and manner of representation are deeply influenced by the model of Homer and Herodotus, two predecessors that function both as antagonists and as guiding lights.[72] In Homer and Herodotus, incidental factors play an important role in paving the way towards the realization of fated events such as the homecoming of Odysseus and the downfall of Croesus. When Poseidon is off feasting among the Aethiopians, Athena seizes the opportunity to launch the sequence of events that will eventually make Odysseus' homecoming possible. Nothing suggests that Poseidon's absence and Athena's harangue before the gathered Olympians happen according to an ineluctable plan of destiny. They are rather, to use the above terminology, the triggers that make the homecoming possible at this particular point in time. Similar considerations apply to the downfall of Croesus: for instance, the reader is in no way given to understand that it has been fated from the outset that Croesus' downfall must come through the Persians. Thucydides' presentation offers a precise analogy. Major events, such as the outbreak of the Peloponnesian War and the Athenian attack on Sicily, are bound to

---

[71] Williams 1993: 141.
[72] For a foundational account of the Homeric influence, see Strasburger 1966: 62–4, and 1972: 12–14, 33–4. For the influence of Homer and Herodotus on Thucydides' narrative technique, see Rengakos 2006: 279–300, On the Homeric influence, see further Rutherford 2012: 27–31; Joho 2017: 587–604. On thematic links and allusions that connect Thucydides' work with Herodotus, see Rogkotis 2006: 57–86.

happen. However, the specific events that will enable necessity to run its course are contingent, and the same is true of their timing.

Another aspect of Thucydides' flexible necessity is that φύσις, instead of preprogramming every feature of human behaviour, circumscribes the boundaries within which there remains scope for various possibilities. In this respect, too, Thucydides follows a path previously trodden by Homer and Herodotus. 'The Homeric gods...,' writes Adkins, 'make isolated irruptions into human affairs; not all human actions are caused, in whole or in part, by them.'[73] Fate or Zeus impose a wide frame of fatalistic necessity within which scope remains for specific developments. The following observation made by Frede regarding the Greek concept of causation is relevant to what one finds in Thucydides: '[G]iven the kinds of causes and explanations appealed to, the world might remain in our sense causally underdetermined.'[74] Seen against this backdrop, it is plausible that in Thucydides, too, φύσις is conceptualized as a power that imposes constraints, but also leaves leeway. Within the limits imposed by basic necessities and provided that fortunate circumstances obtain, human beings can (as maintained by the Athenians at Sparta and proven by Diodotus) influence the course of events on occasion, mitigating the harshest aspects of the pressure exerted by natural compulsion. Necessity is 'stronger', but it is not so strong as to leave no scope for variation. Cogan is thus generally right to observe that 'the regularity which constitutes τὸ ἀνθρώπινον is a regularity of process rather than of result'.[75] Nonetheless, once certain preconditions are fulfilled (such as the Athenians' assumption of leadership over the allies), the regularity of process, which does not predetermine every action on a small and intermediate scale, enforces the occurrence of the most consequential events.

The interplay between necessity and leeway takes us to the theme of responsibility. In Chapter 6 (pp. 218–22), we saw that Herodotus depicts this as a question of who is αἴτιος, man or god, and that he has Croesus acknowledge that, despite the divine foreordainment, he himself is at fault for his downfall (1.91.6). Thucydides uses αἰτία, the noun derived from the same lexeme, to capture the attributions of blame and responsibility made in connection with the initial outbreak of the Peloponnesian War. Thucydides' subsequent report of the Spartans' bad conscience is likely

---

[73] Adkins 1960: 13.   [74] Frede 2011: 16.   [75] Cogan 1981a: 234.

to suggest that their side bears greater responsibility for the breaking of the treaty (7.18.2). So, in both authors, the question of blame and responsibility is not declared irrelevant, and it belongs firmly to the human (as opposed to the divine or impersonal) level. This, however, is not the final word on the issue of causation. The choices made by Croesus and by the actors unleashing the Peloponnesian War are always qualified by the fact that they open the door to events that are bound to happen at some point.

Individual responsibility can coexist comfortably enough with fatalism because necessitated outcomes occur in such a way that they reflect the established character of the agents involved. Croesus' own personality predisposes him, for instance, first to challenge the Persians and then to misread the oracles. A more wholesome variant of the same interplay is Odysseus' salvation amid the surging waves off Scheria: Athena can only give him presence of mind because Odysseus has it in himself to act with instinctive prudence in moments where people normally lose their head. This aspect of the relationship between Odysseus and Athena is illuminated by their encounter shortly after the hero's return to Ithaca. Delighted by Odysseus' clever craft, Athena caresses him and tells him with obvious satisfaction: 'You are far the best among all mortals / in counsel and speech, but among all the gods / I am famed for cleverness and wiles' (ἐπεὶ σὺ μέν ἐσσι βροτῶν ὄχ' ἄριστος ἁπάντων / βουλῇ καὶ μύθοισιν, ἐγὼ δ' ἐν πᾶσι θεοῖσι / μήτι τε κλέομαι καὶ κέρδεσιν, Od. 13, 297–9). Athena is so especially fond of Odysseus because she recognizes something of herself in him. Her liking does not suggest a relationship between puppeteer and puppet, but one between soulmates.

In Thucydides, too, the major events induced by natural necessity do not unfold according to a uniform mechanism but closely reflect the character of the city involved: as pointed out in Chapter 5 (p. 189), fear dominates at Sparta, whereas hope and desire take precedence at Athens. It is chiefly fear that drives the Spartans into the Peloponnesian War, and desire combined with hope that induces the Athenians to reject the Spartan peace offer during the crisis at Pylos, and to launch the Sicilian Expedition. Yet, notwithstanding the influence of a city's specific character, the contrary impulses can be traced back to a foundational necessity: a predetermined collective quest for self-affirmation that is combined with a predisposition towards irrationality.

Finally, the principle of dual motivation (investigated in Chapter 6 and familiar in Homer, Herodotus, and Greek tragedy) offers a model for the interaction of general human nature and personal action in Thucydides. The outbreak of the War can be analysed along these lines. While the Athenians and the Spartans make decisions for which they are responsible, they simultaneously act under the influence of binding principles laid down by φύσις. Agents make choices, but these choices are always qualified (to a greater or lesser degree) by necessity. Ultimately, human action smooths the way for the necessity to run its course.

Despite the prevalence of necessity, Thucydides pays attention, just as much as Homer and Herodotus, to the contingent human element in the formation of events in his narrative of the War. This level is observable whereas divine forces (in Homer and Herodotus), or natural necessity (in Thucydides), operate beneath the surface. Consider in this connection the following observation made by Pelling with regard to Herodotus: 'It is less paradoxical than it may seem that divine explanations are sometimes inescapable and when they exist can be the ones that matter most, yet the focus and the interest so regularly remains on the human level. The gods are very difficult to know about, beyond the basic fact that they exist and that they can do extraordinary things, some of the time.'[76] The same is true of natural necessity in Thucydides. The insights provided by several speakers and by Thucydides' own occasional comments turn the reader's attention to this level. On the whole, however, the pull of natural necessity can only be gleaned from the struggles that take place on the surface level of cities, war, and politics. Depth hides on the surface.

Lesky observed with regard to the Homeric model of dual motivation that it is the expression of a primordial insight about human experience: 'Everyone has had the feeling more than once in life that some action for which one had to take responsibility did not wholly belong to oneself: something "got into oneself", and one now finds it incomprehensible how that something "could get into one's head".'[77] Compared with this familiar experience, the widespread modern opposition between

---

[76] Pelling 2019: 161.
[77] Lesky 1961: 44 [my translation]. See also Stallmach 1968: 100–1.

determinism and autonomy may well come across as a theoretical superimposition, an abstraction that obstructs a livelier access to phenomena.[78]

A similar point can be made about the interaction of necessity and relatively free initiative found in Thucydides. During the run-up to the outbreak of the War, everybody makes choices that respond to nothing but the situation at hand. At the same time, however, there is a strong impression that these actions lead to an event that enforces itself. If one is to believe the Corinthian speakers, the Spartans are not at all keen on war (1.68.1–2, 69.1–2, 71.1). Nonetheless, they ultimately give in to the pressure of events and vote for war. In the same manner, the Athenians try to avoid the War (1.78), but they find it impossible to put aside the demands that their newly acquired power makes on them. The impetus towards war produces a pull that undermines the notion of an entirely open horizon of possibilities. Thucydides' dual conception reflects just this paradox: the making of deliberate choices is offset by the strong sense that people's actions merely contribute to a slowly gathering tornado, which partly derives from their actions and decisions, but which also forces itself upon the Greek world and ultimately derives from the necessities inherent in human nature.

This image of the emergence of major historical events is hardly far-fetched. Consider the famous lines from Abraham Lincoln's Second Inaugural Address:[79]

> On the occasion corresponding to this four years ago all thoughts were anxiously directed to an impending civil war. All dreaded it – all sought to avert it... Both parties deprecated war but one of them would make war rather than let the nation survive, and the other would accept war rather than let it perish. And the war came.[80]

None of the parties wanted the war, everybody anticipated it with horror, but their actions nonetheless precipitated it. Lincoln's language is

---

[78] See Schadewaldt 1970a [1958]: 51. For a statement of this point made in connection with modern arguments about historical causation, see Carr 1986: 86–92.
[79] Nathan Tarcov has drawn my attention to this passage.   [80] Lincoln 1989: ii. 689.

remarkable. The sequence of clauses, marked by recurring parallelism, conveys the impression of an uncanny undertow. To some extent, form undercuts content: both parties dread the war, but at the same time they are caught up in a maelstrom heading towards catastrophe. The paradoxical interplay between form and content (i.e. between the single-minded sequence of phrases marked by parallelism and the express intention of everyone to avoid the war) serves a specific purpose: it accurately reflects the uncanny circumstance that both sides, while seeking to avoid the war, nonetheless bring it to pass by their *own* actions. The breathless tone conveyed by the short phrases involving parallelism aptly capture the steady movement towards the abyss. At the end, the amplitude of the phrases grows more extensive, rising to a summarizing crescendo. While parallelism continues, a new element is introduced: Lincoln sets up an antithesis that contrasts the different priorities of the two sides. This shift towards antithesis expresses his view that one side ultimately bears more blame than the other for the outbreak of the war, a thought that closely resembles Thucydides' viewpoint on the outbreak of the Peloponnesian War.

After this antithetical summary, the series of parallelisms comes to a sudden halt and gives way to a laconic statement of objective, factual terseness: 'And the war came.' War, the impersonal agent will eventually get its way, regardless of what humans set about. Lincoln's words might just as well have been authored by Thucydides: πόλεμος τοῖς Ἕλλησι κατέστη (1.23.5).

8
Pericles' Containment of Necessity and the Scope for Choice

The flexible variant of necessity, ascribed to Thucydides in Chapter 7, leaves open the possibility that from time to time some exceptional individuals can make a difference for the better of their city. They cannot remove the pull of necessity, but they may be able to modify it—if not for good, then at least for a while. As Pouncey observes, the most notable cases are Pericles, Brasidas, and Hermocrates.[1] Among these, Pericles stands out, not least because Thucydides dedicates the so-called valedictory passage to him, in which he provides a detailed assessment of Pericles' political achievement.

Given the Spartan hostility towards Athenian power, Pericles thinks that the Athenians must accept the coming of the Peloponnesian War, and he has a clearly articulated strategy that he considers a reliable path to success: the Athenians must move inside the city walls, avoid large land battles, and make vigorous use of their supremacy at sea while putting a tight rein on the allies (1.143.5–144.1, 2.13.2, 2.65.7). This strategy requires considerable self-restraint from the ever-reckless Athenians, who will find the loss of their homes in Attica and the sight of the Spartan army ravaging their land exceedingly hard to bear. Nonetheless, the Athenians are willing to follow Pericles' lead, despite this tension between Pericles' plan and the Athenian mentality. Once the War has broken out, however, the Athenians are soon reduced to a mixture of anger and consternation in the wake of the Spartan devastation of Attica and the rampant plague. As a result, they soon wish to give up the war effort and to abandon Pericles' strategy. In this critical

---

[1] Pouncey 1980: 35.

moment, Pericles succeeds, albeit with difficulty, in curbing their impulses and maintaining their commitment to his strategy.

As this summary shows, Thucydides' account of Pericles' statesmanship provides clear evidence not only that purposeful, rational projects can be conceived but that it is possible for their advocates to prevail over contrary impulses that arise due to the inevitable predisposition for irrationality that besets human collectives. This chapter will analyse the scope, and the limits, of Pericles' success.

Before turning to this investigation, some preliminary reflections on Thucydides' stance vis-à-vis Pericles are in order. The position, once universally accepted, that in Thucydides' view Pericles made a difference for the better to the affairs of Athens has been called into question by various scholars. Beginning with two essays by Hermann Strasburger and Hellmut Flashar, and inspired, in some cases, by the work of Leo Strauss,[2] several studies have set out to demonstrate that Thucydides was in fact critical of Pericles' political programme. Proponents of this line of interpretation primarily highlight three potential failings on the part of Pericles: first, Pericles' endorsement of a war that Athens lost; second, his single-minded prioritization of Athenian naval power; and, third, the glorification of Athenian democracy and its overseas empire, achievements that Pericles considers worthy of any sacrifice.[3] While the proponents of this position do not belong to a single school of thought, one shared aspect of their work is their attention to details in Thucydides' account that seem like challenges to, or untoward consequences of, Pericles' strategy outlined above. Although much of the cited evidence merits serious consideration, Thucydides' strong and explicit expression of esteem for Pericles' statecraft in the so-called valedictory passage (2.65)

---

[2] Strasburger 1968b [1958] 523; Strauss 1964: 228; Flashar 1989 [1969] 464, 471, 480. Notice, however, that, according to Strauss, '[w]e must not forget ... the kinship between the universalism of thought (Thucydides) and the universalism of the city (Athens) ... There is indeed a profound kinship between Thucydides' thought and the daring which is characteristic of Athens' (1964: 229). Not least on Strauss' interpretation, the foremost representative of Athenian universalism and daring is Pericles.

[3] Since large portions of the following works are dedicated to the issue of Pericles, I refer to specific sections in which the various authors give a succinct statement of their argument with regard: Forde 1989: 14–15, 29–33, 54–6; Palmer 1992: 19, 32–3, 38–9; Orwin 1994: 28–9; Crane 1998: 315–22; Ober 1998: 88–9; Grethlein 2005: 63–4; Foster 2010: 3–4, 217, 220; Taylor 2010: 1–3, 73, 81; Kopp 2017: 206.

poses a considerable challenge to this approach. It would be an illusion to believe that a comprehensive examination of this issue is possible here. Nonetheless, I will try to state in summarizing fashion what considerations I think run counter to the position that Thucydides adopted a critical attitude vis-à-vis Pericles.

The first thing to note is the extraordinary status of the valedictory passage. It stands in marked contrast to Thucydides' general reticence, his reluctance to infuse his account with explicit authorial assessments of individual characters and their actions.[4] No other appraisal of a specific individual has the same scale: most of Thucydides' ad hominem comments, whether approving or critical, consist in no more than a few words. If on this one occasion Thucydides sits down to draw the balance of an individual's achievement in such extended fashion, it seems reasonable to attach overriding importance to this authorial exposition.

The valedictory passage shows no signs of criticism with regard to Pericles' political actions. Thucydides writes that, 'when the War had broken out, he [sc. Pericles] evidently made, also with regard to this issue, a right forecast about [the city's] power' (ἐπειδή τε ὁ πόλεμος κατέστη, ὁ δὲ φαίνεται καὶ ἐν τούτῳ προγνοὺς τὴν δύναμιν, 2.65.5). Already in the following sentence, Thucydides underlines this point about Pericles' power to foresee the future by pointing out that after Pericles' death 'his foresight with regard to the War was still more fully recognized' (ἐπὶ πλέον ἔτι ἐγνώσθη ἡ πρόνοια αὐτοῦ ἡ ἐς τὸν πόλεμον, 2.65.6). In what follows, Thucydides explains what he means by the reference to Pericles' foresight: after reviewing the central features of the strategy, he reports Pericles' claim that the Athenians 'would prevail' (περιέσεσθαι, 2.65.7). On Thucydides' view, then, Pericles' confidence that the Athenians would be victorious due to their naval superiority was entirely justified.

Yet, if that is so, why did the Athenians lose the War? Thucydides' answer is that they 'acted contrary to [Pericles' plan] in all these points [i.e. with regard to all the aspects of his war strategy]' (οἱ δὲ ταῦτα ... πάντα ἐς τοὐναντίον ἔπραξαν, 2.65.7). The implication is that, if the

---

[4] Westlake (1968: 5): '[E]xplicit judgements [sc. about individuals] are few and mostly brief. Thucydides is evidently chary of expressing his own views about leading individuals, and where he does so, there is often some special reason.'

Athenians had not been so foolish to disregard Pericles' advice, then they would have prevailed. This may still leave open the possibility that Pericles' promotion of the War, along with his conviction that the Athenians should try to hold on to the empire under all circumstances (1.144.4, 2.43.1, 2.63, 2.64.4–6), might have been misguided in the first place. However, according to Thucydides, 'during peacetime' (ἐν εἰρήνῃ) Pericles 'led the city with moderation and kept it safe' (μετρίως ἐξηγεῖτο καὶ ἀσφαλῶς διεφύλαξεν αὐτήν, 2.65.5). It is hard to see why Thucydides should emphasize Pericles' promotion of Athenian safety in such strong terms if he also thought that Pericles' outspoken advocacy of the Peloponnesian War, which fell into peacetime, was jeopardizing the fortunes of the city.

Should Pericles not, however, have foreseen that, in case of his premature death, the Athenians would abandon his war strategy, because it required an unlikely degree of restraint from a city always burning for action? Moreover, should he not have guessed that, in this case, Athenian politicians would be embroiled in fierce quarrels over the leading position, incited by their deep-rooted striving for individual pre-eminence? Thucydides does not go into these issues. Nevertheless, it is worth noting that Pericles is in fact quite aware of the risk that the Athenians might abandon his plan for the War. In his first speech, immediately after presenting the Athenians with the central tenets of his strategy, he remarks: 'I am more afraid of our own mistakes than of the plans of our enemies' (μᾶλλον... πεφόβημαι τὰς οἰκείας ἡμῶν ἁμαρτίας ἢ τὰς τῶν ἐναντίων διανοίας, 1.144.1). At the same time, Pericles knows that, sooner or later, the War will be inevitable (εἰδέναι δὲ χρὴ ὅτι ἀνάγκη πολεμεῖν, 1.144.3). The most plausible explanation is that Thucydides agreed with Pericles that the War would happen anyway, and that, once this premise is granted, Thucydides thought that the path taken by Pericles was Athens' only chance.

What then about the claim that Thucydides was critical of Pericles' account of the ideal character of the Athenian life in the Funeral Oration, especially its use as justification for Athenian power and the empire? A proponent of this view observes that Thucydides 'unmasks the thought' of Pericles, juxtaposing the lofty picture of the Funeral Oration with the darker depiction of domestic affairs at Athens in the narrative.[5] The image of Athens given in the Funeral Oration is certainly in tension with the passages that attest to a sometimes uncontrolled Athenian mentality: obvious examples are the general mindset prevailing during the run-up to the Sicilian Expedition as well as the Athenians' intractability in the wake of the first Spartan invasions, not to mention the collapse of morals in the wake of the plague, whose effects directly contradict, as scholars have shown, some of the central aspirations of the Funeral Oration.[6] Despite these tensions, it is hard to believe that Thucydides tries to debunk the account of Athens given by the politician whom he held in uniquely high regard. It is more plausible to assume that Pericles' portrayal of Athens is meant to be neither a straightforward image of reality nor mere calculated propaganda. As Wohl has pointed out, Pericles' image of Athens in the Funeral Oration represents a higher self of the city, an 'ideal-ego',[7] that 'sets the direction for the subject's correct...development'.[8] In a similar vein, Loraux observes that 'in Thucydides' work, Athens has more than one face; there are at least two cities, which, like the real and the paradigm, sometimes coexist and sometimes are mutually exclusive'.[9] The Funeral Oration shows what Athens can be when at its best, a potential towards which Pericles wishes to turn the Athenians' minds before this legacy will necessarily be obfuscated by the convulsions soon to be brought by the War.[10] Pericles' idealism in the Funeral Oration is not simply at odds with reality but rather interacts with it in the manner of a variable dialectic: while it sometimes lifts reality to the higher plane of the ideal paradigm, on other occasions the dialectic interplay may lose its grip so that both realms, the ideal and the real, become separated by a profound gulf.

With regard to Thucydides' assessment of Pericles, Yunis remarks: '[G]iven Thucydides' unqualified admiration for Pericles and his leadership of the *dēmos*, we have no basis for inferring that Thucydides had any

---

[5] Flashar 1989 [1969]: 466.
[6] Flashar 1989 [1969]: 463–4; Loraux 2006 [1981]: 513 n. 88; Connor 1984: 63–4; Palmer 1992: 30; Orwin 1994: 174–5.
[7] Wohl 2002: 33.   [8] Wohl 2002: 35.   [9] Loraux 2006 [1981]: 365.
[10] See the observations made by Pouncey (1980: 32) on the relationship between Funeral Oration and plague: 'Pericles may be speaking for Athens in its prime...In this case the Plague would prefigure, by a kind of physical concentration of the principle of decay, the long process of Athenian decline.'

reservations about Pericles at all.'[11] On Thucydides' view, even the plan that was best in the given circumstances, and that was conceived by the most intelligent and most incorruptible statesman, cannot but involve pitfalls and drawbacks. On the final reckoning, not even Pericles' brilliant power of conception can prevent the downfall of Athens. This awareness of the ultimate futility of the most well-wrought endeavours bears witness to the tragic strand running through Thucydides' thought, a notion that we will revisit towards the end of this chapter.[12]

8.1 The Athenians Exposed to Invasion and Plague: Human Nature on the Rise

In the second year of the Peloponnesian War, the devastation of the Athenian countryside as well as the spread of the plague in over-crowded and confined conditions weigh heavily on the Athenians. As a result, they come to regret their decision to have entered the War at Pericles' behest. On the brink of giving up the War, they vent their anger on Pericles. Confronted with widespread anger and fear, Pericles tries to revive the Athenians' awareness that their original decision was correct.[13]

Commenting on the situation at Athens, Thucydides writes that 'the disease and the War, in unison, pressed hard on [sc. the Athenians]' (ἡ νόσος ἐπέκειτο ἅμα καὶ ὁ πόλεμος, 2.59.1). Like ἐπιπίπτω and ἐμπίπτω, ἐπίκειμαι and ἔγκειμαι are words that are used of an attacking enemy, but also of diseases and other troublesome physical conditions. As shown in previous chapters, the characteristic manifestations of the War (viz.

---

[11] Yunis 1996: 69–70. See also de Romilly 1965: 574.
[12] See Macleod 1983f, 152: 'The imperial city is not more secure than the tragic hero.'
[13] Anger: χαλεπαίνοντας ('being angry', 2.59.3); τὸ ὀργιζόμενον τῆς γνώμης ('the state of anger that had seized their mind', 2.59.3); τὰ τῆς ὀργῆς ('outbursts of anger', 2.60.1); ὀργίζεσθε ('you are angry', 2.60.5); ἐμὲ δι' ὀργῆς ἔχετε ('you vent your anger against me', 2.64.1); ὀργῆς παραλύειν ('release from anger;' 2.65.1); ἐν ὀργῇ ἔχοντες ('holding on to anger', 2.65.3). Fear: πρὸς τὸ ... ἀδεέστερον καταστῆσαι ('bring in a less fearful state', 2.59.3); δεδιότας αὖ ἀλόγως ('unreasonably afraid', 2.65.9).

the plague, stasis, the ἔρως for Sicily, and the slaughter at Mycalessus) tend to figure as subjects of compounds of πίπτω (see Chapters 2, pp. 67–70, and 5, pp. 187–8). The compound of κεῖμαι with the prefix ἐπί- belongs to the same register. With the expression ἡ νόσος ἐπέκειτο ἅμα καὶ ὁ πόλεμος still on the reader's mind, a synonymous compound of κεῖμαι follows, this time with the Athenians as subject (2.59.2):

πανταχόθεν τε τῇ γνώμῃ ἄποροι καθεστῶτες ἐνέκειντο τῷ Περικλεῖ.

Having been reduced to a perplexed state of mind from all sides, they pressed hard on Pericles.

As the resumption of ἐπέκειτο by ἐνέκειντο indicates, both destructive forces, the plague and the War, have now merged with the Athenian demos. Thus, the Athenians at large have become yet another concrete embodiment of the destructive energies of the War.

The perfect form καθεστῶτες, in combination with the local adverb πανταχόθεν, indicates the settling of state: a mood of anger and despair has solidified and becomes an inescapable condition constricting the Athenians, a constraint imposed on them 'from all sides'. In the *History*, this phrasing resurfaces in two other passages that combine a form of καθίσταμαι and cognates of ἀπορία. After the fall of Plataea, the captured Plataeans are confronted with the futile task of self-defence before the Spartan judges. They describe their situation as follows: 'Being reduced to a perplexed state from all sides, we are compelled, and it seems to be safer, to speak up and take the risk' (πανταχόθεν δὲ ἄποροι καθεστῶτες ἀναγκαζόμεθα καὶ ἀσφαλέστερον δοκεῖ εἶναι εἰπόντας τι κινδυνεύειν, 3.53.3). Not only the phrase ἄποροι καθεστῶτες, but also the adverb πανταχόθεν recalls 2.59.2. The other passage comes from a speech by Gylippus and his generals before the decisive battle in the Great Harbour of Syracuse. Gylippus and his colleagues bring the difficulties confronting the Athenians to the attention of the Syracusan soldiers: 'They [*sc*. the Athenians], compelled by their present dire straits, are reduced to a state of desperation in which they run any risk... they possibly can' (βιαζόμενοι ὑπὸ τῆς παρούσης ἀπορίας ἐς ἀπόνοιαν καθεστήκασιν... ἀποκινδυνεῦσαι οὕτως ὅπως δύνανται, 7.67.4). Both here and at 3.53.3, phrases involving perfect forms of καθίσταμαι and vocabulary drawn from the lexeme of ἄπορος are combined with language suggesting that the incumbent situation 'compels' (ἀναγκαζόμεθα, βιαζόμενοι) people to run a risk (κινδυνεύειν, ἀποκινδυνεῦσαι). Each time, the resulting action is a futile attempt to escape what has become inevitable. The verbal parallels between these two passages and the section dealing with the Athenians' anger at Pericles (also featuring a perfect of καθίσταμαι and the adjective ἄπορος) suggest that the Athenians experience a similar kind of compulsion in the wake of the second Spartan invasion. Indeed, the Athenians find that they have 'fallen in with disasters' (ταῖς ξυμφοραῖς περιπεπτωκότες, 2.59.2), a phrase capturing passivity in the face of adversity in a manner typical of Thucydides' general representation of the War.

In the speech that Pericles delivers in response to this emergency situation, he observes that the pressure of their present circumstances has reduced the Athenians to irrationality (2.61.2):

ξυνέβη...τὸν ἐμὸν λόγον ἐν τῷ ὑμετέρῳ ἀσθενεῖ τῆς γνώμης μὴ ὀρθὸν φαίνεσθαι, διότι τὸ μὲν λυποῦν ἔχει ἤδη τὴν αἴσθησιν ἑκάστῳ, τῆς δὲ ὠφελίας ἄπεστιν ἔτι ἡ δήλωσις ἅπασι...

It has happened...that, given the weakness of your resolution, my reasoning no longer seems correct because right now grief has the perception of each of you in its grip, but the clear proof of our advantage still escapes you all...

The passage features phrasing that is typical of Thucydides' general depiction of the impact of adverse circumstances on actions and decisions: the impersonal main verb ξυνέβη stresses the occurrence of an event as opposed to the activity of personal subjects; the nominal phrase ἐν τῷ ὑμετέρῳ ἀσθενεῖ τῆς γνώμης suggests the priority of a collective mindset, represented as an impersonal state, over the initiatives of personal agents; the passion of grief, likewise captured by a nominalized neuter phrase, occupies the subject position and 'holds' the Athenians' perception 'in its grip' (τὸ μὲν λυποῦν ἔχει...τὴν αἴσθησιν...).

In this situation, the isolated personal agent Pericles might easily be thrust aside by the onslaught of collective passions and unfavourable circumstances, thus suffering the same fate that Nicias will later experience on the eve of the Sicilian Expedition. In fact, another phrase used by Pericles suggests that Pericles is exposed to the power of collective passions in the face of which individual agents are usually hard put (2.60.1):

Καὶ προσδεχομένῳ μοι τὰ τῆς ὀργῆς ὑμῶν ἔς με γεγένηται (αἰσθάνομαι γὰρ τὰς αἰτίας)...
Your outbursts of anger against me have in fact happened just as I expected (for I can perceive the causes prompting them[14])...

The phrase τὰ τῆς ὀργῆς belongs to the group of substantivized neuter constructions by which Thucydides (or a specific speaker) signals the impact of collective impulses evocative of rampant impersonal forces. Moreover, the verb γεγένηται, which suggests the idea of occurrence and a settled situation due to its perfect aspect, underscores the analogy between these passions and external events. Anger and despair have seized the Athenians, entrenched themselves, and run their course. This account suggests that Pericles agrees with Thucydides' aforementioned presentation of the situation at Athens (2.59.1–2), which immediately precedes the assessment that Pericles gives in his speech.[15]

8.2 Pericles Face to Face with Human Nature

The phrases analysed in the previous section imply that forces beyond anyone's control have beset the Athenians soon after the onset of the Peloponnesian War. These findings, however, are not the full story. They are offset by other stylistic choices, which suggest that Pericles is in fact not entirely passive in the face of the unleashed force of collective human nature. Pericles states that he has 'expected' the Athenians' anger

[14] Based on the opposition between πρόφασις and αἰτία (see 7.5 [pp. 257–9]), I translate αἰτία as 'prompting cause' in this passage.
[15] As mentioned in the Introduction (see p. 16 n. 38) and Chapter 6 (see p. 206 n. 13), Tompkins (1972, 1993a, 1993b, 2013) has convincingly shown Thucydides' effort to differentiate the style of different speakers—Nicias, Alcibiades, Diodotus, Archidamus, and Pericles—so as to suit their particular character. On this occasion, however, one finds clear continuity of style, which suggests that the historian and Pericles agree about the driving forces in the present situation.

(προσδεχομένῳ, 2.60.1), and he insists on himself as a standard of reference (προσδεχομένῳ μοι τὰ τῆς ὀργῆς ὑμῶν ἔς με γεγένηται). He thus signals that, even if confronted with the frantic general atmosphere, he is not submerged by it.

In Chapter 7, we saw that Thucydides, in a manner typical of Greek thought, conceives of the constraint exercised by human nature not as strict casual determinism, but as a contest between unevenly matched opponents. As I argued there, this conception is reflected in a set of passages in which nature and its proxies are said to 'defeat' human beings, or to be forces that 'are stronger' (pp. 250–2). This latter notion is usually expressed by κρείσσων. In this way, Diodotus calls ἔρως and ἐλπίς 'stronger' than seen dangers (3.45.5), and observes that every situation in which people find themselves is mastered 'by something incurable and stronger' (3.45.4).

In Thucydides' entire work, just one *human individual* appears as the subject of κρείσσων when this adjective governs a dependent genitive referring to impersonal factors, whether material or psychological: Pericles. In his last speech, Pericles says that he is 'inferior to none in determining on the right course of action and in explaining it, being a patriot and *stronger than money*' (οὐδενὸς ἥσσων ... εἶναι γνῶναί τε τὰ δέοντα καὶ ἑρμηνεῦσαι ταῦτα, φιλόπολίς τε καὶ χρημάτων κρείσσων, 2.60.5). Far from being an empty boast, the veracity of this claim is attested by Thucydides' acknowledgment of Pericles' supreme incorruptibility in the valedictory passage (χρημάτων ... διαφανῶς ἀδωρότατος γενόμενος, 2.65.8). By withstanding desire for private enrichment, Pericles is superior to πλεονεξία, which is one of the principal natural urges that lead to a city's self-undoing in the chapters on stasis (3.82.8). Thus, Pericles insists on his capacity to resist the urges rooted in φύσις.

As Holmes has pointed out, phrases suggesting that passions are 'stronger' than human beings (or, less often, vice versa) became idiomatic in classical Greek.[16] The fact that this is the only occurrence of this

---

[16] Holmes expresses some uncertainty as to when this happened (2010: 210). Several passages from Euripides (*Andr.* 629–31; *Hipp.* 475; *TrGF* 5.187.6 and 282.5) and line 1081

phrase with a person as a subject in all of Thucydides gives it special weight. Thucydides' normal assumption is that φύσις, and the passions arising from it, are stronger than human beings, a view shared by most of his contemporaries. There is, however, one case in which the personal subject is used with κρείσσων, namely Pericles.

Thucydides systematically develops the notion of Pericles as a worthy adversary of human nature. This can be gleaned from Thucydides' employment of stylistic features in his depiction of Pericles that otherwise tend to capture the overpowering influence of human nature. Thucydides writes that, when the Athenians are hard pressed by the plague, Pericles 'wanted to... bring them into a milder and less fearful state' (ἐβούλετο... πρὸς τὸ ἠπιώτερον καὶ ἀδεέστερον καταστῆσαι, 2.59.3). A compound of ἵστημι with Pericles in subject position, in combination with substantivized neuter phrases, also occurs in the valedictory passage, where Thucydides stresses Pericles' ability to thwart the extreme tendencies of the Athenian temperament: '[W]hen, in turn, they [sc. the Athenians] were unreasonably fearful, he restored them to boldness again' (δεδιότας αὖ ἀλόγως ἀντικαθίστη πάλιν ἐπὶ τὸ θαρσεῖν, 2.65.9). Conversely, Thucydides says Pericles would 'strike them into fear' (κατέπληξεν ἐπὶ τὸ φοβεῖσθαι, 2.65.9) when perceiving them to become 'over-confident out of insolence' (παρὰ καιρὸν ὕβρει θαρσοῦντας, 2.65.9). The verb καταπλήσσω, and the cognate noun κατάπληξις, bear connotations of shock and are repeatedly used to capture the terror that comes to prevail among the Athenians in response to the string of setbacks that they suffer at Sicily (7.24.3, 7.72.4, 7.77.4, 8.1.2). Just like dire circumstances, Pericles is able to strike shock into human beings.

Pericles is thus able to call forth enduring mental states, which are expressed by substantivized neuter adjectives and infinitives (πρὸς τὸ ἠπιώτερον καὶ ἀδεέστερον, 2.59.3; ἐπὶ τὸ φοβεῖσθαι, 2.65.9; ἐπὶ τὸ θαρσεῖν, 2.65.9). Such nominalized neuters usually refer to the constraining factors and passions that lead to irrational decisions. Thucydides also

---

from Aristophanes' *Clouds* (originally staged in 423) provide examples of the idiom. This suggests that it was well established by the time of Thucydides. For further examples of the idiom in extant Greek sources, see Holmes 2010: 210, esp. n. 63.

uses forms of καθίστημι in connection with Pericles' ability to counterbalance the Athenians' impulses (καταστῆσαι, 2.59.3; ἀντικαθίστη, 2.65.9). Yet instead of being used intransitively and suggesting people's entanglement in circumstances and seizure by passionate impulses, these verbs are now used transitively, and with the individual Pericles in subject position.

The use of the prepositions πρός and ἐπί with the accusative shows that Pericles is not replacing one irrational passion with another: without taking them all the way to the opposite extreme, Pericles leads the Athenians *in the direction of* the passion that marks the opposite of the state that prevails in excess. In this way, contrary to human nature's innate tendency towards the extreme, Pericles ultimately aims at balance and equilibrium between the poles of boldness and fearfulness, even when he induces intense mental states.[17]

Pericles' quest for balance is also reflected in the contrary measures that he adopts on the occasion of the first and second Spartan invasions, respectively: in the case of the first invasion, when the Athenians are frantically eager for a sortie, he calms them down (τήν... δι᾽ ἡσυχίας μάλιστα ὅσον ἐδύνατο εἶχεν, 2.22.1), while during the second, when they are on the verge of despair, he emboldens them (θαρσῦναι, 2.59.3). Although Pericles adopts opposite measures, Thucydides uses almost identical phrases on each occasion, a fact pointed out by Emily Greenwood:[18] 'seeing them getting angry in the face of the present situation' (ὁρῶν μὲν αὐτοὺς πρὸς τὸ παρὸν χαλεπαίνοντας, 2.22.1) and 'seeing them getting angry in the face of present circumstances' (ὁρῶν αὐτοὺς πρὸς τὰ παρόντα χαλεπαίνοντας, 2.59.3). The neuters τὸ παρόν and τὰ παρόντα highlight the impersonal force of circumstances that have the tendency to constrain human choices. The parallel phrasing indicates that the predisposition towards extreme reactions to adverse circumstances is not occasional but anchored in a general human

---

[17] Commenting on the cited passages at 2.65.9, de Romilly (1965: 567) observes: 'Devant ces deux excès contraires,... Périclès agit comme le modérateur: il rappelle la crainte là où on l'oublie, la confiance là où elle manque.' See also Connor (1984: 62): 'Periclean leadership is effective not only because it represents tendencies at Athens, but also because it is able to check those tendencies when they become unbalanced.'

[18] Greenwood 2006: 53.

constitution. By the repetition of ὁρῶν, these phrases also suggest Pericles' steadfast alertness to the risk that the Athenians might be overcome by rash impulses. By contrast, the contrary measures taken by Pericles show that the specific manifestation of this general tendency depends on the situation at hand. In each case, Pericles is similarly capable of counterbalancing the different states of anger, which can both be traced back, despite their apparent difference, to the same basic natural predisposition.

8.3 Realization of the Periclean Ideal in Language

Thucydides' presentation of Pericles' political agency reveals a pervasive antithesis, an opposition between Pericles and the Athenian demos: Pericles is the paragon of γνώμη, whereas the forces besetting the Athenians can be summed up by the term ὀργή.[19] As scholars have stressed, the distinctive token of γνώμη is that it denotes, not the exercise of pure and abstract thought, understood as a self-sufficient faculty, but thought that engages with practical reality by conceiving a rational plan directed at the world of action.[20] As a result, the word γνώμη covers various shades of meaning. When it is applied to Pericles, in particular in opposition to the Athenians' affliction by passion, the term can be rendered in four ways, of which the first three have primarily intellectual, the fourth volitional connotations. In this way, the word suggests, first, the mind in general; second, the mind's signal capacity, namely power of judgment and intelligence; third, the specific result produced by the exercise of this faculty, namely an intelligent judgment or plan of action; and, fourth, the resolve to execute what one has intelligently conceived.[21]

---

[19] On the antithesis between γνώμη and ὀργή as representing the opposition between Pericles and the Athenians, see Edmunds 1975: 9–14; Rawlings 1981: 131; Wohl 2017: 447. The relevant passages for the Athenians' ὀργή (including ὀργίζομαι) are: ἐν ὀργῇ εἶχον, 2.21.3; ὀργῇ, 22.1; τὸ ὀργιζόμενον, 59.3; τὰ τῆς ὀργῆς, 60.5; ὀργίζεσθε, 60.5; δι' ὀργῆς, 64.1; τῆς...ὀργῆς 65.1. Γνώμη (also expressed by the verb γιγνώσκω) functions as counteracting force against ὀργή in the following places: ὀρθῶς γιγνώσκειν, 2.22.1; γνώμῃ, 22.1; γνῶναι...τὰ δέοντα, 60.5; τὴν γνώμην, 65.1.

[20] Snell 1924: 33–5; Parry 1972: 60; Huart 1973: 70–1; Dihle 1982: 28–9.

[21] Müri 1968 [1947]: 145–7; Huart 1973: 83, 85–8; Edmunds 1975: 8–10; Rawlings 1981: 131; Dihle 1982: 29; Rengakos 1984: 41, 45–6; Tompkins 2013: 450 n. 8.

From a modern point of view, the conjunction that one finds with γνώμη between intellect and volition is surprising because mental and volitional activity tend to belong to separate faculties in modern accounts.[22] By contrast, the capacity denoted by γνώμη usually contains the stimulus towards action within itself: a genuinely intelligent plan entails the determination to carry it out, so that intelligence and will-power amount to the same thing,[23] an aspect of particular importance for Thucydides' account of Pericles.[24] Thucydides' contemporaries did not take this unity of thought and determination for granted. Instead, they made the experience that reflection often leads to indecision, a mechanism often highlighted in modernity (and associated in particular with Shakespeare's *Hamlet*). Evidence for the circulation of this idea can be found in Pericles' Funeral Oration: Pericles observes that for most non-Athenians 'ignorance involves boldness, but reasoning hesitation' (ἀμαθία μὲν θράσος, λογισμὸς δὲ ὄκνον φέρει, 2.40.3).

This unification of powers (i.e. intellect and resolve) that are potentially at odds with each other does not only belong to the internal structure of γνώμη, but it also manifests itself externally in the relationship between γνώμη and dispositions that are in tension with it. Γνώμη enters into a dialectical relationship with the forces confronting it. This type of engagement is reflected in the style of Pericles' speeches. They are marked by an elaborate system of antitheses organized around the word γνώμη, which occurs twelve times in Pericles' speeches. Eight times, the

---

[22] From an ancient Greek point of view, this combination is to be expected because, as many scholars have observed, the Greeks of the classical era did not posit an independent faculty of the will, distinct from both reason and emotion. Whereas according to many modern accounts the free will lies at the heart of the capacity to make choices, the evidence from Greek authors of the fifth and fourth century, not least from Plato and Aristotle, suggests that they conceived of human motivation without any reference to the notion of the will. For them, human beings make genuine choices if they act in accordance with reason. Thus, whereas the notion of choice is present in both classical Greek and in modern thought, the Greeks (at least those of the classical era) did not locate the power to make choices in sheer volition understood as a distinct human faculty. On the lack of the notion of will, and on the Greek tendency to identify choice with action in accordance with reason, see Dodds 1951: 26 n. 105; Dirlmeiner 1956: 327–8; Fränkel 1962: 87–8 and 446 n. 52; Vernant 1988 [1972]: 54–9; Arendt 1978: 15–17, 57–62; Dihle 1982: 20–7; Kahn 1988: 239–45; Frede 2011: 19–21; Brann 2014: 1–13.

[23] Snell 1924: 35; Dihle 1982: 28–9. See also Bender (1938: 10): 'Wenn wir Moderne immer wieder betonen müssen, daß Politik ein Umsetzen von Erkenntnissen und Erfahrungen in den Willen bedeutet und daß Erkenntnis, für sich allein genommen, ohne Wert ist, so bildet für den Griechen, dessen ganzes Wesen von einer wunderbaren rationalen Klarheit durchstrahlt ist..., die Sphäre des Erkennens und des Wollens noch eine ungebrochene Einheit.'

[24] Bender 1938: 11–14; Edmunds 1975: 12; Rawlings 1981: 131; Rengakos 1984: 55.

word is set against an antithetical term. The terms that are contrasted with γνώμη invariably fall into either of two categories: they either indicate a mental state (1.144.4, 2.62.4, 2.62.5), typically in the guise of a passion, or they refer to external reality, whether by denoting circumstances or deeds (1.140.1, 1.144.4, 2.13.2, 2.38.1, 2.43.3, 2.62.4 [ἀπὸ ἀμαθίας εὐτυχοῦς ... γνώμῃ], 2.62.5, twice at 2.64.6). Pericles' style makes a crucial contribution to the impact that his speeches have on the Athenians: the system of antitheses gives tangible shape to the all-important notion, which Pericles tries to impress on the Athenians, that the intellect has the power to infuse reality and organize its raw material. Thucydides qua narrator sustains the same notion that γνώμη, as represented by Pericles, involves antitheses with either other mental states (2.22.1, 59.3, 65.1) or external reality (2.65.1). Such overlap between the style of Pericles and that of the narrator may cut across our expectations regarding character speech. These different suppositions notwithstanding, there is no getting around the fact that Thucydides tends to sustain a specific verbal style associated with Pericles even outside the speeches.

The syntactic form taken by the antithesis again features two variants. In the first variant, the antithetical term (whether referring to a mental state or external reality) is found in parallel grammatical position with γνώμη, usually placed in a coordinated clause or phrase. The following passage provides an example:[25] 'In each man, an unwritten memorial [*sc.* of the fallen soldiers' deed] abides, resting in the **mind** rather than a physical monument' (ἄγραφος μνήμη παρ' ἑκάστῳ **τῆς γνώμης** μᾶλλον ἢ τοῦ ἔργου ἐνδιαιτᾶται, 2.43.3). In the second variant, the antithesis is not underscored by parallelism, but involves syntactical variation: the antithetical term is often directly contrasted with γνώμη, for instance by a prepositional phrase or a dependent (often separative) genitive. An example of this form is provided by Pericles' remark in the Funeral Oration: 'We have furnished countless opportunities for the **spirit** to rest from toil' (τῶν πόνων πλείστας ἀναπαύλας **τῇ γνώμῃ** ἐπορισάμεθα, 2.38.1). 'Toil', which belongs to the external realm of ἔργον, forms a

---

[25] In what follows, I use three different forms of underlining to distinguish the three types of terms involved in the antitheses from a semantic point of view: **γνώμη**—external reality—mental state.

contrast with the mental capacity described by γνώμη. The antithesis, unassisted by verbal parallelism, nonetheless leaps to the reader's eye because of Thucydides' frequent habit of contrasting the mental sphere with either passion or fact.

We have already noted the systematic opposition between γνώμη and ὀργή in Thucydides' account of the interaction between Pericles and the Athenians. The other antithesis, the opposition between γνώμη and external reality, refers to one of the key elements of Thucydides' thought and style, the chief subject of Parry's engagement with Thucydides.[26] Thucydides trains the reader to look out for these two recurring antitheses. He systematically organizes antitheses involving Pericles and γνώμη along two axes: one semantic (γνώμη set against passion and γνώμη set against external reality) and one formal (antithesis expressed by parallelism and antithesis involving syntactic variation).

The mental states that Pericles contrasts with γνώμη through antithesis are τόλμα (1.144.4), ἀμαθία (2.62.4), and ἐλπίς (2.62.5). In addition, Thucydides himself contrasts Pericles' γνώμη three times with ὀργή (ὀργῇ, 2.22.1; τὸ ὀργιζόμενον, 59.3; ὀργῆς, 65.1). When γνώμη stands in opposition to external reality, the following terms occur: ἔργον (2.43.3, 64.6), ξυμφοραί (1.140.1, 2.64.6), τύχη (1.144.4), χρημάτων περιουσία (2.13.2), πόνοι (2.38.1), εὐτυχές (2.62.4), and τὰ ὑπάρχοντα (2.62.5). Again, the narrator sustains the antithesis when summarizing Pericles' last speech through a direct contrast between the terms γνώμη and τὰ παρόντα δεινά ('present evils', 2.65.1). In combination, the two sets of terms that are antithetical to γνώμη represent the internal and the external obstacles that φύσις places in the way of sound decision-making. Pericles thus represents γνώμη as a power that is constantly set against contrary forces. The systematic organization percolating through Pericles' language suggests that the antitheses are not incidental, but that the struggle with opposite powers is intrinsic to γνώμη.

The antitheses express, first and foremost, the antagonistic stance between γνώμη and the powers opposed to human intelligence. In some

---

[26] Parry (1970: 11): 'The distinction between thought and reality, between *logos* and *ergon* or more or less obvious equivalents, is the real idiosyncrasy of Thucydides' style.' See also Parry 1981: 6, and Denniston 1952: 13.

instances, however, the antitheses imply that the factors contrasted with γνώμη cooperate with it, acting as complementary partners of γνώμη. In his last speech Pericles remarks that 'intelligence... trusts less in hope... but [that it] puts its trust in **reasoned judgment** proceeding from the actual facts' (ἡ ξύνεσις... ἐλπίδι... ἧσσον πιστεύει..., **γνώμῃ** δὲ ἀπὸ τῶν ὑπαρχόντων, 2.62.5). In this passage, γνώμη is set against the unreliable power of ἐλπίς by antithesis through parallelism. At the same time, however, it achieves a clear-sighted assessment of the situation by taking its bearings 'from the actual facts' (ἀπὸ τῶν ὑπαρχόντων), a term that belongs to the other set of terms against which γνώμη is usually set. Thus, the antithesis with ἐπλίδι is negative, but the antithesis with ἀπὸ τῶν ὑπαρχόντων suggests congruence between thought and external reality. The reversal of this constellation can be observed in a passage from Pericles' first speech. Pericles remarks apropos the generation triumphant at Salamis: 'Our fathers, at any rate, drove away the barbarian with more **intelligent resolve** than luck and with greater boldness than power' (οἱ γοῦν πατέρες... **γνώμῃ** τε πλέονι ἢ τύχῃ καὶ τόλμῃ μείζονι ἢ δυνάμει τόν... βάρβαρον ἀπεώσαντο, 1.144.4). On this occasion, γνώμη is set against external circumstance (τύχῃ), but it cooperates with passion (τόλμῃ), which is coordinated with it through parallelism.

In the Funeral Oration, the verb γιγνώσκω, from which the noun γνώμη is derived, is also used to underscore these systematic antitheses. On all three occurrences in the Funeral Oration, the verb is part of an antithesis that contrasts 'knowing' with words signifying either passion or external reality (πρὸς ἔργα, 2.40.2; ἐκ τῶν κινδύνων, 40.3; τολμῶντες... καὶ ἐν τοῖς ἔργοις αἰσχυνόμενοι, 43.1). From a formal point, too, these antitheses are analogous to the antithetical statements organized around γνώμη: they are expressed in the form of either parallelism (**γιγνώσκοντες** καὶ... μὴ ἀποτρεπόμενοι, 2.40.3) or syntactical variation (ἑτέροις πρὸς ἔργα τετραμμένοις τὰ πολιτικὰ μὴ ἐνδεῶς **γνῶναι**,[27] 2.40.2).

In keeping with the idealizing character of the Funeral Oration, the antitheses structured around γιγνώσκω highlight the ability to harmonize

---

[27] The printed text, which diverges from Alberti, is based on the unanimous manuscript tradition and the evidence of a papyrus. The soundness of the transmitted text has been convincingly defended by Edmunds (1972: 171–2) and Rusten (1989, on 2.40.2).

contrary dispositions (theoretical versus practical, intellectual versus emotional) and contrary spheres (thought versus external reality), thus achieving a unique realization of human potential. For example, Pericles singles out the combination of knowledge and vigorous action as a distinctive trait of the past generations that were responsible for acquiring the immense power of Athens: 'Men acquired these things who were venturesome and **knew** what was necessary and were moved by a sense of shame in their deeds' (τολμῶντες καὶ γιγνώσκοντες τὰ δέοντα καὶ ἐν τοῖς ἔργοις αἰσχυνόμενοι ἄνδρες αὐτὰ ἐκτήσαντο, 2.43.1). Immerwahr observes with respect to this passage that 'the central idea of the Oration is the definition of democratic courage as a kind of knowledge',[28] a remark that aptly summarizes γνώμη as Pericles conceives it. The central term γιγνώσκοντες marks the centre of two antitheses that are formally structured by parallelism. It is thus coordinated with τολμῶντες and αἰσχυνόμενοι, which both refer to emotions. However, the insertion of ἐν τοῖς ἔργοις into the participial phrase based on αἰσχυνόμενοι effects a shift of the semantic antithesis: the contrast with γιγνώσκοντες centres less on the opposition between knowledge and shame, but on the more evident contrast between the mind and external reality, a notion familiar through the frequent opposition of λόγος versus ἔργον. Pericles' point at 2.43.1 is that the Athenians acquired their power by closing the gap between the intellect and realms that are usually antithetical to it: passionate impulse and the external world of fact.

Pericles employs the various antitheses to suggest that γνώμη is the nub of the Athenians' mastery over reality. The rationale underlying the antitheses leads the reader, as well as the Athenians listening to Pericles' speeches, to understand that γνώμη imposes order on the waywardness of reality. The ultimate goal is the triumph of γνώμη over the contrary realms of passion and external reality. However, γνώμη prevails not by erasing the powers set against it, but by drawing them in a dynamic relationship in which they prove beneficial under the guidance of intelligence. The system of antitheses does not suggest an effortless triumph, but it also highlights that the forces opposed to γνώμη tend to resist. Pericles also acknowledges the possibility that they will oust γνώμη: in his first speech, for instance, he

---

[28] Immerwahr 1960: 285.

stresses the danger of fickleness, observing 'that in response to circumstances people change their **judgments**, too' (τοὺς ἀνθρώπους ... πρὸς ... τὰς ξυμφορὰς καὶ **τὰς γνώμας** τρεπομένους, 1.140.1).

In his speeches, Pericles tells the Athenians on two occasions what makes people 'strongest'. Each statement involves either γνώμη or the verb γιγνώσκω, and each also features the familiar antitheses. In the Funeral Oration, Pericles points out that 'strongest in spirit' (κράτιστοι ... τὴν ψυχήν) are those who '**recognize** most clearly what is to be feared and what is pleasant' (οἱ τά τε δεινὰ καὶ ἡδέα σαφέστατα **γιγνώσκοντες**) and who simultaneously do 'not shrink from dangers' (μὴ ἀποτρεπόμενοι ἐκ τῶν κινδύνων, 2.40.3). The phrase 'not shrinking from dangers' resumes the words τολμᾶν and θράσος from the preceding sentences. It follows that Pericles has the combination of two contrary dispositions in mind: clarity of thought and courage. At the same time, the reference to 'dangers' highlights pressures that arise in the external world. Those are 'strongest' whose intellect masters the realms set against it: the sphere of passion and the realm of external circumstances.

In the concluding sentence of his last speech, Pericles again highlights, in his final words in the *History*, what makes people 'strongest' (2.64.6):

ὡς οἵτινες πρὸς τὰς ξυμφορὰς **γνώμῃ** μὲν ἥκιστα λυποῦνται, **ἔργῳ** δὲ μάλιστα ἀντέχουσιν, οὗτοι καὶ πόλεων καὶ ἰδιωτῶν κράτιστοί εἰσιν.

For, those who suffer least distress **in their spirit**[29] when confronted with misfortunes but in action resist most vigorously—these are the strongest whether they be cities or individuals.

Here, 'being strongest' springs from the integration of the antithesis between mind (γνώμη) and action in the external world (ἔργῳ). Notice that Thucydides could also have skipped the nouns γνώμῃ and ἔργῳ and have written: 'Those who when confronted with misfortunes suffer least distress but resist most vigorously—these are strongest.' In that case, however, the antithesis through parallelism between γνώμῃ and ἔργῳ would be lost. Again, the idea is that the greatest achievement requires

---

[29] The phrase γνώμῃ λυπέομαι seems to mean 'to lose heart'. Γνώμη here denotes, in Huart's terms, '*sentiment*... au sens de *état d'esprit, mentalité*' (1973: 12).

that one succeeds at bridging the gulf between realms separated by an antithetical relationship. At the same time, the passage features a further reference to external circumstances ($\pi\rho\grave{o}s$ $\tau\grave{a}s$ $\xi\upsilon\mu\varphi o\rho\acute{a}s$), a phrase that reminds the audience that the intellect and the world of facts are usually at odds with each other. Congruence of mind and action presupposes that the spirit successfully asserts itself against the thrust of adverse circumstances.

According to Pelling, the interaction of conflicting forces plays an important role in Greek philosophical and medical writings: '[S]uch tension and balancing can be productive and can even be an indispensable ingredient for health and success providing – what is not easy – that the balance can be maintained.'[30] Here, just as in Pericles' speeches, it turns out that antithetical forces do not undermine each other but activate each other's potential to the full if they are brought into the right balance. For Pericles, the Athenians' achievement of cooperation between these charged antithetical forces is the cornerstone of their success in the realm of political action.

In sum, the systematic antitheses that mark Pericles' oratorical style sustain a specific idea: they give shape to the notion that $\gamma\nu\acute{\omega}\mu\eta$ is a power that realizes itself through engagement with antithetical forces. Only by mastery over antagonistic factors can the highest innate potential of $\gamma\nu\acute{\omega}\mu\eta$ become reality. Parry has stressed that '[t]he central problem of history is, How, and when, can man impose his *gnōmē* on things outside himself?'[31] The antithesis organized around Pericles' references to $\gamma\nu\acute{\omega}\mu\eta$ draw attention to precisely this theme. Due to the system of antitheses, Pericles creates a tangible image in language of the struggle of $\gamma\nu\acute{\omega}\mu\eta$. In summarizing Pericles' last speech, Thucydides points out: 'By saying such things, Pericles attempted to ... divert [*sc.* the Athenians'] $\gamma\nu\acute{\omega}\mu\eta$ from the present terrors' ($\tau o\iota a\hat{\upsilon}\tau a$ $\acute{o}$ $\Pi\epsilon\rho\iota\kappa\lambda\hat{\eta}s$ $\lambda\acute{\epsilon}\gamma\omega\nu$ $\dot{\epsilon}\pi\epsilon\iota\rho\hat{a}\tau o$ ... $\dot{a}\pi\grave{o}$ $\tau\hat{\omega}\nu$ $\pi a\rho\acute{o}\nu\tau\omega\nu$ $\delta\epsilon\iota\nu\hat{\omega}\nu$ $\dot{a}\pi\acute{a}\gamma\epsilon\iota\nu$ $\tau\grave{\eta}\nu$ $\gamma\nu\acute{\omega}\mu\eta\nu$, 2.65.1). Language provides the instrument by which Pericles paves the way for enlightened decisions. Faced with the system of antitheses, the Athenians vividly experience the ordering of unruly reality, which is brought into alignment with the unified faculty of intelligence and zest for action. The ideal conceived in thought translates itself into the sphere of fact through the spoken word: it captivates the Athenians and restores their willingness to resist. In this way, Pericles' oratory closes the gap between conception and action in the medium of language. For once, the gulf between $\lambda\acute{o}\gamma os$ and $\check{\epsilon}\rho\gamma o\nu$ is overcome.

[30] Pelling 2019: 87.   [31] Parry 1970: 20.

8.4 Restoring the Athenians' Power of Choice

The ascendancy of γνώμη is anything but a matter of course. In light of the frequent representation of passion as an indomitable dynamic force, it is hardly surprising that, even in Periclean Athens, passion does not automatically submit to the guidance of reason. Pericles delivers his last speech in view of the fact that the Athenians have been seized by passions that threaten to shed the guidance of γνώμη.

Various phrases used by Pericles in his last speech show that passion seizes the leading role when γνώμη proves 'weak'. After the Athenians have succumbed to anger and despair in reaction to the suffering brought by the plague, Pericles tells them: 'Given the weakness of your γνώμη, my reasoning no longer seems correct [sc. to you]' (τὸν ἐμὸν λόγον ἐν τῷ ὑμετέρῳ ἀσθενεῖ τῆς γνώμης μὴ ὀρθὸν φαίνεσθαι, 2.61.2). Pericles' reference to γνώμη implies that a single power is responsible for what we would probably consider two separate failures (one intellectual, the other volitional): in Pericles' view, the Athenians' resolve is eroded by the pressure of circumstances, a weakening that he considers tantamount to a breakdown of their capacity to recognize the right course of action. The 'weakening' affecting the Athenians is captured by a substantivized neuter adjective (τῷ ὑμετέρῳ ἀσθενεῖ) of the kind that Thucydides, or his speakers, often use to describe conditions that overtake human collectives.

Pericles' last speech features further passages in which Pericles equates the Athenians' seizure by passion with a breakdown of the integrated faculty of thought and resolve. Highlighting the general breakdown of γνώμη in the wake of the plague, Pericles tells the Athenians: 'And since a great reversal has struck, and suddenly at that, your spirit[32] is too

---

[32] Just like γνώμη, διάνοια is an intellectual term that can often be translated as 'intelligence' or 'understanding' (LSJ s.v. διάνοια A.III). At the same time, the word extends to the sphere of intention and practical decision: it can be rendered as 'intention' or 'purpose' (LSJ s.v. διάνοια A. I). Huart points out that in references to διάνοια 'the exercise of ratiocination' is usually in play, although the meaning 'intention' and 'design' tends to predominate in Thucydides (1968: 317). In the present passage, it denotes the faculty from which concrete 'intentions' and 'purposes' arise, rendered by Huart as 'l'esprit' and 'l'état d'esprit' (1968: 317). Huart translates ταπεινὴ... ἡ διάνοια ἐγκαρτερεῖν as 'n'avoir pas la pensée assez ferme' (317 n. 8), thus indicating that διάνοια resembles γνώμη in being an intellectual capacity at root, notwithstanding its primarily practical and volitional connotations.

dejected to persevere in the plan that you decided to adopt' (καὶ μεταβολῆς μεγάλης, καὶ ταύτης ἐξ ὀλίγου, ἐμπεσούσης ταπεινὴ ὑμῶν ἡ διάνοια ἐγκαρτερεῖν ἃ ἔγνωτε, 2.61.2). The verb γιγνώσκω, which has both intellectual and volitional connotations in this passage,[33] alludes to γνώμη. The terms ταπεινός and ἐγκαρτερεῖν belong to the semantic field of strength and weakness, thus recalling ἀσθενής in the previous passage. Where moderns might typically speak of strength, or weakness, of the will, Pericles applies the same terms to the intellect. The force that proves stronger than the intellect (viz. the μεταβολή of the plague) appears as subject in combination with a compound of πίπτω in a genitive absolute construction. An impersonal force in the guise of a larger-than-life-sized attacker has overwhelmed the Athenians' brilliant intelligence.

Since the Athenians have (at least momentarily) forsaken the ability to act in accordance with rational insight, they are reduced to a state of unfreedom (2.61.3):

δουλοῖ γὰρ φρόνημα τὸ αἰφνίδιον καὶ ἀπροσδόκητον καὶ τὸ πλείστῳ παραλόγῳ ξυμβαῖνον.

For what is sudden and unexpected and happens with the greatest unexpectedness enslaves the spirit.

Pericles uses a series of substantivized neuter adjectives and participles to capture the external forces enslaving the mind (τὸ αἰφνίδιον καὶ ἀπροσδόκητον καὶ τὸ...ξυμβαῖνον). These impersonal factors fill the position of the subject. The passage provides an instance of personification insofar as the verb governed by these neuter phrases refers to a human activity (viz. 'to enslave'). A further abstract noun (πλείστῳ παραλόγῳ) has been incorporated into the participial neuter substantive τὸ ξυμβαῖνον. In terms of both form and content, this last nominalized phrase stresses the notion of things happening over personal action. The passage is an exemplary version of Thucydides' depersonalizing style: an occurrence of events takes precedence over human agency and impersonal states (instead of personal agents) are used as grammatical subjects.

---

[33] On γιγνώσκω in a volitional sense, see LSJ s.v. A.II.1.

Parry points out that the unfreedom in question is not 'political slavery, but that other kind to which all men are subject – the slavery to outside things which break in on human calculation, subdue the judgment and **annihilate decision** [my emphasis]'.[34] The style of the passage expresses the aspect of events highlighted by Parry: the unpredictability of external occurrences is represented as an alien force, simultaneously agent and mindless, and unresponsive to human plans and aspirations.

The notion of enslavement, coupled with the depersonalizing implications of Thucydides' style, shows that the question at stake in Pericles' last speech is whether the Athenians can preserve their power of choice or whether they will forsake it. Michael Frede stresses that the Greeks tended to conceive of choice by analogy with political freedom, and he explains this notion as follows:

> It is crucial that this freedom [i.e. the political freedom that provides the blueprint for the Greek notion of choice]...almost invariably seems to be understood as a freedom from external constraints which go beyond the acceptable constraints involved in living in a political community and which would systematically prevent one from doing what it takes to have a good life. Living under a tyrant and being a slave are regarded as involving such constraints.[35]

These ideas shed light on Pericles' last speech. The adverse external circumstances that Pericles says 'enslave' (δουλοῖ) the Athenians' spirit (φρόνημα) play an analogous role to that held by the tyrant who enslaves people on the political plain. Just as people living under a tyrant are no longer capable of performing the actions necessary for a good life, so the Athenians cease to be capable of what it would mean to direct their city well: they are on the brink of making poor decisions that threaten to wreak havoc upon Athens. Consider in this connection the following observation made by Dihle: 'The freedom to choose, individually and collectively, the means and ends of action by intellectual effort can be drastically restricted in consequence of unfavorable conditions in the outside world such as war, hunger, or pestilence.'[36] In this way, the

---

[34] Parry 1981: 175.   [35] Frede 2011: 9.   [36] Dihle 1982: 43.

Athenians' enslavement to passion amounts to a significant diminishment of their freedom of choice.

Based on modern presumptions, one might easily misconstrue the faculty of freedom in Thucydides as the ability to do as one likes. On this view, what counts is the unencumbered freedom of the will, regardless of whether a choice is sensible or not. At the extreme, this includes the possibility to act absurdly, irrationally, wickedly, or self-destructively. By contrast, the Greeks (including Pericles in Thucydides) conceive of choice differently. For them, it is not a matter of doing as one likes but of acting in accordance with reason. It follows that human beings exercise their power of choice when they act based on their reason-based cognition of the right (and therefore good) course of action.[37] The power to make choices is forsaken when one acts, not according to reason, but from irrational passions that arise in concert with dramatic shifts in external circumstances.

When φρόνημα, which refers to spiritedness in the sense of confidence anchored in rational discernment,[38] is no longer able to assert itself, human beings are reduced to a state in which powers other than reason (exemplified by the various nominalized neuters at 2.61.3) come to dominate them. Whereas the exercise of reason enables human beings to realize their power of choice, the prevalence of passion signifies their subjection to an alien force that Pericles captures through language whose impersonal character highlights the breakdown of choice. As Dodds observes, this view of passion as external to the personal self

---

[37] Frede (2011: 27) exemplifies this deeply rooted view with regard to Aristotle's notion of choice: '[C]hoices are not explained in terms of a will but in terms of the attachment of reason to the good, however it might be conceived of, and the exercise of reason's cognitive abilities to determine how in this situation the good might best be attained.' See also Dihle (1982: 45): 'The freedom, then, to choose the ends and means of action which human beings seem to enjoy is not primarily, in the Greek view, the freedom to direct one's intention wherever one pleases. Free will does not exist in its own right as it does according to St. Augustine's anthropology. It depends on man's alleged potential ability to reach an adequate understanding of reality by his own intellectual effort.'

[38] Huart observes (1968: 469 n. 1) that in Thucydides φρόνημα never means 'thought', but suggests what LSJ renders as 'high spirit, resolution, pride' (s.v. A.II.1). However, given the wording of the preceding sentence (ταπεινὴ ὑμῶν ἡ διάνοια ἐγκαρτερεῖν ἃ ἔγνωτε, 2.61.2), for which the claim about the enslavement of φρόνημα provides an explanation (marked as such by γάρ), it is clear that φρόνημα, just like γνώμη and διάνοια, refers to resolve anchored in thought: the intellectual resonances of διάνοια (see n. 33 of this chapter) and γιγνώσκω suggest this conclusion.

originates in the Greek identification of character and knowledge, a coupling already found in Homer:

> If character is knowledge, what is not knowledge is not part of the character, but comes to a man from outside. When he acts in a manner contrary to the system of conscious dispositions which he is said to 'know,' his action is not properly his own, but has been dictated to him. In other words, unsystematised, nonrational impulses, and the acts resulting from them, tend to be excluded from the self and ascribed to an alien origin.[39]

Thucydides does not locate this alien origin of passion in divine forces, but in the universal disposition of human nature. Γνώμη must always assert itself against this force, which threatens to overwhelm the self.

Faced with the struggle between γνώμη and the forces opposed to it, Pericles prevents the Athenians' reason-based resolve from enslavement in his last speech. It is worth noting how Thucydides summarizes the effect of Pericles' speech (2.65.1):

> Τοιαῦτα ὁ Περικλῆς λέγων ἐπειρᾶτο τοὺς Ἀθηναίους τῆς τε ἐς αὐτὸν ὀργῆς παραλύειν καὶ ἀπὸ τῶν παρόντων δεινῶν ἀπάγειν τὴν γνώμην.
>
> By saying such things, Pericles sought to free the Athenians from their anger against him and to divert their mind from their present terrors.

Three key terms occur in this passage: ὀργή, τὰ παρόντα, and γνώμη. In summarizing the effect of Pericles' speech, Thucydides highlights the system of antitheses that have marked Pericles' dealings with the Athenians throughout. Another noteworthy aspect concerns the verb παραλύω that Thucydides uses to point out that Pericles 'frees' or 'releases' the Athenians from their anger.[40] As observed above, the prevalence of passion over the mind amounts to a state of enslavement: it is an alien power that dominates the mind. By contrast, the Athenians'

---

[39] Dodds 1951: 17.
[40] The usage of the verbum simplex shows that these connotations are not far to seek; see LSJ s.v. λύω A.I.2.b.

'release' from anger in the wake of Pericles' speech restores their freedom. This freedom is based on the breakthrough of intelligent resolve, which must assert itself against the perennial opponents of the power of rational choice: irrational passion and the pressure exerted by circumstances.

8.5 The Power of Choice: An Ever-Imperiled Faculty

Pericles' affirmation of choice challenges the emphasis on necessity that one finds in many other passages of Thucydides' work. This triumph of γνώμη over contrary forces, however, provides a rare exception to the general course of things. The extraordinary nature of this achievement becomes apparent in light of one of the rare authorial statements made by Thucydides on the factors that usually prevail in decision-making. The passage is found in Thucydides' account of Brasidas' instigation of rebellion among the Athenian allies in Thrace. Faced with Brasidas' attractive promises of freedom and protection, the allies badly misjudge the remaining military clout of the Athenians. Thucydides explains the reasons for the allies' heedlessness as follows (4.108.4):

τὸ δὲ πλέον βουλήσει κρίνοντες ἀσαφεῖ ἢ προνοίᾳ ἀσφαλεῖ, εἰωθότες οἱ ἄνθρωποι οὗ μὲν ἐπιθυμοῦσιν ἐλπίδι ἀπερισκέπτῳ διδόναι, ὃ δὲ μὴ προσίενται λογισμῷ αὐτοκράτορι διωθεῖσθαι.
[They underestimated the power of the Athenians] basing their judgment more on wishfulness wrapped in obscurity than on foresight based on certainty—for human beings are accustomed to entrust whatever they desire to ill-considered hope, but to thrust aside that which they do not welcome, due to the influence of calculation, which acts as an absolute ruler.

The phrase εἰωθότες ἄνθρωποι indicates that the mentality rampant among the allies reflects a constant of human nature. The allies' attitude is another example of the collective mindset that is described in general terms by Diodotus and epitomized by the Athenians on the eve of the Sicilian Expedition. For one thing, the adjective ἀσαφής should not be translated by English 'unclear' because the word does not connotate the vagueness of desire's object in the present passage. This is the case because the objective of the allies' wish (i.e. independence from Athens) is well defined. Instead, ἀσαφής evokes the same connotations conveyed by terms signifying 'absence' and 'invisibility' (the latter being an approximate byword for ἀσαφής[41]) when applied to the Athenians' obsession with Sicily:[42] all these word suggest the impenetrability of the future. The 'obscurity' that marks the allies' wishful thinking does not concern the object of their desire, but the practical circumstances that will be involved, based on a realistic estimate, in the attempt to attain this object. This kind of obscurity gives free rein to the unbridled projections of hope and desire, the passions that lure the Athenians into the realm of absent and invisible things associated with Sicily.[43] It is no coincidence that the passage about the Athenian allies also features words for hope (ἐλπίδι) and desire (ἐπιθυμοῦσιν).

The most striking element in the cited passage is the phrase λογισμὸς αὐτοκράτωρ. It is an instance of personification, depicting the allies' λογισμός (their 'calculation' or 'reasoning') as a ruler with absolute powers. Thucydides suggests that the relevant type of calculation, considering itself all-powerful (cf. αὐτοκράτωρ), overrules the obstacles that reality puts in the way of its projections. Yet, in despising what is real and limiting, the intellect becomes an instrument of illusion, a faculty that offers sham justifications. Thus, λογισμός denotes a lower mode of intellectual operation in this passage: the mind's ability to concoct speciously plausible rationalizations. In this way, 'calculation' cooperates with desire and hope by lending credence to their projections.

---

[41] Classen-Steup (iv, on 4.108.4.20) illustrate the relevant meaning of ἀσαφής by comparison with a passage from the Melian Dialogue: τὰ ἀφανῆ τῷ βούλεσθαι ὡς γιγνόμενα ἤδη θεᾶσθε ('You look at invisible things as if they were already taking place, just out of your wish for them,' 5.113). The connotations of ἀσαφής in the present passage can also be gleaned from the phrase that directly precedes the quoted excerpt: Thucydides writes that the allies were mistaken about the reality of Athenian power, specifically about 'how great it subsequently proved to be' (ὅση ὕστερον διεφάνη, 4.108.4). Thucydides sets up an antithesis between this phrase and βουλήσει κρίνοντες ἀσαφεῖ: the revelation of the reality of Athenian power, which is the decisive fact that the allies should consider in assessing their chances, is contrasted with the dimness of wishful thinking, which allows the allies to avoid facing up to the facts.

[42] The relevant passages are: περὶ τῶν ἀφανῶν καὶ μελλόντων κινδυνεύειν, 6.9.3; τὰ γὰρ διὰ πλείστου πάντες ἴσμεν θαυμαζόμενα, 11.4; δυσέρωτας εἶναι τῶν ἀπόντων, 13.1; τῆς τε ἀπούσης πόθῳ ὄψεως καὶ θεωρίας, 24.3. On the implications of the theme of 'absence' and 'invisibility' for Thucydides' account of the Sicilian Expedition, see Strauss 1964: 229; Wohl 2002: 189–90; Taylor 2010: 137–40, 154–5; Joho 2019: 142–50.

[43] On the Athenians' infatuation with hope and desire, see Chapters 4, pp. 121–3 and 133, and 6, pp. 196–201.

It is instructive to compare the idea of λογισμὸς αὐτοκράτωρ with the depiction of γνώμη as championed by Pericles. As pointed out above, γνώμη is engaged in a continual struggle with the forces opposing it: the antitheses that mark Pericles' style give visual expression to this agonistic quality. Intelligence that masters recalcitrant reality through contest and struggle is at the heart of the power of choice as Pericles conceives it. By contrast, 'calculation' playing the role of an 'absolute ruler' does not confront reality. Instead, it elevates itself above hard facts and subjects reality to idle projections. Thus, absolute rule is not the token of rationality but a symptom of wilfulness, a condition in which mental projections work in unison with hope and desire. In this connection, it deserves to be stressed that the role of λογισμός, unlike the function of γνώμη, is entirely negative: it offers justifications for *putting aside* whatever is contrary to the allies' aspirations. By contrast, the positive motives on which people act are provided by desire.

In Plato's *Republic*, it is precisely the tyrant, the bearer of absolute political power, who is enslaved to passion (573a4–b4, d7–8, e3–7). The parallel with Plato's image of the tyrant can still be taken further: the tyrant in Plato's *Republic*, just as the allies in Thucydides, is under the spell of ἐλπίς (οὐ μόνον ἀνθρώπων ἀλλὰ καὶ θεῶν ... ἐλπίζει δυνατὸς εἶναι ἄρχειν 573c4–5) and ἔρως, with the latter even being identified with a tyrant (573b6–7, c7–9, d4–5, e6–7).[44] In this way, both Thucydides and Plato highlight the same paradox: unbounded despotic power, whether it is wielded by the mind or by a political ruler, ultimately reduces its bearers to unfreedom. Moreover, Thucydides' observation that the allies have become subject to the autocratic regime of calculation recalls Frede's above-mentioned observation that the Greeks conceived of the faculty of choice as the opposite of subjection to tyrannical rule. It looks as if the allies have in fact forsaken their power of choice.

The Melian Dialogue offers an interesting parallel for the use of λογισμός. Drawing on a verb of the same lexeme (viz. λογίζομαι), the Athenian ambassadors point out that the whole parley is doomed to failure if the Melians 'have met in order to concoct suspicions about

---

[44] On the relation between ἔρως and tyranny in the passage from the *Republic* and its significance for Thucydides, see also Cornford 1907: 207–9.

future things or for any reason other than to hold counsel about the safety of your city based on things that are present and which you see' (ὑπονοίας τῶν μελλόντων λογιούμενοι ἢ ἄλλο τι ξυνήκετε ἢ ἐκ τῶν παρόντων καὶ ὧν ὁρᾶτε περὶ σωτηρίας βουλεύσοντες τῇ πόλει, 5.87). The verb λογίζομαι suggests that the mind generates unfounded rationalizations, thus recalling the use of λογισμός in the passage about the Thracian allies. Λογίζομαι is tellingly opposed to βουλεύω, the term that Diodotus uses to capture his ideal of decision-making based on rational reflection (βουλεύω and βουλεύομαι in Diodotus' speech: 3.42.1, 42.5, 44.3, 44.4, 46.1, 48.2; εὐβουλία: 42.1, 44.1). In the Melian Dialogue and in Thucydides' comment about the allies, the kind of ratiocination expressed by λογισμός and λογίζομαι is directed towards a realm that eludes verifiability: the adjective ἀσαφής in the earlier passage corresponds to the neglect of 'things that are present and which you see' (ἐκ τῶν παρόντων καὶ ὧν ὁρᾶτε) in the Melian Dialogue. A further parallel between the two passages is that this pseudo-rational make-believe cooperates with irrational impulses. In the case of the Melians, the irrational element consists in their infatuation with delusive hope (5.103.2, 113).

As Dihle has stressed, the Greeks thought that the power of choice was not simply available, but that it had to be attained, and that this accomplishment required the ascendancy of the intellect:

[T]he free use of one's own intellectual faculties which leads to...free choice or intention is...extremely rare in human life...[M]an's intellectual activity is often hindered or led astray by necessities and compulsions from outside, from his own desires, emotions, and passions.[45]

This account recalls an observation made with regard to Homeric epic in Section 7.2 (pp. 238–9): in Homer scope for independent choices is not a natural endowment of every mortal, but a hallmark of the greatest heroes. In a similar way, Pericles' aptitude for decision-making is exceptional. It is far more common that passion rules and that the intellect is

---

[45] Dihle 1982: 45–6.

not in abeyance. In this case, thought becomes subservient to irrational impulse, which capitalizes on reasoning to achieve its goals. Under these circumstances, thought loses its way. People, instead of authoring their decisions by following the lead of rational thought that has mastered passion, fall under the sway of the 'absolute ruler'. The Melians and the Athenian allies are both caught up in this situation and have forsaken the power of choice. The necessities in the outside world and within human nature have become the powers driving human action. As Dihle writes, Greek writers thought that this situation obtained far more frequently than genuine freedom of choice. Commenting on the Athenian allies in Thrace, Thucydides points out that human beings customarily surrender themselves to hope and desire and enthrone wishful thinking as an absolute ruler. Thus, despite the Periclean exception, he regards people's loss of the capacity to make rational choices as the default situation.

8.6 The Equivocalness of γνώμη

Thucydides' account of Pericles features some passages in which the word γνώμη is best rendered as 'frame of mind', a significance that is less determinate than the more specific 'intelligence', 'judgment', or 'resolve'. Huart points out that γνώμη does not necessarily bear the connotations of rationality when it suggests 'frame of mind', and that the word can refer to a mindset dominated by passion.[46] In the account of Pericles' struggle with the Athenians' angry impulses, Thucydides points out that the Athenians are 'reduced to a perplexed state of mind' (τῇ γνώμῃ ἄποροι καθεστῶτες, 2.59.2) and highlights, in one of the distinctive neuter phrases, the 'angry state affecting [*sc.* the Athenians'] frame of mind' (τὸ ὀργιζόμενον τῆς γνώμης, 2.59.3). Against the background of the repeated reference in the same section to Pericles' γνώμη in the sense of 'intelligence', 'judgment', and 'resolve' (1.140.1, 2.22.1, 2.34.6, 2.55.2, 2.65.8), Thucydides' choice of the same word for the Athenians' irrational state of mind is likely to be meaningful.

[46] Huart 1973: 28–9.

Thucydides uses γνώμη in yet a further sense, which again bears on the juxtaposition between Pericles and the Athenians. Edmunds notes a sustained opposition between Pericles' single and steadfast γνώμη, understood as rational judgment with positive normative connotations, and the many γνῶμαι of the Athenians, which denote the Athenians' divided or shifting 'opinions' (1.139.4, 2.59.1).[47] The following point made by Dihle sheds light on this opposition: 'A change in one's intention...is in general not very favorably looked upon..., regardless from which kind of influence [sc. whether rational or irrational] it results, for it always implies that one of the two intentions is or was based on error.'[48] Thus, Pericles' steadfast and unitary γνώμη does not change because it is based on cognition of the truth, whereas the multiplicity of the Athenians' γνῶμαι suggests that their actions proceed from mere opinions, which are disconnected from rational insight.[49]

It is remarkable that Thucydides characterizes contrary tendencies that come into open conflict with each other by one and the same word (i.e. γνώμη), which he applies to both Pericles and the Athenians. This pointed equivocalness draws attention to a connection between the opposite poles marked by Pericles' intelligence and by the mental states of the demos (i.e. their impassionate mindset and their shifting opinions). The modus operandi distinctive of Athens is based on the ideal of mastering the outside world by putting mind in charge over matter. The Athenians do not filter their decisions through a strict code of conduct sanctioned by tradition, but they require people to make up their mind about the affairs of their city in response to each new situation. This approach stands in glaring contrast with the Spartans' steadfast reliance on their inherited ways.[50] The problem with the Athenian approach is

---

[47] Edmunds 1975: 10. For γνώμη in the sense of 'opinion', see also Snell 1924: 32–3; Huart 1973: 120–8.

[48] Dihle 1982: 30–1.

[49] Apropos Pericles' dealings with the Athenians, Wohl (2017: 450) rightly draws attention to the connection between the unimpaired exercise of human intelligence and the steadfastness that is part and parcel of such intelligence: '[I]t is by adhering steadfastly to his policy in the face of their anger that he proves his superior intelligence.' Once again, intelligent insight and steadfast resolution amount to the same thing, both aspects expressed by the Periclean variant of the γνώμη.

[50] Archidamus' speech at the Spartan assembly in book 1 provides evidence for this conception of the Spartans' principle of action. According to Archidamus, the Spartans are 'well-advised because we are educated with too little learning to be capable of contempt of our laws

that the direction taken by such mental projections is fundamentally open: the mind can manifest itself as intelligent judgment, but it can also be dominated by lack of insight or even raging passion. Thus, the Athenians run the risk of fluctuating between the extremes of intelligent design and rampant folly. In equal measure, the high and the low rest on the enthronement of the mind over the city's affairs. For this reason, γνώμη captures both the supreme insight of Pericles and the irrational forces opposing his political wisdom. Thucydides implies that the power capable of conquering irrationality and achieving freedom can easily change into its opposite. Given this ambiguity, it seems unlikely that Athens will master the spectre of necessity once and for all, notwithstanding the intermittent ascendancy of rationality that Pericles achieves.

A similar equivocalness as the one between the different variants of γνώμη attaches itself to the term ὀργή. As observed in Section 8.3 (p. 282), Thucydides repeatedly uses this word to capture the Athenians' affliction by collective anger, a state that incites them to rebel against Periclean γνώμη. This methodical antithesis between ὀργή and γνώμη can also be found at the opening of Pericles' first speech: '[I know],' says Pericles, 'that human beings do not display the same mindset when they are persuaded to go to war as when they are in the midst of the action, but that in response to circumstances they also change their opinions' (εἰδὼς τοὺς ἀνθρώπους οὐ τῇ αὐτῇ ὀργῇ

---

and customs (τῶν νόμων) and with too much self-restraint, combined with severity, to disobey them' (εὔβουλοι δὲ [γιγνόμεθα] ἀμαθέστερον τῶν νόμων τῆς ὑπεροψίας παιδευόμενοι καὶ ξὺν χαλεπότητι σωφρονέστερον ἢ ὥστε αὐτῶν ἀνηκουστεῖν, 1.84.3). In translating τῶν νόμων as 'laws and customs', I follow Gundert's rendition of the passage (1968 [1940]: 117). Archidamus goes on to point out that the Spartans think 'that he is strongest whoever is educated amid the severest compulsions' (κράτιστον...εἶναι ὅστις ἐν τοῖς ἀναγκαιοτάτοις παιδεύεται, 1.84.4). According to Classen-Steup (i, on 1.84.4.24), this phrase refers to Spartan education, which operates 'in a manner that leaves no freedom to the will' ('so dass seinem Willen keine Wahl gelassen bleibt') and 'by imposing the most unrelenting precepts and demands' ('unter den unerbittlichsten Vorschriften und Forderungen'). In contrast to a system that leaves hardly any room to the independent initiative of the human intellect, Pericles considers those to be 'strongest' (κράτιστοι, 2.40.3) who combine knowledge (οἱ τά τε δεινὰ καὶ ἡδέα σαφέστατα γιγνώσκοντες) with courage (μὴ ἀποτρεπόμενοι ἐκ τῶν κινδύνων). Whereas Archidamus considers 'lack of learning' (expressed by the adjective ἀμαθής) an asset of the Spartans, Pericles takes recourse to the adverbial variant of the same word (ἀμαθῶς, 1.140.1) in order to envision the forces, the folly of events as well as the bad human planning, that might oppose the aspirations of Athens. The issue of 'lack of learning' marks out the fundamental difference between Sparta and Athens: it is anathema to the Athenian spirit, but an intrinsic component of Spartan identity.

ἀναπειθομένους τε πολεμεῖν καὶ ἐν τῷ ἔργῳ πράσσοντας, πρὸς δὲ τὰς ξυμφορὰς καὶ τὰς γνώμας τρεπομένους, 1.140.1). In this passage, ὀργή does not suggest 'anger' but 'mindset' or 'mentality'.[51] As compared with the conflict between Pericles and the Athenians in book 2, γνώμη and ὀργή play reversed roles: ὀργή captures a sober mindset aligned with rational thought whereas γνῶμαι are the changing opinions that lose sight of the right course of action. Just prior to the quoted passage, Pericles has pointed out that his γνώμη is the same as always (τῆς ... γνώμης ... αἰεὶ τῆς αὐτῆς ἔχομαι, 1.140.1). Not least through the shared stress on sameness (τῆς γνώμης ... τῆς αὐτῆς and τῇ αὐτῇ ὀργῇ), ὀργή and the type of γνώμη represented by Pericles are aligned. Therefore, just as γνώμη can suggest two contrary states, one enlightened and one irrational, the same holds true of ὀργή.

Exploring the ambiguity of the terms γνώμη and ὀργή, Thucydides gives the reader a subtle hint that the greatest achievements and the most severe dangers are intimately related. They represent two sides of one and the same phenomenon. Along similar lines, the Chorus of Sophocles' *Antigone* observes that nothing is more δεινόν than man (332-3): a creature that inspires 'awe', thus equally evoking wonder and inspiring terror. Another example of this thought can be found in Aeschylus' *Agamemnon*, where the Chorus conclude their song of victory with the wish that they may never become sackers of cities (472-4). In this way, the Chorus forge a link between the conquest of Troy and the acts of sacrilege committed in its wake. The former marks the height of heroic achievement and is carried out at the behest of Zeus, whereas the latter inevitably attracts divine punishment. Aeschylus lets these stark contrasts stand next to each other: the dark underside of superlative deeds does not render their positive counterpart invalid. Instead, ambiguity is part and parcel of the very greatest achievements.

According to Thucydides, the same tragic ambivalence holds true of the highpoint of human achievement reached by Athenian γνώμη under the aegis of Pericles. It is a hallmark of the Athenians to entrusts the

---

[51] See LSJ s.v. A.I. Huart offers the translation 'disposition d'esprit' (1968: 157). Classen-Steup suggest 'Sinnesweise' (i, on 1.130.2.11) as a rendition of ὀργή at 1.130.2, citing 1.140.1 as evidence for the same significance.

affairs of their city to the power of conception. This endeavour can lead either to the triumph of thought over reality or to the chaos of ill-conceived decisions induced by passion and volatile opinions. The extremes are related to each other. For the time being, Pericles carries the day. Nonetheless, Thucydides does not let the reader lose sight of the fact that this victory is unlikely to be permanent: it is won by a force that may flip and morph into its opposite all too easily.

8.7 Conclusion: Intimations of Periclean Pessimism

It is noteworthy, and perhaps no coincidence, that in his last speech Pericles makes a statement that ranks among the strongest acknowledgements of necessity in Thucydides' work.

Just when he stresses the eternal perpetuity of Athenian fame, Pericles makes an aside that reveals that he considers Athens no exception to the general drift of all things (2.64.3):

πάντα γὰρ πέφυκε καὶ ἐλασσοῦσθαι
For all things are predisposed by nature also to decline.

This is a surprising turn given that this speech represents Pericles' largely successful effort to strengthen the reason-based resolve of his fellow countrymen.[52] Hunter has drawn attention to the statement's strong implications of necessity: 'The biological metaphor of natural decline...is one of the first hints of inevitability in the *History*. For once the destructive force of *anthropeia physis* is released, the process of history, which began in unity and growth, must "run its course", and end in division, disintegration, and decline. This is *ananke*, inherent necessity.'[53]

---

[52] Compare Pouncey's (1980: 32) summary of the general impression that this speech conveys: '[T]he speaker Pericles is not, in Thucydides' judgment, diminished by the plague, but rather has his status enhanced by it, emerging at the end of a final uncompromising speech with his consistency intact, in splendid isolation as the "First Man".'

[53] Hunter 1982: 173. On the same passage, see also Hunter 1973: 181.

In expounding this general rule, Pericles draws on several features that are characteristic of the depersonalizing style: a substantivized neuter (πάντα) is combined with an intransitive perfect verb that has the same root as φύσις. Moreover, the phrase is suggestive of process as opposed to agency: the word ἐλασσοῦσθαι ('become small') belongs to the same register as, for instance, the point about the Athenians' 'becoming great' (μεγάλους γιγνομένους, 1.23.6) from the passage on the true causes of the War. Rise and fall are represented as processes that happen to cities, developments that are rooted in the way things are. They are expressions of the perennial growth and vanishing that the Greeks called φύσις.[54] Yet there is also another aspect to φύσις, which is to some extent contrary to the notion of growth: reflecting the settled outcome of a process, φύσις also refers to the constitution of an entity, designating the limits within which it behaves. The perfect aspect of the intransitive form πέφυκε highlights this aspect: the structural set-up of all entities predetermines that they will eventually decline. Thus, in the very speech in which Pericles vigorously calls on the Athenians to withstand the urges of human nature, he acknowledges that φύσις will prevail in the long run, and that the Athenian empire, like all other things, will fade away.

Even Pericles' first speech, which is emphatically optimistic with regard to the Athenians' prospects in the War, contains a striking observation about the wilful quasi-agent that directs the course of events in defiance of human purposes (1.140.1):

ἐνδέχεται γὰρ τὰς ξυμφορὰς τῶν πραγμάτων οὐχ ἧσσον ἀμαθῶς χωρῆσαι ἢ καὶ τὰς διανοίας τοῦ ἀνθρώπου.

For it is possible for the vagaries of events to proceed no less ignorantly than the plans of humans do as well.[55]

---

[54] On the meaning of φύσις, in particular its double significance (growth vs. constitution), see Schadewaldt 1970b [1960]: 514–15; Bremer 1989: 242–50; Rechenauer 1991: 116–19; Naddaf 2005: 3; Hadot 2006: 17–19.

[55] As Classen-Steup (i, on 1.140.1.10) and Poppo-Stahl i, 1, ad loc. point out, τοῦ ἀνθρώπου is used generically here.

It is not easy to understand what exactly Pericles is claiming in this passage. The immediate context provides some important cues. The passage serves as a justification for Pericles' claim, which precedes the quoted passage, that those Athenians who support Pericles' uncompromising stance now should continue to do so even if Athens were to fail in some venture during the upcoming War (1.140.1).[56] Pericles anticipates that, in case of failure, they will renounce their previous support and blame Pericles: they will say that his plan has 'proceeded ignorantly', i.e. that his plan was ill-conceived and is therefore responsible for their failure. Pericles takes the notion that 'the plans of humans proceed ignorantly' to be common sense: the comparison between 'events proceeding ignorantly' no less than 'plans of humans' implies that the latter notion is familiar, but that the former is not. The point of the analogy is that one must not overlook the fact that an irrationality of events exists 'as well' (καὶ τὰς διανοίας τοῦ ἀνθρώπου).[57]

The conclusion of the very same sentence shows what exactly Pericles has in mind when referring to the 'ignorance' of events: 'it is in fact because of this [i.e. because events run ignorantly] that we tend to blame τύχη for whatever comes to pass contrary to rational calculation' (δι' ὅπερ καὶ τὴν τύχην, ὅσα ἂν παρὰ λόγον ξυμβῇ, εἰώθαμεν αἰτιᾶσθαι, 1.140.1). Pericles' point is that people's normal name for the 'ignorance of events' is τύχη, unpredictable 'chance'. It follows that Pericles' reference to the ignorance of events denotes the unforeseeable, even absurd, course that they might take. The adverb ἀμαθῶς suggests that events have not learned what they should if they were reason-guided, namely that they should run according to rational forecast. To quote Pelling's paraphrase: events apparently 'haven't read the script'.[58] The most prudent

---

[56] Note that the conditional clause in which Pericles mentions the possibility of Athenian failure is introduced by ἢν ἄρα (ἢν ἄρα τι καὶ σφαλλώμεθα, 1.140.1). The construction expresses that Pericles considers it unlikely or undesirable that the hypothesis will come true: 'if it so happens that we fail in anything' (cf. K-G ii. 324; Sm. 2796). Given the prophetic quality of Pericles' statement (see below), it seems more appropriate that ἢν ἄρα conveys undesirability rather than unlikelihood in this passage.

[57] The following paraphrase by Gomme boils Pericles' statement down to its essence: '"we may suffer disaster (ἢν ἄρα τι καὶ σφαλλώμεθα), for (though a man make a wise decision) the turn of events may prove as unwise as the plans of men", "fortune may support the wrong side"' (HCT i, on 1.140.1).

[58] Pelling 2019: 49. Notice also Sir Ronald Syme's (1962: 56) summary of the issue: '[Pericles] reminds them that events can turn out stupidly, just like the designs of men (i.140.1)...You cannot teach events. They are stubborn, but reason is all we have.' See also Parry 1981: 155, and Hornblower i, ad loc. (citing Syme approvingly).

policy, such as Pericles' war plan, may come to naught when faced with this irreducible irrationality of events.

Pericles' ascription of ignorance and planning to events involves an unusual idea: impersonal, objective occurrences are depicted as if they were conscious beings. Pericles likens events to independent agents over which human control is limited. He can influence the Athenians in order to prevent them from letting their plans 'proceed ignorantly', but he has no ultimate influence over the freakishness of events. Reality pursues its own erratic purposes, which override the rational conceptions of human agents.

In the final analysis, there is an ironic twist to Pericles' statement. The Athenians will soon be confronted with the recalcitrant refusal of events to learn when Athens is struck by the plague, which Thucydides says is 'stronger than λόγος' (2.50.1),[59] and which Pericles calls both 'stronger than expectation' (2.64.1) and an example of τὰ δαιμόνια (2.64.2). Given the failure of the plague to conform to Pericles' rational planning, it is a paradigmatic case of 'the vagaries of events proceeding ignorantly'. The irony consists in the fact that the irreducible irrationality of external events will ultimately not be responsible for the Athenians' defeat in the War. Instead, the responsibility will rest with the Athenians' own folly, which is reflected in their failure to adhere closely to Pericles' plan. In the valedictory passage, Thucydides observes that the Athenians acted contrary to Pericles' war strategy in all its various aspects (2.65.7), and that this caused their ultimate defeat in the War.

Verbal parallels between the passage from Pericles' first speech and the valedictory passage show that Pericles' remarks about the ignorance of events and human plans are meant to anticipate the eventual defeat of Athens. As already mentioned, in the sentence preceding the claim about the ignorance of events, Pericles calls on those Athenians who will follow his advice to continue supporting the collective decision, 'if it so happens that we fail in some way' (ἢν ἄρα τι καὶ σφαλλώμεθα, 1.140.1), 'or else not to

---

[59] Connor draws attention to the polysemy of the phrase: while the standard translation ('the nature of the distemper was such as to baffle all description', Connor 1984: 100) reflects the meaning of λόγος as 'speech', the other sense of λόγος (namely 'rational analysis') is in play as well. Thus, the phrase also suggests 'that the plague surpasses the faculty for rational discourse' (Connor 1984: 100).

lay claim to intelligent insight if we are successful' (μηδὲ κατορθοῦντας τῆς ξυνέσεως μεταποιεῖσθαι, 1.140.1). The antithesis between the possibilities of failure and success, between ἤν... σφαλλώμεθα and κατορθοῦντας, recurs, with the identical wording, in Thucydides' remarks about Pericles' short-sighted successors in the valedictory passage: the successors' policies were merely advantageous to individual leaders 'as long as they were successful' (κατορθούμενα μέν, 2.65.7); but 'when they failed' (σφαλέντα δέ, 2.65.7), they brought ruin to the entire state. The verbal parallel shows that Pericles' acknowledgement of the possibility of defeat is prophetic, but with a twist: it is the 'plans of humans', and not 'the vagaries of events', whose inability to be instructed results in the defeat. The strand of irrationality that inevitably besets human nature causes the ultimate downfall of the city.

Pericles in fact foresees this twist. At another place in his first speech, he calls on the Athenians not to extend the empire while at war and not to incur self-chosen danger. In this connection, he voices the following concern: 'For I fear our own mistakes more than the plans of our opponents' (μᾶλλον γὰρ πεφόβημαι τὰς οἰκείας ἡμῶν ἁμαρτίας ἢ τὰς τῶν ἐναντίων διανοίας, 1.144.1). In this passage, the word for 'plans' (διανοίας) recalls the 'plans of humans' at 1.140.1. Pericles does not worry about their opponents' 'planning': given the Spartans' self-identification with 'ignorance' (ἀμαθέστερον... παιδευόμενοι, 1.84.3) and their disdain of cleverness (τὰ ἀχρεῖα ξυνετοὶ ἄγαν ὄντες, 1.84.3), their 'plans' certainly proceed 'ignorantly'. Yet Pericles worries, and with no little justification, that Athenian mistakes will ultimately come down to the same result: 'mistakes' and 'plans proceeding ignorantly' are two different names for the same thing—the eternal spectacle of human folly.

Edith Foster has highlighted a paradox that runs through Thucydides' presentation of Pericles. On the one hand, Pericles displays clear awareness of the fragility of Athenian power; on the other hand, he highlights the Athenians' impregnable control of an entire element of the world (viz. the sea), an achievement bursting the limits that reality ordinarily imposes on human endeavours.[60] Against the background of Pericles' rational leadership, the account presented in the foregoing paragraphs amounts to a similar paradox. In several passages, Pericles asserts the

---

[60] Foster 2010: 186–7.

ultimate priority of wilful events over human action: events are represented as intractable agents pursuing an erratic agenda of their own (1.140.1); all things are by nature bound to decline (2.64.3); and thought and judgment tend to be enslaved by the unpredictable waywardness of chance (2.61.3, cf. Section 8.4, pp. 291–2). In addition, Thucydides' stress on the ambiguity that affects the terms γνώμη and ὀργή highlights the fragility of Pericles' achievement: the faculty that achieves freedom is likely to undermine itself, succumbing to irrational outbursts and the volatility of fluctuating opinions. And yet, Pericles' success in eliciting rational action proves that human beings are not entirely impotent. Pericles combines clear awareness of the ultimate futility of human efforts with a forceful determination to leave his mark in the here and now. He proves that natural necessity does not render reason-guided agency simply impossible. Yet even Pericles must acknowledge that in the long run the forces of necessity will carry the day.

Conclusion

The Exception of Pericles and the Persistence of Necessity

This book has argued that necessity prevails in the world of interstate politics according to Thucydides. Yet Pericles' effective political leadership might seem to pose a challenge to this argument. In order to address this, let us consider the results of the preceding chapters together and explain how the two polar opposites of agency and necessity can coexist.

As we saw in Chapter 7, the version of necessity applicable to Thucydides does not imply predetermination of every single event, a view that would entail Thucydides' belief in a mechanistic universe. In Thucydides, just as in Homer and Herodotus, necessity can be compared to a frame that settles what happens at the most far-reaching junctions. The inevitability of these events is based on innate natural dispositions that weigh on political communities: the quest for power combined with a predisposition for sprawling irrational impulses and a proneness to domination by the pressure of circumstances. These inevitable predispositions will sooner or later wreak havoc. According to Hunter, their release gives rise to the logic of process.[1] In this way, necessity manifests itself, not in a deterministic causal chain that preordains every event, but in the inevitability of specific dispositions that will erupt at some point, thus causing mad decisions and thereby inducing a process that leads to disaster. The coming of the Peloponnesian War or the downfall of Athens are examples of this. These momentous occurrences inevitably take place due to underlying conditions. To be unleashed, these dispositions

---

[1] Hunter 1982: 231.

require specific events to play the role of catalysts. The 'reasons' or 'complaints' (αἰτίαι, 1.23.6) facilitating the outbreak of the Peloponnesian War are a prime example: in the terminology introduced by Pelling, they are the 'triggers' that enable an underlying disposition to come forth.[2]

Nevertheless, considerable scope remains within the context of a predetermined final outcome. The empty spaces left by necessity typically concern the timing and the road towards the most consequential occurrences. Flexibility in these areas affords scope for the intervention of agents and gives them an opportunity to influence the specific course of events. The pull of necessity qualifies the choices of these agents, but it does not erase the possibility that choices take place.

Based on these premises, Pericles is able to direct the Athenians to choose the opportune moment for the inevitable war with Sparta and to fight it on terms that suit Athens: namely, the Athenians should exercise control over the sea, keep a tight rein on the allies, withdraw behind the walls of city, and avoid large land battles against the invading force. The downfall of Athens might well have been put off for a considerable time if Pericles had lived longer, or if at least some of his successors had adhered to his high standard, which combines political wisdom and personal authority.

The intervention of Pericles presupposes a model of causation different from the theory of cause and effect, a specifically modern notion often taken to imply determinism. The alternative model of explaining events, presupposed not just by Thucydides but also by other Greek authors, is based on the idea that entities with inherent properties interact with each other, and that one of these items ultimately asserts itself over the other. By approaching Thucydides with these ideas in mind, one finds that natural impulse is usually stronger than reason and moderation, yet it is not impossible (though rare) that individual agents are capable of restraining irrationality and excess. In this role, individuals act as opponents of human nature and help to assert temporarily the predominance of reason. In counteracting disruptive natural forces, the Athenians favour the method of encouraging exceptional individual

---

[2] Pelling 2000: 88.

leaders to devise an intelligent plan that is suited to the particular situation that confronts the city. This model is best exemplified by Pericles and Themistocles. Thucydides explicitly highlights the exceptional qualities of both men in some of his rare authorial statements (Themistocles: 1.138.3; Pericles: 1.139.4, 2.65.5–13). Sparta presents an alternative model: according to Archidamus (1.84.3–4), the Spartan method is based on the collective inculcation of an obligatory code of conduct geared towards the suppression of the innate forces that threaten to throw the Spartan state into turmoil.

It is crucial that Thucydides emphasizes the rare qualities of Pericles. It requires political leadership of an exceptional calibre to make good use of the scope for agency. It is tantamount to the unlikely triumph of mind over matter, a feat enacted by the antitheses that mark Pericles' oratorical style, with γνώμη systematically set against the forces that oppose it: passion and external circumstances. For this reason, it would be wrong to conclude from Pericles' largely successful interventions that Thucydides gives general priority to the agency of reason-guided individuals over the impersonal forces that run contrary to it. Individuals of Pericles' mould do not emerge frequently enough to become the dominant factor in Thucydides' account. Pericles shows the possibility of exceptions, but he does not disprove the thesis concerning necessity. The presence of destructive dispositions is permanent: the quest for power is predisposed to overreach and spin out of control, and irrational impulses always lie in wait for their chance to burst forth. In addition, the thrust of circumstances provides temptations that lead cities astray (e.g. the Sicilian Expedition, the secession of Mytilene, or the revolt of the Athenian allies at Thrace) and catastrophic reversals that reduce them to panic and anger (e.g. the plague or the Spartan defeat at Pylos). These tendencies are always operative, whether subdued or fully unleashed. They may be temporarily controlled and redirected, and individual agents may play a crucial role in containing them provided that they are capable of elevating themselves beyond these general dispositions so as to follow the insights provided by unimpaired reason. According to Thucydides, rational action thus understood means freedom, a faculty that is not a matter of course, but that must constantly be achieved (see Section 8.5). Free agency capable of rational self-assertion requires an exceptional degree of intelligence and discipline, whereas the craving for power and the susceptibility to collective impulses are ever-present. Sooner or later, these dispositions will come out on top: if not in every specific individual, then certainly in political collectives.

Against the thesis concerning necessity, one might argue that an infinite series of leaders following the Periclean model might have been able to guarantee the permanence of Athenian success. Yet, this position fails to take account of the engrained general disposition of human nature: it is not humanly possible for a city to produce the required number of outstanding individuals. What is more, the Spartan ambassadors at Athens advance the thesis that the more successful a city is, the more prone it becomes to succumb to the irrational impulses threatening to erupt at any time (4.17.3–4). As we saw in Chapter 5 (pp. 170 and 181–2), Diodotus' deliberations about human nature (3.45.4–5) have much in common with the view expressed by the Spartan ambassadors. Moreover, their account resonates with Thucydides' own representation of the mentality that prevails at Athens in the wake of Pylos (4.65.4, see Chapter 5, pp. 179–80). The insights of the Spartan ambassadors applied to the case of Pericles lead to the conclusion that the more successfully a city adopts wholesome, reason-based policies, the harder it will become to sustain this path. This paradoxical situation obtains because success calls forth the inclination to give free rein to impulses such as hope and desire. As Pouncey puts it, 'human nature carries within itself drives that are destructive of its own achievements..., so that in a sense the way up and the way down are one and the same.'[3]

The constellation of these factors leads to an inevitable downward spiral: while the task of guiding a city becomes ever more formidable, the prevailing conditions constantly undermine the likelihood that the required type of political leader will emerge. Perhaps Diodotus provides the only example of a post-Periclean statesman who could possibly guide Athens on the right path if circumstances were to permit it. According to Didodotus, however, at Athens the speakers wishing to promote 'the

---

[3] Pouncey 1980: xiii. Pelling (2019: 198) notes that the same idea emerges from Herodotus' presentation of Persian history: 'Persia's story has shown one way in which strengths and weaknesses can combine, even interact: the same qualities that generate Persian success can persuade a ruler to overreach.'

better course' for the city (τὸν τὰ ἀμείνω λέγοντα, 3.43.2) must speak deceitfully if they want to succeed. As Manuwald has argued, this requirement of deception applies not least to Diodotus himself.[4] The constraints faced by a speaker in these circumstances stands in sharp contrast with Pericles' forthrightness in addressing the Athenians (2.65.8). It seems that a speaker's room for manoeuvre has been drastically reduced in the few years that separate the Periclean speeches from the Mytilenean Debate. Diodotus can merely have an isolated effect on one particular occasion, but he cannot provide continuous guidance in the footsteps of Pericles. It stands to reason that circumstances have made it considerably harder for personal agents to restrain the destructive potentials of human nature.

So much for the problem of necessity. What are the implications of Thucydides' account of Pericles for our other topic: the question of style? Pericles' oratory is marked by a set of distinctive antitheses: γνώμη, intelligence combined with resoluteness in action, is systematically contrasted with words for passion and for external circumstances, and these antitheses are expressed either through parallelism or through contrast with syntactic variation (see Chapter 8, pp. 283–5). These antitheses fall into place according to a rationally organized, comprehensive system. They imply that Pericles imposes a similarly systematic order on the waywardness of political reality. In addition, they also suggest that the mind functions as the focal point of this Periclean scheme by holding the various antitheses together. The system of antitheses suggests that mind pervades raw matter and domesticates the recalcitrant forces of pure φύσις. The implications of this feature of Pericles' oratory stand in marked contrast to the depersonalizing style that contains impersonal subjects, emphasis on things happening over people acting, and suggestions of passivity. The picture that Pericles projects presents mind, not as subject to impersonal forces, but as capable of resisting and channelling them. According to Pericles, the prior faculty of mind capitalizes on the

---

[4] Manuwald 1979: 409–10.

factualness of the external world and the vigour of passions, drawing contrary forces into a cooperation that ultimately energizes each of the two opposite poles (see Chapter 8, pp. 285–9). Pericles' style expresses the idea that room remains to oppose and modify the necessities confronting political life: although φύσις cannot be rendered inoperative, the intellect can domesticate it, at least for a while and to some extent. Pericles offers the Athenians an internal perspective on this struggle of mind with matter by making it an integral component of his language. Language shapes reality by presenting a vivid picture of mind's self-assertion, thus giving tangible shape to an energizing ideal, which the Athenians internalize as they listen to Pericles' speeches. As a result, λόγος, encompassing intellect and language, comes to dominate the outside world, a reversal of the situation prevailing under stasis when external forces subdue both thought and language.

At various places, Pericles himself stresses the intractability of reality in the face of rational planning (1.140.1, 2.64.1–2) and accepts the ultimate necessity of decline as a given (2.64.3). In a similar vein, Diodotus holds that it is impossible to overcome human nature when it is unleashed (3.45.7). Nevertheless, Pericles and Diodotus clearly show that interventions of individual agents can, in fact, have a salutary impact on the course of events. This tension between a pessimistic theoretical outlook and successful practical action is reminiscent of a thesis advanced by Jacob Burckhardt and Friedrich Nietzsche. They both thought that one of the distinguishing features of Greek mentality was its reconciliation of a high degree of pessimism in thought with powerful optimism in practical matters.[5] Thucydides' presentation of Pericles provides evidence for this conjunction of optimism and pessimism: in

---

[5] Burckhardt 1977, ii.363: 'The most baffling aspect of the entire phenomenon of Greek pessimism is the staunch optimism of the Greek temperament. At its deepest root, it is creative, plastic, and worldly; in addition, it is very much given (at least on the surface) to the full use and enjoyment of the present moment' [my translation]. In one of his posthumously published notes, Nietzsche (*NL* 1875: 5 [70], *KSA* viii. 60) describes the character of the Greeks as follows: 'Their way of intuitively grasping misery, combined with the happy genius of their temperament' [my translation]. See also the following passage from the *Birth of Tragedy* (*KSA* i. 35–6): 'Greek man knew and felt the horror and the direness of existence: in order to be able to live at all, he had to overlay these things with the brilliant product of a dream: the Olympians... He considers living under the bright sunshine of these gods as the paragon of everything worth striving for' [my translation].

his last speech he ultimately contains the irrational impulses that have come to beset the Athenians (2.65.1) while acknowledging in the same speech that all things human are bound to fall apart in the long run (2.64.3). To use a summary formula coined by Henning Ritter:[6] intellectual pessimism coexists alongside temperamental optimism. Thus, thanks to Pericles, a moderately uplifting thought concludes this study of the sombre implications of Thucydides' depersonalizing style.

---

[6] Ritter (2011: 263): 'Pessimismus des Intellekts und Optimismus des Temperaments.'

Bibliography

Abbreviations

Alberti — G. B. Alberti (ed.), *Thucydidis historiae*, 3 vols. (Istituto Poligrafico e Zecca dello Stato: Rome, 1972–2000)
Boehme-Widmann — G. Boehme and S. Widmann (eds.) *Thukydides*, 6th ed., 9 vols. (Leipzig: Teubner, 1894)
Classen-Steup — J. Classen and J. Steup (eds.), *Thukydides*, 8 vols. (Berlin: Weidmann; vols. 1 and 2: 5th ed., 1914–19; vols. 3–8: 3rd ed., 1892–1922)
Crawley — R. Crawley, *The Complete Writings of Thucydides: The Peloponnesian War*, tr. R. Crawley, ed. J. H. Finley, Jr (New York: Modern Library, 1951)
DK — H. Diels and W. Kranz (eds.), *Die Fragmente der Vorsokratiker*, 3 vols. 6th ed. (Berlin: Weidmann, 1951–2)
GP — J. D. Denniston, *The Greek Particles*, 2nd ed. (Oxford: Oxford University Press, 1954)
HCT — A. W. Gomme, A. Andrewes, and K. J. Dover, *A Historical Commentary on Thucydides*, 5 vols. (Oxford: Oxford University Press, 1945–81)
Hornblower — S. Hornblower, *A Commentary on Thucydides*, 3 vols. (Oxford: Oxford University Press, 1991–2008)
K-G — R. Kühner and B. Gerth, *Ausführliche Grammatik der griechischen Sprache, zweiter Teil: Satzlehre*, 2 vols. (Hannover: Hahnsche Buchhandlung, 1898–1904)
Krüger — K. W. Krüger (ed.), Θουκυδίδου ξυγγραφή, 2 vols. (Berlin: Krüger's Verlagsbuchhandlung; vol. 1.1: 3rd ed., 1860; vols. 1.2–2: 2nd ed., 1858–61)
LSJ — H. Liddell and R. Scott, revised by H. S. Jones, *Greek–English Lexicon*, 9th ed. (Oxford: Oxford University Press, 1940), with suppl. by P. G. W. Glare et al., 1996
OCT — H. Stuart Jones, *Thucydides historiae*, rev. by J. E. Powell, 2 vols. (Oxford: Oxford University Press, 1942)
Poppo-Stahl — E. F. Poppo and J. M. Stahl (eds.), *Thucydidis de bello Peloponnesiaco libri octo*, 4 vols. in 8 (Leipzig: Teubner; vol. 1: 3rd ed., 1886–9; vol. 2–4: 2nd ed., 1875–83)
Smith (Loeb) — C. F. Smith (tr.), *Thucydides*, 4 vols. (Cambridge, MA: Harvard University Press, 1919–23)
Sm. — H. W. Smyth, *Greek Grammar*, revised by G. M. Messing (Cambridge, MA: Harvard University Press, 1956)

TrGF	B. Snell, R. Kannnicht, and S. L. Radt (eds.), *Tragicorum Graecorum fragmenta*, 5 vols. in 6 (Göttingen: Vandenhoeck & Ruprecht, 1971–2004)

Secondary Literature

Adkins, A. W. H. (1960) *Merit and Responsibility: A Study in Greek Values*. Oxford: Oxford University Press.
Allison, J. W. (1989) *Power and Preparedness in Thucydides*. Baltimore: Johns Hopkins University Press.
Allison, J. W. (1997) *Word and Concept in Thucydides*. Atlanta: Scholars Press.
Arendt, H. (1978) *The Life of the Mind*, vol. 2: *Willing*. San Diego: Harcourt.
Auerbach, E. (1967) 'Passio als Leidenschaft', in *Gesammelte Aufsätze zur romanischen Philologie*. Bern: Francke, 161–75. Originally published in *Publications of the Modern Language Association* 56 (1941): 1179–96.
Avery, H. C. (1973) 'Themes in Thucydides' Account of the Sicilian Expedition', *Hermes* 101: 1–13.
Avery, H. C. (1979) 'A Poetic Word in Herodotus', *Hermes* 107: 1–9.
Babut, D. (1982) 'Six discours de Thucydide au livre IV: caractère et fonction dans l'exposé historique', *Bulletin de l'Association Guillaume Budé* 1: 41–71.
Babut, D. (1986) 'L'épisode de Pylos-Sphactérie chez Thucydide: l'agencement du récit et les intentions de l'historien', *Revue de philologie* 60: 59–79.
Badian, E. (1993) 'Thucydides and the Outbreak of the Peloponnesian War: A Historian's Brief', in *From Plataea to Potidaea: Studies in the History and Historiography of the Pentecontaetia*. Baltimore: Johns Hopkins University Press, 125–62.
Balot, R. K, S. Forsdyke, and E. Foster (2017) *The Oxford Handbook of Thucydides*. Oxford: Oxford University Press.
Barrett, W. S. (1964) (ed.) *Euripides: Hippolytos*. Oxford: Oxford University Press.
Beekes, R. (2010) *Etymological Dictionary of Greek*, 2 vols. Leiden: Brill.
Bender, G. F. (1938) *Der Begriff des Staatsmannes bei Thukydides*. Würzburg: Konrad Triltsch.
Benseler, G. E. (1832) (ed.) *Isocratis Areopagiticus*. Leipzig: Kollmann.
Berlin, I. (2002) 'Historical Inevitability', in *Liberty*. Oxford: Oxford University Press. Originally published as an individual volume by Oxford University Press in 1954.
Blass, F. (1887–98) *Die attische Beredsamkeit*, 4 vols., 2nd ed. Leipzig: Teubner.
Bloedow, E. F. (1993) 'Hermocrates' Strategy Against the Athenians in 415 B.C', *Ancient History Bulletin* 7: 115–24.
Bosworth, A. B. (1993) 'The Humanitarian Aspect of the Melian Dialogue', *JHS* 113: 30–44.
Brann, E. (2014) *Un-willing: An Inquiry into the Rise of Will's Power and an Attempt to Undo it*. Philadelphia: Paul Dry Books.

Bremer, D. (1989) 'Von der Physis zur Natur: Eine griechische Konzeption und ihr Schicksal', *Zeitschrift für philosophische Forschung* 43: 241-64.
Browning, R. (1958) 'Greek abstract nouns in *-sis, -tis*', *Philologus* 102: 60-73.
Bruell, C. (1974) 'Thucydides' View of Athenian Imperialism', *American Political Science Review* 68: 11-17.
Bruhn, E. (1891) (ed.) *Euripides: Die Bakchen.* Berlin: Weidmannsche Buchhandlung.
Bruns, I. (1896) *Das literarische Porträt der Griechen.* Berlin: Wilhelm Hertz.
Brunt, P. A. (1993) 'Introduction to Thucydides', in *Studies in Greek History and Thought.* Oxford: Oxford University Press, 137-80. Previously published as introduction to *Thucydides: the Peloponnesian Wars*, trans. B. Jowett (New York: Washington Square Press, 1963).
Bruzzone, R. (2017) '*Polemos, Pathemata,* and Plague: Thucydides' Narrative and the Tradition of Upheaval', *Greek, Roman, and Byzantine Studies* 57: 882-909.
Burckhardt, J. (1977) *Griechische Kulturgeschichte*, 4 vols. Munich: Deutscher Taschenbuchverlag.
Burger, A. (1925) *Les mots de la famille de φύω en grec ancient: Bibliothèque de l'École des Hautes Études; Sciences Historiques et Philologiques* 246. Paris: Librairie Ancienne Honoré Champion.
Carr, E. H. (1986) *What is History?* 2nd ed. Basingstoke: Macmillan.
Clark, C. A., E. Foster, and J. P. Hallett (eds.) (2015) *Kinesis: The Ancient Depiction of Gesture, Motion, and Emotion; Essays for Donald Lateiner.* Ann Arbor: University of Michigan Press.
Cogan, M. (1981a) *The Human Thing: The Speeches and Principles of Thucydides' History.* Chicago: The University of Chicago Press.
Cogan, M. (1981b) 'Mytilene, Plataea, and Corcyra: Ideology and Policy in Thucydides, Book Three', *Phoenix* 35: 1-21.
Cohen, D. (1984) 'Justice, Interest, and Political Deliberation in Thucydides', *Quaderni Urbinati di Cultura Classica*, n.s., 16: 35-60.
Collingwood, R. G. (1946) *The Idea of History.* Oxford: Oxford University Press.
Connor, W. R. (1984) *Thucydides.* Princeton: Princeton University Press.
Connor, W. R. (1985) 'Narrative Discourse in Thucydides', in *The Greek Historians: Literature and History; Papers presented to A. E. Raubitschek.* Saratoga: ANMA Libri, 1-18.
Cornford, F. M. (1907) *Thucydides Mythistoricus.* London: Arnold.
Crane, G. (1998) *Thucydides and the Ancient Simplicity: The Limits of Political Realism.* Berkeley: University of California Press.
Denniston, J. D. (1952) *Greek Prose Style.* Oxford: Oxford University Press.
Denniston, J. D., and D. Page (1957) (eds) *Aeschylus: Agamemnon.* Oxford: Oxford University Press.
Desmond, W. (2006) 'Lessons of Fear: A Reading of Thucydides', *Classical Philology* 101: 359-79.
Dietrich, B. C. (1965) *Death, Fate and the Gods: The Development of a Religious Idea in Greek Popular Belief and in Homer.* London: Athlone Press.

Dihle, A. (1982) *The Theory of the Will in Classical Antiquity*. Berkeley: University of California Press.
Dirlmeiner, F. (1956) (tr.) *Aristoteles: Nikomachische Ethik*, vol. 6 of *Aristoteles: Werke in deutscher Übersetzung*, ed. E. Grumach. Berlin: Akademie-Verlag.
Dodds, E. R. (1929) 'Euripides the Irrationalist', *Classical Review* 43: 97–104.
Dodds, E. R. (1951) *The Greeks and the Irrational*. Berkeley: University of California Press.
Dodds, E. R. (1960) (ed.) *Euripides: Bacchae*, 2nd ed. Oxford: Oxford University Press.
Dover, K. J. (1965a) (ed.) *Thucydides: Book VI*. Oxford: Oxford University Press.
Dover, K. J. (1965b) (ed.) *Thucydides: Book VII*. Oxford: Oxford University Press.
Dover, K. J. (1997) *The Evolution of Greek Prose Style*. Oxford: Oxford University Press.
Doyle, R. E. (1984) Ἄτη: *Its Use and Meaning; A Study in the Greek Poetic Tradition from Homer to Euripides*. New York: Fordham University Press.
Duckworth, G. E. (1933) *Foreshadowing and Suspense in the Epics of Homer, Apollonius, and Vergil*. Princeton: Princeton University Press.
Dunn, F. M. (2007) *Present Shock in Late Fifth-Century Greece*. Ann Arbor: University of Michigan Press.
Easterling, P. E. (1973) 'Presentation of Character in Aeschylus', *Greece and Rome* 20: 3–19.
Edmunds, L. (1975) *Chance and Intelligence in Thucydides*. Cambridge, MA: Harvard University Press.
Edmunds, L. (1972) 'Thucydides ii.40.2', *Classical Review*, n.s., 22: 171–2.
Egermann, F. (1972) 'Thukydides über die Art seiner Reden und über seine Darstellung der Kriegsgeschehnisse', *Historia* 21: 575–602.
Ehrenberg, V. (1947) 'Polypragmosyne: A Study in Greek Politics', *Journal of Hellenic Studies* 67: 46–67.
Ellis, A. (2016) 'A Socratic History: Theology in Xenophon's Rewriting of Herodotus' Croesus "Logos"', *Journal of Hellenic Studies* 136: 73–91.
England, E. B. (1891) (ed.) *The Iphigeneia at Aulis of Euripides*. London: Macmillan.
Erbse, H. (1968) 'Zur Geschichtsbetrachtung des Thukydides', in *Thukydides: Wege der Forschung* 98, ed. H. Herter, 594–619. Originally published in *Antike und Abendland* 10 (1961): 19–34.
Euben, J. P. (1990) *The Tragedy of Political Theory: The Road not Taken*. Princeton: Princeton University Press.
Finley, J. H., Jr (1942) *Thucydides*. Cambridge, MA: Harvard University Press.
Finley, J. H., Jr (1967) *Three Essays on Thucydides*. Cambridge, MA: Harvard University Press.
Finley, J. H., Jr (1967a) 'Euripides and Thucydides', in *Three Essays on Thucydides*, 1–54.
Finley, J. H., Jr (1967b) 'The Origins of Thucydides' Style', in *Three Essays on Thucydides*, 55–117.
Fisher, M., and K. Hoekstra (2017) 'Thucydides and the Politics of Necessity', in *Oxford Handbook of Thucydides*, ed. Balot, Forsdyke, and Foster, 373–90.

Fisher, N. R. E. (1992) *Hybris: A Study in the Values of Honour and Shame in Ancient Greece*. Warminster: Aris & Phillips.
Flashar, H. (1989) 'Der Epitaphios des Perikles: Seine Funktion im Geschichtswerk des Thukydides', in *Eidola: Ausgewählte kleine Schriften*. Amsterdam: B. R. Grüner, 435–84. Originally published as Sitzungsberichte der Heidelberger Akademie der Wissenschaften, Philosophisch-historische Klasse, 1969, no. 1 (Heidelberg: Winter).
Forde, S. (1989) *The Ambition to Rule: Alcibiades and the Politics of Imperialism in Thucydides*. Ithaca: Cornell University Press.
Fornara, C. W. (1983) *The Nature of History in Ancient Greece and Rome*. Berkeley: University of California Press.
Fornara, C. W. (1990) 'Human History and the Constraint of Fate in Herodotus', in *Conflict, Antithesis, and the Ancient Historian*, ed. J. W. Allison. Columbus: Ohio State University Press, 24–45.
Foster, E. (2010) *Thucydides, Pericles, and Periclean Imperialism*. Cambridge: Cambridge University Press.
Foster, E., and D. Lateiner (2012) (ed.) *Thucydides and Herodotus*. Oxford: Oxford University Press.
Fraenkel, E. (1950) (ed.) *Aeschylus: Agamemnon*, 3 vols. Oxford: Oxford University Press.
Fränkel, H. (1962) *Dichtung und Philosophie des frühen Griechentums*. Munich: Beck.
Frede, M. (2011) *A Free Will*. Berkeley: University of California Press.
Freundlich, R. (1987) *Verbalsubstantive als Namen für Satzinhalte in der Sprache des Thukydides: Beiträge zur Klassischen Philologie* 52. Frankfurt am Main: Athenäum.
Fritz, K. von. (1967) *Die griechische Geschichtsschreibung*, 2 vols. Berlin: de Gruyter.
Frohberger, H. (1866–71) (ed.) *Ausgewählte Reden des Lysias*, 3 vols. Leipzig: Teubner.
Gagné, R. (2013) *Ancestral Fault in Ancient Greece*. Cambridge: Cambridge University Press.
Gildersleeve, B. L. (1878) 'Contributions to the History of the Articular Infinitive', *Transactions of the American Philological Association* 9: 5–19.
Gildersleeve, B. L. (1887) 'The Articular Infinitive again', *American Journal of Philology*: 329–37.
Gomme, A. W. (1937) 'The Speeches in Thucydides', in *Essays in Greek History and Literature*. Oxford: Blackwell, 156–89.
Gomme, A. W. (1954) *The Greek Attitude to Poetry and History*. Berkeley: University of California Press.
Greenwood, E. (2006) *Thucydides and the Shaping of History*. London: Duckworth.
Grégoire, H. (1961) (ed.) *Les Bacchantes*, vol. 6.2 of *Euripide*. Paris: Les Belles Lettres.
Grethlein, J. (2005) 'Gefahren des λόγος: Thukydides' "Historien" und die Grabrede des Perikles', *Klio* 87: 41–71.
Grethlein, J. (2013) *Experience and Teleology in Ancient Historiography: 'Futures Past' from Herodotus to Augustine*. Cambridge: Cambridge University Press.
Gribble, D. (1999) *Alcibiades and Athens: A Study in Literary Presentation*. Oxford: Oxford University Press.

Gribble, D. (2006) 'Individuals in Thucydides', in *Brill's Companion to Thucydides*, ed. A. Rengakos and A. Tsakmakis. Leiden: Brill, 439–68.

Griffin, J. (2004) [1987] *Homer: The Odyssey*. Cambridge: Cambridge University Press.

Griffin, J. (1990) 'Characterization in Euripides: *Hippolytus* and *Iphigenia at Aulis*', in *Characterization and Individuality*, ed. Pelling, 128–49.

Grube, G. M. A. (1950) 'Dionysius of Halicarnassus on Thucydides', *Phoenix* 4: 95–110.

Grube, G. M. A. (1961) *A Greek Critic: Demetrius on Style*. Toronto: University of Toronto Press.

Gundert, H. (1940) 'Charakter und Schicksal homerischer Helden', *Neue Jahrbücher für Antike und deutsche Bildung* 3: 225–37.

Gundert, H. (1968) 'Athen und Sparta in den Reden des Thukydides', in *Thukydides: Wege der Forschung* 98, ed. H. Herter. Darmstadt: Wissenschaftliche Buchgesellschaft, 114–34. Originally published in *Die Antike* 16 (1940): 98–114.

Hadot, P. (2006) *The Veil of Isis: An Essay on the History of the Idea of Nature*, trans. M. Chase. Cambridge, MA: Harvard University Press. Originally published as *Le Voile d'Isis* (Paris: Gallimard, 2004).

Harrison, T. (2000) *Divinity and History: The Religion of Herodotus*. Oxford: Oxford University Press.

Hartung, J. A. (1852) (ed.) *Iphigenia in Aulis*, vol. 14 of *Euripides' Werke*. Leipzig: Engelmann.

Heidegger, M. (2001) *Sein und Zeit*, 18th ed. Tübingen: Niemeyer.

Heinimann, F. (1945) *Nomos und Physis*. Basel: Reinhardt.

Heiny, S. B. (1973) 'The Articular Infinitive in Thucydides'. PhD diss., Indiana University.

Heitsch, E. (1967) '*ΤΑ ΘΕΩΝ*: Ein Epigramm des Euripides', *Philologus* 111: 21–6.

Hellmann, F. (1934) *Herodots Kroisos-Logos*. Berlin: Weidmann.

Herter, H. (1968) (ed.) *Thukydides: Wege der Forschung* 98. Darmstadt: Wissenschaftliche Buchgesellschaft.

Herter, H. (1968a) 'Freiheit und Gebundenheit des Staatsmannes bei Thukydides', in *Thukydides: Wege der Forschung* 98, ed. H. Herter. Darmstadt: Wissenschaftliche Buchgesellschaft, 260–81. Originally published in *Rheinisches Museum* 93 (1950): 133–53.

Herter, H. (1968b) 'Pylos und Melos: Ein Beitrag zur Thukydides-Interpretation', in *Thukydides: Wege der Forschung* 98, ed. H. Herter. Darmstadt: Wissenschaftliche Buchgesellschaft, 369–99. Originally published in *Rheinisches Museum* 97 (1954): 316–43.

Heubeck, A. (1980) '*Πρόφασις* und kein Ende', *Glotta* 1980: 222–36.

Holmes, B. (2010) *The Symptom and the Subject: The Emergence of the Physical Body in Ancient Greece*. Princeton: Princeton University Press.

Hornblower, S. (1987) *Thucydides*. London: Duckworth.

Huart, P. (1968) *Le Vocabulaire de l'analyse psychologique dans l'oeuvre de Thucydide*. Paris: Klincksieck.

Huart, P. (1973) *Γνώμη chez Thucydide et ses contemporains*. Paris: Klincksieck.

Hulswit, M. (2002) *From Cause to Causation*. Dordrecht: Kluwer Academic Publishers.
Hunter, V. (1973) *Thucydides. The Artful Reporter*. Toronto: Hakkert.
Hunter, V. (1982) *Past and Process in Herodotus and Thucydides*. Princeton: Princeton University Press.
Immerwahr, H. R. (1954) 'Historical Action in Herodotus', *Transactions and Proceedings of the American Philological Association* 85: 16–45.
Immerwahr, H. R. (1956) 'Aspects of Historical Causation in Herodotus', *Transactions and Proceedings of the American Philological Association* 87: 241–80.
Immerwahr, H. R. (1960) 'Ergon: History as a Monument in Herodotus and Thucydides', *American Journal of Philology* 81: 261–90.
Immerwahr, H. R. (1966) *Form and Thought in Herodotus*. Cleveland: Press of Western Reserve University.
Jaeger, W. (1934–55) *Paideia: Die Formung des griechischen Menschen*, 3 vols. Berlin: de Gruyter.
Jaffe, S. N. (2017) *Thucydides on the Outbreak of War: Character and Contest*. Oxford: Oxford University Press.
Joho, T. (2017) 'Thucydides, Epic, and Tragedy', in *Oxford Handbook of Thucydides*, ed. Balot, Forsdyke, and Foster, 587–604.
Joho, T. (2019) 'Alcibiadean Mysteries and Longing for "Absent" and "Invisible Things" in Thucydides' Account of the Sicilian Expedition', *Harvard Studies in Classical Philology* 110: 115–58.
Joho, T. (2021) 'The Peloponnesian War and the State of Nature in Thucydides: The Coincidence of Motion and Rest', in Polemos *and His Children: War, Its Repercussions, and Narrative in Ancient Greek Literature*, Histos Supplement 12, ed. R. Bruzzone, 17–45. Available online at: https://histos.org/documents/SV12.02.Joho.pdf
Kagan, D. (1969) *The Outbreak of the Peloponnesian War*. Ithaca: Cornell University Press.
Kagan, D. (1975) 'The Speeches in Thucydides and the Mytilene Debate', *Yale Classical Studies* 24: 71–94.
Kahn, C. H. (1979) (ed.) *The Art and Thought of Heraclitus: An Edition of the Fragments with Translation and Commentary*. Cambridge: Cambridge University Press.
Kahn, C. H. (1988) 'Discovering the Will: From Aristotle to Augustine', in *The Question of Eclecticism: Studies in Later Greek Philosophy*, ed. J. M. Dillon and A. A. Long. Berkeley: University of California Press, 234–60.
Kallet, L. (1993) *Money, Expense, and Naval Power in Thucydides' History 1–5.24*. Berkeley: University of California Press.
Kallet, L. (2001) *Money and the Corrosion of Power in Thucydides: The Sicilian Expedition and its Aftermath*. Berkeley: University of California Press.
Kapp, E. (1930) Review of *Die Geschichtsschreibung des Thukydides: Ein Versuch*, by W. Schadewaldt, *Gnomon* 6: 76–100.
Kindt, J. (2006) 'Delphic Oracle Stories and the Beginning of Historiography: Herodotus' Croesus Logos', *Classical Philology* 101: 34–51.

Kirkwood, G. M. (1952) 'Thucydides' Words for "Cause"', *American Journal of Philology* 73: 37–61.
Knox, B. M. W. (1979) 'The *Hippolytus* of Euripides', in *Word and Action: Essays on the Ancient Theater*. Baltimore: Johns Hopkins University Press, 205–30. Originally published in *Yale Classical Studies* 13 (1952): 1–31.
Kohn, M. (1891) *De usu adjectivorum et participiorum pro substantivis, item substantivorum verbalium apud Thucydidem*. Berlin: Mayer und Müller.
Konstan, D. (2006) *The Emotions of the Ancient Greeks: Studies in Aristotle and classical literature*. Toronto: University of Toronto Press.
Kopp, H. (2017) *Das Meer als Versprechen: Bedeutung und Funktion von Seeherrschaft bei Thukydides*. Göttingen: Vandenhoeck & Ruprecht.
Kosch, B. D. (2017) 'Reading Demosthenes'. PhD diss., University of Chicago.
Kovacs, D. (1987) *The Heroic Muse: Studies in the Hippolytus and Hecuba of Euripides*. Baltimore: Johns Hopkins University Press.
Krause, W. (1949) 'Zeus und Moira bei Homer', *Wiener Studien* 64: 10–52.
Langholf, V. (1990) *Medical Theories in Hippocrates: Early Texts and the 'Epidemics'*. Berlin: de Gruyter.
Lateiner, D. (1977) 'Pathos in Thucydides', *Antichthon* 11: 42–51.
Lateiner, D. (1989) *The Historical Method of Herodotus*. Toronto: University of Toronto Press.
Lateiner, D. (2018) '*Elpis* as Emotion and Reason (Hope and Expectation) in Fifth-century Greek Historians', in *Hope in Ancient Literature, History, and Art*, ed. G. Kazantzidis and D. Spatharas. Berlin: de Gruyter, 131–49.
Lebow, R. N. (2007) 'Thucydides and Deterrence', *Security Studies* 16: 163–88.
Lefkowitz, M. (2016) *Euripides and the Gods*. New York: Oxford University Press.
Lesky, A. (1960) 'Psychologie bei Euripides', in *Euripide: Entretiens sur l'antiquité classique* 6. Vandœuvres-Geneva, 123–68.
Lesky, A. (1961) *Göttliche und menschliche Motivation im homerischen Epos*. Sitzungsberichte der Heidelberger Akademie der Wissenschaften, Philosophisch-historische Klasse, no. 4. Heidelberg: Winter.
Lesky, A. (1964) *Die tragische Dichtung der Hellenen*, 2nd ed. Göttingen: Vandenhoeck & Ruprecht.
Lévy, E. (1995) 'Le rêve chez Hérodote', *Ktèma* 20: 17–27.
Liebeschuetz, W. (1968) 'The Structure and Function of the Melian Dialogue', *Journal of Hellenic Studies* 88: 73–7.
Liegle, J. (1923) 'Untersuchungen zu den Platonischen Lebensformen'. PhD diss., Ruprecht-Karls-Universität Heidelberg.
Lincoln, A. (1989) 'Second Inaugural Address', in *Speeches and Writings*, ed. D. E. Fehrenbacher, 2 vols. New York: Library of America.
Lloyd-Jones, H. (1983) *The Justice of Zeus*, 2nd ed. Berkeley: University of California Press.
Lohmann, J. (1952) 'Das Verhältnis des abendländischen Menschen zur Sprache', *Lexis* 3: 5–50.
Long, A. A. (1968) *Language and Thought in Sophocles: A Study of Abstract Nouns and Poetic Technique*. London: Athlone Press.

Loraux, N. (2006) *The Invention of Athens: The Funeral Oration in the Classical City*, trans. A. Sheridan. New York: Zone Books. Originally published as *L'invention d'Athènes: l'histoire de l'oraison funèbre dans la cité classique* (Paris: Mouton, 1981).

Loraux, N. (2009) 'Thucydides and Sedition among Words', on *Oxford Readings in Classical Studies: Thucydides*, ed. J. S. Rusten. Oxford: Oxford University Press, 261–94. Originally published as 'Thucydide et la sédition dans les mots', *Quaderni di Storia* 23 (1986): 95–134.

Luginbill, R. D. (1999) *Thucydides on War and National Character*. Boulder: Westview Press.

Macleod, Colin. (1983) *Collected Essays*. Oxford: Oxford University Press.

Macleod, Colin. (1983a) 'Form and Meaning in the Melian Dialogue', in *Collected Essays*, 52–67. Originally published in *Historia* 23 (1974): 385–400.

Macleod, Colin. (1983b) 'Rhetoric and History (Thucydides 6.16-18)', in *Collected Essays*, 68–87. Originally published in *Quaderni di Storia* 2 (1975): 39–65.

Macleod, Colin. (1983c) 'Reason and Necessity: Thucydides III 9–14, 37–48', in *Collected Essays*, 88–102. Originally published in *Journal of Hellenic Studies* 98 (1978): 64–78.

Macleod, Colin. (1983d) 'Thucydides' Plataean Debate', in *Collected Essays*, 103–22. Originally published in *Greek, Roman, and Byzantine Studies* 18 (1977): 227–46.

Macleod, Colin. (1983e) 'Thucydides on Faction', in *Collected Essays*, 123–39. Originally published in *Proceedings of the Cambridge Philological Society* 205, n.s., 25 (1979): 52–68.

Macleod, Colin. (1983f) 'Thucydides and Tragedy', in *Collected Essays*, 140–58.

Maddalena, A. (1950) 'L'umano e il divino in Erodoto', in *Studi di filosofia greca*, ed. V. E. Alfieri and M. Untersteiner. Bari: Laterza, 57–84.

Manuwald, B. (1979) 'Der Trug des Diodotos', *Hermes* 107: 407–22.

Marg, W. (1965) '"Selbstsicherheit" bei Herodot', in *Herodot: Wege der Forschung* 26, ed. W. Marg. Darmstadt: Wissenschaftliche Buchgesellschaft, 290–301. Originally published in *Studies Presented to David Moore Robinson*, vol. 2, ed. G. E. Mylonas and D. Raymond (St Louis: Washington University, 1953), 1103–11.

Marinatos, N. (1981) *Thucydides and Religion: Beiträge zur Klassischen Philologie* 129. Königstein: Anton Hain.

Marinatos, N. (1982) 'Wahl und Schicksal bei Herodot', *Saeculum* 33: 258–64.

Matthaiou, A. (2016) "Ὁ ἐνεπίγραφος σκύφος τῆς Κηφισιᾶς', *Grammateion* 5: 53–65.

Meier, C. (1980) 'Prozeß und Ereignis in der griechischen Historiographie des 5. Jahrhunderts vor Christus', in *Die Entstehung des Politischen bei den Griechen*. Frankfurt am Main: Suhrkamp, 326–59.

Meyer, E. (1899) 'Thukydides', in *Forschungen zur Alten Geschichte*, vol. 2: *Zur Geschichte des fünften Jahrhunderts*. Halle: Niemeyer, 269–436.

Mikalson, J. D. (2003) *Herodotus and Religion in the Persian Wars*. Chapel Hill: The University of North Carolina Press.

Morrison, J. V. (1999) 'Preface to Thucydides: Rereading the Corcyrean Conflict (1.24–55)', *Classical Antiquity* 18: 94–131.

Munson, R. (2015) 'Natural Upheavals in Thucydides (and Herodotus)', in *Kinesis*, ed. Clark, Foster, and Hallett, 41–59.
Müri, W. (1968) 'Beitrag zum Verständnis des Thukydides', in *Thukydides: Wege der Forschung* 98, ed. H. Herter. Darmstadt: Wissenschaftliche Buchgesellschaft, 135–70. Originally published in *Museum Helveticum* 4 (1947): 251–75.
Myres, J. L. (1953) *Herodotus: Father of History*. Oxford: Oxford University Press.
Naddaf, G. (2005) *The Greek Concept of Nature*. Albany: State University of New York Press.
Nietzsche, F. (1980) *Sämtliche Werke: Kritische Studienausgabe* (= *KSA*), 15 vols., ed. M. Montinari and G. Colli. Munich: Deutscher Taschenbuch Verlag.
Nilsson, M. (1967–74) *Geschichte der griechischen Religion*, 2 vols., 3rd ed., in *Handbuch der Altertumswissenschaften*, Fünfte Abteilung, Zweiter Teil, ed. I. von Müller, W. Otto, and H. Bengtson. Munich: Beck.
Norden, E. (1898) *Die antike Kunstprosa*, 2 vols. Leipzig: Teubner.
Ober, J. (1998) 'Public Speech and Brute Fact: Thucydides', in *Political Dissent in Democratic Athens: Intellectual Critics of Popular Rule*. Princeton: Princeton University Press, 52–121.
Orwin, C. (1994) *The Humanity of Thucydides*. Princeton: Princeton University Press.
Ostwald, M. (1979) 'Diodotus, Son of Eucrates', *Greek, Roman, and Byzantine Studies* 20: 5–13.
Ostwald, M. (1988) *Ananke in Thucydides*. Atlanta: Scholars Press.
Otto, W. F. (1987) *Die Götter Griechenlands*, repr. of the 2nd ed. from 1934. Klostermann: Fankfurt.
Palmer, M. (1992) *Love of Glory and the Common Good: Aspects of the Political Thought of Thucydides*. Lanham, MD: Rowman & Littlefield.
Parry, A. (1969) 'The Language of Thucydides' Description of the Plague', *Bulletin of the Institute of Classical Studies London* 16: 106–18.
Parry, A. (1970) 'Thucydides' Use of Abstract Language', *Yale French Studies* 45: 3–20.
Parry, A. (1972) 'Thucydides' Historical Perspective', *Yale Classical Studies* 22: 47–61.
Parry, A. (1981) *Logos and Ergon in Thucydides*. New York: Arno Press.
Patzer, H. (1937) *Das Problem der Geschichtsschreibung des Thukydides und die thukydideische Frage*. Berlin: Junker und Dünnhaupt.
Pearson, L. (1952) 'Prophasis and Aitia', *Transactions and Proceedings of the American Philological Association* 83: 205–23.
Pearson, L. (1972) 'Prophasis: A Clarification', *Transactions and Proceedings of the American Philological Association* 103: 381–94.
Pelling, C. B. R. (1990) (ed.) *Characterization and Individuality in Greek Literature*. Oxford: Oxford University Press.
Pelling, C. B. R. (1990a) 'Conclusion,' in *Characterization and Individuality*, ed. Pelling, 245–62.
Pelling, C. B. R. (1991) 'Thucydides' Archidamus and Herodotus' Artabanus', in *Georgica: Greek Studies in Honour of George Cawkwell; Bulletin of the Institute of Classical Studies Suppl.* 58. London: University of London, 120–42.
Pelling, C. B. R. (2000) *Literary Texts and the Greek Historian*. London: Routledge.

Pelling, C. B. R. (2006) 'Educating Croesus: Talking and Learning in Herodotus' Lydian *Logos*', *Classical Antiquity* 25: 141–77.
Pelling, C. B. R. (2008) "Why Read Thucydides?" Unpublished Lecture presented at the University of Wisconsin-Madison, April 2008.
Pelling, C. B. R. (2012) 'Aristotle's *Rhetoric*, the *Rhetorica ad Alexandrum*, and the Speeches in Herodotus and Thucydides', in *Thucydides and Herodotus*, ed. Foster and Lateiner, 281–315.
Pelling, C. B. R. (2019) *Herodotus and the Question Why*. Austin: University of Texas Press.
Pelling, C. B. R. (2021a) (ed.) *Thucydides: The Peloponnesian War Book VI*. Cambridge: Cambridge University Press.
Pelling, C. B. R. (2021b) (ed.) *Thucydides: The Peloponnesian War Book VII*. Cambridge: Cambridge University Press.
Porzig, W. (1942) *Die Namen für Satzinhalte im Griechischen und im Indogermanischen: Untersuchungen zur indogermanischen Sprach- und Kulturwissenschaft* 10. Berlin: de Gruyter.
Pötscher, W. (1988) 'Götter und Gottheit bei Herodot', in *Hellas und Rom: Beiträge und kritische Auseinandersetzung mit der inzwischen erschienen Literatur*. Hildesheim: Olms, 3–36. Originally published in *Wiener Studien* 71 (1958): 5–29.
Pouncey, P. R. (1980) *The Necessities of War: A Study of Thucydides' Pessimism*. New York: Columbia University Press.
Price, J. J. (2001) *Thucydides and Internal War*. Cambridge: Cambridge University Press.
Pritchett, W. K. (1975) (tr.) *Dionysius of Halicarnassus: On Thucydides*. Berkeley: University of California Press.
Radford, R. S. (1901) *Personification and the use of abstract subjects in the Attic orators and Thucydides*. Baltimore: Johns Hopkins University Press.
Raubitschek, A. E. (1973) 'The Speech of the Athenians at Sparta', in *The Speeches in Thucydides*, ed. P. A. Stadter. Chapel Hill: The University of North Carolina Press, 32–48.
Rawlings, H. R., III (1975) *A Semantic Study of Prophasis to 400 B.C.: Hermes Einzelschriften* 33. Wiesbaden: Franz Steiner.
Rawlings, H. R., III (1977) 'Thucydides on the Purpose of the Delian League', *Phoenix* 31: 1–8.
Rawlings, H. R., III (1981) *The Structure of Thucydides' History*. Princeton: Princeton University Press.
Rechenauer, G. (1991) *Thukydides und die hippokratische Medizin: Naturwissenschaftliche Methodik als Modell für Geschichtsdeutung*; Spudasmata 47. Hildesheim: Olms.
Rehdantz, C. (1873–78) (ed.) *Demosthenes: Neun Philippische Rede*, 2 vols. (vols. 1 and 2.1: 4th ed.; vol. 2.2: 3rd ed.). Leipzig: Teubner.
Reinhardt, K. (1966) 'Thukydides und Machiavelli', in *Vermächtnis der Antike: Gesammelte Essays zur Philosophie und Geschichtsschreibung*. Göttingen: Vandenhoeck & Ruprecht, 184–218.
Reiske, J. J. (1791) (ed.) *Libanii Sophistae Orationes et Declamationes*, vol. 1. Altenburg: Richter.
Rengakos, A. (1984) *Form und Wandel des Machtdenkens der Athener bei Thukydides*: Hermes Einzelschriften 48. Stuttgart: Franz Steiner.

Rengakos, A. (2006) 'Thucydides' Narrative: The Epic and Herodotean Heritage', in *Brill's Companion to Thucydides*, ed. A. Rengakos and A. Tsakmakis. Leiden: Brill, 279–300.
Rhodes, P. J. (1992) 'The Delian League to 449 B.C.', in *The Cambridge Ancient History*, 2nd ed., vol. 3. Cambridge: Cambridge University Press, 34–61.
Rijksbaron, A. (1991) *Grammatical Observations on Euripides' Bacchae*. Amsterdam: Gieben.
Ritter, H. (2011) *Notizhefte*. Berlin: Berlin Verlag.
Rivier, A. (1975) *Essai sur la tragique d'Euripide*. Paris: Baccard.
Roberts, W. R. (1901) (tr.) *Dionysius of Halicarnassus: The three literary letters*. Cambridge: Cambridge University Press.
Roettig, K. (2010) *Die Träume des Xerxes: Zum Handeln der Götter bei Herodot*. Nordhausen: Bautz.
Rogkotis, Z. (2006) 'Thucydides and Herodotus: Aspects of their Intertextual Relationship', in *Brill's Companion to Thucydides*, ed. A. Rengakos and A. Tsakmakis. Leiden: Brill, 57–86.
Romilly, J. de (1963) *Thucydides and Athenian Imperialism*, trans. P. Thody. Oxford: Oxford University Press. Originally published as *Thucydide et l'impérialisme athénien* (Paris: Les Belles Lettres, 1947).
Romilly, J. de (2012) *The Mind of Thucydides*, trans. E. Trapnell Rawlings. Ithaca: Cornell University Press. Originally published as *Histoire et raison chez Thucydide* (Paris: Les Belles Lettres, 1956).
Romilly, J. de (1956) 'La crainte dans l'œuvre de Thucydide', *Classica et Mediaevalia* 17: 119–27.
Romilly, J. de (1958) 'L'utilité de l'histoire selon Thucydide', in *Histoire et historiens dans l'antiquité: Entretiens sur l'antiquité classique* 4. Vandœuvres-Geneva, 41–81.
Romilly, J. de (1965) 'L'optimisme de Thucydide et le jugement de l'historien sur Périclès (Thuc. 2.65)', *Revue des Études Grecques* 78: 557–75.
Romilly, J. de (1971) 'La notion de nécessité dans l'histoire de Thucydide', in *Mélanges en l'honneur de Raymond Aron: Science et conscience de la société*, vol. 1, ed. J.-C. Casanova. Paris: Calmann-Lévy, 111–28.
Rood, T. (1998) *Thucydides: Narrative and Explanation*. Oxford: Oxford University Press.
Ros, J., S.J. (1938) *Die μεταβολή (variatio) als Stilprinzip des Thukydides*. Paderborn: Schöningh.
Roux, J. (1970-2) (ed.) *Euripide: Les Bacchantes*, 2 vols. Paris: Les Belles Lettres.
Ruijgh, C. J. (1971) *Autour de 'te épique'*. Amsterdam: Hakkert.
Rusten, J. S. (1989) (ed.) *Thucydides: The Peloponnesian War; Book II*. Cambridge: Cambridge University Press.
Rusten, J. S. (2015) '*Kinesis* in the Preface to Thucydides', in *Kinesis*, ed. Clark, Foster, and Hallett, 27–40.
Rutherford, R. B. (2012) 'Structure and Meaning in Epic and Historiography', in Foster and Lateiner, 13–38.
Ste. Croix, G. E. M. de (1972) *The Origins of the Peloponnesian War*. Ithaca: Cornell University Press.

Ste. Croix, G. E. M. de (1977) 'Herodotus', *Greece and Rome* 24: 130–48.
Scardino, C. (2007) *Gestaltung und Funktion der Reden bei Herodot und Thukydides*. Berlin: de Gruyter.
Schadewaldt, W. (1959) *Von Homers Welt und Werk: Aufsätze und Auslegungen zur homerischen Frage*. Stuttgart: Koehler.
Schadewaldt, W. (1970a) 'Der Prolog der Odyssee', in *Hellas und Hesperien* 1. Zürich: Artemis, 42–58. Originally published in *Festschrift für Werner Jaeger: Harvard Studies in Classical Philology* 63 (1958): 13–32.
Schadewaldt, W. (1970b) 'Die Begriffe "Natur" und "Technik" bei den Griechen', in *Hellas und Hesperien* 2. Zürich: Artemis, 523–4. Originally published in *Natur—Technik—Kunst: Drei Beiträge zum Selbstverständnis der Technik in unserer Zeit*. Göttingen: Musterschmidt (1960), 35–53.
Schäublin, C. (1971) 'Wieder einmal πρόφασις', *Museum Helveticum* 28: 133–44.
Schäublin, C. (1979) Review of *Zur Bedeutung von* πρόφασις *in der altgriechischen Literatur* 1, by A. A. Nikitas, and of *A Semantic Study of Prophasis to 400 B. C.*, by H. R. Rawlings III, *Gnomon* 6: 76–100.
Schäublin, C. (1989) 'Prophasis', in *Historisches Wörterbuch der Philosophie*, vol. 7, ed. J. Ritter and K. Gründer. Basel: Schwabe, 1472–3.
Schein, S. (1984) *The Mortal Hero: An Introduction to Homer's* Iliad. Berkeley: University of California Press.
Schmid, W. (1948) *Die griechische Literatur zur Zeit der attischen Hegemonie nach dem Eingreifen der Sophistik*, vol. 5, no. 2, section 2 of *Geschichte der griechischen Literatur*, Part One: *Die klassische Periode der griechischen Literatur*, ed. W. Schmid and O. Stählin, in *Handbuch der Altertumswissenschaften*, Siebente Abteilung, ed. I. von Müller and W. Otto. Munich: Beck.
Schmitt, A. (2013) 'Gibt es eine aristotelische Herodotlektüre?', in *Herodots Quellen—Die Quellen Herodots*, ed. B. Dunsch and K. Ruffing. Wiesbaden: Harrassowitz, 285–322.
Schneider, C. (1974) *Information und Absicht bei Thukydides*: Hypomnemata 41. Göttingen: Vandenhoeck & Ruprecht.
Schuller, S. (1956) 'About Thucydides' Use of Αἰτία and Πρόφασις', *Revue belge de philologie et d'histoire* 34: 971–84.
Schwartz, E. (1919) *Das Geschichtswerk des Thukydides*. Bonn: Cohen.
Sealey, R. (1957) 'Thucydides, Herodotos, and the Causes of War', *Classical Quarterly*, n.s., 7: 1–12.
Segal, C. P. (1971) 'Croesus on the Pyre: Herodotus and Baccylides', *Wiener Studien*, n.s., 5: 39–51.
Sewell-Rutter (2007) *Guilt by Descent: Moral Inheritance and Decision Making in Greek Tragedy*. Oxford: Oxford University Press.
Shapiro, S. O. (1996) 'Herodotus and Solon', *Classical Antiquity* 15: 348–64.
Sihler, E. G. (1881) 'On the Verbal Abstract Nouns in -σις in Thucydides', *Transactions and Proceedings of the American Philological Association* 12: 96–104.
Simonton, M. (2018) 'Who Made Athens Great? Three Recent Books on Pericles and Athenian Politics', *Polis: The Journal for Ancient Greek Political Thought* 35: 220–35.

Smith, C. F. (1918) 'Personification in Thucydides', *Classical Philology* 13: 241–50.
Snell, B. (1924) *Die Ausdrücke für den Begriff des Wissens in der vorplatonischen Philolosophie*. Berlin: Weidmann.
Snell, B. (1952) *Der Aufbau der Sprache*. Hamburg: Classen.
Sorabji, R. (1980) *Necessity, Cause and Blame: Perspectives on Aristotle's Theory*. Duckworth: London.
Stadter, P. A. (1993) 'The Form and Content of Thucydides' Pentecontaetia', *Greek, Roman, and Byzantine Studies* 34: 35–72.
Stahl, H.-P. (2003) *Thucydides: Man's Place in History*. Swansea: Classical Press of Wales. Pp. 1–172 originally published as *Thukydides: Die Stellung des Menschen im geschichtlichen Prozeß*; Zetemata 40 (Munich: Beck, 1966). Pp. 173–88 originally published as 'Speeches and Course of Events in Books Six and Seven of Thucydides', in *The Speeches in Thucydides*, ed. P. A. Stadter. (Chapel Hill: The University of North Carolina Press, 1973), 60–77.
Stahl, H.-P. (1975) 'Learning through Suffering? Croesus' Conversation in the History of Herodotus', *Yale Classical Studies* 24: 1–36.
Stallmach, J. (1968) *ATE: zur Frage des Selbst- und Weltverständnisses des frühgriechischen Menschen; Beiträge zur Klassische Philologie* 18. Meisenheim am Glan: Anton Hain.
Stockert, W. (1992) (ed.) *Euripides: Iphigenie in Aulis*, 2 vols. Vienna: Verlag der österreichischen Akademie der Wissenschaften.
Strasburger, H. (1966) *Die Wesensbestimmung der Geschichte durch die antike Geschichtsschreibung*. Sitzungsberichte der Wissenschaftlichen Gesellschaft an der Johann Wolfgang von Goethe-Universität Frankfurt am Main, vol. 5, no. 3. Wiesbaden: Franz Steiner.
Strasburger, H. (1968a) 'Die Entdeckung der politischen Geschichte durch Thukydides', in *Thukydides: Wege der Forschung* 98, ed. H. Herter. Darmstadt: Wissenschaftliche Buchgesellschaft, 412–76. Originally published in *Saeculum* 5 (1954): 395–428.
Strasburger, H. (1968b) 'Thukydides und die politische Selbstdarstellung der Athener', in *Thukydides: Wege der Forschung* 98, ed. H. Herter. Darmstadt: Wissenschaftliche Buchgesellschaft, 498–530. Originally published in *Hermes* 86 (1958): 17–40.
Strasburger, H. (1972) *Homer und die Geschichtsschreibung*. Sitzungsberichte der Heidelberger Akademie der Wissenschaften, Philosophisch-historische Klasse, no. 1. Heidelberg: Winter.
Strasburger, H. (1982) 'Der Geschichtsbegriff bei Thukydides', in *Studien zur alten Geschichte*, vol. 2. Hildesheim: Olms, 777–800.
Strauss Clay, J. (1983) *The Wrath of Athena: Gods and Men in the Odyssey*. Princeton: Princeton University Press.
Strauss, L. (1964) *The City and Man*. Chicago: The University of Chicago Press.
Strauss, L. (1974) 'Preliminary Observations on the Gods in Thucydides', *Interpretation* 4: 1–16.
Swain, S. (1994) 'Man and Medicine in Thucydides', *Arethusa* 27: 303–27.

Syme, R. (1962) 'Thucydides', *Proceedings of the British Academy* 48: 37–56.
Taylor, M. (2010) *Thucydides, Pericles, and the Idea of Athens in the Peloponnesian War*. Cambridge: Cambridge University Press.
Tompkins, D. P. (1972) 'Stylistic Characterization in Thucydides: Alcibiades and Nicias', *Yale Classical Studies* 22: 181–214.
Tompkins, D. P. (1993a) 'Thucydides constructs his speakers: the case of Diodotus', *Electronic Antiquity* 1.1. Available online at: http://scholar.lib.vt.edu/ejournals/ElAnt/V1N1/tompkins.html
Tompkins, D. P. (1993b) 'Archidamus and the Question of Characterization in Thucydides', in *Nomodeiktes: Greek Studies in Honor of Martin Ostwald*, ed. R. M. Rosen and J. Farrell. Ann Arbor: University of Michigan Press, 99–111.
Tompkins, D. P. (2013) 'The Language of Pericles and Modern International Politics', in *Thucydides Between History and Literature*, ed. A. Tsakmakis and M. Tamiolaki. Berlin: de Gruyter, 447–64.
Topitsch, E. (1943–7) '*Ἀνθρωπεία φύσις* und Ethik bei Thukydides', *Wiener Studien* 61: 50–67.
Tsakmakis, A. (1995) *Thukydides über die Vergangenheit: Classica Monacensia* 11. Tübingen: Narr.
Usher, S. (1974) (tr.) *Dionysius of Halicarnassus: Critical Essays*, 2 vols., Loeb Classical Library. Cambridge, MA: Harvard University Press.
Vernant, J.-P. (1988) 'Intimations of the Will in Greek Tragedy', in *Myth and Tragedy in Ancient Greece*, ed. J.-P. Vernant and P. Vidal-Naquet, trans. J. Lloyd. New York: Zone Books, 49–84. Originally published as 'Ébauches de la volonté dans la tragédie grecque', in *Mythe et tragédie en Grèce ancienne*, vol. 1., ed. J.-P. Vernant and P. Vidal-Naquet (Paris: Maspero, 1972), 43–74.
Verrall, A. W. (1913) *Euripides the Rationalist: A Study in the History of Art and Religion*. Cambridge: Cambridge University Press.
Visser, E. (2000) 'Herodots Kroisos-Logos: Rezeptionssteuerung und Geschichtsphilosophie', *Würzburger Jahrbücher für die Altertumswissenschaft*, neue Folge, 24: 5–28.
Visvardi, E. (2015) *Emotion in Action: Thucydides and the Tragic Chorus; Mnemosyne Supplements* 377. Leiden: Brill.
Vlastos, G. (1975) *Plato's Universe*. Seattle: University of Washington Press.
Wagner, R. (1885) *De infinitivo apud oratores Atticos cum articulo coniuncto*. Schwerin: Bärensprungsche Hofbuchdruckerei.
Wassermann, F. M. (1956) 'Post-Periclean Democracy in Action: The Mytilenean Debate (Thuc. III 37–48)', *Transcactions and Proceedings of the American Philological Association* 87: 27–41.
Weidauer, K. (1954) *Thukydides und die Hippokratischen Schriften: Der Einfluß der Medizin auf Zielsetzung und Darstellungsweise des Geschichtswerks*. Heidelberg: Winter.
Weil, H. (1930) (ed.) *Euripide: Iphigénie à Aulis*, 2nd ed. by G. Dalmyeda. Paris: Hachette.

Westlake, H. D. (1958) 'Hermocrates the Syracusan', *Bulletin of the John Rylands Library* 41: 239–68.
Westlake, H. D. (1968) *Individuals in Thucydides*. Cambridge: Cambridge University Press.
Williams, B. (1993) *Shame and Necessity*. Berkeley: University of California Press.
Wilson, J. (1982a) ' "The Customary Meanings of Words Were Changed" – Or Were They? A Note on Thucydides 3.82.4', *Classical Quarterly*, n.s., 32: 18–20.
Wilson, J. (1982b) 'What Does Thucydides Claim for his Speeches?', *Phoenix* 36: 95–103.
Winnington-Ingram, R. P. (1960) 'Hippolytus: A Study in Causation', *Euripide: Entretiens sur l'antiquité classique* 6. Vandœuvres-Geneva, 169–97.
Winnington-Ingram, R. P. (1965) '*TA ΔEONTA EIΠEIN*: Cleon and Diodotus', *Bulletin of the Institute of Classical Studies* 12: 70–82.
Wohl, V. (2002) *Love among the Ruins: The Erotics of Democracy in Classical Athens*. Princeton: Princeton University Press.
Wohl, V. (2017) 'Thucydides on the Political Passions', in *Oxford Handbook of Thucydides*, ed. Balot, Forsdyke, and Foster, 443–58.
Wolcott, J. D. (1898) 'New Words in Thucydides', *Transactions and Proceedings of the American Philological Association* 29: 104–57.
Woolf, V. (1925) 'On Not Knowing Greek', in *The Common Reader*. New York: Hartcourt, 39–59.
Yunis, H. (1996) *Taming Democracy: Models of Political Rhetoric in Classical Athens*. Ithaca: Cornell University Press.

Index of Passages

For the benefit of digital users, indexed terms that span two pages (e.g., 52–53) may, on occasion, appear on only one of those pages.

Aelianus
　Varia Historia
　　4.17: 128n.39
Aeschylus
　Agamemnon
　　160: 151n.98
　　341–2: 133n.51
　　472–4: 302
　　1084: 143
　Choephori
　　957: 143
Alexander
　De Figuris
　　32.15–18: 34
Aristophanes
　Clouds
　　1081: 279n.16
Aristotle
　Poetics
　　1460a7: 87
Cicero, M. Tullius
　Brutus
　　7.29: 25
　Orator
　　9.30: 25
Demetrius
　On Style
　　40: 10n.16
　　45: 10n.16
　　65: 10n.16
　　72: 10n.16
Demosthenes
　4.37: 98n.56
　4.47: 98n.56
　5.5: 262n.70
Dionysius of Halicarnassus
　On Demosthenes
　　1.130.1–3: 11n.28
　　10.148.14–20: 10
　　10.148.19–149.1: 1
　　10.148.20–149.3: 10
　　10.149.1–3: 1
　　10.149.3–13: 10
　　10.149.9–11: 11n.28
　　10.149.9–13: 10n.17
　　10.149.11–12: 11n.20, 13
　　39.213.19–21: 10n.17
　　39.214.17–19: 10n.17
　On Imitation
　　207.14 (fr. VI, iii Usener): 11n.21
　Letter to Ammaeus II
　　5.426.15–16: 9
　　6.427.7–8: 166n.17
　　6.427.12–16: 164
　　6.427.14–16: 9n.15
　　14.433.6: 52
　　14.433.15–16: 53
　　14.433.18–19: 47, 76
　　14.434.12: 47n.2, 76
　Letter to Pompey
　　3.239.11–13: 25
　　3.239.14: 11n.23
　　3.239.19: 11n.21, 12
　　3.240.9: 11n.20
　　3.240.19–20: 11n.19

Dionysius of Halicarnassus (cont.)
  On Thucydides
    15.347.15–16: 13
    15.347.17: 11n.20
    15.347.17–18: 12
    15.347.17–20: 13
    15.347.18: 11n.21
    15.347.21: 11n.20
    24.361.9: 11n.22
    24.361.20–1: 9
    24.361.21–2: 9n.15
    24.361.9–10: 11n.26
    24.362.16–17: 47
    24.362.16–18: 124
    24.362.17–18: 52
    24.362.20–1: 1, 11n.27
    24.363.4–9: 25
    24.363.12–15: 13
    24.363.13: 11nn.23,26
    24.363.14: 11nn.20,22,24
    24.363.15: 11nn.19,21
    24.363.18–19: 1
    24.363.20–3: 1
    24.363.23–364.2: 1
    27.371.3–4: 14
    28.372.3: 1, 11n.27
    28.372.6–33.381.8: 1
    28.372.9–11: 36
    29.373.22–3: 5
    29.373.24–374.1: 8
    29.374.8: 2
    29.374.14: 40
    29.374.14–16: 2
    29.375.3–4: 5
    29.375.13–15: 7
    29.375.18–19: 48
    33.381.5–6: 11n.27
    40.394.6–7: 116n.16
    51.410.17–411.3: 8
    51.411.3–5: 1
    51.411.5–7: 1
    53.412.24: 11nn.23,24,26
    53.412.25: 11nn.21,26
    53.412.25–6: 11n.20, 13

Euripides
  Andromache
    629–31: 279n.16
    1227: 143n.76
  Bacchae
    4: 152
    274–5: 152
    275–6: 152
    882–96: 149
    883–4: 149
    886: 150, 149n.95
    890: 149n.95
    890–2: 149n.95
    891: 149n.95
    893: 150
    893–6: 146–8
    894: 143n.78, 149n.94, 153
    895: 149nn.93,94
    895–6: 149nn.93,94, 150n.96, 153
    896: 149n.93
    1001: 151
    1388–9: 152
  Cyclops
    411: 143n.76
  Helen
    560: 145
  Herakles
    1263: 151n.98
  Hippolytus
    22–3: 251
    27–8: 132–3
    38–9: 134
    40: 135
    41–50: 256
    172–5: 129
    198–202: 129
    238: 134
    269: 129, 135
    272–6: 130
    296: 136
    323: 132
    337: 131
    339: 131
    341: 131

341–2: 134
343: 131
349: 135
359–61: 144
392: 136
394: 135
398–9: 134
399: 251
400–1: 134
437–8: 130
438: 134–5
439: 135
443: 144
464: 132
474–5: 134–5
475: 251, 279n.16
477: 135
507: 132
527: 134
530–4: 134
615: 132
965–7: 135
1082–3: 131
1434: 132
Iphigenia at Aulis
24–7: 146
30–4: 147, 153
31: 153–4
33–4: 153
394a: 143n.76
808–9: 133–4, 133n.51
Iphigenia among the Taurians
352–3: 51
911: 143n.76
Medea
331: 66n.35
Orestes
420: 143n.76
Phoenician Women
352: 143n.78
Rhesus
65: 143n.76
Suppliant Women
159: 143n.76

Trojan Women
885–6: 136, 151n.98
886: 149–50
889: 136n.55
Fragments
TrGF 2.623.2 = 5.1130 N.²:
143n.76
TrGF 5.62.1: 143n.76
TrGF 5.150.2: 143n.76
TrGF 5.152.1: 143n.78
TrGF 5.187.6: 279n.16
TrGF 5.282.5: 279n.16
TrGF 5.491.5: 143n.76
TrGF 5.584.2: 143n.76
Heraclitus (ed. Diels-Kranz)
22 B 53: 54
22 B 119: 220n.51, 239
Hermogenes
On types of style
249.12: 26n.2
249.12–19: 9–10
Herodotus, *Histories*
Book 1
1.13.2: 194, 208, 213
1.15–26.1: 209
1.28–29.1: 212
1.30.5: 38n.43
1.32.1: 140–2, 208, 221
1.32.4: 211
1.32.9: 221
1.39.2: 38n.43
1.46.1: 213
1.46.2: 209
1.47.3: 210, 216
1.48.1: 209
1.50.1: 210, 211n.22
1.53.3: 211
1.54.1: 211, 211n.22
1.55.1: 211
1.55.2: 212
1.56.1: 211n.22, 212, 213n.27
1.70.1: 213n.27
1.71.1: 211n.22, 219
1.71.2: 215

336 INDEX OF PASSAGES

Herodotus, *Histories* (cont.)
  1.71.4: 215
  1.73.1: 213
  1.73.2: 213
  1.75.2: 211n.22, 219
  1.77.4: 211n.22
  1.79.1: 38n.43
  1.80.5: 211n.22
  1.86.2: 216n.41, 244
  1.86.3: 245
  1.87.2: 216n.41, 245–6
  1.87.3: 215, 218, 243
  1.87.4: 215, 218, 221
  1.89.1: 221, 243
  1.89.3: 243
  1.90.2: 243
  1.90.3: 215, 243
  1.90.4: 215, 219, 242–3
  1.91: 242
  1.91.1: 213, 219, 242
  1.91.1–2: 194
  1.91.2: 243
  1.91.2–3: 143n.75
  1.91.3: 243
  1.91.4: 220
  1.91.4–5: 219
  1.91.5: 219
  1.91.6: 219, 265
  1.193.4: 111n.8
  1.207.1: 221
  1.214.1: 38n.43
  Book 2
    2.32.6: 111n.8
    2.38.2: 111n.8
    2.56.2: 111n.8
    2.63.3: 38n.43
    2.74: 111n.8
    2.91.2: 111n.8
    2.120.3: 38n.43
    2.120.5: 140
    2.138.4: 111n.8
  Book 3
    3.39.3: 81
    3.39.4: 82
    3.40.2: 140–2
    3.80.4: 111, 111n.7
    3.82.3: 38n.45
    3.108.1–2: 140–1
  Book 4
    4.3.3: 38n.43
    4.172.1: 111n.8
  Book 5
    5.87.2: 140
  Book 6
    6.84.1: 140
    6.136.2: 38n.43
  Book 7
    7.1.1: 38n.43
    7.2.1: 38n.45
    7.17.2: 140
    7.46.3: 111
    7.132.2: 262n.70
    7.153.4: 111, 111n.7
    7.167.1: 39n.46
    7.188.3: 255n.56
    7.226.2: 38n.43
    7.230: 38n.43
    7.235.4: 38n.43
  Book 8
    8.60γ: 246
    8.144.2: 61
  Book 9
    9.16.4: 140, 142
    9.16.5: 38n.43
    9.23.1: 38n.43
    9.62.2: 38n.43
    9.69.1: 38n.43
    9.101.1: 38n.43
Hippocratic Corpus (ed. Littré)
  De aere aquis et locis
    ch. 10: II 46.14–48.3: 68
    ch. 24: II 92.6–9: 115
  De affectionibus
    ch. 18: VI 226.5–6: 111n.6
  De articulis
    ch. 47: IV 206.9: 111n.6
  De diaeta
    Bk. 1, ch. 2: VI 470.2: 111n.6
    Bk. 2, ch. 40: VI 538.4: 111n.6
    Bk. 2, ch. 56: VI 568.4: 111n.6
  De diaeta in morbis acutis
    ch. 4: II 246.3–4: 111n.6

De flatibus
  ch. 14: VI 112.1: 111n.6
  ch. 14: VI 112.3: 111n.6
De locis in homine
  ch.1: VI 276 1.4: 111n.6
  ch. 9: VI 292.24: 111n.6
Epistulae
  27: IX 418.13: 111n.6
Prognosticon
  ch. 20: II 170.2: 111n.6
Prorrheticon
  Bk. 2, ch. 24: IX 54.6–7: 111n.6
Homer
  Iliad
    1.5: 237
    19.86–9: 215
    24.525–33: 87
  Odyssey
    1.22–7: 237
    1.68–70: 236
    1.74–5: 236
    1.322: 214n.31
    2.174–6: 236
    5.30–4: 237
    5.34: 240
    5.41–2: 235
    5.113–15: 235
    5.137–8: 237
    5.203–10: 238
    5.279: 238
    5.288–9: 237
    5.288–90: 235
    5.342: 241
    5.342–5: 239
    5.345: 235, 237
    5.346–50: 239
    5.356–7: 239
    5.358–64: 239
    5.370–5: 239
    5.382–7: 240
    5.388–9: 238
    5.391–2: 240
    5.426: 240
    5.427–8: 240
    5.436–7: 240
    7.259: 236
    9.530: 234
    9.532–3: 236
    9.532–5: 234–5
    9.534: 238
    13.297–9: 266
Isocrates
  2.9: 98
  7.9: 98n.56
  8.31: 98n.56
Longinus
  On the sublime
    14.11: 10n.16
Lysias
  5.3: 98n.56
Marcellinus
  Life of Thucydides
    35–9: 10n.16
    41: 10n.16
    50: 10n.16
    56: 10n.16
Plato
  Euthydemus
    291a4: 128n.39
  Republic
    573a4–b4: 297
    573b6–7: 297
    573c4–5: 297
    573c7–9: 297
    573d4–5: 297
    573d7–8: 297
    573e3–7: 297
    573e6–7: 297
  Symposium
    176e1–3: 204
    213a1–4: 205
    217a2–e1: 202
    218a2–7: 202
    219b3–e5: 202
    222a8–c3: 202
Plutarch
  Life of Nicias
    1.1: 14
    1.2: 14
    11–12: 75n.60
    24: 75n.60
Sophocles
  Antigone
    332–3: 302
    616–25: 123n.29

338   INDEX OF PASSAGES

Sophocles (cont.)
  Oedipus Tyrannus
    776–7: 66n.35
  Philoctetes
    88: 114n.12
Thucydides, History of the
    Peloponnesian War
  Book 1
    1.1.2: 14, 79
    1.2–11: 81n.15
    1.2.2: 79
    1.2.3: 79
    1.2.6: 96
    1.5.2: 56
    1.7: 83
    1.8.2: 84
    1.12–19: 81n.15
    1.12.1: 83n.19, 96
    1.13.1: 83
    1.13.5: 84
    1.13.6: 82
    1.15.1: 83n.19
    1.15.3: 83n.19
    1.16.1: 83n.19, 96
    1.17: 96
    1.19: 83n.19
    1.20.1: 16
    1.21.1: 15
    1.22.1: 16, 85n.24
    1.22.2: 16, 139
    1.22.3: 255n.56
    1.22.4: 18, 76–9, 115, 117,
      137, 139
    1.23: 14n.33
    1.23.1: 15, 66, 119
    1.23.3: 70, 72n.56
    1.23.4–5: 163
    1.23.5: 260–3, 269
    1.23.6: 9n.15, 33, 88, 160–1,
      161n.8, 162, 168, 257–63,
      258nn.59,60, 304, 309–10
    1.33.2: 104, 123
    1.33.3: 168
    1.41.2: 31
    1.44.1: 227
    1.44.2: 104–5
    1.49.7: 98
    1.68.1: 253n.50
    1.68.1–2: 268
    1.69.1–2: 268
    1.69.4: 28
    1.70: 26n.2
    1.70.2: 188n.54
    1.70.3: 47n.2, 188n.55
    1.70.4: 188n.54
    1.70.7: 188n.55
    1.70.9: 112n.10
    1.71.1: 268
    1.71.4: 28, 188n.54
    1.71.7: 52
    1.72.1: 92
    1.73–88: 78
    1.73.3: 169n.24
    1.75.1: 106
    1.75.1–2: 95
    1.75.2: 92, 95
    1.75.3: 91, 106, 189, 190n.58, 230,
      252, 255
    1.75.4: 90, 127
    1.75.5: 255
    1.76.1–2: 230
    1.76.2: 20, 89, 127–8, 134, 189,
      190n.58, 229, 250, 252
    1.76.3: 92, 105–6, 118, 135,
      230, 252
    1.76.4: 103, 254
    1.77.2: 103, 254
    1.78: 268
    1.78.3: 174
    1.78.4: 92, 161, 166, 169n.24, 174
    1.81.5: 172
    1.81.6: 172, 190
    1.84.1: 28
    1.84.3: 169n.24, 301n.50, 307
    1.84.3–4: 311
    1.84.4: 169n.24, 190, 301n.50
    1.85.2: 166, 169n.24
    1.87.2: 227

INDEX OF PASSAGES 339

1.87.3: 227
1.88: 161n.8, 166, 168
1.89–118: 93
1.89.1: 93
1.89.2: 94, 96–7
1.89.3: 96
1.90.3: 96
1.91.4: 96
1.93.3: 97n.52
1.94–96.1: 95
1.95.1: 95
1.95.3: 94
1.95.7: 95
1.96.1: 95, 100
1.97.2: 94
1.99.1: 95
1.99.2: 95
1.99.3: 96–7
1.109.1: 59, 59n.22
1.110.4: 68n.39
1.117.1: 68n.39
1.118.2: 93, 97, 99
1.121.3: 191
1.122.1: 32–3, 54, 190–1
1.124.2: 164
1.125.1: 166
1.125.2: 160
1.130.2: 302n.51
1.138.3: 97n.52, 311
1.139.4: 300, 311
1.140.1: 93n.44, 284–5, 288, 299, 301n.50, 301–2, 302n.51, 304–8, 314
1.140.4: 160
1.141.1: 160
1.143.5–144.1: 270
1.144.1: 103, 273, 307
1.144.2: 166
1.144.3: 160, 164, 273
1.144.4: 273, 284–6
1.145: 160
Book 2
  2.1: 262
  2.13.2: 270, 284–5
2.19.1: 59n.23
2.21.2: 31
2.21.3: 282n.19
2.22.1: 281, 282n.19, 284–5, 299
2.34.6: 299
2.37.2: 30
2.38.1: 284–5
2.38.2: 304
2.40.2: 286
2.40.3: 283, 286, 288, 301n.50
2.42.4: 19
2.43.1: 273, 286–7
2.43.2: 19
2.43.3: 284–5
2.43.5–6: 19
2.48.3: 66n.36, 68n.42, 78
2.49.4: 68n.42
2.49.6: 68n.42
2.50.1: 68n.42, 251, 306
2.51.5: 19, 252
2.53.1: 15, 66n.36
2.53.4: 68n.42
2.55.2: 299
2.59.1: 275, 300
2.59.1–2: 278
2.59.2: 276–7, 299
2.59.3: 227, 275n.13, 280–1, 282n.19, 284–5, 299
2.60.1: 227, 275n.13, 278–9, 282n.19
2.60.5: 275n.13, 279, 282n.19
2.61.2: 66n.36, 68n.42, 277, 290–1, 293n.38
2.61.3: 291, 293, 308
2.62.4: 284–5
2.62.5: 284–6
2.63: 273
2.63.2: 101, 190n.58
2.64.1: 251, 275n.13, 282n.19, 306
2.64.1–2: 314
2.64.2: 252, 306
2.64.3: 112n.10, 154, 303, 308, 314–15

340 INDEX OF PASSAGES

Thucydides, *History of the Peloponnesian War* (cont.)
 2.64.4–6: 273
 2.64.6: 284–5, 288
 2.65: 271
 2.65.1: 275n.13, 282n.19, 284–5, 289, 294, 315
 2.65.3: 275n.13
 2.65.5: 272–3
 2.65.5–13: 311
 2.65.6: 272
 2.65.6–7: 103
 2.65.7: 103, 270, 272, 306–7
 2.65.8: 279, 299, 313
 2.65.9: 275n.13, 281n.17, 280–1
 2.65.11: 196
 2.77.2: 59n.23
 2.90.4: 255n.56
 2.93.4: 68n.39
Book 3
 3.3.1: 157
 3.3.3: 68n.39
 3.10.1: 30
 3.12.3: 28
 3.36.2: 227, 232
 3.36.4: 228
 3.38.1: 180, 231–2
 3.39.4: 180
 3.39.5: 109–10, 112n.10, 154, 189, 230n.5
 3.42.1: 227, 229, 231, 298
 3.42.5: 298
 3.43.2: 313
 3.43.4: 229, 231
 3.44.1: 230, 298
 3.44.2: 229
 3.44.3: 298
 3.44.4: 230, 298
 3.45: 129
 3.45.2: 132
 3.45.3: 112n.10, 120–1, 230
 3.45.3–7: 232
 3.45.4: 125, 128, 132, 134, 170, 174, 232, 251, 255, 279
 3.45.4–5: 170, 312
 3.45.4–6: 121–3
 3.45.5: 129, 133–4, 170, 173, 182, 189, 198, 251, 279
 3.45.5–6: 182n.42
 3.45.6: 21, 170, 229–31
 3.45.7: 78n.6, 121, 125, 135, 198n.7, 199–200, 230, 232, 314
 3.46–7: 230
 3.46.1: 298
 3.48.2: 298
 3.49.1: 227
 3.53.3: 276–7
 3.57.3: 98
 3.58.1: 140
 3.58.5: 140
 3.59.2: 140
 3.70–81: 36
 3.70.1: 44
 3.70.4: 37n.40, 39
 3.70.5: 41
 3.71.2: 37n.40, 39n.47
 3.74.1: 37n.40, 38, 39n.47, 41
 3.74.2: 37n.40, 38, 39n.47, 42–3, 44n.54
 3.75.3: 44n.54
 3.75.4: 41–2
 3.75.5: 37n.40, 38n.42, 44n.54
 3.76.1: 37n.40, 38, 39n.47, 44
 3.77.2: 37n.40, 39n.47, 140
 3.77.3: 140
 3.77.4: 140
 3.78.1: 44n.54, 67
 3.78.2: 44n.54
 3.78.4: 37n.40, 39n.47
 3.79.1: 44n.54
 3.80.2: 41
 3.81.4: 37n.40, 39
 3.81.5: 37n.40, 39, 59, 90
 3.82.1: 15, 37nn.38,39, 40, 61
 3.82.2: 14, 18, 24, 37n.39, 40, 41n.51, 53, 65, 67, 68n.44, 70–1, 76–7, 93n.44, 106, 117, 171
 3.82.3: 1, 37n.39, 40, 41n.51, 45

3.82.4: 5, 7, 37n.39, 40n.50, 47–8, 61
3.82.4–5: 61
3.82.6: 37n.39, 40, 41n.51, 48, 61, 61n.28
3.82.7: 37n.39, 41, 41n.51
3.82.8: 37n.39, 41n.51, 50, 56–9, 56n.18, 61n.28, 63, 90, 106, 127, 279
3.83.1: 37n.39, 55, 59–62, 90
3.83.2: 37n.39, 41, 41n.51
3.83.3: 41n.51, 42–3, 106
3.84.1: 103n.62
3.84.2: 251
3.87.1: 68n.42
3.98.3: 59, 59n.22
3.112.3: 68n.39
3.112.5: 68n.39
3.112.7: 59, 59n.22
3.115.4: 179

Book 4
4.10.1: 187
4.12.3: 187
4.14.2: 187
4.14.3: 171, 178
4.17.3: 169
4.17.3–4: 312
4.17.4: 169–71, 173, 175, 197, 181, 184n.45, 185, 187
4.17.5: 171, 181
4.18.3: 170–1, 178
4.18.4: 172, 181–2
4.19.4: 112n.10
4.20.1: 173–5
4.21.2: 175, 185
4.21.3: 180–1
4.22.3: 184n.44
4.25.9: 68n.39
4.26.4: 180–1
4.26.5: 162
4.34.3: 187
4.38.1: 27n.8
4.40.1: 19, 180–1
4.41.3: 193
4.41.3–4: 184n.44
4.41.4: 175, 185

4.55.1: 176–8, 187
4.55.3: 177–8
4.55.4: 178, 184
4.59.2: 198n.7
4.60.1: 192, 198
4.60.2: 192, 262n.70
4.61.1: 192
4.61.2: 192
4.61.3: 112n.10
4.61.5: 109–10, 112n.10, 115, 154, 189
4.62.3: 183
4.62.4: 182–3
4.65.3: 179
4.65.4: 171, 179–85, 312
4.72.2: 68n.39
4.92.2: 175n.32
4.108.4: 295

Book 5
5.9.8: 114, 114n.12
5.14.2: 184
5.14.3: 171, 191
5.25.3: 262–3
5.61.2: 262n.70
5.70.1: 138n.57
5.87: 298
5.91.1: 118n.18
5.91.2: 118n.18
5.95: 118n.18
5.97: 118n.18, 190
5.99: 118n.18
5.103.1: 123, 135, 157, 189
5.103.2: 124, 157, 189, 298
5.104: 138
5.105.1: 138
5.105.2: 20, 109, 116–17, 135, 137–9, 153, 253n.50
5.105.2–3: 153
5.105.3: 138–9
5.111.2: 157
5.112.2: 140
5.113: 157, 296n.41, 298

Book 6
6.1.1: 156
6.6.1: 191, 199, 254
6.6.2: 199

Thucydides, *History of the Peloponnesian War* (*cont.*)
  6.8.2: 197
  6.8.4: 191, 200
  6.9.3: 190, 199, 296n.42
  6.10.1: 197
  6.10.5: 185, 190, 197
  6.11.2: 189
  6.11.4: 296n.42
  6.12.1: 97
  6.12.2: 190, 202
  6.13.1: 135, 156, 184, 187, 190, 197, 296n.42
  6.14: 136
  6.15.2: 156, 184, 196, 198–9, 202
  6.15.3: 197, 253n.50
  6.15.4: 197
  6.16.2: 30
  6.16.4: 203
  6.16.6: 185, 197
  6.17.1: 202
  6.17.2–5: 198
  6.17.6: 198
  6.18.2: 190
  6.18.3: 102, 190, 198
  6.18.4: 97, 192
  6.18.5–6: 201
  6.18.6: 200, 202
  6.18.7: 190
  6.19.1: 195, 199, 203–4
  6.19.2: 200
  6.20.1: 199
  6.24.1: 200
  6.24.2: 185–7, 197, 199
  6.24.3: 69, 133, 156, 184, 188, 191, 296n.42
  6.24.4: 197
  6.26.1: 193
  6.30.2: 156, 184
  6.31.3: 197
  6.31.6: 156, 184
  6.33.2: 197
  6.33.6: 97
  6.46.2: 162
  6.54.2: 51n.8
  6.83.4: 189
  6.90.3: 192
  6.92.4: 204
  6.93.1: 204
  6.93.1–2: 166
  6.97.3: 255n.56
  6.105.1: 166
Book 7
  7.2.1: 255n.56
  7.18.2: 166–7, 266
  7.18.3: 166–7, 187
  7.24.3: 280
  7.28.4: 70n.50
  7.29.3: 68n.39, 69
  7.29.5: 59, 59n.22, 60, 68n.39, 69
  7.57.1: 255, 255n.56
  7.67.4: 276
  7.69.2: 140
  7.72.4: 280
  7.75.5: 35
  7.77.2: 140
  7.77.3: 140
  7.77.4: 140, 280
  7.85.1: 19
  7.86.5: 98
Book 8
  8.1.2: 280
  8.2.4: 191
  8.24.4: 22n.58
  8.40.2: 22n.58
  8.84.4: 68n.39
  8.96.5: 188–9, 188nn.54,55
Xenophon
 Anabasis
  1.8.25: 39n.46
  2.1.1: 38n.44
  2.1.6: 38n.44
  2.2.21: 38n.44
  4.8.21: 39n.46
  5.2.9: 38n.44
  6.1.29: 38n.45
 Cynegeticus
  13.10: 106n.64
 Cyropaedia
  1.6.54: 262n.70
  5.1.11: 113
  5.1.16: 112n.9

de Equitandi ratione
   5.4: 112n.9
   7.12: 112n.9
   10.14: 112n.9
Hiero
   3.9: 113
   3.9: 116
Historica Graeca
   1.1.32: 38n.45
   1.7.35: 38n.45
   3.1.2: 38n.44
   3.2.29: 38n.44
   3.4.25: 38n.44
   3.5.19: 38n.44
   4.2.18: 38n.44
   4.2.23: 38n.44
   4.8.29: 38n.44
   6.3.6: 262n.70
   6.4.9: 38n.44
   7.5.20: 38n.44
   7.5.26: 38n.44
   7.5.27: 38n.44
Memorabilia
   1.2.64: 145n.84
Oeconomicus
   9.19: 113
de Vectigalibus
   5.2: 112n.9

Subject Index

For the benefit of digital users, indexed terms that span two pages (e.g., 52–53) may, on occasion, appear on only one of those pages.

Abstract nominal forms (in ancient Greek generally)
   adjectival vs. verbal 8, 27
   definition of 8, 27
   indications of time of day frequent in subject position 37
   overview of 26–8
   and substantivized adjectives 28
Abstract nominal phrases in Thucydides
   accumulations of 4, 6, 30–1, 40–2, 51–2, 55–6, 65–6, 178–9
   vs. active / personal phrasing 173–5, 183, 231–2, 260–3, 313–14
   agency of humans called into question / deemphasized by 6–7, 51–2, 54–8, 62–3, 69–73, 76, 94–6, 122–3, 170–1, 177–9, 182–3, 185–8, 277, 291–2
   circumstances / conditions / states of affairs stressed by 2–3, 49–52, 54–5, 65–7, 72, 90–1, 102–3, 110, 114, 120, 124, 170–1, 176–9, 231–2, 253–4, 262–3, 277, 281–2
   and coinages of abstract nouns by Thucydides 27, 29, 31
   vs. 'common style': See *vs. 'plain style'*
   and dative of person 167–8, 173–5, 177, 187
   depersonalizing 2–4, 45, 48, 52–3, 58, 63, 69, 73, 76, 114, 119–20, 124, 291–2
   and dominant participle ('*ab-urbe-condita* construction') 161–2
   and events and circumstances presented as quasi-agents 2–3, 45, 53–5, 69–70, 172–3, 177–8, 186, 231–2, 251–2, 304–8
   generalizing 16, 59, 61–5, 115, 124
   and 'grand style' 9–10
   and Hippocratic Corpus 68–9, 110–11, 115, 119, 155
   idiosyncratic by standards of Greek prose 8–9, 26, 30–2, 34–5
   and nouns becoming hub of sentence 7, 55–7
   and passive phrases / shades of meaning 7, 20–1, 57–8, 61–3, 89, 91–2, 95–6, 123–4, 167–70, 176–80, 183, 186, 231–2, 253–4, 263, 276–7
   and perfect forms with static implications 90, 110, 114, 124, 167–8, 171, 176–9, 186–7, 231–2, 276–8, 304
   and personification 32–3, 53–5, 89–90, 104–5, 121–4, 132–3, 172–3, 177, 180–3, 291–2
   vs. 'plain style' 36–46, 67, 73–5, 193–4
   and poets 114n.12
   preferred to personal constructions 2–3, 31–2, 44–5, 47–52, 62, 114, 116, 277
   preferred to verbal constructions 3–5, 29–32, 40, 42–4, 51–2, 71, 157–8
   processes suggested by 4, 6–7, 82–4, 97–9, 119, 162–3, 165–6, 304
   and strategies used by Thucydides to foster abstraction 29–36
   as subjects 2–3, 32–3, 37–40, 50–1, 55–6, 67, 70, 162–3, 174–5, 176–7, 182–3, 231–2, 262, 275–7, 290–2
   unremarkable instance of 37–9

SUBJECT INDEX 345

summary of implications of 73, 119, 124
thought of Thucydides channeled
  by 15–17, 47, 73–5
Thucydides' fondness for 2, 8–9, 28–9,
  45–6
unwieldiness of 30–1, 43–4, 102, 178–9
See also *Archaeology: abstract nominal
  style in; Articular infinitive;
  Impersonal passive; Nominal
  periphrasis; Substantivized neuter
  phrases; πάσχω; πίπτω, compounds
  of; φύομαι, perfect forms of; χράομαι*
Aeschylus 143, 217, 302
  and Thucydides 133–4
Alcibiades
  and Athenian decision in favour of
    Sicilian Expedition 96–7, 185,
    189–90, 191–2, 195–8, 200, 222
  conciliatory personality of 202–3
  and desire 196–8, 200–3, 207, 222–5
  on equality 203
  and human nature 196, 212, 222–5
  individualized representation of 195,
    201–7 (esp. 205), 222, 224–5
  liked by everyone 203–5
  on necessities of power 102–4
  vs. Nicias 16n.38, 189–90, 195–6, 200,
    201–2, 206n.13
  vs. Pericles 103–4
  in Plato's *Symposium* 202–5
  at Sparta 203–4
  See also *Quest for power: and Alcibiades;
    ἐλπίς: and Alcibiades*
Archaeology
  abstract nominal style in 82–4
  and τὸ ἀνθρώπινον 79
  αὐξάνω in 96–7
  as blueprint for process 22–3, 80–1
  individuals in 81–2
  and material factors 22–3,
    79–84
  See also: *Fear: in Archaeology;
    Pentecontaetia: and Archaeology;
    Quest for power: and Archaeology;
    τὸ ἀνθρώπινον: and Archaeology*
Archidamus 88n.29, 169, 172–3, 190–1,
  300n.50, 310–11
Articular infinitive 4, 27–8, 43, 48, 55–6,
  72, 102–3, 157–8, 165–6, 178–9

dominant participle equivalent to 161
  rare before Thucydides 71
Asthenic verbs: see *Impersonal passive: and
  asthenic verbs; Nominal
  periphrasis: and asthenic verbs*
Athenians at Melos (Speech of)
  and 'divine' 138–40, 156
  on necessity 116–18, 153, 156
  self-confident tone of...about
    necessity 156–7
  See also *ἐλπίς: and Melian Dialogue*
Athenians at Sparta (Speech of)
  apologetic of Athens 92–3
  and depersonalizing style 89–92
  and 'greatest things' (fear, honour, and
    advantage) 20–2, 89–93, 101,
    105–8, 118, 127–8, 134, 151–2,
    190n.58, 230, 250–2
  on moderation of necessity 103–4,
    252–4
  on necessity of Athenian empire 88–93,
    101, 106–7
  and *Pentecontaetia* 93–5, 101
  self-confident tone of 105–7
  See also: *Necessity: of Athenian empire*
Athens and Athenians
  and Corcyrean alliance 105, 227
  exposed to forces beyond their
    control 92, 93–4, 96–7, 106–7,
    175–6, 179–88, 192–3, 275–7,
    303–4
  and fear 189–90
  justice as concern of 228–9, 252–3
  mentality of...in the wake of
    Pylos 175, 179–84
  and Mytilenean revolt 157–8, 227–30,
    232–3
  vs. Spartans 173–4, 176, 179, 184,
    188–9, 191–2, 229, 266, 305n.50,
    310–11
  See also *Desire: Athenian...(mostly for
    Sicily); Diodotus: lessons
    of...applicable to Athens;
    Irrational impulses: Athenians beset
    by; Pentecontaetia: Athenians
    presented as purposeful?; Sicilian
    Expedition: Athenian motivation
    for; ἐλπίς: and Athenians after
    Pylos; ἐλπίς: and Sicilian Expedition*

346 SUBJECT INDEX

Brasidas 23–4, 114–15, 205–7, 270, 296
Burckhardt, Jacob 314–15

Causation in Thucydides
 and collective passions 222, 254–5
 and disposition and trigger 257–60, 309–10
 and idea of contest 250–2, 257–9, 279–80, 310–11
 vs. modern ideas 247–9, 257, 265
 and 'truest cause of Peloponnesian War' 160–6, 257–65
Character: See *Necessity: and character*
Chios 22n.58
Choice (primarily in Thucydides)
 and freedom 23–4, 232–3, 253–4, 292–5, 298–9, 307–8, 311–12
 Greek vs. modern conception of 292–3
 impairment / erasure of 72–3, 173–5, 232–3, 291–3, 296–9
 qualified by necessity 23–4, 98–9, 207, 222, 224–5, 233, 265–9, 307–10
 and rationality 293–5, 311–12
 scope for 169–70, 173–4, 227–8, 230–3, 265, 270, 307–8, 310
 See also *Desire: as threat to rational choice*; *Diodotus: and choice*; *Irrational Impulses: and choice*; *Necessity (in Thucydides): and responsibility*; *Peloponnesian War: choice erased by*; *Pericles: and agency*; *Sicilian Expedition: individual agency intertwined with necessity*; *Sparta and Spartans: on scope for choice*; γνώμη: *as choice*
Cleon
 irrationality championed by 231–3
 on necessity 109–10, 113–16, 180–1
 See also *Diodotus: vs. Cleon*
Corcyreans at Athens (Speech of) 104–5, 123–4, 168
Corinthians (Speeches of)
 at Athens 5–6
 at Congress of Spartan allies 32–3, 164, 190–1

 at Sparta 52–3, 188–9, 268
Croesus (in Herodotus)
 and ἄτη 215–16
 caution displayed by 214
 character of... and necessity 208–9, 212, 216–17, 220–3, 266
 deceived by Apollo? 219–22, 242–3
 and Delphic oracle 209–11, 213–16, 218–19, 242
 and ἐλπίς 210–12
 and excess 211–12
 and Gyges 208, 213–14, 219, 246
 and layers of superhuman influence 242–3, 246
 personal labels for divine used by 243–4
 personal traits of 208–9, 212, 214
 preconceived opinions of 210–12, 215–16
 and predestination of his downfall 208–9, 213–14, 219, 243–4
 reaction of... to rise of Persia 208–9
 responsible for his downfall? 218–22
 See also *Herodotus*

Daemons and δαίμονες 128–9, 133–4, 136–7, 220–1, 238–9, 250–2
Demosthenes (Athenian general) 205–7
Depersonalizing style: See *Abstract nominal phrases in Thucydides*
Desire
 Athenian... (mostly for Sicily) 185–9, 191–2, 196–8, 266
 'for more' (πλεονεξία) 22–3, 58, 63–4, 105–6, 125–8, 159–60, 175, 185, 279
 and human nature 189, 196, 266, 295–7
 See also *Alcibiades: and desire*; ἔρως
Diodotus
 vs. Cleon 229
 and Euripidean tragedy 129, 132–7
 as 'gift of Zeus' 232–3
 and 'greatest things' (freedom or dominion over others) 229–31
 on human nature 120–7

SUBJECT INDEX 347

lessons of... applicable to
    Athens 157-8, 198-200
ὀργή defeated by 227-8
and 'stronger ones' 128-9
rhetorical strategy of 229-31, 312-13
See also *Sicilian Expedition, Decision for:
and Diodotus; Spartans at Athens:
and Diodotus;* ἐλπίς: *Diodotus on;*
ἔρως: *Diodotus on;* κρείσσων: *in
Diodotus' speech;* τύχη: *Diodotus
on*

Dionysius of Halicarnassus
    on abstract style in Thucydides 9
    on ἀληθεστάτη πρόφασις 164-6
    on 'common style' of Thucydides 36
    on continuity between Thucydides' style
        and subject matter 12-15
    critical of Thucydides' style 1-6, 10, 25
    on grandeur of Thucydides 10
    on idiosyncrasy of Thucydides' style 8,
        11, 15, 34-5
    labels used by... to characterize
        Thucydides' Style 1-2, 4-5, 11
    on 'persons replacing things' 52-3
    rewriting Thucydidean passages 1-7, 48
    on 'things replacing persons' 47, 76
    See also: δεινός *and* δεινότης: *applied by
ancient literary critics to
Thucydides;* πάθος, πάθημα, *and*
παθητικός: *applied by Dionysius to
Thucydides;* φόβος, φοβερός, *and*
φοβέομαι: *applied by Dionysius to
Thucydides*

'Divine, The' (τὸ θεῖον, τὸ δαιμόνιον etc.)
    in Euripides 143-54
    in Herodotus 140-3, 154-5, 243-4
    vs. 'the human' 137-40, 143, 155
    in Melian Dialogue 137-41
    vs. personal labels 140, 243-4
    rare in Aeschylus and Sophocles 143
    See also: *Athenians at Melos: and
'divine'; Necessity (in Thucydides):
and divine*

Dual Motivation: See *Herodotus: on
human and divine level of
causation; Homer: and dual
motivation; Necessity (in
Thucydides): and dual motivation*

Euripides:
    and naturalistic representation of
        divine forces 129-33, 136-7, 144,
        149-52, 154
    parallels between... and
        Thucydides 129, 132-7, 153-5
    See also *'Divine, The': in Euripides;
Necessity (in Thucydides): and
Euripides; Sicilian Expedition,
Decision for: and Euripides on* ἔρως;
*Substantivized neuter phrases: in
Euripides compared with
Thucydides;* ἀνάγκη: *in Euripides;*
ἔρως: *in Euripides (compared with
Thucydides)*

Fear
    in *Archaeology* 22-3
    and human nature 189, 190n.58, 266
    as motivation for Sicilian
        Expedition 189-90
    Pericles confronted with 275, 280-1
    and stasis at Corcyra 42-4, 106
    See also *Athens and Athenians: and fear;
Athenians at Sparta: and 'greatest
things'; Sparta and Spartans: and
Fear;* φόβος

'Greatest things' (τὰ μέγιστα): See
    *Athenians at Sparta: and 'greatest
things'; Diodotus: and 'greatest
things'*
Greek Pessimism 314-15

Hermocrates
    on Athenian concern with Sicily 191-2,
        197-8
    and Athenian mentality after
        Pylos 182-4
    on necessity of human
        behaviour 109-10, 112-16
    successful as leader 23-4, 270
    Thucydides' depiction of 205-7

348 SUBJECT INDEX

Hermogenes
  on Thucydides' abstract style 9–10
Herodotus
  and dual motivation: See *on human and divine level of causation*
  and τὸ Ἑλληνικόν 61
  on fate or 'Fates' 143n.75, 242–4
  and flexible necessity 242–3, 245–7, 264–5
  on human and divine level of causation 207–8, 212–18, 220–2, 225–6, 244–6
  and immanent causation 193–4, 209, 212–13, 217
  and predestination of decisive events 208–9, 213–14, 219, 243–4, 246–7
  See also *Croesus*; *'Divine, The': in Herodotus*; *Individuals: in Herodotus vs. Thucydides*; *Necessity (in Thucydides): and Herodotus*
Homer
  character and divine influence in 238–43, 266
  and dual motivation 240–1, 267–8
  homecoming of Odysseus in 234–8
  individuals in 223–4
  layers of superhuman influence in 236–8, 240, 242
  momentous events foreordained in 234, 240
  and Odysseus' contribution to his rescue off Scheria 239–41
  plan of Zeus in 229
  Polyphemus' prayer in 234–8
  scope for agency in 234, 236, 238–42, 264–5
  See also: *Necessity (in Thucydides): and Homer*; *Speeches in Thucydides: and Homeric model*

Impersonal passive
  and asthenic verbs 57, 66–7, 69
  definition of 35–6
  and emotional states 57–8
  and nominal periphrasis 35

  unremarkable instances of 38–9
  See also *Nominal periphrasis*; ἵστημι, *compounds of*
Individuals
  appraisal of... in Thucydides 272
  depersonalizing presentation of... in Thucydides 75, 81–2, 205–7
  depiction of... in Greek literature 223–4
  in Herodotus vs. Thucydides 81–2
  withstanding necessity 19–20, 23–4, 227–8, 270, 279–82, 289, 294–5, 307–8, 310–11
  See also *Alcibiades: individualized representation of*; *Sicilian Expedition, Decision for: and individual agents*
Inner vs. outer
  distinction of... collapsed 54–5, 122–8
Invisible things (τὰ ἀφανῆ) 128–9, 157–8, 198–9, 295–8
Irony 180–1, 184–5
Irrational impulses
  as agents 122–4
  Athenians beset by 132–6, 175, 157–8, 183–4, 181–8, 189–90, 196–200, 270–1, 276–82, 299–301, 306–7
  and choice 231–3, 271, 290–9, 310–12
  and circumstances 54–5, 192–3
  dominating intellect 296–9
  and human nature 105–8, 121–8, 132, 189–93, 199–201, 230–1, 233, 253–4, 263–4, 266, 271, 295–9, 309–12
  and Plato on tyrant 297
  See also *Causation in Thucydides: and collective passions*; *Cleon: irrationality championed by*; *Desire*; *Fear*; *Pericles: prevailing over irrationality*; γνώμη: *vs. passion*; ἔρως; ἐλπίς; κρείσσων: *passions as*

Lincoln, Abraham 268–9

Mycalessus
  and compounds of πίπτω 69–70, 187–8, 275–6
  and πᾶσα ἰδέα 60

Mytilene
  secession of 108–9, 121, 157–8, 180–1, 200–1, 228, 230–1, 311–12
  See also *Athens and Athenians: and Mytilenean revolt*

National character: See *Nature: and national character*
Nature (φύσις)
  as agent 116, 121
  continuous with moral order 116–17, 119–20
  and drives 121–3
  and dynamic forces 124, 128
  and Hippocratic Corpus 65, 110–11, 119, 155
  hostile, presented as 122–3
  mechanistic conception of 249, 257
  vs. national character 188–93
  and νόμος 148–9, 153
  pessimistic view of 120–1
  as predisposition 110–11, 128, 249–50, 304
  as process 304
  two perspectives on 108–9
  See also *Alcibiades: and human nature; Desire: and human nature; Diodotus: on human nature; Euripides: and naturalistic representation of divine forces; Fear: and human nature; Irrational impulses: and human nature; Necessity (in Thucydides): and nature*
Necessity (in Thucydides)
  of Athenian empire 88–93, 95–101
  vs. causal determinism 20, 23–4, 265, 309–11
  and character 212, 217, 222–6, 266
  and circular pattern of events 18, 65, 76, 117–18
  and circumstances / material conditions / states of affairs 72–3, 76–7, 80–2, 92–7, 124–8, 169–74, 181–4, 277
  vs. contingency 17–18, 23–4, 259–60, 267

and divine 136–7, 154–5
and dual motivation model 20, 225–8, 257–9, 267–8, 310
and Euripides 153–4, 225, 251, 256–7
flexible 23–4, 118, 228, 252–7, 263–5, 310–11
'hard' vs. 'practical' 19–21, 89–90
and Herodotus 222–3, 264–7
and Homer 264–8
impersonal element in 80–1, 89–90, 109, 124, 137, 143, 155, 162–3, 192–3, 293–4
of momentous events 257–66, 309–10
and nature (φύσις) 18, 22–3, 65, 72–3, 92, 105–6, 116–17, 136–7, 153, 249–50, 263–4, 303–4, 309–10
'practical': See *'hard' vs. 'practical'*
and processes 22–3, 90–2, 95–101, 162–3, 259–60, 265, 268, 303–4, 309–10
pull exerted by 92, 253–4, 268
and responsibility 222, 265–6
scholarly approaches to 18–23
and style 75
See also *Athenians at Melos: on necessity; Athenians at Melos: and self-confident tone about necessity; Athenians at Sparta: on moderation of necessity; Athenians at Sparta: and 'greatest things'; Athenians at Sparta: on necessity of Athenian empire; Choice: qualified by necessity; Cleon: on necessity; Hermocrates: on necessity of human behaviour; Individuals: withstanding necessity; Peloponnesian War: necessity of; Quest for power: as necessity; Sicilian Expedition: and individual agency intertwined with necessity; Spartan and Spartans: necessity withstood by?;* ἀνάγκη; τὸ ἀνθρώπινον: *and necessity;* κρείσσων: *necessity captured by;* τύχη: *and necessity in Thucydides*

Nicias
  and Athenian decision for Sicilian
      Expedition 135–6, 185–92,
      197–200, 277–8
  inadequacy of 195–6
  and personal gods 140
  and retreat at Sicily 19–20
  Thucydides' depiction of 205–7
  See also *Alcibiades: vs. Nicias*
Nietzsche, Friedrich 314–15
Nominal periphrasis
  and asthenic verbs 33–4, 49
  compounds of ἵστημι in 33–4
  definition of 33–4
  fondness of Thucydides for 3–4,
      34–5, 39
  unremarkable instances of 38–9
  See also *Impersonal passive*; *ἵστημι,
      compounds of*

Pale verbs: See *Impersonal passive:
    and asthenic verbs*;
    *Nominal periphrasis: and asthenic
    verbs*
Pathology of war
  kinship disrupted in 48–9
  locus classicus for abstract style 26
  and stasis as attacker 68–9
  and stasis as disease 68–9
  stylistic comparison with preceding
      narrative 36–45, 67
  See *Abstract nominal phrases in
      Thucydides*; *Fear: and stasis at
      Corcyra*
Peace of Nicias 159–60, 166–7, 184n.45,
      190–1, 262
Peloponnesian War
  and American Civil War 268–9
  as attacker 70, 177, 275–6
  choice erased by 173–4
  as commonly characterized by
      Thucydides 14–15
  as cosmic principle 53–4
  encapsulated by various forces 69–70,
      187–8
  necessity of 164–6, 257–65, 268

  personified 33, 53–5
  See also *Plague: and character of
      Peloponnesian War*; *Sparta and
      Spartans: reopening the
      Peloponnesian War*; *Sparta and
      Spartans: responsibility for
      Peloponnesian War*
Pentecontaetia
  and *Archaeology* 96–7
  Athenians presented as purposeful
      in? 94–6, 99–101
  depersonalizing style in 93–9
  process (as opposed to action)
      highlighted by 95–9, 101
  See: *Athenians at Sparta: and
      Pentecontaetia*
Pericles
  and agency 23–4, 271, 289, 294–5,
      307–8
  antitheses involving γνώμη in speeches
      of 283–9, 313–14
  and balance 281–2, 285–7, 289, 313–14
  on empire as tyranny 100–1
  exceptionality of 298–9, 311–12
  and ideal 273–4, 289
  and pessimism 303–8, 314–15
  prevailing over irrationality 23–4,
      227–8, 279–82, 287–8
  on soldiers overcoming survival
      instinct 19–20
  and strategy in Peloponnesian
      War 103–4, 270–1, 310
  and "stronger" 279–80
  and "strongest" 288–9
  Thucydides' view of 271–5
  See also: *Alcibiades: vs. Pericles*; *Fear:
      Pericles confronted with*;
      *Substantivized neuter phrases: and
      Pericles*; *Γνώμη: championed by
      Pericles*; *ἐλπίς: in Pericles' speeches*;
      κρείσσων: Pericles as; *τύχη: and
      Pericles*
Plague
  and character of Peloponnesian War 15
  and compounds of πίπτω 68–70,
      187–8, 275–6

SUBJECT INDEX 351

and κρείσσων 251–2, 306
as μεταβολή 66n.36, 290–1, 311–12
'usefulness' of Thucydides' description of 77–8
Plain style of Thucydides: See *Abstract nominal phrases in Thucydides: vs. plain style; Dionysius of Halicarnassus: on 'common style' of Thucydides*
Plataea and Plataeans 140, 229, 276–7
Plutarch
  on style of Thucydides 14
'Present things / circumstances' (τὰ παρόντα, τὰ ὑπάρχοντα, τὰ πράγματα etc.) 53–5, 93–4, 120, 170–2, 179–80, 252–4, 281–2, 285–9, 294–5
Pylos
  significance of events at 159–60
  See also *Athens and Athenians: mentality of... in the wake of Pylos; Hermocrates: and Athenian mentality after Pylos; Sicilian Expedition, Decision for: and Pylos; Sparta and Spartans: after Pylos; ἐλπίς: and Athenians after Pylos; τύχη: and Pylos*

Quest for power
  and Alcibiades 196–7
  and *Archaeology* 22–3, 80–4
  as bare fact 127–8
  as insatiable 80–1, 99
  mainsprings of 22–3, 105–6
  as necessity 20–2, 63–4, 81–2, 89–93, 102–4, 119, 127–8, 153, 250, 263–4, 266, 309–10
  and scope for moderation 118, 253–4, 256
  self-destructive 22–3, 105–8, 122, 311–12
  and self-preservation 102–3, 230–1, 253–4
  as uncontrollable 20–1, 95–105, 118
  See also *Alcibiades: on necessities of power; Athenians at Sparta: on necessity of Athenian empire;*
  Sicilian Expedition, Decision for: and wish to rule Sicily in its 'entirety'; Sparta and Spartans: wishing to rule Greece in its 'entirety'

Reversal: See μεταβολή
Rigour, Thucydides' concern with 73–4

Sicilian Expedition, Decision for
  Athenian motivation for 133–4, 184–8, 254–5
  and Euripides on ἔρως 200–1
  and Diodotus 198–200, 222, 225–6
  and individual agents 195–6
  and Pylos 185–6
  and responsibility 222
  and transpersonal forces 200–1
  and wish to rule Sicily in its 'entirety' 191–2
  See also *Alcibiades: and Athenian decision in favour of Sicilian Expedition; Desire: Athenian ... (mostly for Sicily); Fear: as motivation for the Sicilian Expedition; Hermocrates: on Athenian concern with Sicily; Nicias: and Athenian decision for Sicilian Expedition; ἐλπίς: and Sicilian Expedition; ἔρως: and Sicilian Expedition*

Sparta and Spartans
  after Pylos 176–9
  character of... reflected by necessity 266
  exposed to forces beyond their control 167–9, 176–9, 184
  and fear 160–4, 161n.8, 168–9, 176–8, 188–9, 257–62, 266
  and hope 190–1
  necessity withstood by? 19–20, 22n.58
  and Plataea 229
  reopening Peloponnesian War 166–7
  responsibility for Peloponnesian War 166, 168–9, 227–8, 265–6
  wishing to rule Greece in its 'entirety' 191–2
  See also: *Athens and Athenians: vs. Spartans; ἐλπίς: Spartans affected by*

352 SUBJECT INDEX

Spartans at Athens (Speech of)
  on chance 171-3
  on dangers of good fortune 169-71
  and Diodotus 170, 174-5
  proven right 175-6, 312
  on scope for choice 169-70, 173-5
  and speeches at debate at Sparta in book 1 172-4
  stylistic implications of... summarized 176
  See also ἐλπίς: *in speech of Spartans at Athens*
Speeches in Thucydides (generally) 84-8
  and ancient vs. modern assumptions 86-8
  higher-order insights afforded by 85
  and Homeric model 86-8
  issues for reflection raised by 86
  and objectivity 86-8
  rhetorical function of 85
Stasis, Excursus on: See *Pathology of war*
Style of Thucydides, General features of 25
Substantivized neuter phrases
  abstract vs. collective sense of 48-50, 60-1
  based on adjectives 48-50, 60-3, 67, 70, 76-7, 83-4, 115-16, 137-55, 172-3, 176-7, 182-3, 186, 290-2, 304
  based on nominal phrases (i.e. with article governing genitive or prepositional phrase) 172, 178, 183, 278
  based on participles (= *schema Thucydideum*) 27, 114-15, 185-6, 277, 291-2
  in Euripides compared with Thucydides 153-4
  frequent in Thucydides 29
  and Pericles 280-1
  vivid compared to abstract nouns 28-9
  See also: τὸ ἀνθρώπινον *and* τὸ ἀνθρώπειον: and implications of neuter
Success
  resulting in loss of control 169-71
  unexpected 169-70, 180-1
Syracuse and Syracusans 14, 188-90, 276-7

Thracian allies of Athens 296-9, 311-12
  See also ἐλπίς: *and Thracian allies*
Tragic perspective of Thucydides 22-3, 106-7, 274-5, 302-3

Greek Terms

For the benefit of digital users, indexed terms that span two pages (e.g., 52-53) may, on occasion, appear on only one of those pages.

ἀνάγκη
  in Euripides 135-7
  meaning of... in Thucydides 19-22, 92
  See also *Necessity*
ἀνήκεστος 135, 174-5
τὸ ἀνθρώπινον and τὸ ἀνθρώπειον ('the human')
  and *Archaeology* 79
  beyond human control 156-8, 192-3
  and necessity 18, 76, 137, 265
  and implications of neuter 76-7, 80-2, 115-16, 120, 137, 192-3
  in Melian Dialogue 139, 157-8
  See also *'Divine, The'*: vs. *'the human'*
αὐξάνω 96-7
Γνώμη (and γιγνώσκω)
  and antithesis 283-8, 313-14
  championed by Pericles 282-4, 313-14
  as choice 291-2, 294-5
  enslavement of 291-2
  equivocalness of 299-303
  vs. external circumstances 283-9, 294-5
  and Hippocratic ideas 289
  meaning of 282-3, 299
  vs. passion 282-91, 294-5
  struggling with contrary impulses 285-91, 297
  volitional connotations of 290-1
  weakness of 290-1
  See also *Pericles: antitheses involving γνώμη in speeches of*
τὸ δαιμόνιον: See *'Divine, The'*
δαίμων: See *Daemons*

δεινός and δεινότης:
  as term applied by ancient literary critics to Thucydides 11-14
τὸ Ἑλληνικόν 60-3
ἐλπίς ('hope' or 'expectation') and ἐλπίζω and εὔελπις:
  and Alcibiades 196, 198, 205, 222
  and Athenians after Pylos 159-60, 181-3
  Diodotus on 121-6, 128-9, 132, 134-5, 157-8, 189, 198-9, 233, 250-1
  and Melian Dialogue 123-4, 135, 156-7, 189
  in Pericles' speeches 285-6
  and Sicilian Expedition 133-6, 156-7, 184-5, 195, 198-201, 222, 266
  Spartans affected by 190-2
  and Thracian allies 295-9
  in speech of Spartans at Athens 170, 176
ἐμπίπτω: See πίπτω: *compounds of*
ἐπιπίπτω: See πίπτω: *compounds of*
ἔργον
  'fact' rather than 'deed' denoted by 91
  vs. λόγος 120, 286-7
ἔρως
  Diodotus on 121-6, 128-9, 132, 172-3, 198-9, 222, 250-1, 279
  in Euripides (compared with Thucydides) 129, 132-6
  and Sicilian Expedition 69-70, 156-7, 184-5, 187-91, 195, 198, 200-1, 207, 222, 233, 254-5, 275-6
  and tyrant in Plato's *Republic* 297
  See also *Desire*

354 GREEK TERMS

εὐβουλία 169, 173–4, 297–8
τὸ θεῖον: See 'Divine, The'
ἰδέα, πᾶσα 59–60
ἵστημι, compounds of 58–60, 65–6, 82–4,
  90, 94, 102–5, 123–4, 167–8, 177,
  186–7, 261–3, 276–7, 279–80
  and κατάστασις 90–1, 263
κατέχω ('to possess', typically of daemonic
  agents possessing humans) 128–9,
  132–3
κρείσσων ('stronger')
  in Diodotus' speech 128–9
  as label for daemons 128–9, 134–5
  necessity captured by 135, 250–2
  passions as 279–80
  Pericles as 279–80
  See also: Plague: and κρείσσων
μεταβολή ('reversal') 65–6, 68–9, 171,
  177–9, 181–2, 186–7, 290–1, 311–12
νικάω 89–90, 134, 151–2, 250–2
νόμος: See Nature: and νόμος
ὀργή and ὀργίζομαι 54–5, 125–6, 227–8,
  232–3, 275n.13, 278, 282, 285, 294–5,
  299, 301–2, 307–8
πάθος, πάθημα, and παθητικός
  applied by Dionysius to
    Thucydides 11–12, 14

as attacker 70
  definition of 12, 70, 126–7
  in Thucydides 59–60, 119–20, 177
πάσχω 123–4, 135, 169–70,
  173–4, 187
πέφυκα: See φύομαι, perfect forms of
πίπτω
  compounds of 67–70, 133–4, 290–1
  verbum simplex 71
προσπίπτω: See πίπτω: compounds of
πρόφασις: See Causation in Thucydides
τύχη ('chance', 'fortune')
  Diodotus on 122–3
  in Melian Dialogue 138–40
  and necessity in Thucydides 259–60
  and Pericles 285–6, 305–6
  and Pylos 171–3, 177–8
φόβος, φοβερός, and φοβέομαι
  applied by Dionysius to
    Thucydides 11
  vs. δέος 168, 189–90
  See also Fear
φύομαι, perfect forms of 110–14,
  116–17, 121, 124, 148–9, 153–4, 304
χράομαι (in sense 'experience, suffer, be
  subject to') 92, 123–4, 135, 179–80,
  253–4